# CIMA

STUDY TEXT

MANAGERIAL

# PAPER P4

## ORGANISATIONAL MANAGEMENT AND INFORMATION SYSTEMS

**In this edition we:**

- Highlight the most important elements in the syllabus and the key skills you will need

- Signpost how each chapter links to the syllabus and the learning outcomes

- Provide lots of exam focus points demonstrating what the examiner will want you to do

- Emphasise key points in regular fast forward summaries

- Test your knowledge of what you've studied in quick quizzes

- Examine your understanding in our exam question bank

- Reference all the important topics in our full index

BPP Learning Media's **i-Learn** and **i-Pass** products also support this paper.

FOR EXAMS IN NOVEMBER 2008, MAY 2009 AND NOVEMBER 2009

LEARNING MEDIA

First edition 2004

Fifth edition May 2008

ISBN 9780 7517 5287 8
(previous edition 9780 7517 4214 5)

British Library Cataloguing-in-Publication Data
A catalogue record for this book
is available from the British Library

Published by

BPP Learning Media Ltd
BPP House, Aldine Place
London W12 8AA

www.bpp.com/learningmedia

Printed in Great Britain by

WM Print Ltd
45-47 Frederick Street
Walsall
West Midlands
WS2 9NE

We are grateful to the Chartered Institute of Management
Accountants for permission to reproduce past
examination questions. The suggested solutions in the
exam answer bank have been prepared by BPP Learning
Media Ltd.

Your learning materials, published by BPP
Learning Media Ltd, are printed on paper sourced
from sustainable, managed forests.

ii

# Contents

## Distance Learning from BPP Professional Education

You can access our exam-focused interactive e-learning materials over the **Internet**, via BPP Learn Online, hosted by BPP Professional Education.

BPP Learn Online offers **comprehensive tutor support**, **revision guidance** and **exam tips**.

Visit www.bpp.com/cima/learnonline for further details.

## Learning to Learn Accountancy

BPP Learning Media's **Learning to Learn Accountancy** book is designed to be used both at the outset of your CIMA studies and throughout the process of learning accountancy. It can help you **focus your studies on the subject and exam**, enabling you to **acquire knowledge, practise and revise efficiently and effectively**.

## Important – changes to IAS 1

Recent changes to IAS 1 *Presentation of financial statements* will be reflected in CIMA exams from May 2009. The main changes are to the terminology used for the financial statements.

| Old terminology – examinable November 2008 exam | New terminology – examinable 2009 exams |
|---|---|
| Income statement | Income statement and Statement of comprehensive income |
| Balance sheet | Statement of financial position |
| Cash flow statement | Statement of cash flows |

In this Study Text we have used the old and new terminology. The Practice and Revision Kit, published in January 2009, will use the new terminology and will give further guidance on the changes. If you are taking your exam in 2009, you must buy the 2009 Practice and Revision Kit.

# How the BPP Learning Media Study Text can help you pass

## Tackling studying

We know that studying for a number of exams can seem daunting, particularly when you have other commitments as well.

- We provide guidance on how to cover chapters **quickly.**

- We explain the **purposes** of the **different features** in the Study Text, demonstrating how they help you and improve your chances of passing.

## Developing exam awareness

We never forget that you're aiming to pass your exams, and our Texts are completely focused on helping you do this.

- In the section **Studying P4** we introduce the key themes of the syllabus, describe the skills you need and summarise how to succeed.

- The **Introduction** to each chapter sets the chapter in the context of the syllabus and exam.

- We provide specific tips, **Exam focus points**, on what you can expect in the exam and what to do (and not to do!) when answering questions.

**And** our Study Text is **comprehensive**. It covers the syllabus content. No more, no less.

## Using the Learning outcomes and Syllabus

CIMA's website sets out the Learning outcomes and Syllabus in full:
http://www.cimaglobal.com/cps/rde/xchg/SID-0AAAC564-1C631D43/live/root.xsl/1377.htm

The **Learning outcomes** will show you what **capabilities** (skills) you'll have to demonstrate. The topics listed in the **Syllabus** are the **key topics** in this exam. By quickly looking through the Syllabus, you can see the breadth of the paper.

- Don't worry if the Syllabus seems large when you look through it; the Study Text will **carefully guide you** through it all.

- Remember the Study Text shows, at the start of every chapter, which **Learning outcomes** and **Syllabus areas** are covered in the chapter.

## Testing what you can do

Testing yourself helps you develop the skills you need to pass the exam and also confirms that you can recall what you have learnt.

- We include **Questions** within chapters, and the **Exam Question Bank** provides lots more practice.

- Our **Quick Quizzes** test whether you have enough knowledge of the contents of each chapter.

# Skim study technique

If you have limited time to cover a chapter, follow the **Skim study** technique below.

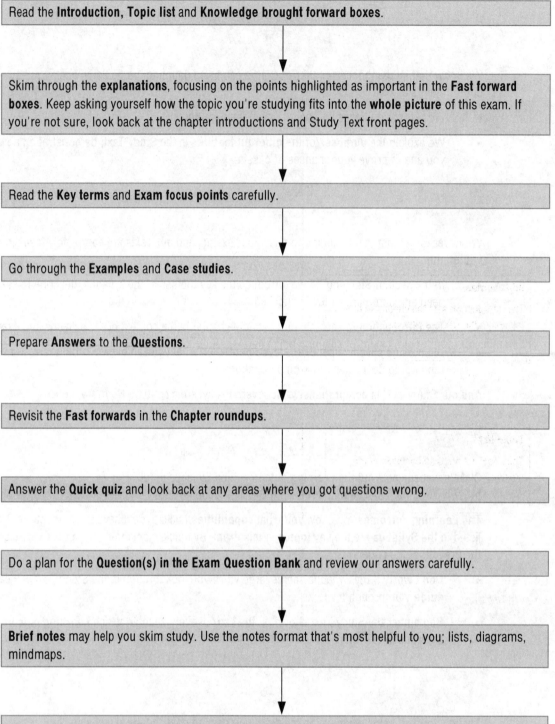

Read the **Introduction, Topic list** and **Knowledge brought forward boxes**.

Skim through the **explanations**, focusing on the points highlighted as important in the **Fast forward boxes**. Keep asking yourself how the topic you're studying fits into the **whole picture** of this exam. If you're not sure, look back at the chapter introductions and Study Text front pages.

Read the **Key terms** and **Exam focus points** carefully.

Go through the **Examples** and **Case studies**.

Prepare **Answers** to the **Questions**.

Revisit the **Fast forwards** in the **Chapter roundups**.

Answer the **Quick quiz** and look back at any areas where you got questions wrong.

Do a plan for the **Question(s) in the Exam Question Bank** and review our answers carefully.

**Brief notes** may help you skim study. Use the notes format that's most helpful to you; lists, diagrams, mindmaps.

When you are ready to start revising, you should still refer back to this Study Text.
- As a source of **reference** (you should find the Index particularly helpful for this)
- As a way to **review** (the Fast forwards, Exam focus points, Chapter Roundups and Quick Quizzes help you here)

# Example chapter

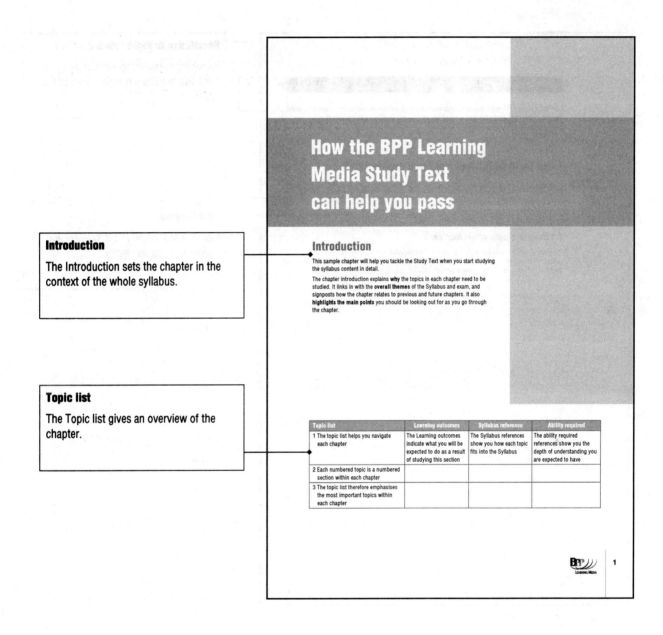

**Introduction**

The Introduction sets the chapter in the context of the whole syllabus.

**Topic list**

The Topic list gives an overview of the chapter.

## How the BPP Learning Media Study Text can help you pass

### Introduction

This sample chapter will help you tackle the Study Text when you start studying the syllabus content in detail.

The chapter introduction explains **why** the topics in each chapter need to be studied. It links in with the **overall themes** of the Syllabus and exam, and signposts how the chapter relates to previous and future chapters. It also **highlights the main points** you should be looking out for as you go through the chapter.

| Topic list | Learning outcomes | Syllabus reference | Ability required |
|---|---|---|---|
| 1 The topic list helps you navigate each chapter | The Learning outcomes indicate what you will be expected to do as a result of studying this section | The Syllabus references show you how each topic fits into the Syllabus | The ability required references show you the depth of understanding you are expected to have |
| 2 Each numbered topic is a numbered section within each chapter | | | |
| 3 The topic list therefore emphasises the most important topics within each chapter | | | |

## Knowledge brought forward

Knowledge brought forward shows you what you need to remember from previous exams.

> Knowledge brought forward from earlier studies

Knowledge brought forward boxes summarise information and techniques that you are **assumed to know** from your earlier studies. As the exam may test your knowledge of these areas, you should **revise** your previous study material if you are unsure about them.

# 1 Key topic which has a section devoted to it

**FAST FORWARD**  Fast forwards give you a **summary** of the content of each of the main chapter sections. They are listed together in the roundup at the end of each chapter to allow you to review each chapter quickly.

## Fast forward

Fast forwards allow you to preview and review each section easily.

## 1.1 Important topic within section

The headings within chapters give you a good idea of the **importance** of the topics covered. The larger the header, the more important the topic is. The headers will help you navigate through the chapter and locate the areas that have been highlighted as important in the front pages or in the chapter introduction.

2

## Example

Examples show you how theory is put into practice.

## Key term

Key terms are the core vocabulary.

## Exam focus point

Exam focus points provide specific links to the exam.

## Formula to learn

You must remember these formulae in the exam.

## Question

Questions provide vital practice of what you've learnt.

## Case Study

Case Studies link what you've learnt with the business environment.

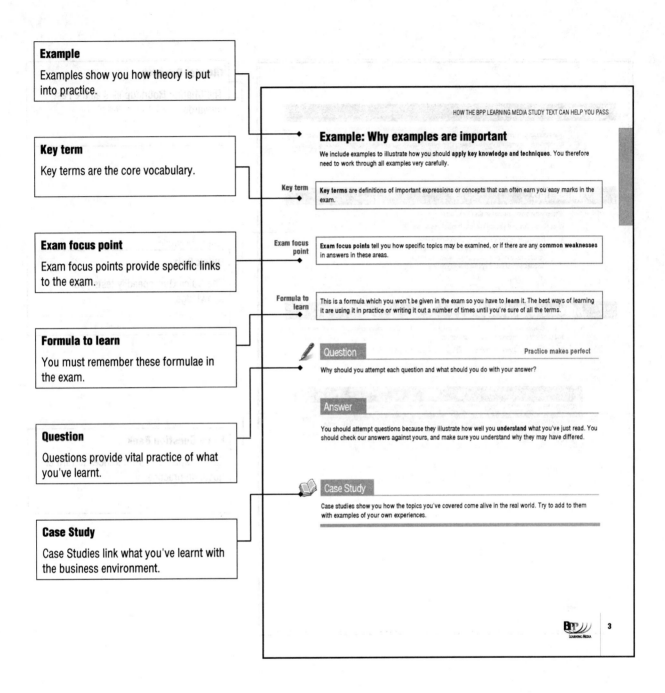

### Example: Why examples are important

We include examples to illustrate how you should **apply key knowledge and techniques**. You therefore need to work through all examples very carefully.

**Key term** — **Key terms** are definitions of important expressions or concepts that can often earn you easy marks in the exam.

**Exam focus point** — **Exam focus points** tell you how specific topics may be examined, or if there are any **common weaknesses** in answers in these areas.

**Formula to learn** — This is a formula which you won't be given in the exam so you have to **learn** it. The best ways of learning it are using it in practice or writing it out a number of times until you're sure of all the terms.

**Question** — Practice makes perfect

Why should you attempt each question and what should you do with your answer?

**Answer**

You should attempt questions because they illustrate how well you **understand** what you've just read. You should check our answers against yours, and make sure you understand why they may have differed.

**Case Study**

Case studies show you how the topics you've covered come alive in the real world. Try to add to them with examples of your own experiences.

3

## Chapter Roundup

- Fast forwards give you a **summary** of the content of each of the main chapter sections. They are listed together in the roundup at the end of each chapter to allow you to review each chapter quickly.

## Quick Quiz

1   What are the main purposes of the Quick Quiz?

2   What should you do if you get Quick Quiz questions wrong?

   A   Nothing as you now know where you went wrong
   B   Note the correct answer and go on to the next chapter
   C   Practise full questions on this topic when you revise
   D   Go back and look through the topic again to ensure you know it

## Answers to Quick Quiz

1   The main purposes of the Quick Quiz are to check how much you've remembered of the topics covered and to practise questions in a variety of formats.

2   D   Go back and look through the topic again to ensure that you know it.

Now try the questions below from the Exam Question Bank

| Number | Level | Marks | Time |
|---|---|---|---|
| Questions that give you practice of what you've learnt in each chapter | Examination | 25 | 45 mins |

4

**Chapter Roundup**

The Chapter Roundup lists all the Fast forwards.

**Quick Quiz**

The Quick Quiz speedily tests your knowledge.

**Exam Question Bank**

Each chapter cross-references to further question practice.

# Studying P4

# 1 What P4 is about

The Organisational Management and Information Systems paper covers five areas:

- Information systems (20%)
- Operations management (20%)
- Managing human capital (30%)
- Marketing (20%)
- Managing change (10%)

Questions requiring knowledge from each of these five areas are likely to be included in each examination.

## 1.1 Information systems

You aren't expected to be an information systems (IS) or information technology (IT) expert. However, you are expected to be able to evaluate an organisation's information systems and recommend appropriate solutions. This requires an awareness of the business uses and benefits of IS/IT, but without detailed technical know-how.

## 1.2 Operations management

The key learning outcome here is to be able to explain how the quality of products and services can be assessed, measured and improved. The link between product/service design and the operations required to deliver a product/service of the quality level required is important.

## 1.3 Managing human capital

Human resource management is the largest area of this syllabus (30%). It also links very easily to all of the other syllabus areas, so is highly likely to feature in scenario questions. The key learning outcome in this is to 'explain the role of the human resource management function'.

## 1.4 Marketing

It will become clear to you as you study that 'marketing' in P4 is a wide concept that incorporates all aspects of product and service design and delivery. Marketing therefore links closely with the operations management part of the syllabus. After studying this material, you need to be able to 'evaluate the marketing processes of an organisation'.

## 1.5 Managing change

The key learning outcome here is to be able to 'evaluate various means of introducing change'. In longer questions, change management is likely to be examined together with another syllabus area. Organisational development is also covered under the change management heading.

# 2 What is required

Section A questions test knowledge retention. Section B and Section C questions are likely to require you to **apply** knowledge. Responses to essay style questions may be in straightforward essay style, or may also be in the form of memorandum, letter, briefing notes, presentation slides or a report.

The preparation for this exam will therefore need to be different to the work done for numerical papers. You will need to learn key syllabus areas and practise all of the different types of question that appear in this exam.

It would also be useful to keep up to date with developments in business thinking in general (especially the uses of information technology) by regularly reviewing the business pages of a quality newspaper.

# 3 Passing P4

## 3.1 Cover the whole syllabus

70% of the marks available in this exam are for compulsory questions. This gives the examiner plenty of opportunity to test all major areas of the syllabus on **every** paper, but sadly doesn't give you much opportunity to avoid questions you don't like.

## 3.2 Practise

This Text includes Questions within chapters, Quick Quiz questions and an Exam Question Bank. In addition, the BPP Learning Media Practice and Revision Kit provides lots more question practice. It is particularly important to practise:

- Banks of MCQs and '50-word' objective test questions so that you get used to these
- Section B 30-mark questions (six 5 markers)
- Longer written questions that appear in Section C (30 marks each)

## 3.3 Develop time management skills

The examiner has identified time management as being a problem, with some candidates not leaving themselves enough time to produce fully explained written answers. Attempting questions under exam conditions is essential preparation for the P4 exam.

## 3.4 Develop business awareness

Although this is not a higher level paper, candidates with good business awareness can score well in a number of areas.

- Reading articles in CIMA's *Financial Management* magazine and the business press will help you understand practical business issues and make it easier for you to make reasonable suggestions to scenario style problems
- Being aware of the work of different departments in your own organisation or others you know about will help you discuss the practical management issues involved in running a business; for P4 particularly HR, operations, information systems and marketing.

## 3.5 Develop examination and application skills

The examiner recently altered the style of the Section C questions. These questions now require an evaluation of a particular scenario or the discussion of various issues from a number of syllabus areas. It is highly likely that this style of question will continue and that several areas of the syllabus will be examined in each Section C question. The following contains advice on how to approach Section C questions.

### 3.5.1 Reading the requirements

When you first see a scenario question, it can be useful to have an initial quick look through the information given to you before looking at the question requirements, to gain an idea of what the main issues are likely to be. However, you should read the question requirements carefully before analysing the scenario in detail. You need to identify what the requirements tell you about:

- The **syllabus areas** to be addressed
- What information will be **most significant** in the scenario
- The **techniques** you will need to analyse the data
- **Possible links and overlaps** between different parts of the question
- What the question is asking you to **provide** (determined by the question verb), also whether the requirements specify the way you should **structure** your answer
- **How long** to spend on each part (determined by the mark allocation)

## 3.5.2 Application skills

What application skills do you need? Many questions will include detail in a scenario about a specific organisation. The following skills are particularly important when you're dealing with question scenarios.

- **Identifying the most important features** of the organisation and the organisation's environment; clues to these will be scattered throughout the scenario. The technical knowledge that you have should help you do this, but you will also need business awareness and imagination
- **Using analysis techniques** that will give you more insight into the data that you're given
- **Selecting real-life examples** that are relevant to the scenario
- **Making informed judgements** that follow from your analysis about what the organisation is doing and should be doing
- **Communicating clearly and concisely** your analysis and recommendations. Perhaps you will be reporting to a specific individual; if so you should take into account the needs of this individual

## 3.5.3 Evaluation questions

Evaluation questions also test your ability to do the following:

| Identify what's relevant to the organisation | Consider what the organisation's strategy is, and whether the organisation will be easily able to do what it wants to do |
|---|---|
| Select appropriate methods of assessment | This means choosing appropriate numerical techniques or theoretical models – assume you won't be told what method or model to use |
| Interpret fairly the results of your analysis | What does the analysis suggest about what the organisation is doing and should do? |
| Discuss the limitations of what you have done | What are the shortcomings of the data and problems with the techniques you've used (these should be relevant to the scenario)? Would other techniques give you additional insights? |
| Discuss the problems with the results you have obtained | Do the strategic decisions suggested by the results appear sensible? If not what other key factors are influencing strategy? You also need to consider the links between the decisions and implementing the decisions. What will be the impact upon management accounting, information and control systems? |

## 3.5.4 Advise and recommend

Don't be afraid to give advice. Even if you analyse a situation well, you will fail to pick up marks if you're told to recommend but don't provide any recommendations. The examiner may also want you to make a number of recommendations, rather than focusing exclusively on a single suggestion.

Other important qualities your recommendations or advice should have are:

- They should be in terms that the recipient(s) will **understand**. They shouldn't be too technical
- It should be **clear** what the recipient **has to do**. For example, it wouldn't be enough to say – 'Improve recruitment procedures' as you haven't explained how to improve them. Instead you would say improve recruitment procedures by appointing an HR officer, carefully wording adverts and selecting appropriate locations to advertise vacancies.
- The recommendations must be **appropriate** for the organisation's circumstances. For example, if the organisation is small, that limits the sources of funding it can use and means that certain suggestions, such as a large, state-of-the-art IT department, will not be suitable

### 3.5.5 Analysing the situation

Even when you're reading the scenario carefully, don't get too stuck in the detail, but look for the **key issues and information** in each paragraph. The importance of different information will be determined by the question requirements, but the following information will normally be important if it's included in the scenario:

- Financial and non-financial objectives
- Business strategies
- Financial and non-financial resources available to the organisation
- Constraints on the organisation or its directors
- Key persons/stakeholders within the organisation
- The organisation's size, structure and culture
- Products, markets and competition
- Recent financial trends
- Likely changes in the business environment
- Other problems and weaknesses

Often the question requirements will require you to consider the implementation and consequences of **significant changes**. Anything that will give you insights into the effects of change (the opportunities that will be provided, and the internal consequences on the organisation) will be important. You'll need to consider how far to analyse the **consequences** of the change. The level of **uncertainty** involved may be very significant, affecting the reliability of the techniques you use and meaning that you have to make reasonable estimates of what will happen.

## 4 The good news

Generally the pass rates for paper P4 have been excellent. Most candidates seem to have a good knowledge of most of the syllabus and are comfortable with the range of question formats.

## The exam paper

### Format of the paper for Paper P4

The format of this paper changed in May 2007.

|  |  | Number of marks |
|---|---|---|
| Section A: | Around 20 multiple choice and other objective test questions, 2-4 marks each | 40 |
| Section B: | 6 compulsory questions, 5 marks each | 30 |
| Section C: | 1 out of 2 questions, 30 marks each/1 compulsory question 30 marks | 30 |
|  |  | 100 |

Time allowed: 3 hours

**Section A** will always contain some multiple choice questions but will not consist solely of them. It may contain types of objective test question that are different from those included in the pilot paper.

Further guidance on objective test questions and multiple choice questions is included on pages xvi and xvii.

**Section B** questions will be mainly written discussion, although some calculations may be included. This section will require breadth of syllabus knowledge and also good time management skills.

**Section C** questions will be in various different styles including more complex calculations and analysis of data. Most questions will require calculation and written evaluation. Questions may include issues from a number of areas of the syllabus. Careful planning of answers will be essential.

# Analysis of past papers – Managerial level

| Covered in Text chapter | | Nov 2007 | May 2007 | Nov 2006 | May 2006 | Nov 2005 | May 2005 | Pilot paper |
|---|---|---|---|---|---|---|---|---|
| | **INFORMATION SYSTEMS** | | | | | | | |
| 1 | Systems theory | B | B | | | | | |
| 1 | Information systems | B | B | | | | | |
| 2 | Systems development | | | B | B | | | |
| 3 | Hardware, software and the internet | | B | | B | B | | |
| 3 | Information systems department | B | | B | | | | |
| | **OPERATIONS MANAGEMENT** | | | | | | | |
| 4 | Operations strategy and product/service design | | B | | | | | |
| 5 | Capacity management, supply chains and inventory management | | *O* | | | B | | |
| 6 | Quality management and business process re-engineering | B | *O* | B | | B | | |
| | **MANAGING HUMAN CAPITAL** | | | | | | | |
| 7 | Human resource management theory and the HR plan | *O* | *O* | B | | *O* | B/*O* | *O* |
| 7 | Recruitment, selection and legal/ethical issues | *O* | | *O* | | *O* | *O* | |
| 8 | Motivation and performance | *O* | | | *O* | *O* | B/*O* | *O* |
| 9 | Training, development and career management | B | B/*O* | | | *O* | | |
| | **MARKETING** | | | | | | | |
| 10 | Marketing theory | B | B | *O* | *O* | *O* | B | B |
| 10 | Marketing strategy and pricing | B | B | *O* | | B/*O* | | |
| 11 | Market segmentation, buyer behaviour and market research | *O* | | *O* | | | | |
| 12 | Marketing and information technology: Online marketing, E-commerce and 'M-Marketing' | | B | *O* | | | B | |
| 12 | Managing customer relationships | | | | *O* | | | |
| | **MANAGING CHANGE** | | | | | | | |
| 13 | Organisational development | | B | | *O* | | | |
| 14 | Human behaviour towards change | *O* | *O* | B | B | | | *O* |
| 14 | Overcoming resistance to change | *O* | *O* | B | | | *O* | |
| 14 | Information technology and change management; Successfully implementing change | | | B | | | *O* | *O* |

**B**: Examined in compulsory Section B question
*O*: Examined in optional Section C question

# Tackling multiple choice questions

The MCQs in your exam will contain four or five possible answers. You have to **choose the option that best answers the question**. The three or four incorrect options are called distracters. There is a skill in answering MCQs quickly and correctly. By practising MCQs you can develop this skill, giving yourself a better chance of passing the exam.

You may wish to follow the approach outlined below, or you may prefer to adapt it.

**Step 1**      Skim read all the MCQs and identify which appear to be the easier questions and which questions you will not need a calculator to answer.

**Step 2**      Remember that the examiner will not expect you to spend an equal amount of time on each MCQ; some can be answered instantly but others will take time to work out.

**Step 3**      Attempt each question **The questions** identified in Step 1 are questions which you should be able to answer during the 20 minutes reading time. Read the question thoroughly. You may prefer to work out the answer before looking at the options, or you may prefer to look at the options at the beginning. Adopt the method that works best for you.

         You may find that you recognise a question when you sit the exam. Be aware that the detail and/or requirement may be different. If the question seems familiar, read the requirement and options carefully – do not assume that it is identical.

**Step 4**      Read the five options and see if one matches your own answer. Be careful with numerical questions, as the distracters are designed to match answers that incorporate **common errors**. Check that your calculation is correct. Have you followed the requirement exactly? Have you included every stage of the calculation?

**Step 5**      You may find that none of the options matches your answer.

- Re-read the question to ensure that you understand it and are answering the requirement

- Eliminate any obviously wrong answers

- Consider which of the remaining answers is the most likely to be correct and select that option

**Step 6**      If you are still unsure, make a note and continue to the next question. Likewise if you are nowhere near working out which option is correct, leave the question and come back to it later.

**Step 7**      Revisit unanswered questions. When you come back to a question after a break, you often find you can answer it correctly straightaway. If you are still unsure, have a guess. You are not penalised for incorrect answers, so **never leave a question unanswered!**

**Step 8**      **Rule off answers** to each MCQ in the answer booklet.

# Tackling objective test questions

## What is an objective test question?

An objective test (**OT**) question is made up of some form of **stimulus**, usually a question, and a **requirement** to do something.

- **MCQs.** Read through the information on page 38 about MCQs and how to tackle them.
- **Data entry**. This type of OT requires you to provide figures such as the answer to a calculation, words to fill in a blank, single word answers to questions, or to identify numbers and words to complete a format.
- **Word-limited answers**. You may be asked to state, define or explain things in no more than a certain number of words or within a single line in the answer booklet.
- **Multiple response.** These questions provide you with a number of options and you have to identify those that fulfil certain criteria.
- **Matching.** This OT question format could ask you to classify particular costs into one of a range of cost classifications provided, to match descriptions of variances with one of a number of variances listed, and so on.

## Dealing with OT questions

Again you may wish to follow the approach we suggest, or you may be prepared to adapt it.

| | |
|---|---|
| **Step 1** | Work out **how long** you should allocate to each OT, taking into account the marks allocated to it. Remember that you will not be expected to spend an equal amount of time on each one; some can be answered instantly but others will take time to work out. |
| **Step 2** | **Jot down answers, workings or ideas** for as many OTs as possible on the question paper during the 20 minutes reading time. |
| **Step 3** | **Attempt each question**. Read the question thoroughly, and note in particular what the question says about the **format** of your answer and whether there are any **restrictions** placed on It (for example the number of words you can use). |
| | You may find that you recognise a question when you sit the exam. Be aware that the detail and/or requirement may be different. If the question seems familiar read the requirement and options carefully – do not assume that it is identical. |
| **Step 4** | Read any options you are given and select which ones are appropriate. Check that your calculations are correct. Have you followed the requirement exactly? Have you included every stage of the calculation? |
| **Step 5** | You may find that you are unsure of the answer. |
| | • Re-read the question to ensure that you understand it and are answering the requirement |
| | • Eliminate any obviously wrong options if you are given a number of options from which to choose |
| **Step 6** | If you are still unsure, **continue to the next question**. |
| **Step 7** | Revisit questions you are uncertain about. When you come back to a question after a break you often find you are able to answer it correctly straightaway. If you are still unsure have a guess. You are not penalised for incorrect answers, so **never leave a question unanswered!** |
| **Step 8** | Make sure you show your **workings** clearly on calculation OTs, as you may gain some credit for workings even if your final answer is incorrect. |
| **Step 9** | Rule off answers to each OT in the answer booklet. |

# Information systems

# Systems and information theory

## Introduction

In this chapter we look at **systems and information theory**, and how these concepts can be applied to information systems.

Much of the material in this chapter is theoretical. In the exam you may be required to show you have learnt and understood the theory (perhaps in an objective test question) or you may be required to apply this theory to a practical scenario.

So, it is important to ensure you learn the theory and you also learn how to apply it or even adapt it. As with many topics, the key is extensive question practice during the revision phase of your studies.

| Topic list | Learning outcomes | Syllabus references | Ability required |
|---|---|---|---|
| 1 General systems theory | A(vii) | A(3) | Evaluation |
| 2 Types of system | A(iv), A(vi) | A(3), A(10) | Evaluation |
| 3 Systems concepts | A(vii) | A(3) | Evaluation |
| 4 Information theory | A(iv), A(vii) | A(3) | Evaluation |
| 5 Information systems | A(iii), A(vii) | A(3), A(10) | Evaluation |

# 1 General systems theory

The term **system** is widely used – the 'respiratory system', the 'political system', the 'long ball system', and so on. Any definition of a 'system' must therefore be wide ranging.

> Any system can be thought of in terms of **inputs**, **processing** and **outputs**.

**Key terms**

> A **system** is set of interacting components that operate together to accomplish a purpose.
>
> A **business system** is a collection of people, machines and methods organised to accomplish a set of specific functions.
>
> **Information systems (IS)** include all systems and procedures involved in the collection, storage, production and distribution of information.
>
> **Information technology (IT)** describes the equipment used to capture, store, transmit or present information. IT provides a large part of the information systems infrastructure.

## 1.1 The component parts of a system

A system has three component parts: inputs, processes and outputs. Other key characteristics of a system are the environment and the system boundary – as shown in the following diagram.

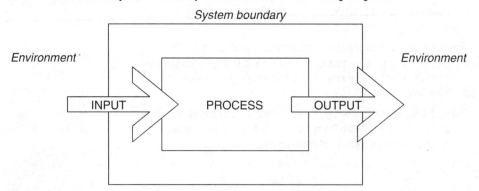

### 1.1.1 Inputs

Inputs **provide the system with what it needs** to be able to operate. Input may vary from matter, energy or human actions, to information.

- Matter might include, in a manufacturing operation, adhesives or rivets.
- Human input might consist of typing an instruction booklet or starting up a piece of machinery.

Inputs may be **outputs from other systems**, for example, the output from a transactions processing system forms the input for a management information system.

### 1.1.2 Processes

A process **transforms an input into an output**. Processes may involve tasks performed by humans, plant, computers, chemicals and a wide range of other actions.

Processes may consist of **assembly**, for example where electronic consumer goods are being manufactured, or **disassembly**, for example where oil is refined.

There is **not necessarily a clear relationship** between the number of inputs to a process and the number of outputs.

### 1.1.3 Outputs

Outputs are the **results of the processing**. They could be said to represent the **purpose** for which the system exists.

Many outputs are used as **inputs to other systems**.

Alternatively outputs may be discarded as **waste** (an input to the ecological system) or **re-input** to the system which has produced them, for example, in certain circumstances, defective products.

### 1.1.4 The system boundary

FAST FORWARD

A system exists in an environment. An environment surrounds the system but is not part of it. **A system boundary** separates the system from its environment.

The concept of the system boundary is explained above. For example, a cost accounting department's boundary can be expressed in terms of who works in it and what work it does. This boundary will separate it from other departments, such as the financial accounts department.

System boundaries may be natural or artificially created (an organisation's departmental structures are artificially created).

There may be **interfaces** between various systems, both internal and external to an organisation, to allow the exchange of resources. In a commercial context, this is most likely to be a reciprocal exchange, for example money for raw materials.

### 1.1.5 The environment

Anything which is outside the system boundary belongs to the system's environment and not to the system itself. A system **accepts inputs** from the environment and **provides outputs** into the environment. The parts of the environment from which the system receives inputs may not be the same as those to which it delivers outputs.

The environment exerts a considerable influence on the behaviour of a system; at the same time the system can do little to **control** the behaviour of the environment.

### Question
The environment

Learning outcome: A (vii)

The environment affects the performance of a system. Using a business organisation as an example of a system, give five examples of environmental factors which might affect it. (5 marks)

### Answer

(a) Policies adopted by the government or ruling political body.

(b) The strength of the domestic currency of the organisation's country of operation.

(c) Social attitudes: concern for the natural environment.

(d) The regulatory and legislative framework within which the company operates.

(e) The number of competitors in the marketplace and the strategies they adopt (eg products, price, quality).

You may have thought of other valid factors.

## 1.2 Subsystems

A system itself may contain a number of systems, called **subsystems**. Each subsystem consists of a process whereby component parts interact to achieve an objective. Separate subsystems **interact** with each other, and **respond** to each other by means of **communication** or observation. The goals of subsystems must be consistent with the goal of the overall system.

Often, whether something is a system or a subsystem is a matter of definition, and depends on the context of the **observer**. For example, an organisation is a social system, and its 'environment' may be seen as society as a whole. Another way of looking at an organisation would be to regard it as a subsystem of the entire social system. **Information** links up the different subsystems in an organisation.

## 1.3 The systems approach

The theory we have covered in this section may applied to a wide range of situations. For example, a computerised information system may also be thought of in terms of inputs, processed outputs and subsystems.

Organisations can also be viewed as a system. **Inputs** are received and **processed** to produce **outputs** of goods and services. The **objectives** of the organisation are thereby fulfilled.

The systems approach uses three steps.

- Identify what the **whole system** is
- Identify the overall **objectives** of the system as a whole
- Make **plans** with these objectives in mind

## 1.4 Socio-technical systems

Another point of view suggests that an organisation is a 'structured **socio-technical** system', that is, it consists of at least **three subsystems**.

(a)  A structure.

(b)  A technological system (concerning the work to be done, and the machines, tools and other facilities available to do it).

(c)  A social system (concerning the people within the organisation, the ways they think and the ways they interact with each other).

# 2 Types of system

**FAST FORWARD**

An **open** system has a relationship with its environment which has both prescribed and uncontrolled elements. A **closed** system is shut off from its environment and has no relationship with it.

## 2.1 Open systems and closed systems

In systems theory a distinction is made between open systems and closed systems.

**Key term**

> A **closed system** is a system which is isolated from its environment and independent of it. No environmental influences affect the behaviour of the system, nor does the system exert any influence on its environment.

Some scientific systems might be described as closed systems. An example of a closed system is a chemical reaction in a sealed, insulated container. Another is the operation of a thermostat. However, all **social** systems, including business organisations, have some interaction with their environment, and so cannot be closed systems.

**Key term**

An **open system** is a system connected to and interacting with its environment. It takes in influences (or 'energy') from its environment and also influences this environment by its behaviour (it exports energy).

Open and closed systems can be described by diagram as follows.

*Closed system*

Shut off from its environment

*Open system*

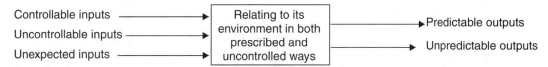

Controllable inputs ⟶
Uncontrollable inputs ⟶
Unexpected inputs ⟶
Relating to its environment in both prescribed and uncontrolled ways
⟶ Predictable outputs
⟶ Unpredictable outputs

For example, a **business** is an open system where management decisions are influenced by or have an influence on suppliers, customers, competitors, society as a whole and the government.

Employees are obviously influenced by what they do in their job, but as members of society at large, they are also a part of the **environment**, just as their views and opinions expressed within the business are often a reflection of their opinions as members of society at large.

Every system has a boundary. An open system will have considerable cross-influences with its environment **across its boundary**, whereas a closed system's boundary would shut it off from its environment.

### 2.1.1 Semi-closed systems

Some writers also refer to semi-closed systems. A semi-closed system interfaces with the environment and reacts in a predictable controlled way. This differs from an open system as open systems interact with the environment in both a controlled and uncontrolled way.

*Semi-closed system*

Predictable inputs ⟶ PROCESS ⟶ Predictable outputs

## 2.2 Feedback control and feedforward control systems

### 2.2.1 Feedback control systems

Feedback control systems describe the situation where part of system output is returned (fed-back) as an input. An example is an accounting budgetary control system as the output (eg variance analysis) may result in changes to input and/or processes.

## 2.2.2 Feedforward control systems

Feedforward control systems involve the monitoring of the environment, the process and the output – and taking any corrective action on the basis of these factors.

This involves a predictive element as the corrective action is based upon both current and future events.

# 2.3 Feedback control loops

The term 'feedback control loop' describes a situation where feedback is gathered and then used to influence future performance (ie exercise control) by adjusting input.

### 2.3.1 A single feedback loop

Single loop feedback follows a 'simple' path comparing actual results against expected results.

### 2.3.2 A double feedback loop

Double loop feedback involves making changes to the actual plans or systems as a result of changes in both internal and external conditions.

**Single and double loop feedback**

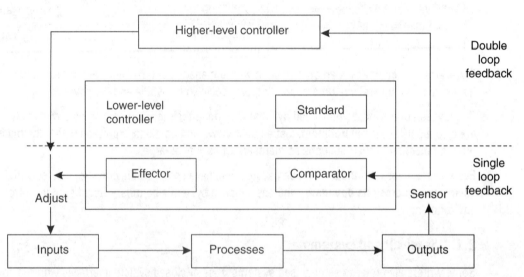

The diagram includes other elements of systems theory as explained in the table below.

| Element | Description |
|---|---|
| Sensor | Measuring or recording device – may be an automated or manual checking process. |
| Comparator | Compares the actual result (obtained by the sensor) against the plan (or standard). |
| Effector | This is usually a manager or supervisor acting upon the comparison by issuing new instructions relating to input. |

If a higher-level controller is involved (ie double feedback loop) this would usually be senior management who revise plans, budgets and the control systems themselves.

# 3 Systems concepts

## 3.1 Filtering

**Filtering** means ensuring information is relevant and required before disseminating.

**Key term**

> **Filtering** means removing 'impurities' such as excessive detail from data as it is passed up the organisation hierarchy.

We met this concept in the context of good information. Operational staff may need all the detail to do their jobs, but when they report to higher and higher subsystems the data can be progressively **summarised**. Extraneous detail is filtered out leaving only the important points.

The **problem** with this is that sometimes the 'filter' may let through unimportant information and/or remove important information, with the result that the message is **distorted** at the next level.

### Question

**Filtering**

Which one of the following is an example of 'filtering'?

A     Deleting all accounts not used within the past three years from the accounts receivable ledger.
B     Ensuring all e-mail messages are forwarded to another employee while on holiday.
C     The transfer of information from one system to another.
D     The inclusion of an executive summary at the start of a report.

### Answer

D     Filtering involves changing the way information is presented or displayed to make it suitable for use higher up the hierarchy.

## 3.2 Coupling and decoupling

The terms **coupling** and **decoupling** relate to how closely one system depends on another.

If systems or subsystems are very closely linked or **coupled** this may cause difficulties.

For example, in order to sell goods, a manufacturing company must first of all make them. If the sales and production subsystems are closely coupled, the company may be able to produce almost exactly the amount required for a given period's sales. However, the system would be prone to inefficiency through a 'mishap', such as a late delivery of raw materials, a machine breakdown, or a strike, as then goods would not be available to meet sales demand.

From a traditional point of view, greater efficiency is achieved between the production and sales systems by **decoupling** them. In the example above, this would mean reducing the interaction between sales and production by creating finished goods stock.

From a modern point of view, holding finished goods stock is expensive, and greater efficiency is achieved by adopting **quality management** philosophies to try to ensure that mishaps do not occur. For example, the adoption of a **just-in-time (JIT)** approach to production and purchasing closely couples the sales and production subsystems and closely couples one organisation's purchasing function with another's supplying function.

## 3.3 Requisite variety

FAST FORWARD

> If there is variety in the environmental influences in the system, then the system itself must be suitably varied and variable to adapt itself successfully to its environment. This is the principle behind the **law of requisite variety**.

The 'law' of requisite variety is a principle of general systems theory, developed by *Ross Ashby*.

**Key term**

> The **law of requisite variety** states that the variety *within a system* must be at least as great as the *environmental variety* against which it is attempting to regulate itself.

If a system does not have the requisite amount of variety, it will be **unable to adapt to change** and will eventually die or be replaced. History is full of examples of political systems that could not adapt to social, economic or political changes, and so were overthrown.

The law of requisite variety applies to self-regulating systems in general, but one application of the law relates to control systems. A control system (which is a sub-system of a larger system) must be sufficiently flexible to be able to deal with the variety that occurs naturally in the system that it is attempting to control.

### Case Study

A company making heavy equipment suddenly found its raw materials and in-process inventory climbing, but, at the same time, it was experiencing reduced sales and reduced production. The system was out of control.

The cause was traced to the materials analysts who made the detailed inventory decisions. They had been furnished with decision rules for ordering, cancelling, etc, under normal conditions, but they had no rules governing how to handle the inventory when production was decreasing and production lots were being cancelled.

In other words, the system did not provide the requisite variety of control responses. In this case, the urgency of remedy did not allow new rules to be formulated and validated. Instead, each materials analyst was treated as a self-organising system, given a target inventory, and told to achieve it. With the analysts given the freedom to generate control responses, the inventory was reduced in a few months.

Ways of introducing the requisite variety into a control system include the following.

(a)     **Allowing a controller some discretion**, to judge what control action is needed.

In a business system, managers should not be instructed that a problem must be handled in a particular way, especially when the problem involves labour relations, disciplinary procedures, motivating the workforce or any other such 'behavioural' matters. The response of individuals to control action by managers will be variable because people are different, and even one person's moods change from day to day. The control system must be flexible enough to use different methods to achieve the same ends.

(b)     **Introducing tolerance limits.**

When actual results differ from planned results, control action should not be instigated automatically in every instance. Control action should only be applied when the variance becomes excessive and exceeds allowable tolerance limits. Tolerance limits recognise that plans are based on an 'average' or 'norm' of what is expected to happen, and some variation around this average will be due to 'natural' causes which there should be no reason to get alarmed about.

## 3.4 Entropy

A final important term in information and systems theory is entropy.

**Entropy** arises because of the natural tendency of objects, and systems, to fall into a state of disorder.

**Key term**

**Entropy** is the amount of disorder or randomness present in any system.

All inanimate systems display this tendency to move towards a state of disorder. If they remain unattended they will gradually lose all motion and degenerate into an inert state. When this state is reached and no observable systems activity can be discerned, the system has reached maximum entropy.

The term **entropy is therefore used as a measure of disorganisation**. A system will increase its entropy unless it receives **negative entropy** in the form of information or inputs from the environment.

For instance if a business does not listen to its customers' complaints about its products it will eventually fail because it will not be able to sell what it produces. The system will fall into a state of disorder, in the sense that it is ignoring its purpose, which is to sell things and not just to produce them. Negative entropy is needed in the form of new or improved products or perhaps new, more open-minded management.

# 4 Information theory

## 4.1 Why do organisations need information?

Organisations require **information** for a range of **purposes**.

- Planning
- Controlling
- Recording transactions
- Performance measurement
- Decision making

### 4.1.1 Planning

Once any decision has been made, it is necessary to plan **how to implement** the steps necessary to make it effective. Planning requires a knowledge of, among other things, available **resources**, possible **time-scales** for implementation and the likely **outcome under alternative scenarios**.

### 4.1.2 Controlling

Once a plan is implemented, its actual performance must be controlled. Information is required to assess **whether it is proceeding as planned** or whether there is some unexpected deviation from plan. It may consequently be necessary to take some form of corrective action.

### 4.1.3 Recording transactions

Information about **each transaction or event** is required for a number of reasons. Documentation of transactions can be used as **evidence** in a case of dispute. There may be a **legal requirement** to record transactions, for example for accounting and audit purposes. Detailed information on production costs can be built up, allowing a better **assessment of profitability**. Similarly, labour utilised in providing a particular service can be measured. Structured systems can be installed to capture transactions data.

### 4.1.4 Performance measurement

Just as individual operations need to be controlled, so overall performance must be measured in order to enable **comparisons against budget or plan** to be carried out. This may involve the collection of information on, for example, costs, revenues, volumes, time-scale and profitability.

### 4.1.5 Decision making

Information is also required to make informed decisions. This completes the full circle of organisational activity.

## 4.2 Internal information

> Data can be **collected** from **within** and **beyond an organisation**. **Information systems** are used to convert this **data into information** and to **communicate** it to management at all levels.

Data and information come from sources both inside and outside an organisation, and an information system should be designed so as to obtain – or **capture** – all the relevant data and information from whatever source. Capturing data/information from **inside** the organisation involves the following.

(a)     A **system** for collecting or measuring **transactions** data – for example sales, purchases, stock turnover etc – which sets out procedures for **what** data is **collected**, how frequently, by whom, and by what methods, and how it is **processed**, and **filed** or **communicated**.

(b)     **Informal communication** of information between **managers and staff** (for example, by word-of-mouth or at meetings).

(c)     **Communication between managers**.

## 4.3 Internal data sources

### 4.3.1 The accounting records

Accounts receivable ledgers, accounts payable ledgers, general ledgers and cash books etc hold information that may be of great value outside the accounts department, for example, sales information for the marketing function.

To maintain the integrity of its accounting records, an organisation operates **controls** over transactions. These also give rise to valuable information. A stock control system for example will include details of purchase orders, goods received notes, goods returned notes and so on, which can be analysed to **provide management information** about speed of delivery, say, or the quality of supplies.

### 4.3.2 Other internal sources

Organisations record information to enable them to carry out operations and administrative functions.

(a)     Information about **personnel** will be held, possibly linked to the **payroll** system. Additional information may be obtained from this source if, say, a project is being costed and it is necessary to ascertain the availability and rate of pay of different levels of staff, or the need for and cost of recruiting staff from outside the organisation.

(b)     Much information will be produced by a **production** department about machine capacity, fuel consumption, movement of people, materials, work in progress, set up times, maintenance requirements and so on.

(c)     Many **service** businesses, notably accountants and solicitors, need to keep detailed records of the **time spent** on various activities, both to justify fees to clients and to assess the efficiency and profitability of operations.

**Staff** themselves are one of the primary sources of internal information. Information may be obtained either informally in the course of day-to-day business or through meetings, interviews or questionnaires.

## 4.4 External information

Capturing information from **outside** the organisation might be entrusted to particular individuals, or might be 'informal'.

**Routine formal** collection of data from outside sources includes the following.

(a)     A company's **tax specialists** will be expected to gather information about changes in tax law and how this will affect the company.

(b)     Obtaining information about any new legislation on health and safety at work, or employment regulations, must be the responsibility of a particular person – for example the company's **legal expert** or **company secretary** – who must then pass on the information to other managers affected by it.

(c)     Research and development (R & D) work often relies on information about other R & D work being done by another company or by government institutions.

(d)     **Marketing managers** need to know about the opinions and buying attitudes of potential customers. To obtain this information, they might carry out market research exercises.

**Informal** gathering of information from the environment **goes on all the time, consciously or unconsciously**, because the employees of an organisation learn **what is going on in the world around** them – perhaps from newspapers, television reports, meetings with business associates or the trade press.

## 4.5 External data sources

An organisation's files (paper and computerised) include information from external sources such as invoices, letters, e-mails, advertisements and so on **received from customers and suppliers**. Sometimes additional external information is required, requiring an active search outside the organisation. The following sources may be identified.

(a)     The government.
(b)     Advice or information bureaux.
(c)     Consultancies of all sorts.
(d)     Newspaper and magazine publishers.
(e)     There may be specific reference works which are used in a particular line of work.
(f)     Libraries and information services.
(g)     Increasingly businesses can use each other's systems as sources of information, for instance via electronic data interchange (EDI).
(h)     Electronic sources of information are becoming ever more important.

  (i)     Companies like **Reuters** offer access to a range of predominantly business related information.

  (ii)    Many information provision services are now provided via the **Internet**. As the rate of Internet use increases, greater numbers of people and organisations are using it to source information on a vast range of topics.

**Key term**

> The phrase **environmental scanning** is often used to describe the process of gathering external information, which is available from a wide range of sources.

| Question | Information |

(a)     Think about the relative importance of internally-produced and external information. What sort of problems might, say, Marks and Spencer face if it decided **not** to collect external information?

(b)     Also think about how information needs vary for different types of organisation, such as commercial, public sector and charities.

# 5 Information systems

## 5.1 Types of information system

FAST FORWARD

> Different **types of information systems** exist with different characteristics – reflecting the different roles they perform.

### 5.1.1 Executive Information Systems (EIS)

**Key term**

> An **Executive Information System (EIS)** pools data from internal and external sources and makes information available to senior managers in an easy-to-use form. EIS help senior managers make strategic, unstructured decisions.

An EIS should provide senior managers with easy access to key **internal** and **external** information. The system summarises and tracks strategically critical information, possibly drawn from internal MIS and DSS (see below), but also including data from external sources eg competitors, legislation, and external databases such as Reuters.

Executive Information Systems are sometimes referred to as **Executive Support Systems** (ESS). An ESS/EIS is likely to have the following **features**.

- Flexibility
- Quick response time
- Sophisticated data analysis and modelling tools

A model of a typical EIS follows.

**An Executive Information System (EIS)**

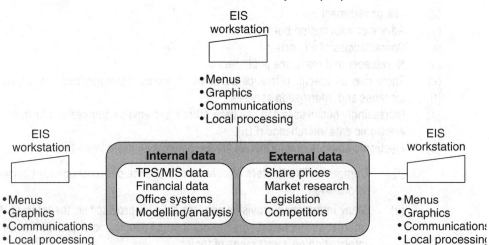

### 5.1.2 Management Information Systems (MIS)

**Key term**

> **Management Information Systems (MIS)** convert data from mainly internal sources into information (eg summary reports, exception reports). This information enables managers to make timely and effective decisions for planning, directing and controlling the activities for which they are responsible.

An MIS provides regular reports and (usually) on-line access to the organisation's current and historical performance.

MIS usually transform data from underlying transaction processing systems (TPS) into summarised files that are used as the basis for management reports.

MIS have the following characteristics:

- Support **structured** decisions at operational and management control levels
- Designed to report on **existing** operations
- Have little analytical capability
- Relatively **inflexible**
- Have an **internal** focus

**Exam focus point**

> The November 2007 exam required candidates to explain the value of good MIS and EISs. To gain good marks candidates were expected to think about the benefits these systems bring to an organisation.

### 5.1.3 Decision Support Systems (DSS)

**Key term**

> **Decision Support Systems (DSS)** combine data and analytical models or data analysis tools to support semi-structured and unstructured decision making.

DSS are used by management to assist in making decisions on issues which are subject to high levels of uncertainty, the various **responses** which management could undertake, or the likely **impact** of those actions.

Decision support systems are intended to provide a wide range of alternative information gathering and analytical tools with a major emphasis upon **flexibility** and **user-friendliness**.

DSS have more analytical power than other systems, enabling them to analyse and condense large volumes of data into a form that aids managers' decision making. The objective is to allow the manager to consider a number of **alternatives** and evaluate them under a variety of potential conditions.

### 5.1.4 Knowledge Work Systems (KWS)

**Key terms**

> **Knowledge Work Systems (KWS)** are information systems that facilitate the creation and integration of new knowledge into an organisation.
>
> **Knowledge Workers** are people whose jobs primarily involve creating new information and knowledge. They are often members of a profession such as doctors, engineers, lawyers and scientists.

KWS help knowledge workers create new knowledge and expertise. Examples include:

- Computer Aided Design (CAD)
- Computer Aided Manufacturing (CAM)
- Specialised financial software that analyses trading situations

### 5.1.5 Office Automation Systems (OAS)

**Key term**

> **Office Automation Systems (OAS)** are computer systems designed to increase the productivity of data and information workers.

OAS support the major activities performed in a typical office such as document management, facilitating communication and managing data. Examples include:

- Word processing, desktop publishing, and digital filing systems
- E-mail, voice mail, videoconferencing, groupware, intranets, schedulers
- Spreadsheets, desktop databases

## 5.1.6 Transaction Processing Systems (TPS)

> A **Transaction Processing System (TPS)** performs and records routine transactions.

TPS are used for **routine tasks** in which data items or transactions must be processed so that operations can continue. TPS support most business functions in most types of organisation. The following table shows a range of TPS applications.

| Transaction processing systems | | | | | |
|---|---|---|---|---|---|
| | Sales/ marketing systems | Manufacturing/ production systems | Finance/ accounting systems | Human resources systems | Other types (eg university) |
| **Major functions of system** | • Sales management<br>• Market research<br>• Promotion pricing<br>• New products | • Scheduling<br>• Purchasing Shipping/ receiving<br>• Engineering<br>• Operations | • Budgeting<br>• General ledger<br>• Billing<br>• Management accounting | • Personnel records<br>• Benefits<br>• Salaries<br>• Labour relations<br>• Training | • Admissions<br>• Student academic records<br>• Course records<br>• Graduates |
| **Major application systems** | • Sales order information system<br>• Market research system<br>• Pricing system | • Materials resource planning<br>• Purchase order control<br>• Engineering<br>• Quality control | • General ledger<br>• Accounts receivable /payable<br>• Budgeting<br>• Funds management | • Payroll<br>• Employee records<br>• Employee benefits<br>• Career path systems | • Registration<br>• Student record<br>• Curriculum/ class control systems<br>• Benefactor information system |

## 5.1.7 Expert systems

Expert systems are a form of DSS that allow users to benefit from expert knowledge and information. The system will consist of a **database** holding specialised data and **rules** about what to do in, or how to interpret, a given set of circumstances.

For example, many financial institutions now use expert systems to process straightforward **loan applications**. The user enters certain key facts into the system such as the loan applicant's name and most recent addresses, their income and monthly outgoings, and details of other loans. The system will then:

(a)   **Check the facts** given against its database to see whether the applicant has a good credit record.

(b)   **Perform calculations** to see whether the applicant can afford to repay the loan.

(c)   **Match up other criteria**, such as whether the security offered for the loan or the purpose for which the loan is wanted is acceptable, and to what extent the loan applicant fits the lender's profile of a good risk (based on the lender's previous experience).

A decision is then suggested, based on the results of this processing. This is why it is now often possible to get a loan or arrange insurance **over the telephone**, whereas in the past it would have been necessary to go and speak to a bank manager or send details to an actuary and then wait for him or her to come to a decision.

> Do not just learn what these systems are; you need to understand which levels of an organisation's hierarchy would use them and how they support its operations.

There are many other **business applications** of expert systems.

(a)   **Legal** advice.

(b)   **Tax** advice.

(c)   **Forecasting** of economic or financial developments, or of market and customer behaviour.

(d)   **Surveillance**, for example of the number of customers entering a supermarket, to decide what shelves need restocking and when more checkouts need to be opened, or of machines in a factory, to determine when they need maintenance.

(e)   **Diagnostic systems**, to identify causes of problems, for example in production control in a factory, or in healthcare.

(f)   **Project management**.

(g)   **Education** and **training**, diagnosing a student's or worker's weaknesses and providing or recommending extra instruction as appropriate.

An organisation can use an expert system when a number of conditions are met.

(a)   The problem is **reasonably well-defined**.

(b)   The expert can define some **rules** by which the problem can be solved.

(c)   The problem cannot be solved by **conventional** transaction processing or data handling.

(d)   The **expert could be released** to more difficult problems. Experts are often highly paid, meaning the value of even small time savings is likely to be significant.

(e)   The **investment** in an expert system is **cost-justified**.

| Question | Expert systems |
|---|---|

Explain why organisations use expert systems for decision-making tasks which humans are naturally better able to perform than computers?                                                    (5 marks)

| Answer |
|---|

The primary reason has to do with the relative costs. A 'human' expert is likely to be more expensive either to employ or to use on a consultancy basis.

Secondly, enshrining an expert's accumulated wisdom in a computer system means that this wisdom can be accessed by more people. Thus, the delivery of complicated services to customers, decisions whether or not to extend credit and so forth, can be made by less experienced members of staff. If a manufacturing company has a complicated mixture of plant and machinery, then the repair engineer may accumulate a lot of knowledge over a period of time about the way it behaves: if a problem occurs, the engineer will be able to make a reasoned guess as to where the likely cause is to be found. If this accumulated expert information is made available to less experienced staff, it means that some of their learning curve is avoided.

An expert system is advantageous because it saves time, like all computer systems (in theory at least) but it is particularly useful as it possesses both knowledge and limited reasoning ability.

### 5.1.8 Intranets and Extranets

Organisations are increasingly using **intranets** and **extranets** to **disseminate information**.

(a)   An **intranet** is like a mini version of the Internet. Organisation members use networked computers to access information held on a server. The user interface is a browser – similar to those used on the Internet. The intranet offers access to information on a wide variety of topics.

(b)   An **extranet** is an intranet that is accessible to **authorised outsiders**, using a valid username and password. The username will have access rights attached – determining which parts of the extranet can be viewed. Extranets are becoming a very popular means for business partners to exchange information.

An **intranet** is a private network inside a company or organisation accessed through web-browser like software. Intranets are for the use of staff only, they are not accessible by the public. Intranets are used to provide and distribute information.

An **extranet** allows customers and suppliers to gain limited access to an intranet in order to enhance the speed and efficiency of their business relationship. Put another way, it is an intranet that allows some access by authorised outsiders.

## Question                                                          Types of systems

Which of the following statements is **incorrect**?

A     Expert systems exist that can help decide credit worthiness.

B     A management information system is normally capable of producing exception reports.

C     Batch processing systems are not appropriate if information is required to be up-to-date at all times.

D     An expert system always provides the correct solution to a problem.

## Answer

D     An expert system can produce an incorrect answer. The answer produced by the system depends on the quality of the data and rules held by the system. The other statements are all correct.

**Exam focus poin**

This area of the syllabus is developing quickly. Ensure you keep up to date by reading the articles in *Financial Management*. In particular an article by Camilla Berens in November 2006 considers the online auction house eBay.

## 5.2 Summary

The diagram below shows how information systems may be utilised at different levels within an organisation, and how these systems may interact.

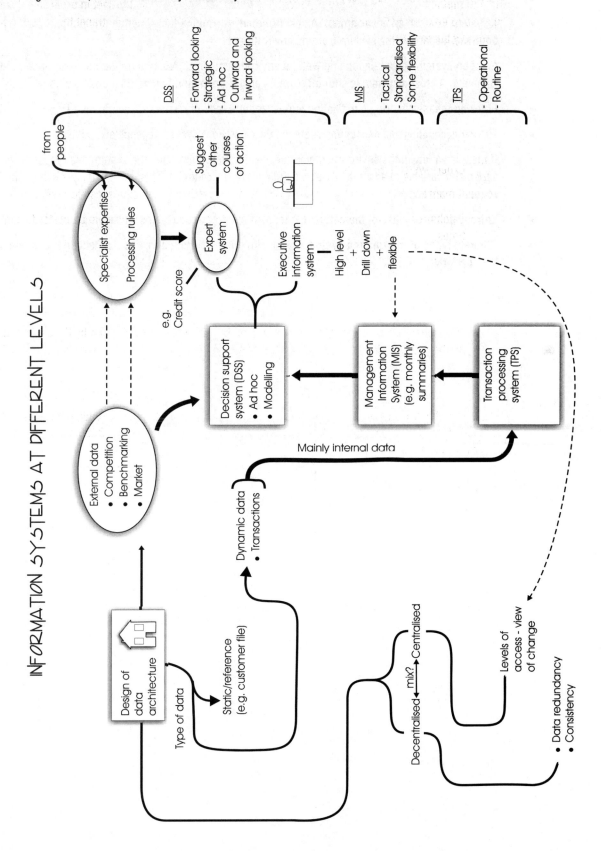

INFORMATION SYSTEMS AT DIFFERENT LEVELS

# Chapter Roundup

- Any system can be thought of in terms of **inputs**, **processing** and **outputs**.

- A system exists in an environment. An environment surrounds the system but is not part of it. A **system boundary** separates the system from its environment.

- An **open** system has a relationship with its environment which has both prescribed and uncontrolled elements. A **closed** system is shut off from its environment and has no relationship with it.

- **Filtering** means ensuring information is relevant and required before disseminating.

- The terms **coupling** and **decoupling** relate to how closely one system depends on another.

- If there is variety in the environmental influences in the system, then the system itself must be suitably varied and variable to adapt itself successfully to its environment. This is the principle behind the **law of requisite variety**.

- **Entropy** arises because of the natural tendency of objects and systems, to fall into a state of disorder.

- Different **types of information systems** exist with different characteristics – reflecting the different roles they perform.

# Quick Quiz

1    What are the three component parts of a system?

    1 ....................................................

    2 ....................................................

    3 ....................................................

2    Define the terms open system and closed system.

3    Why do coupled systems have increased potential for problems?

4    How can requisite variety be introduced into a control system?

5    'The more entropy present in a system the more efficient the system is likely to be'.

    True ☐

    False ☐

6    Which of the following is not a type of information system?

    A    EIS
    B    MIS
    C    DWS
    D    OAS

# Answers to Quick Quiz

1    Inputs, processes and outputs.

2    An open system is a system connected to and interacting with its environment. A closed system is a system which is isolated from its environment and independent of it.

3    Linking systems together may improve efficiency when things go to plan, but also means that the impact of any 'mishap' is likely to spread to coupled systems.

4    Two examples are: by allowing a controller discretion over what control action is needed, or by introducing tolerance limits.

5    False. Entropy is disorder. A system in disorder is less efficient.

6    C    The others are: Executive Information System, Management Information System and Office Automation System.

Now try the question below from the Exam Question Bank

| Number | Level | Marks | Time |
|--------|-------|-------|------|
| 1 | Examination | 30 | 54 mins |

# Systems development

## Introduction

In this chapter we look in detail at the stages and activities involved in **systems development**.

We provide an **overview**, as the examiner **does not expect you to be an expert systems analyst** or to have computer programming knowledge.

However, you should understand the concept and main principles of systems development.

Exam questions in this area are likely to focus on the importance of **user involvement** in system design – and upon the wider organisation benefits an information system may bring.

| Topic list | Learning outcomes | Syllabus references | Ability required |
|---|---|---|---|
| 1 The systems development cycle | A(v) | A(9) | Evaluation |
| 2 The feasibility study | A(iii), A(iv), A(v) | A(9) | Evaluation |
| 3 Systems investigation | A(iii), A(v) | A(9) | Evaluation |
| 4 Analysis and design methods | A(iii), A(iv) | A(4) | Evaluation |
| 5 Implementation | A(v), A(vi) | A(8), A(9), A(11) | Evaluation |
| 6 System maintenance | A(iv) | A(6), A(13) | Evaluation |
| 7 System evaluation and performance measurement | A(iv), A(vi) | A(6), A(11) | Evaluation |
| 8 Post-implementation review | A(iv), A(vi) | A(6), A(10), A(11) | Evaluation |

# 1 The systems development cycle

The **systems development life cycle** is a formal model of the stages involved in **systems development**.

## 1.1 The formal systems development life cycle (SDLC)

**Key term**

The **systems development life cycle** is the process of conceiving, designing and implementing an information system.

**In the early days of computing**, systems were developed in a fairly haphazard fashion. **The development of systems was not properly planned**. The consequences were often poorly designed systems, which cost too much to make and which were not suited to users' needs.

As early as the 1960s, developers attempted to bring order to the development process. Since then, a number of systems development life cycle (SDLC) models have been created. The original 'typical' SDLC is sometimes referred to as the **waterfall model** – this is because it involves a **sequence** of stages in which the **output of each stage** becomes the **input for the next stage**. One example of a 'typical' SDLC model is explained below (this one has seven stages, some analysts prefer to combine various stages such as Analysis and Design).

| Stage | Comment |
| --- | --- |
| **Identification of a problem or opportunity** | This starts with the initial suggestion that 'things could be done better' and may involve an analysis of the organisation's information requirements. |
| **Feasibility study** | This involves a review of the existing system and the identification of a range of possible alternative solutions. A feasible (technical, operational, economic, social) solution will be selected – or a decision not to proceed made. |
| **System investigation** | A fact finding exercise which investigates the existing system to assess its problems and requirements and to obtain details of data volumes, response times and other key indicators. |
| **System analysis** | Once the workings of the existing system have been documented, they can be analysed. This process examines why current methods are used, what alternatives might achieve the same, or better, results, and what performance criteria are required from a new system. |
| **System design** | System design will examine existing computerised and manual procedures, addressing, in particular, inputs, outputs, program design, file design and security. New processes will also be considered allowing a detailed specification of the new system to be produced. |
| **System implementation** | This stage carries development through from design to operations. It involves acquisition (or writing) of software, program testing, file conversion or set-up, acquisition and installation of hardware and 'going live'. |
| **Review and maintenance** | This is an ongoing process which ensures that the system meets the objectives set during the feasibility study, that it is accepted by users and that its performance is satisfactory. |

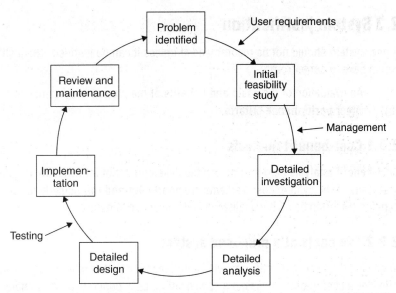

In the remainder of this chapter, we will look in greater detail at the activities undertaken during each stage of systems development.

**Exam focus point**

Your knowledge of systems development could be tested in an objective test question, which would most likely test you have **learnt the theory**. On the other hand, systems development may be relevant to a scenario question, which would most likely require you to **apply the theory** to the situation described.

# 2 The feasibility study

**FAST FORWARD**

A **feasibility study** is carried out to ensure that a system is viable or feasible. It normally includes a **cost-benefit analysis**.

**Key term**

A **feasibility study** is a formal study to decide what type of system can be developed which best meets the needs of the organisation.

## 2.1 Feasibility study team

A **feasibility study team** should be appointed to carry out the study (although individuals might be given the task in the case of smaller projects). The team should include people from departments affected by the project as well as those with the required technical and business knowledge. With larger projects it may well be worthwhile for a small firm to employ a **professional systems analyst** and then appoint a management team to work with the analyst.

## 2.2 Conducting the feasibility study

The feasibility study should be conducted within a well-defined  terms of reference that makes it clear exactly what the study aims to achieve, and sets boundaries that ensures the study remains focussed.

### 2.2.1 Problem definition

In some circumstances the '**problem**' (for example the necessity for a real-time as opposed to a batch-processed application) may be quite **exact**; in others it may be characterised as '**soft**' (related to people and the way they behave).

### 2.2.2 Option evaluation

The study may uncover or suggest a number of possible **options** for a new system. The study should evaluate these and recommend one for adoption, usually in the **feasibility study report**.

## 2.3 System justification

A new system should not be recommended unless it can be justified. The justification for a new system would have to come from:

(a)     An evaluation of the **costs and benefits** of the proposed system, and/or
(b)     Other **performance criteria**.

### 2.3.1 Cost-benefit analysis

**Cost-benefit analysis** before or during the development of information systems is complicated by the fact that many of the system cost elements are **poorly defined** (particularly for development projects) and that benefits can often be highly qualitative and subjective in nature.

### 2.3.2 The costs of a proposed system

In general the best cost estimates will be obtained for systems bought from an **outside vendor** who provides a cost quotation against a specification. Less concrete cost estimates are generally found with development projects where the work is performed by the organisation's own employees.

The costs of a new system will include costs in a number of different categories – see the following table.

| Cost | Example |
|---|---|
| **Equipment costs** | • Computer and peripherals<br>• Ancillary equipment<br>• The initial system supplies (disks, tapes, paper etc) |
| **Installation costs** | • New buildings (if necessary)<br>• The computer room (wiring, air-conditioning if necessary) |
| **Development costs** | • Measuring and analysing the existing system<br>• Software/consultancy work<br>• Systems analysis and programming<br>• Changeover costs such as file conversion |
| **Personnel costs** | • Staff training<br>• Staff recruitment/relocation<br>• Staff salaries and pensions<br>• Redundancy payments<br>• Overheads |
| **Operating costs** | • Consumable materials (tapes, disks, stationery etc)<br>• Maintenance<br>• Accommodation costs<br>• Heating/power/insurance/telephone<br>• Standby arrangements, in case the system breaks down |

### 2.3.3 The benefits of a proposed system

The benefits from a proposed new system must also be evaluated. These should include:

(a)     **Savings** because an inefficient **old system** will no longer be operated.
(b)     Extra **savings** or revenue benefits because of the improvements or enhancements that the **new system** should bring, for example better inventory control (with a new inventory control system) and so fewer inventory losses from obsolescence or lost sales due to stock-outs.

Some benefits might be **intangible**, or impossible to give a money value to.

(a)     Greater **customer satisfaction**, arising from a more prompt service.
(b)     Improved **staff morale** from working with a 'better' system.
(c)     **Better decision making** is hard to quantify, but may result from better MIS, DSS or EIS.

The main **financial selection** techniques are listed below. The syllabus does not include a detailed analysis of these techniques – although you may draw on your knowledge of these techniques when discussing feasibility.

- The payback method
- Discounted cashflow
- Accounting rate of return
- Return on investment

# 3 Systems investigation

FAST FORWARD

> The **systems investigation** is a detailed **fact-finding exercise** about the areas and system under consideration. Methods employed include the use of **interviews** and **questionnaires**.

The project team has to determine the **inputs, outputs, processing methods** and **volumes** of the current system. It reviews the organisational structure and examines controls, staffing and costs. It should also consider the expected growth of the organisation and its **future requirements**.

## 3.1 Systems investigation tools

### 3.1.1 Interviews

**Interviews** with members of staff can be an effective method of fact finding. Although they can be **time consuming** for the analyst, who may have several to conduct, and therefore expensive.

(a)    In an interview **attitudes** not apparent from other sources may be obtained.

(b)    **Immediate clarification** can be sought to unsatisfactory/ambiguous responses.

(c)    Interviews require a response – some staff may ignore a questionnaire.

(d)    A well-conducted interview should provide staff with **reassurance** regarding the upcoming change.

Some guidelines to consider when conducting fact-finding interviews are explained below.

(a)    **Employees ought to be informed** before the interview that a systems investigation is taking place, and its **purpose explained**.

(b)    The interviewer's approach should be **adapted** to suit the individual interviewee.

(c)    The interviewer should be **fully prepared** with a plan of questions.

(d)    The interview should **not be too formal**, but should be allowed to develop into a **conversation**.

(e)    The interview should be long enough for the interviewer to obtain the information required and to ensure an understanding of the system, but short enough to ensure that concentration does not wander.

### 3.1.2 Questionnaires

The use of questionnaires may be useful whenever a **limited** amount of **information** is required from a large number of individuals. Questionnaires may be used as the **groundwork for interviews** with some respondents being interviewed subsequently.

Many respondents find questionnaires **less imposing than interviews** and may therefore be more prepared to express their opinion.

(a)    Employees ought to be informed of the questionnaire's **purpose**. This should remove any staff suspicion and encourage sensible responses.

(b)    **Question design** is important. Questions should obtain the specific information required.

(c)    Questionnaires must not be too long – a questionnaire of many pages is likely to end up in a 'pending' tray indefinitely, or worse, the bin. They should be **organised in a logical sequence**.

(d)    Ideally, they should be designed so that each question can be answered with a limited range of answers, such as **'yes'** or **'no'** or a 'tick' in a numbered box, eg 1 = Strongly agree, 4 = Strongly disagree.

(e)   They should be **tested independently** before being issued. This should enable the systems analyst to establish the effectiveness of the questions.

(f)   Questionnaires should take into account the **sensitivity** of individuals in respect of any threat to their job security, change of job definition etc.

(g)   Staff may prefer **anonymity**. This should result in greater honesty, but has the disadvantage of preventing follow-up of uncompleted questionnaires, and of 'interesting' responses.

Questionnaires, by themselves, are useful for gathering specific information. In a systems development context, it is likely that further methods of gathering information, such as interview or observation, would also be required.

### 3.1.3 Observation

An analyst, after establishing the methods and procedures used in the organisation, may wish to undertake further investigation through **observing operations**. Observation may be used to check facts obtained by interview or questionnaire.

The observer must remember that staff may act differently simply because they know they are being observed – this is a difficult problem to overcome as observing staff without their knowledge may not be **ethical**.

### 3.1.4 User workshops

A workshop is a meeting with the emphasis on **practical exercises**. User workshops are often used in systems analysis to help establish and record user requirements.

User workshops should be facilitated by a **facilitator**. The facilitator co-ordinates the workshop activities with the aim of ensuring the objectives of the session are achieved.

### 3.1.5 Document review

The systems analyst should investigate existing **documents** in use. This may be a wide ranging investigation, using for example organisation charts, procedures manuals and standard operational forms.

### 3.1.6 Existing computerised systems

User requirements for a new computerised system can also be collected from existing computerised systems. It is important to take into account changes in the way work is being carried out – it is unlikely that the new system will be performing an identical role to the old system.

With this in mind, areas where the existing system can provide useful information include:

- File structures
- Transaction volumes
- Screen design
- User satisfaction
- User complaints
- Help desk/Information centre records
- Causes of system crashes
- Processor speed

It is important to remember however, that a duplicate of the existing system is not required. The aim is to produce a better system – which is likely to involve changes to existing working methods.

**Exam focus point**

> You need to understand these methods of systems investigation and be able to generate advantages and disadvantages for each.

## 3.2 Requirements creep

If user requirements are investigated and established effectively, an accurate picture should be established of what the new system should achieve. This should prevent a common problem occurring later in the project, the problem of 'requirements creep'.

Requirements creep refers to the situation where **users appear to change their requirements** throughout the development process. Requirements creep may be due to actual changes in user requirements, but the real cause is often an inaccurate original system specification.

# 4 Analysis and design methods

FAST FORWARD

**Systems analysis** examines why **current methods** are used, what **alternatives** are available, what **restricts the effectiveness** of the system and what **performance criteria** are required from a new system.

The **systems analysis** process examines why **current methods** are used and what **alternatives** might achieve the same or better results. A variety of fact-finding techniques are available to determine how a system operates, what document flows occur, what work processes are involved and what personnel are involved.

FAST FORWARD

**Data flow diagrams** are used to show how data is processed. **Entity relationship models** provide an understanding of a system's logical data requirements independently of the system's processes. **Entity life history** shows the processes that happen to an entity and **decision tables** define the logic of a process.

## 4.1 Data flow diagrams (DFD)

Data flow diagrams show the ways in which data is processed. The production of a data flow diagram is often the first step in a structured systems analysis, because it provides a **basic understanding of how the system works**. The following four symbols are used in data flow diagrams.

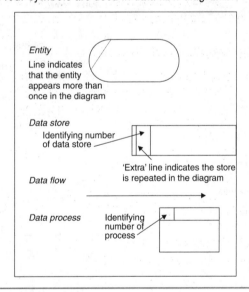

**Key terms**

An **external entity** is a **source** or **destination** of data which is considered **external to the system** (not necessarily external to the organisation). It may be people or groups who provide data or input information or who receive data or output information.

A **data store** is a point which receives a data flow and holds data. Most data stores would be either digital (ie computer files) or paper.

A **data flow** represents the movement or transfer of data from one point in the system to another.

**Data processes** involve data being used or altered. The processes could be manual, mechanised or computerised.

A **data flow** could 'physically' be anything – for example a letter, a telephone call, a fax, an e-mail, a link between computers, or a verbal statement. When a data flow occurs, a copy of the data transferred may also be retained at the transmitting point.

A **process** could involve changing the data in some way, or simply using the data. For example, a mathematical computation or a process such as sorting would alter data, whereas printing data out does not change it – the process makes the same data available in a different form.

**Exam focus point**

CIMA have stated that students will not be required to produce a data flow diagram in the examination. However, **knowledge of data flow diagrams is examinable**.

## 4.2 Example: data flow diagram

The following example is based upon a system used for purchasing in a manufacturing company.

Within this organisation, the **Stores department** places requests for purchases and accepts delivery of the goods, the **Purchasing department** places orders, and receives and pays invoices. A **DFD** for the purchasing department is shown below. The top section of the diagram starts with the Purchase request being sent from Stores to Purchasing. The bottom section starts with the Supplier sending an Invoice.

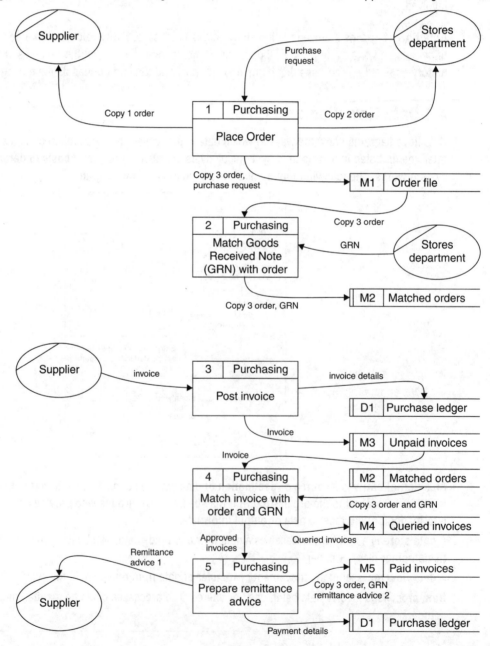

The following points may be observed.

(a)  Each process is numbered, but this is only for ease of identification: the numbers are not meant to show the strict sequence of events.

(b)  Each process box has a heading, showing where the process is carried out or who does it. The description of the process should be a clear verb like 'prepare', 'calculate', 'check' (not 'process', which is too vague).

(c)  The same entity or store may appear more than once on the same diagram (to prevent diagrams becoming overly complicated with arrows crossing each other). When this is done an additional line is put within the symbol. The supplier entity and several of the data stores have extra lines for this reason.

(d)  Data stores are given a reference number (again sequence is not important). Some analysts like to use 'M' with this number if it is a **manual** store, and a 'D' if it is a digital or **computerised** store.

## Question

Data source/destination

In a data flow diagram (DFD), a source and/or destination is known as:

A    A root node.
B    An entity.
C    A data store.
D    A data process.

## Answer

B    A data flow diagram is constructed to show entities, data flows, data processes and data stores. An entity is a source or destination of data from which or to which data or information will flow. For example, in an online stock-broker system, entities will include clients of the stockbroker and market dealers in securities with which the broker makes transactions on behalf of clients.

## 4.3 Entity relationship modelling

An **entity**, as we have seen, is an item (a person, a job, a business, an activity, a product or stores item etc) about which information is stored.

**Key terms**

> An **entity** is any item, role, object, organisation, activity or person that is relevant to the data held in a system.
>
> An **Entity Relationship Model (ERM)** (also known as an **entity model** or a **Logical Data Structure (LDS)**) provides an understanding of the logical data requirements of a system independently of the system's organisation and processes.

An **attribute** is a characteristic or property of an entity. For a customer, attributes include customer name and address, amounts owing, date of invoices sent and payments received, credit limit etc. The following **relationships** may be identified between attributes and entities.

### 4.3.1 One-to-one relationship (1:1)

With a one-to-one relationship, an entity is related to only one other entity. For example, a one-to-one relationship exists between *company* and *finance director*. The model below shows one company which employs one finance director. (These diagrams are sometimes called Bachmann diagrams.)

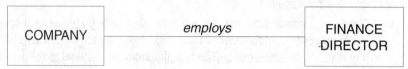

### 4.3.2 One-to-many relationship (1:M)

For example, the relationship '**employs**', also exists between *company* and *director*. The company employs more than one director.

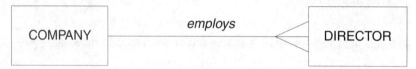

### 4.3.3 Many-to-one relationship (M:1)

This is really the same as the previous example, but **viewed from the opposite direction**. For example, many *sales managers* report to one *sales director*.

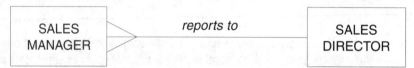

### 4.3.4 Many-to-many relationship (M:M)

The relationship between *product* and *part* is **many-to-many**. A product is composed of many parts, and a part might be used in many products.

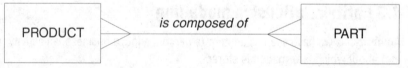

When analysing relationships the correct classification is important. If the one-to-many relationship, 'customer order', contains part numbers incorrectly described as one-to-one, a system designed on the basis of this ERM might allow an order to be entered with one item and one item only.

## 4.4 Example: building an ERM

A diagram modelling part of a warehousing and despatch system is shown below. This indicates that:

(a)   A customer may make many orders.

(b)   That an order form can contain several order lines.

(c)   That each line on the order form can only detail one product, but that one product can appear on several lines of the order.

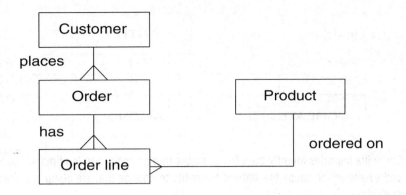

Learning outcome: A (iii)

Use the following narrative to construct an appropriate entity-model.          (10 marks)

| Entity | Relationship | Entity |
|---|---|---|
| Customer | Places many | Orders |
| Order | Has many | Deliveries |
| Product | Is ordered on many | Orders |
| Product | Is ordered on many | Purchase orders |
| Supplier | Receives many | Purchase orders |
| Invoice | Is for one | Delivery |
| Customer | Receives many | Invoices |

Answer

## 4.5 Entity life histories (ELH)

As we have seen, **Entity Relationship Models** take a **static** view of data. We will now look at a modelling tool that focuses on data processes.

**Key term**

An **Entity Life History** (**ELH**) is a diagram of the *processes* that happen to an *entity*. An entity life history gives a **dynamic** view of the data.

Data items do not always remain unchanged – they may come into existence by a specific operation and be destroyed by another. For example, a customer order forms part of a number of processes, and is affected by a number of different events. At its simplest, an entity life history displays the following structure.

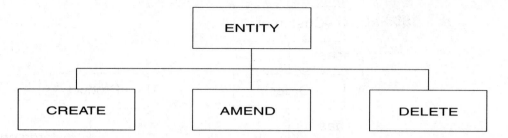

Entity life histories identify the various states that an entity can legitimately be in. It is really the functions and events which cause the state of the entity to change that are being analysed, rather than the entity itself.

The following notation rules are used for Entity life histories.

(a)     Three symbols are used. The main one is a rectangular box. Within this may be placed an asterisk or a small circle, as explained below.

(b)     At the top level the first box (the '**root node**') shows the entity itself.

(c)     At lower levels the boxes represent events that affect the life of the entity.

(d)     The second level is most commonly some form of 'create, amend, delete', as explained earlier (or birth, life, death if you prefer). The boxes are read in **sequence** from top to bottom and left to right.

(e)     If an event may affect an entity many times (**iteration**) this is shown by an **asterisk** in the top right hand corner of the box. A customer account, for example, will be updated many times.

(f)     If events are alternatives (**selection**) – for example accept large order or reject large order – a **small circle** is placed in the top right hand corner.

Note the three types of process logic referred to:

•     Sequence
•     Iteration (or repetition)
•     Selection

Here is a very simple example.

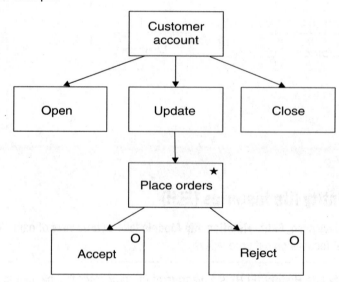

# 4.6 Decision tables

Decision tables are used as a method of defining the logic of a process (ie the processing operations required) in a compact manner. They are particularly useful in situations where a **large number of logical alternatives exist**. The basic format consists of four quadrants divided by intersecting double lines.

| Condition stub | Condition entry |
|---|---|
| Action stub | Action entry |

## 4.6.1 Simple example: a decision table

We start by considering a very simple decision that most of us face every day: whether to get up or stay in bed.

Suppose you have to get up at around 8 am during the week to enable you to get to work on time. You go to work on Monday to Friday only. If you woke up one Tuesday morning at 8.02 you would be faced with the following appalling dilemma. An X marks the action you should take.

| Conditions | Entry |
|---|---|
| Is it 8 o' clock yet? | Yes |
| Is it the weekend? | No |
| Actions | Entry |
| Get up | X |
| Stay in bed | |

We can expand this table so that it takes account of **all the possible combinations** of conditions and shows the action that would be taken in each case.

(a) Because a condition can only apply or not apply (Yes or No), the number of combinations (or 'rules') is $2^n$, where n is the number of conditions.

Here there are two conditions (n = 2) so the number of combinations is $2^2 = 4$. There are four columns.

| | 1 | 2 | 3 | 4 |
|---|---|---|---|---|
| Is it 8 o' clock yet? | | | | |
| Is it the weekend? | | | | |
| Get up | | | | |
| Stay in bed | | | | |

(b) The conditions can either have a Yes or No answer (Y or N).

(i) As there are **two** possible outcomes, fill **half** of each row with Ys and the other half with Ns. So, write in Y for the first half of the columns in row 1 (columns 1 and 2) and N for the other half (columns 3 and 4).

(ii) For row 2, write in Ys and Ns for **half** the number of columns of each group in the previous row. In this example row 1 has Ys in groups of twos, so row 2 will have Ys in groups of one.

(iii) If there are more conditions continue **halving** for each row until you reach the final condition, which will always be consecutive Ys and Ns.

| | 1 | 2 | 3 | 4 |
|---|---|---|---|---|
| Is it 8 o' clock yet? | Y | Y | N | N |
| Is it the weekend? | Y | N | Y | N |
| Get up | | | | |
| Stay in bed | | | | |

(c) Now **consider what action** you would take if the condition(s) specified in each column applied. For column 1 it is 8 o'clock but it is the weekend so you can stay in bed. For column 2 it is 8 o' clock but it is not the weekend so you must get up. Explain the logic of columns 3 and 4 yourself.

| | 1 | 2 | 3 | 4 |
|---|---|---|---|---|
| Is it 8 o' clock yet? | Y | Y | N | N |
| Is it the weekend? | Y | N | Y | N |
| Get up | | X | | |
| Stay in bed | X | | X | X |

(d) In more complicated problems you may find that there are some columns that do not have any Xs in the Action entry quadrant because **this combination of conditions is impossible**.

## Question

Learning outcome: A(iii)

Mr L Bones decided to draw up a decision table demonstrating the decision-making process he executed when he woke up each day.

He identified three conditions, mirroring his early-morning thought processes, and two possible actions.

*Conditions*    Is it 8 o' clock yet? Is it a weekday? Is it the weekend?

*Actions*    Get up. Stay in bed.

*Required*

Draw up and complete the decision table.                    (10 marks)

## Answer

There are three conditions so there will be $2^3$ = 8 columns.

| | 1 | 2 | 3 | 4 | 5 | 6 | 7 | 8 |
|---|---|---|---|---|---|---|---|---|
| Is it 8 o' clock yet? | Y | Y | Y | Y | N | N | N | N |
| Is it a weekday? | Y | Y | N | N | Y | Y | N | N |
| Is it the weekend? | Y | N | Y | N | Y | N | Y | N |
| Get up | | X | | | | | | |
| Stay in bed | | | X | | | | X | X |

Columns 1, 4, 5 and 8 do not have any Xs because it cannot be both a weekday *and* a weekend. In more complex decision situations it may only become clear that certain combinations are impossible once the table has been drawn up.

In this example we could simplify the table by deleting columns 1, 4, 5 and 8. We then end up with the same decision table as the one we saw earlier (although with the columns in a different order).

The very simple example above demonstrates the basics of decision tables. This is sufficient knowledge for the P4 exam, as it is unlikely you will be asked to construct a table. Therefore, don't get too bogged down in the more complicated examples that follow. These are provided to help your understanding, but it is not essential (for the P4 exam) to be able to produce a perfect decision table.

### 4.6.2 A more formal explanation

We can now explain this more formally and look at a business example.

- The purpose of the **condition stub** is to specify the values of the data that we wish to test for.
- The **condition entry** specifies what those values might be.

Between them, the condition stub and condition entry show what values an item of data might have that a computer program should test for. Establishing conditions will be done within a computer program by means of **comparison checks**.

The **action entry** quadrant shows the action or actions that will be performed for each rule. The columns are marked with an 'X' opposite the actions(s) to be taken. In the computer program, instructions specify the action to take, given the conditions established by comparison checks.

## 4.7 Example: a decision table

There are **three conditions** which might be encountered by a sales order processing clerk taking a telephone order.

- The caller may have an existing overdue balance on their account
- The caller's account balance may already be in excess of their credit limit
- The caller may not have an account at all

(Note that the possibility that the customer has an existing account, that is not overdue, and has not exceeded their credit limit, is covered by answering 'N' to these three conditions.)

The number of columns in the decision table is the number of options to the power of the number of conditions. In this example there are two options – 'Y' or 'N' and three conditions. The number of rules is therefore $(2^3)$ – **eight rules**.

| Rule | 1 | 2 | 3 | 4 | 5 | 6 | 7 | 8 |
|---|---|---|---|---|---|---|---|---|
| Account overdue? | Y | Y | Y | Y | N | N | N | N |
| Credit limit exceeded? | Y | Y | N | N | Y | Y | N | N |
| New customer (no account)? | Y | N | Y | N | Y | N | Y | N |

The three conditions in this example are **not** totally **independent**. Therefore some rules can be eliminated as **impossible**. For example, a customer that does not currently have an account cannot have an overdue balance and therefore will not have a credit limit. In cases such as this you should **start with a complete table** like that shown above – and deal with the impossible combinations later.

Continuing the example, suppose that the **actions** are as follows.

Orders from existing customers who do not have an overdue balance and have not exceeded their credit limit should **be processed**.

This organisation decides that customers requiring an account must **provide credit references** for checking before the account can be opened. If these customers attempt to place an order before an account is set up, the order is **placed on hold**.

The policy for orders from existing customers with a balance in **excess of their credit limit** is that these orders are **placed on hold** and **referred to the section head**.

The policy for existing customers who have overdue balances, but are within their credit limit, is to **process the order** but to **also generate a reminder** letter for overdue balances.

From this description we can isolate five actions.

- Process order
- Obtain reference
- Place order on hold
- Refer to head
- Send reminder

Consider the fourth rule in the following table. There is an overdue balance on the account, but the customer would remain within their credit limit. The action entry will therefore show an X against 'Process order' and 'Send reminder'.

| Rule | 1 | 2 | 3 | 4 | 5 | 6 | 7 | 8 |
|---|---|---|---|---|---|---|---|---|
| Account overdue? | Y | Y | Y | Y | N | N | N | N |
| Credit limit exceeded? | Y | Y | N | N | Y | Y | N | N |
| New customer (no account)? | Y | N | Y | N | Y | N | Y | N |
| Process order | | | | X | | | | |
| Obtain reference | | | | | | | | |
| Place order on hold | | | | | | | | |
| Refer to head | | | | | | | | |
| Send reminder | | | | X | | | | |

By considering each rule in turn the table can be completed. The rules that are **logically not possible** are shaded in the lower half of the table – and crossed out in the top half of the table.

| Rule | 1 | 2 | 3 | 4 | 5 | 6 | 7 | 8 |
|---|---|---|---|---|---|---|---|---|
| Account overdue? | Y | Y | Y | Y | N | N | N | N |
| Credit limit exceeded? | Y | Y | N | N | Y | Y | N | N |
| New customer (no account)? | Y | N | Y | N | Y | N | Y | N |
| Process order | | | | X | | | | X |
| Obtain reference | | | | | | | X | |
| Place order on hold | | X | | | | X | X | |
| Refer to head | | X | | | | X | | |
| Send reminder | | | | X | | | | |

## 4.8 Finalising the process of analysis and design

**FAST FORWARD**

**Systems design** is a technical phase which addresses in particular **inputs, outputs, program design, dialogue design, file design** and **security**.

### 4.8.1 The new system

The new system should be built to meet an agreed (by users, developers, management) **requirements specification**.

### 4.8.2 Logical design

Logical design involves describing the purpose of a system – what the system will do. Logical design does not include any specific hardware or software requirements – it is more concerned with the processes to be performed. Models such as data flow diagrams or written descriptions may be used to show and explain what a system will do.

### 4.8.3 Physical design

Physical design refers to the actual 'nuts and bolts' of the system – it includes technical specifications for the hardware and software required.

When the new system design has been finalised, the **next stage** of the system life cycle (**Implementation**) may begin.

# 5 Implementation

The main stages in the implementation of a computer system once it has been designed are as follows.

(a)     Installation of the **hardware and software**.
(b)     Testing.
(c)     Staff training and production of documentation.
(d)     Conversion of files and database creation.
(e)     Changeover.

The items in the list above **do not** necessarily happen in a set **chronological order**, and some can be done at the same time – for example staff training and system testing can be part of the same operation. The requirements for implementation **vary** from system to system.

## 5.1 Installation

Installing a mainframe computer or a large network is a major operation that is carried out by the manufacturer/supplier. If just a few PCs are being installed in a small network, this may be able to be performed by non-specialists.

Most new software is provided on CD-ROM and may be able to be installed by non-specialists, depending upon the complexity of the system and the checks required to ensure all is operating as intended.

## 5.2 Testing

FAST FORWARD

A system must be thoroughly **tested** to ensure it operates as intended. The nature and scope of testing will vary depending on the size and type of the system.

A system must be thoroughly tested before implementation, otherwise there is a danger that the new system will **go live with faults** that might prove costly. The scope of tests and trials will **vary** with the size and complexity of the system. To ensure a coherent, effective approach to testing, a testing plan should be developed.

A testing strategy should cover the following areas.

| Testing strategy area | Comment |
|---|---|
| **Strategy approach** | A testing strategy should be formulated that details the approach that will be taken to testing, including the tests to be conducted and the testing tools/techniques that will be used. |
| **Test plan** | A test plan should be developed that states what will be tested, when it will be tested (sequence), and the test environment. |
| **Test design** | The logic and reasoning behind the design of the tests should be explained. |
| **Performing tests** | Detailed procedures should be provided for all tests. This explanation should ensure tests are carried out consistently, even if different people carry out the tests. |
| **Documentation** | It must be clear how the results of tests are to be documented. This provides a record of errors, and a starting point for error correction procedures. |
| **Re-testing** | The re-test procedure should be explained. In many cases, after correction, all aspects of the software should be re-tested to ensure the corrections have not affected other aspects of the software. |

Four basic stages of testing can be identified: system logic, program testing, system testing and user acceptance testing.

### 5.2.1 Testing system logic

Before any programs are written, the logic devised by the systems analyst should be checked. This process would involve the use of flow charts or data flow diagrams.

The path of different types of data and transactions are manually plotted through the system, to ensure all possibilities have been catered for and that the processing logic is correct. When all results are as expected, programs can be written.

### 5.2.2 Program testing

Program testing involves processing test data through all programs. Test data should be of the type that the program will be required to process and should include invalid/exceptional items to test whether the program reacts as it should. Program testing should cover the following areas.

- Input validity checks
- Program logic and functioning
- Interfaces with related modules/systems
- Output format and validity

The testing process should be fully documented – recording data used, expected results, actual results and action taken. This documentation may be referred to at a later date, for example if program modifications are required. Two types of program testing are unit testing and unit integration testing.

### 5.2.3 Unit testing and unit integration testing

**Key terms**

> **Unit testing** means testing one function or part of a program to ensure it operates as intended.
>
> **Unit integration testing** involves testing two or more software units to ensure they work together as intended. The output from unit integration testing is a debugged module.

Unit testing involves detailed testing of part of a program. If it is established during unit testing that a program is not operating as intended, the cause of the error must be established and corrected. Automated diagnostic routines, that step through the program line by line may be used to help this process.

Test cases should be developed that include test data (inputs), test procedures, expected results and evaluation criteria. Sets of data should be developed for both unit testing and integration testing. Cases should be developed for all aspects of the software.

### 5.2.4 System testing (overall system testing)

When it has been established that individual programs and interfaces are operating as intended, **overall system testing** should begin. System testing has a wider focus than program testing. System testing should extend beyond areas already tested, to cover:

- Input documentation and the practicalities of input eg time taken
- Flexibility of system to allow amendments to the 'normal' processing cycle
- Ability to produce information on time
- Ability to cope with peak resource requirements eg transaction volumes
- Viability of operating procedures
- Ability to produce information on time

System testing will involve testing both before installation (known as off-line testing) and after implementation (on-line testing). As many problems as possible should be identified before implementation, but it is likely that some problems will only become apparent when the system goes live.

### 5.2.5 User acceptance testing

**User acceptance testing** is carried out by those who will use the system to determine whether the system meets their needs. These needs should have previously been stated as acceptance criteria.

The purpose of user acceptance testing is to establish whether users are satisfied that the system meets the system specification when used in the actual operating environment. Users process test data, system performance is closely monitored and users report how they felt the system meets their needs. Test data may include some historical data, because it is then possible to check results against the 'actual' output from the old system.

It is vital that users are involved in system testing to ensure the system operates as intended when used by the people expected to utilise it. Any problems identified should be corrected – this will improve system efficiency and should also encourage users to accept the new system.

### 5.2.6 Types of test

To ensure as many scenarios as possible are tested, testing should include the following three types of test.

(a) **Realistic tests**. These involve using the system in the way it will be used in reality – ie the actual environment, users and types of data.

(b) **Contrived tests**. These are designed to present the system with unusual events to ensure these are handled correctly, for example that invalid data is rejected.

(c) **Volume tests** present the system with large numbers of transactions to see how the system copes.

### 5.2.7 Limitations of testing

The presence of 'bugs' or errors in the vast majority of software/systems demonstrates that even the most rigorous testing plan is unlikely to identify all errors. The limitations of software testing are outlined in the following table.

| Limitation | Comment |
|---|---|
| **Poor testing process** | The test plan may not cover all areas of system functionality. Testers may not be adequately trained. The testing process may not be adequately documented. |
| **Inadequate time** | Software and systems are inevitably produced under significant time pressures. Testing time is often 'squeezed' to compensate for project over-runs in other areas. |
| **Future requirements not anticipated** | The test data used may have been fine at the time of testing, but future demands may be outside the range of values tested. Testing should allow for future expansion of the system. |
| **Inadequate test data** | Test data should test 'positively' – checking that the software does what it should do, and test 'negatively' – that it doesn't do what it shouldn't. It is difficult to include the complete range of possible input errors in test data. |
| **Software changes inadequately tested** | System/software changes made as a result of testing findings or for other reasons may not be adequately tested as they were not in the original test plan. |

## 5.3 Training

**Staff training** is essential to ensure that information systems are utilised to **their full potential**. There are a range of options available to **deliver training** including individual tuition 'at desk', a classroom course, computer-based training (CBT), software reference material and case studies and exercises.

Staff training in the use of a new system is essential if the return on investment is to be maximised. Training should be provided to **all staff** who will use the system. Examples of situations when **significant training is likely to be required** include:

- A new system is implemented
- An existing system is significantly changed
- Job specifications change
- New staff are recruited
- Skills have been forgotten

Training should **focus on the specific tasks the user is required to perform** eg entering an invoice or answering a query. There are a range of options available to deliver training, as shown below.

| Training method | Comment |
|---|---|
| **Individual tuition 'at desk'** | A trainer could work with an employee observing how they use a system and suggesting possible alternatives. |
| **Classroom course** | The software could be used in a classroom environment, using 'dummy' data. |
| **Computer-based training (CBT)** | Training can be provided using CDs, or via an interactive website. |
| **Case studies and exercises** | Regardless of how training is delivered, it is likely that material will be based around a realistic case study relevant to the user. |
| **Software reference material** | Users may find on-line help, built-in tutorials and reference manuals useful. |

The **training method** applicable in a given situation will **depend on the following factors**:

- Time available
- Software complexity
- User skill levels
- Facilities available
- Budget

**User documentation** may be used to **explain** the system to users. Much of this information **may be available online** using context-sensitive help eg 'Push F1 for help'.

## 5.4 File conversion

**File conversion**, means converting **existing files** into a format suitable for the new system.

Most computer systems are based around files containing data. When a new system is introduced, files must be created that conform to the requirements of that system. The various scenarios that file conversion could involve are outlined in the following table.

| Existing data | Comment |
|---|---|
| **Held in manual (ie paper) files** | Data will be keyed into the new system – probably via input forms, so that data entry operators have all the data they require in one document. This is likely to be a time-consuming process. |
| **Held in existing computer files** | How complex the process is in converting the files to a format compatible with the new system will depend on technical issues and the coding systems used. It may be possible to automate much of the conversion process. |
| **Held in both manual and computer files** | Two separate conversion procedures are required. |
| **Existing data is incomplete** | If the missing data is crucial, it must be researched and made available in a format suitable for the new system – or suitable for the file conversion process. |

The file conversion process is shown in the following diagram, which assumes the original data is held in manual files.

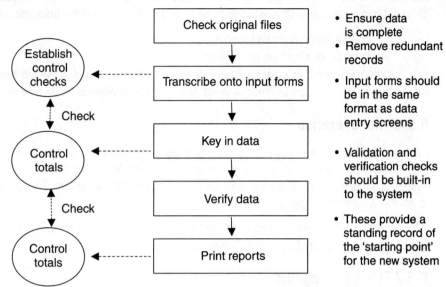

It is essential that the 'new' converted files are accurate. Various controls can be utilised during the conversion process.

(a)     **One-to-one checking** between records on the old and new systems.

(b)     **Sample checking**. Selecting and checking a sample of records, as there are too many to check individually.

(c)     **Built-in data validation** routines in automated conversion processes.

(d)     **Control totals** and **reconciliations**. These checks could include checking the total number of records, and the value of transactions.

**Exam focus point**

You may find it useful to remember the main implementation stages as **FITT**. **F**ile conversion, **I**nstallation, **T**raining and documentation **T**esting.

## 5.5 Changeover

Once the new system has been fully and satisfactorily tested the changeover can be made.

**FAST FORWARD**

There are four approaches to system **changeover**: direct changeover, parallel running, pilot operation and phased implementation. These vary in terms of time required, cost and risk.

### 5.5.1 Direct ('Big Bang') changeover

The old system is **completely replaced** by the new system **in one move**. This may be unavoidable where the two systems are substantially different, or where the costs of parallel running are too great.

While this method is comparatively **cheap** it is **risky** (system or program corrections are difficult while the system has to remain operational). The new system should be introduced during **a quiet period**, for example over a bank holiday weekend or during an office closure.

### 5.5.2 Parallel running

The **old and new** systems are **run in parallel** for a period of time, both processing current data and enabling cross checking to be made. This method provides a **degree of safety** should there be problems with the new system. However, if there are differences between the two systems cross-checking may be difficult or impossible.

Parallel running **delays** the actual implementation of the new system, which may be perceived as a **lack of confidence** in the system. Also, **more staff** are required to cope with systems running concurrently. This cautious approach, if adopted, should be properly planned, and the **plan should include**:

(a)     A firm **time limit** on parallel running.
(b)     Details of **cross-checking** procedures.
(c)     Instructions on how **errors** are to be dealt with eg errors found in the old system.
(d)     Instructions on how to report and act on **any major problems** in the new system.

### 5.5.3 Pilot operation

Pilot operation involves selecting part or parts of an organisation (eg a department or branch) to operate running the new system in parallel with the existing system. When the branch or department piloting the system is satisfied with the new system, they cease to use the old system. The new system is then piloted in another area of the organisation.

Pilot operation is **cheaper** and **easier to control** than running the whole system in parallel, and provides a **greater degree of safety** than a direct changeover.

### 5.5.4 Phased changeover

Phased or modular changeover involves selecting a complete section of the system for a direct changeover, eg in an accounting system the purchase ledger. When this part is running satisfactorily, another part is switched – until eventually the whole system has been changed. A phased series of direct changeovers is less risky than a single direct changeover, as any problems and disruption experienced should be isolated in an area of operations.

### 5.5.5 Advantages and disadvantages

The relative advantages and disadvantages of the various changeover methods are outlined in the following table.

| Method | Advantages | Disadvantages |
|---|---|---|
| **Direct ('Big Bang') changeover** | Quick<br>Minimal cost<br>Minimises workload | Risky<br>Could disrupt operations<br>If fails, will be costly |
| **Parallel running** | Safe, built-in safety<br>Provides way of verifying results of new system | Costly-two systems need to be operated<br>Time-consuming<br>Additional workload |
| **Pilot operation** | Less risky than direct changeover<br>Less costly than complete parallel running | Can take a long time to achieve total changeover<br>Not as safe as complete parallel running |
| **Phased changeover** | Less risky than a single direct changeover<br>Any problems should be in one area – other operations unaffected | Can take a long time to achieve total changeover<br>Interfaces between parts of the system may make this impractical |

 Case Study

Facing frequent outages in the DSL (digital subscriber line) network serving 50-plus corporate-owned Gold's Gyms, Bobby Badugu knew it was time for a significant upgrade. After looking into the various options he opted for a carrier-provided voice VoIP (voice over IP) service.

The plan was to install a T-1 line to each gym and implement voice and data service when the circuits were installed. Badugu figured scheduling the T-1s from various LECs (local exchange carriers) would be the most complicated issue.

At each gym, one contractor would order, configure and install a router. Another configured and installed the firewall and hooked up the VPN tunnel. 'As we did each location, we found more and more complexities in that process,' Badugu said. 'We had six or seven parties involved in putting the phone and data lines in. I really felt like some were pretty much learning the technology or learning the equipment.'

Badugu also admitted to shortcomings on the company's part. 'One of the things we didn't do correctly was we didn't know our environment,' he said. That included the types of phone systems installed in each location and whether they could connect to the T-1 line. Even though he had been installing digital, IP-ready phone systems in all gyms, some didn't have the required T-1 card, which meant an additional expense, and others were still analog. Locating all the wiring closets was another challenge.

If he had to do it again, however, he would take a more phased approach. 'We tried the big-bang theory, doing everything at once,' he said. That decision was driven by business needs, because the DSL network was so unreliable, and because Qwest (the supplier) was urging Gold's to sign a contract that included every gym. 'Even still, I think we should've done two or three gyms first, and made sure that was okay before we did the rest.'

Extracts from Case study: VoIP implementation
The problems of the 'big bang' approach
Paul Desmond, *PC Advisor,* November 18, 2006

# 6 System maintenance

## 6.1 Types of maintenance

FAST FORWARD

> There are three types of systems maintenance. **Corrective** maintenance is carried out to correct an error, **perfective** maintenance aims to make enhancements to systems and **adaptive** maintenance takes account of anticipated changes in the processing environment.

**Key terms**

> **Corrective maintenance** is carried out when there is a systems failure of some kind, for example a defect in processing or in an implementation procedure. Its objective is to ensure that systems remain operational.
>
> **Perfective maintenance** is carried out in order to perfect the software, or to improve software so that the processing inefficiencies are eliminated and performance is enhanced.
>
> **Adaptive maintenance** is carried out to take account of anticipated changes in the processing environment. For example new taxation legislation might require change to be made to payroll software.

**Corrective** maintenance usually consists of action in response to a **problem**. Much **perfective** maintenance consists of making enhancements requested by **users** to improve or extend the facilities available. The user interface may be amended to make software more user friendly.

The key features of system maintenance ought to be **flexibility** and **adaptability**.

(a)    The system, perhaps with minor modifications, should cope with changes in the computer user's procedures or volume of business.

(b)    The computer user should benefit from advances in computer hardware technology without having to switch to another system altogether.

## 6.2 The causes of system maintenance

Besides environmental changes, three factors contribute to the need for maintenance.

| Factor | Comment |
|---|---|
| **Errors** | However carefully and diligently the systems development staff carry out systems testing and program testing, it is likely that **bugs** will exist in a newly implemented system. Most should be identified during the first few runs of a system. The effect of errors can obviously vary enormously. |
| **Poor documentation** | If old systems are accompanied by poor documentation, or even a complete lack of documentation, it may be very difficult to understand their programs. It will be hard to update or maintain such programs. Programmers may opt instead to patch up the system with new applications using newer technology. |
| **Changes in requirements** | Although users should be consulted at all stages of systems development, problems may arise after a system is implemented because users may have found it difficult to express their requirements, or may have been concerned about the future of their jobs and not participated fully in development. |
| | Cost constraints may have meant that certain requested features were not incorporated. Time constraints may have meant that requirements suggested during development were ignored in the interest of prompt completion |

### 6.2.1 Testing the effect of changes

A problem with systems development and maintenance is that it is **hard to predict all the effects of a change** to the system. A 'simple' software change in one area of the system may have unpredicted effects elsewhere. It is important therefore to carry out **regression testing**.

**Key term**

> **Regression testing** involves the retesting of software that has been modified to fix 'bugs'. It aims to ensure that the bugs have been fixed **and** that no other previously working functions have failed as a result of the changes.

Regression testing involves **repeating system tests** that had been executed correctly before the recent changes were made. Only the changes expected as a result of the system maintenance should occur under the regression test – other changes could be due to errors caused by the recent change. Problems with regression testing include:

- Deciding on the extent of testing required
- Envisaging all areas possibly affected
- Convincing users and programmers that the tests are necessary

## 6.3 Hardware maintenance

Provision must also be made to ensure computer hardware is maintained. A **hardware maintenance contract** should specify service response times in the event of a breakdown, and include provision for temporary replacement equipment if necessary. Maintenance services may be provided by the computer manufacturers or suppliers, or by a third-party maintenance company.

# 7 System evaluation and performance measurement

A system should be **reviewed** after implementation, and periodically, so that any unforeseen problems may be solved and to confirm that it is achieving the desired results. The system should have been designed with clear, specified **objectives**, and justification in terms of **cost-benefit analysis** or other **performance criteria**.

## 7.1 Cost-benefit review

A cost-benefit review is similar to a cost-benefit analysis, except that **actual** data can be used. For instance when a large project is completed, techniques such as **DCF appraisal** can be performed **again**, with actual figures being available for much of the expenditure.

Cost-benefit review

Learning outcome: A (iv)

A cost-benefit review might categorise items under the five headings of **direct benefits**, **indirect benefits**, **development costs**, **implementation costs** and **running costs**.

*Required*

Give two examples of items which could fall to be evaluated under each heading.                    (5 marks)

### Answer

**Direct benefits** might include reduced operating costs, for example lower overtime payments.

**Indirect benefits** might include better decision-making and the freeing of human 'brainpower' from routine tasks so that it can be used for more creative work.

**Development costs** include systems analysts' costs and the cost of time spent by users in assisting with fact-finding.

**Implementation costs** would include costs of site preparation and costs of training.

**Running costs** include maintenance costs, software leasing costs and on-going user support.

## 7.2 Measuring system performance

**FAST FORWARD**

Metrics may be used to measure system **performance**. Systems **evaluation** may also use **computer-based monitoring**. Methods include the use of hardware monitors, software monitors and systems logs.

### 7.2.1 Metrics

**Key term**

**Metrics** are quantified measurements used to measure system performance.

The use of metrics enables some aspects of **system quality** to be **measured**. Metrics may also allow the early identification of problems – for example, by highlighting instances of system failure, the causes of which may then be investigated.

Metrics should be carefully thought out, objective and **stated clearly**. They must measure significant aspects of the system, be used consistently and agreed with users. **Examples** of metrics include system response time, the number of transactions that can be processed per minute, the number of bugs per hundred lines of code and the number of system crashes per week.

Many facets of system quality are not easy to measure statistically (eg user-friendliness). Indirect measurements such as the number of calls to the help-desk per month can be used as an indication of overall quality/performance.

## 7.3 Performance reviews

**Performance reviews** can be carried out to look at a wide range of systems functions and characteristics. Technological change often gives scope to improve the quality of **outputs** or reduce the extent or cost of **inputs**.

Some organisations may conduct periodic reviews of the performance of their information systems. **Performance reviews** will vary in content from organisation to organisation, but may include the following.

(a) The **growth** rates in file sizes and the number of transactions processed by the system. Trends should be analysed and projected to assess whether there are likely to be problems with lengthy processing time or an inefficient file structure due to the volume of processing.

(b) The **staffing** requirements of the system, and whether they are more or less than anticipated.

(c) The identification of any **delays** in processing and an assessment of the consequences of any such delays.

(d) An assessment of the efficiency of **security** procedures, in terms of number of breaches, or number of viruses encountered.

(e) A check of the **error rates** for input data. High error rates may indicate inefficient preparation of input documents, an inappropriate method of data capture or poor design of input media.

(f) An examination of whether **output** from the computer is being used to good purpose. (Is it used? Is it timely? Does it go to the right people?)

(g) Operational **running costs**, examined to discover any inefficient programs or processes. This examination may reveal excessive costs for certain items although in total, costs may be acceptable.

# 8 Post-implementation review

During the **post-implementation review**, an evaluation of the system is carried out to see whether the targeted performance criteria have been met and to carry out a review of costs and benefits. The review should culminate in the production of a report and recommendations.

A **post-implementation review** should establish whether the objectives and targeted performance criteria have been met, and if not, why not, and what should be done about it. In appraising the operation of the new system immediately after the changeover, comparison should be made between **actual and predicted performance**.

This will include:

(a) Consideration of **throughput speed** (time between input and output).
(b) Use of computer **storage** (both internal and external).
(c) The number and type of **errors/queries**.
(d) The **cost** of processing (data capture, preparation, storage and output media, etc).

A special **steering committee** may be set up to ensure that post-implementation reviews are carried out, although the **internal audit** department may be required to do the work of carrying out the reviews.

The post-implementation measurements should **not be made too soon** after the system goes live, or else results will be abnormally affected by 'teething' problems, lack of user familiarity and resistance to change. A suitable period is likely to be between one month and one year after completion (the appropriate length of time will depend upon the role of the system, and how complex it is).

## 8.1 The post-implementation review report

The findings of a post-implementation review team should be formalised in a **report**.

(a)   A **summary** of their findings should be provided, emphasising any areas where the system has been found to be **unsatisfactory**.

(b)   A review of **system performance** should be provided. This will address the matters outlined above, such as run times and error rates and whether it meets users' needs.

(c)   A **cost-benefit review** should be included, comparing the forecast costs and benefits identified at the time of the feasibility study with actual costs and benefits.

(d)   **Recommendations** should be made as to any **further action** or steps which should be taken to improve performance. It will also make recommendations on how the project was managed to help future initiatives.

# Chapter Roundup

- The **systems development life cycle** is a formal model of the stages involved in **systems development**.

- A **feasibility study** is carried out to ensure that a system is viable or feasible. It normally includes a **cost-benefit analysis**.

- The **systems investigation** is a detailed **fact-finding exercise** about the areas and system under consideration. Methods employed include the use of **interviews** and **questionnaires**.

- **Systems analysis** examines why **current methods** are used, what **alternatives** are available, what **restricts the effectiveness** of the system and what **performance criteria** are required from a new system.

- **Data flow diagrams** are used to show how data is processed. **Entity relationship models** provide an understanding of a system's logical data requirements independently of the system's processes. **Entity life history** shows the processes that happen to an entity and **decision tables** define the logic of a process.

- **Systems design** is a technical phase which addresses in particular **inputs, outputs, program design, dialogue design, file design** and **security**.

- A system must be thoroughly **tested** to ensure it operates as intended. The nature and scope of testing will vary depending on the size and type of the system.

- **Staff training** is essential to ensure that information systems are utilised to **their full potential**. There are a range of options available to **deliver training** including individual tuition 'at desk', a classroom course, computer-based training (CBT), software reference material and case studies and exercises

- There are four approaches to system **changeover**: direct changeover, parallel running, pilot operation and phased implementation. These vary in terms of time required, cost and risk.

- There are three types of systems maintenance. **Corrective** maintenance is carried out to correct an error, **perfective** maintenance aims to make enhancements to systems and **adaptive** maintenance takes account of anticipated changes in the processing environment.

- Metrics may be used to measure system **performance**. Systems **evaluation** may also use **computer-based monitoring**. Methods include the use of hardware monitors, software monitors and systems logs.

- **Performance reviews** can be carried out to look at a wide range of systems functions and characteristics. Technological change often gives scope to improve the quality of **outputs** or reduce the extent or cost of **inputs**.

- During the **post-implementation review**, an evaluation of the system is carried out to see whether the targeted performance criteria have been met and to carry out a review of costs and benefits. The review should culminate in the production of a report and recommendations.

# Quick Quiz

1   List three reasons why an organisation considering the implementation of a new information system should undertake a feasibility study.

    1   .............................................................

    2   .............................................................

    3   .............................................................

2   List four methods used in systems investigations.

    1   .............................................................

    2   .............................................................

    3   .............................................................

    4   .............................................................

3   List the three types of relationship an Entity Relationship Model (ERM) may portray.

    1   .............................................................

    2   .............................................................

    3   .............................................................

4   What three types of process logic may an Entity Life History (ELH) show?

    1   .............................................................

    2   .............................................................

    3   .............................................................

5   Decision tables consist of four quadrants. Label the four quadrants below.

| | |
|---|---|
| | |

6   Which method of system changeover is usually safest?

7   Which method of system changeover is probably most expensive?

8   What is the purpose of user acceptance testing?

9   Which of the following describes corrective maintenance?

    A   Maintenance carried out when there is a systems failure
    B   Maintenance carried out to perfect the system
    C   Maintenance carried out to adjust the system for changes in the processing environment
    D   Maintenance carried out to improve user-friendliness

10  How does a cost-benefit review differ from a cost-benefit analysis?

11  Briefly explain the purpose of a post-implementation review.

# Answers to Quick Quiz

1   A feasibility study should be undertaken when considering a new information system because new systems can:

    –   Be complicated and cost a great deal to develop.
    –   Be disruptive during development and implementation.
    –   Have far-reaching consequences in the way an organisation conducts its business or is structured.

2   Questionnaires, interviews, observation and document review.

3   One-to-one, one-to-many and many-to-many.

4   Sequence, iteration, selection.

5

| Condition stub | Condition entry |
|---|---|
| Action stub | Action entry |

6   Parallel running.

7   Parallel running.

8   User acceptance testing is carried out by those who will use the system to determine whether the system meets their needs. These needs should have previously been stated as acceptance criteria. The aim is for the customer to determine whether or not to accept the system.

9   A       Option B is perfective maintenance, C is adaptive maintenance, D is also perfective maintenance

10  The review uses actual data. The analysis relies on estimates.

11  A post-implementation review establishes whether the system's objectives and targeted performance criteria have been met and if not, what should be done about it.

Now try the question below from the Exam Question Bank

| Number | Level | Marks | Time |
|---|---|---|---|
| 2 | Examination | 30 | 54 mins |

# Selecting and managing information technology

## Introduction

Management accountants now require a **working knowledge of Information Technology (IT)** to perform their role effectively. This does not mean that the management accountant needs to be an IT expert – just as an IT specialist cannot be expected to possess expert accounting expertise.

What is required is **an understanding of the features and operations of commonly used hardware and software** and an appreciation of how technology may be utilised in a business environment.

Don't make the mistake of thinking you need to be an IT expert to do well in P4 – you don't!

| Topic list | Learning outcomes | Syllabus references | Ability required |
|---|---|---|---|
| 1 Manual systems | A(ii) | A(10) | Comprehension |
| 2 Computes: the processor and memory | A(i), A(ii) | A(1) | Comprehension |
| 3 Computers: input devices | A(ii) | A(1) | Comprehension |
| 4 Computers: output devices | A(ii) | A(1) | Comprehension |
| 5 Computers: storage devices | A(ii) | A(1) | Comprehension |
| 6 Software | A(i), A(ii) | A(1) | Comprehension |
| 7 Database systems | A(ii), A(iii) | A(5) | Comprehension |
| 8 Using IT in manufacturing | A(ii) | A(1) | Comprehension |
| 9 Architectures | A(ii) | A(2) | Comprehension |
| 10 Purchasing hardware and software | A(v) | A(6) | Evaluation |
| 11 Information systems department and outsourcing | A(vii) | A(6), A(12) | Evaluation |
| 12 Office technology | A(ii) | A(1) | Comprehension |
| 13 The Internet | A(ii) | A(1) | Comprehension |

# 1 Manual systems

Many tasks (and people) are still better suited to manual methods of working, for example a single quick calculation may best be done mentally or by using a pocket calculator.

Many people also prefer **communicating face to face** with their colleagues, rather than using tools such as e-mail.

## 1.1 Manual systems v computerised systems

FAST FORWARD

> In **many situations manual systems are inferior to computerised systems** in terms of productivity, speed, accessibility, quality of output, incidence of errors, 'bulk' and when making corrections.

**Disadvantages of manual systems** include the following.

| Disadvantage | Comment |
|---|---|
| **Productivity** | **Productivity** is usually lower, particularly in routine or operational situations such as transaction processing. |
| **Slower** | Processing is **slower** where large volumes of data need to be dealt with. |
| **Risk of errors** | The **risk of errors** is greater, especially in repetitive work like payroll calculations. |
| **Less accessible** | Information on manual systems is generally **less accessible**. Access to information is often restricted to one user at a time. |
| **Alterations** | It is difficult to make **corrections**. If a manual document contains errors or needs updating it is often necessary to recreate the **whole** document from scratch. |
| **Quality of output** | **Quality of output** is less consistent and often not well-designed. At worst, hand-written records may be illegible and so completely useless. |
| **Bulk** | Paper based systems are generally very **bulky** both to handle and to store. |

However, don't assume that computerised systems are best in every situation. For example, a post-it note stuck on a colleague's desk with a brief message may in some cases be quicker than typing up an e-mail message.

**Exam focus point**

> Much of this chapter contains technical terms. You are not expected to become an IT expert, but you should understand computers, systems and hardware in enough detail to enable you to explain how systems work and what options are available when developing a new system.

# 2 Computers: the processor and memory

FAST FORWARD

> The amount of **RAM** and the **processor speed** are key determinants of computer performance.

## 2.1 The processor or CPU

The **processor** or **Central Processing Unit (CPU)** is the collection of circuitry and registers that performs the processing in a computer. The processor is sometimes described as the 'brain' of the computer. The CPU is where most calculations take place.

Two typical components of a CPU are:

- The **arithmetic and logic unit** (ALU) which performs arithmetic and logical operations
- The **control unit** , which extracts instructions from memory and decodes and executes them

### 2.1.1 Chips

The CPU may be housed in a single **chip**. A chip is a small piece of silicon upon which is etched an integrated circuit. The chip is mounted on a carrier unit which in turn is 'plugged' on to a circuit board – called the **motherboard** – with other chips, each with their own functions, such as sound (a 'sound card') and video (a 'video card').

Many PCs carry a sticker saying 'Intel inside' – referring to the chips made by the Intel company. Other manufacturers include AMD and Digital.

## 2.2 Memory

The computer's memory is also known as main store or internal store. The memory will hold the following.

- Program instructions
- The input data that will be processed next
- The data that is ready for output to an output device

The processing capacity of a computer is in part dictated by the capacity of its memory. Capacity is calculated in kilobytes (1 kilobyte = $2^{10}$ (1,024) bytes) and megabytes (1 megabyte = $2^{20}$ bytes) and gigabytes ($2^{30}$). These are abbreviated to Kb, Mb and Gb.

### 2.2.1 RAM

RAM (Random Access Memory) is memory that is directly available to the processing unit. It holds the data and programs in current use. RAM in microcomputers is 'volatile' which means that the contents of the memory are erased when the computer's power is switched off.

### 2.2.2 ROM

ROM **(Read-Only Memory)** is **a memory chip into which fixed data is written permanently** at the time of its manufacture. When you turn on a PC you may see a reference to **BIOS** (basic input/output system). This is part of the ROM chip containing all the programs needed to control the keyboard, screen, disk drives and so on.

### 2.2.3 Peripherals

**Key term**

Technically, any device outside the core components of a computer (CPU and memory) is a **peripheral**. Under this definition, some devices that are physically located inside a computer are peripherals (eg hard drive, floppy disk drive, modem). However, in general usage **peripheral** is used to describe any hardware device attached to a computer that expands functionality eg printers, external disk drives, display monitors, keyboards and mice.

# 3 Computers: input devices

There are a range of **input** devices available. The most efficient method will depend on the circumstances of each situation.

## 3.1 The keyboard

The keyboard is the most often used tool for computer input.

Keying data into a computer using a keyboard can be a **labour-intensive** process. In many cases the process of inputting data is speeded up through some form of automated **data capture**. We will look at automatic input devices later in this section.

## 3.2 The VDU or monitor

A VDU (visual display unit) or 'monitor' displays text and graphics. The screen's **resolution** is the number of pixels that are lit up. A **pixel** is a picture element –a 'dot' on the screen, as it were. The fewer the pixels on screen, the larger each individual pixel will be, so fewer pixels mean lower resolution or image quality. A larger number of smaller pixels will provide a higher resolution display.

**Touch-sensitive screens** have been developed which allow the monitor to be used as an input device. Selections are made by users touching areas of the screen. Sensors, built into the screen surround, detect which area has been touched. These devices are widely used in vending situations, such as the selling of train tickets.

## 3.3 Mice and trackball devices

A **wheeled mouse** is a handheld device with a rubber ball protruding from a small hole in its base. The mouse is moved over a flat surface, and as it moves, internal sensors pick up the motion and convert it into electronic signals which **instruct the cursor on screen to move**.

The wheeled mouse is slowly being replaced by the **optical mouse.** The optical mouse has a small light-emitting diode (LED) that bounces light off the surface the mouse is moved across. The mouse contains sensors that convert this movement into co-ordinates the computer can understand.

A typical mouse has two or three **buttons** which can be pressed (**clicked**) to send specific signals. Newer mice also have a **wheel** used to scroll within pages or documents that can't all be displayed on a single screen.

Similar to the mouse is the **trackball**, which is often found on laptop computers. Trackballs comprise a casing fixed to the computer, and a ball which protrudes upwards. The user moves the ball by hand. Other mobile computers use a **touch sensitive pad** for mouse functions; others have a tiny **joystick** in the centre of the keyboard.

## 3.4 Voice data entry (VDE)

**Voice recognition software** is now sufficiently developed to allow computers to accept **voice input** via a **microphone**. A particularly useful application is the use of VDE software and **translation programs** that allow users from different countries to communicate.

## 3.5 Automatic input devices

In the following paragraphs we explain some of the most common document reading methods. Document reading methods reduce the manual work involved in data input. This **saves time and money** and also **reduces errors**.

### 3.5.1 Magnetic ink character recognition (MICR)

Magnetic ink character recognition (**MICR**) involves the recognition by a machine of special formatted characters printed in magnetic ink. The characters are read using a specialised reading device. The main advantage of MICR is its speed and accuracy, but MICR documents are expensive to produce. The main commercial application of MICR is in the banking industry – on cheques and deposit slips.

### 3.5.2 Optical mark reading (OMR)

**Optical mark reading** involves the marking of a pre-printed form with a ballpoint pen or typed line or cross in an appropriate box. The card is then read by an OMR device which senses the mark in each box using an electric current and translates it into machine code. Applications in which OMR is used include **National Lottery** entry forms and answer sheets for multiple-choice questions.

### 3.5.3 Scanners and Optical Character Recognition (OCR)

A scanner is device that can **read text or illustrations printed on paper** and translate the information into a **form the computer can use**. To edit text read by an optical scanner, you need **optical character recognition (OCR)** software to translate the image into text. You may use a scanner and OCR to obtain 'digital' versions of paper documents. To enable the OCR software to recognise the characters correctly, the copy must be of good quality.

### 3.5.4 Barcoding and EPOS

**Barcodes** are groups of marks which, by their spacing and thickness, indicate specific codes or values. Electronic Point of Sale (**EPOS**) devices, which include barcode readers, enable supermarkets and other retailers to record and manage stock movements – and provide detailed sales information.

### 3.5.5 Digital cameras

These capture images in digital form and allow easy transfer to a computer. Images may then be manipulated by image-processing software.

# 4 Computers: output devices

**FAST FORWARD**

The most often used methods of computer **output** are **printers** and **screen display**.

## 4.1 Printers

**Laser printers** print a whole page at a time, rather than line by line. The **quality** of output is very **high**. Laser printers are relatively expensive to purchase, but compared with inkjet printers, running costs are relatively low.

**Inkjet** printers are small and reasonably cheap. They work by sending a jet of ink on to the paper to produce the required characters.

Older style printers, that use tractor-fed rolls of paper are still used in some organisations for printing high volumes. An example is a **dot matrix** printer, which is a character printer which prints a single character at a time. Their main drawback is their **low-resolution.** They are also relatively **slow** and **noisy**.

## 4.2 The VDU or monitor

Screens were described earlier in this chapter, as they are used together with computer keyboards for **input**. It should also be clear that they can be used as an **output** medium, primarily where the output **volume is low** (for example, a single enquiry) and **no permanent output** is required (for example, the current balance on an account).

## 4.3 The choice of output medium

Choosing a suitable output medium depends on a number of factors.

| Factor | Comment |
|---|---|
| Hard copy | Is a printed version of the output needed? |
| Quantity | For example, a VDU screen can hold a certain amount of data, but it becomes more difficult to read when information goes 'off-screen' and can only be read a 'page' at a time. |
| Speed | For example, if a single enquiry is required it may be quicker to make notes from a VDU display. |

| Factor | Comment |
|---|---|
| Suitability for further use | Output to a file would be appropriate if the data will be processed further, maybe in a different system. |
| Cost | The 'best' output device may not be justifiable on the grounds of cost – another output medium should be chosen. |

### 4.4 Audio output

Speakers provide output for audio files, such as MP3 files.

# 5 Computers: storage devices

> **FAST FORWARD**
>
> Hard disks, flash drives and DVDs are common forms of secondary storage.

Memory is a computer's primary storage, however the information stored will be lost when the machine is turned off. Therefore backing (or secondary) storage is required to save the information for future use.

Hard disks are the most common storage medium but in recent years, flash drives and DVDs (digital video/versatile disks) have become more popular due to high speed access and storage capacity.

# 6 Software

> **FAST FORWARD**
>
> There are five classifications of computer software: operating systems, utilities, programming tools, off-the-shelf applications and bespoke applications.

| Type | Comment |
|---|---|
| Operating systems | The operating system provides the interface between the computer hardware and both the user and the other software. An operating system will typically perform the following tasks.<br><br>• Initial set-up of the computer, when it is switched on<br>• Communication between the user and hardware<br>• Calling up of files from storage into memory<br>• File management<br><br>The most widely-used operating system is Microsoft Windows. Other operating systems include UNIX, the Apple Macintosh O/S system and Linux. |
| Utilities | Software utilities are relatively small software packages, usually designed to perform a task related to the general operation of a computer system. An example of a utility is software designed to perform back-ups. **Communications software** is another example of a utility (or it may be included as part of the operating system). This software helps select a transmission method across a network and manages the transmission of data. |
| Programming tools | Some software is designed specifically to help programmers produce computer programs. Examples include program compilers and assemblers, and Computer Assisted Software Engineering (CASE) tools. |
| Off-the-shelf applications | This term is used to describe software produced by a software manufacturer and released in a form that is ready to use. 'Office' type software (spreadsheet, word-processing, database etc) and integrated accounting systems such as Sage Line 50 are examples. |
| Bespoke applications | Bespoke software is tailor-made to meet the needs of an organisation. Bespoke software is relatively expensive, but may be the only feasible solution in unusual situations. |

# 7 Database systems

FAST FORWARD » The term '**database system**' is used to describe a wide range of systems that utilise a central pool of data.

As shown below, a 'database system' can involve much more than a single database package such as Microsoft Access.

**Key terms**

A **database** is a collection of structured data which may be manipulated to select or sort some or all of the data held. The database provides convenient access to data for a wide variety of users and user needs.

A **database management system (DBMS)** is the software that builds, manages and provides access to a database. It allows a systematic approach to the storage and retrieval of data.

The **logical structure** of a database refers to how various application programs access the data. The **physical structure** relates to how data is organised within the database. In a database environment, the ease with which applications access the central pool of data is referred to as **integration**.

The independence of logical data from physical storage, and the independence of data items from the programs which access them, is referred to as **data independence**. Duplication of data items is referred to as **data redundancy**. **Integrity** relates to data accuracy and consistency. Data independence and integration should reduce data redundancy resulting in improved data integrity.

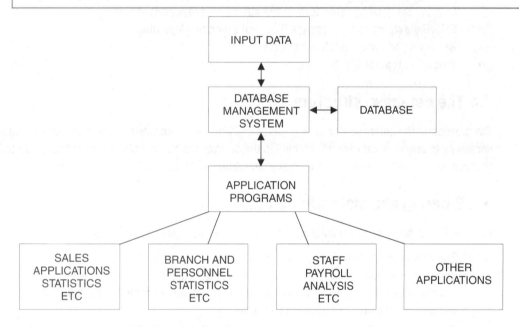

## 7.1 Characteristics of a database

A database has three major **characteristics**.

(a)    It should be **shared**.
(b)    It should provide for the **needs of different users** with different requirements.
(c)    It should be **capable of evolving** to meet **future** needs.

## 7.2 Database administrator (DBA)

FAST FORWARD Control over the database can be facilitated by the appointment of a **database administrator** (DBA).

The DBA controls and sets standards for:

- The input of data
- Its definition, for instance the development of logical data models
- Physical storage structures
- System performance
- Security and integrity of data
- Back-up and recovery strategies

The principal role of a DBA can be described as ensuring that the database **functions correctly and efficiently** at all times. To achieve these aims the DBA will carry out a variety of tasks, including some or all of those discussed below. The DBA must be a person who is **technically competent** and possesses a **good understanding** of the **business and operational needs** of the organisation.

## 7.3 Using a database

There are four main operations in using a database.

(a) Creating the database **structure**, ie the structure of files and records.
(b) **Entering data** on to the database files, and **amending/updating** it.
(c) **Retrieving and manipulating** the data.
(d) Producing **reports**.

## 7.4 The database structure

The creation of the database structure involves carrying out an **analysis** of the data to be included. It is necessary to specify what **files** will be held in the database, what **records** (entities) and the **fields** (attributes) they will contain, and how many **characters** will be in each field.

## 7.5 Entering and maintaining data

When entering data into a new database the following issues may have to be addressed.

(a) The **compatibility** between systems is not just a matter of whether one system's files are computer-sensible to another system. It may extend to matters such as **different systems of coding**, different formats for personal data (with/without a contact name, with/without phone or fax number, and so on), and different field sizes.

(b) **Access to data should not suffer**. Users will be attempting to extract information from a much larger pool. The system must be designed in such a way that they do not have to wade through large amounts of data that is irrelevant.

(c) As well as offering the potential for new kinds of report the system must continue to **support existing reporting**. **Extensive consultation** with users is essential.

(d) Once the data has been amalgamated the business faces the task of ensuring that it is **secure**. A systems failure will now mean that no part of the business can operate, rather than at most just one part.

## 7.6 Retrieval and manipulation of data

Data can be retrieved and manipulated in a variety of ways.

(a) By **specifying the required parameters** – for example, from a database of employee records, records of all employees in the sales department who have been employed for over 10 years and are paid less than £12,000 pa could be extracted. Search and retrieve parameters (queries) can be stored for future use.

(b) Retrieved data can be **sorted** on any specified field (for example, for employees, sorting might be according to grade, department, age, experience, salary level etc).

(c) Some **calculations** on retrieved data can be carried out – such as calculating **totals** and **average** values.

## 7.7 Web applications

Databases are the core element to **online shops** and **shopping carts**. The website is connected to the database via a **database connectivity component** (such as Microsoft ADO and ODBC).

Customers are able to **interrogate** the database via the website to **obtain product information** and availability before **submitting an order**.

## 7.8 Advantages and disadvantages of a database system

The **advantages** of a database system are as follows.

(a) Avoidance of **unnecessary duplication** of data.

(b) Data is looked upon as serving the **organisation as a whole**, not just for individual departments. The database concept encourages management to regard data as a resource that must be **properly managed**.

(c) The installation of a database system encourages management to **analyse data**, relationships between data items, and how data is used in different applications.

(d) **Consistency** – because data is only held once, the possibility of departments holding conflicting data on the same subject is reduced.

(e) Data on file is independent of the user programs that access the data. This allows **greater flexibility** in the ways that data can be used. New programs can be easily introduced to make use of existing data in a different way.

(f) Developing **new application programs** with a database system is easier because the programmer is not responsible for the file organisation.

The **disadvantages** of database systems relate mainly to security and control.

(a) There are problems of **data security** and **data privacy**. There is potential for unauthorised access to data. Administrative procedures for data security must supplement software controls.

(b) Since there is only one set of data, it is essential that the data should be **accurate** and free from corruption.

(c) Since data is held once, but its use is widespread, the impact of **system failure** would be greater.

(d) If an organisation develops its own database system from scratch, **initial development costs** will be high.

# 8 Using IT in manufacturing

Information technology (IT) can be used to **automate** and improve physical tasks in **manufacturing** organisations.

IT may also be used to provide **extra information** about the manufacturing process.

(a) **Product design.** Computer aided design (**CAD**) software helps in the design process. CAD allows the drafting of design drawings, layout (eg of stores, wiring and piping) and electronic circuit diagrams in complex systems. It is easy to change design in CAD systems and to assess ramifications of any changes.

(b) **Process** control. Computer systems enable tighter control over production processes, for example being used to **measure** many aspects of the production process.

(c) **Machine tool control.** Machine tools can be automated and, it is hoped, be made more precise.

(d) **Robots** (computer controlled machines) may be used to automate some of the process.

(e) **Computer-aided manufacturing** (CAM) involves a variety of software modules.

- Production control, supervisory systems
- Materials requirement planning (MRP I) and MRP II systems
- Capacity requirements planning

(f) **Computer-integrated manufacturing** (CIM) integrates all aspects of an organisation's manufacturing activities, using IT to provide integration though communication, effectiveness and efficiency.

(g) **Enterprise Resource Planning** (ERP) systems take MRP II systems a step further, and are not restricted to certain types of organisation (not just manufacturing). ERP systems are used for identifying and planning the **enterprise-wide** resources needed to record, produce, distribute, and account for customer orders.

In both **inbound** logistics and **outbound** logistics IT can have an impact.

(a) The use of IT in **inbound logistics** includes stock control systems such as MRP I, MRP II, ERP and JIT systems (these are covered in later chapters).

(b) **Warehousing**. The use of barcodes can increase knowledge about the quantity and nature of stock in hand.

(c) It is possible to create computer models, or **virtual warehouses**, of stock actually held at **suppliers**.

> Note: We cover technologies used to schedule production and plan operations in Chapter 5 (eg Optimised Production Technology and Enterprise Resource Planning).

# 9 Architectures

The term **system architecture** refers to the way in which the various components of an information system are linked together, and the way they relate to each other. A **centralised** architecture involves all computer processing being carried out on a single central processor. **Distributed** architectures spread the processing power throughout the organisation at several different locations.

In the following paragraphs we discuss the theory behind centralised and distributed systems. However, in reality many systems include elements of both.

## 9.1 Centralised architecture

Key term

A **centralised architecture** involves all computer processing being carried out on a single central processor. The central computer is usually a mainframe or minicomputer designed to be accessed by more than one user.

A centralised system using a central mainframe linked to 'dumb terminals' (which do not include a CPU and therefore rely on the central computer for processing power) is shown below.

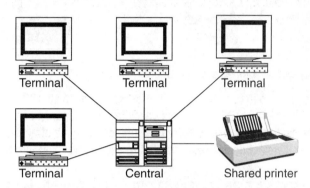

Many centralised systems also have **shared peripherals**, such as printers, linked to the central computer.

Centralised architectures could be based in a **single location** or spread over **multiple locations**. For example, both a **local area network** (LAN) and a **wide area network** (WAN) could utilise a centralised architecture.

A LAN is a network that spans a relatively small area. Most LANs are confined to a single building or group of buildings. A wide area network (WAN) is a computer network that spans a relatively large geographical area. A centralised WAN would have only one computer with processing power. (LANs may be linked to form a WAN – although such a configuration would not be considered a centralised architecture.)

**Advantages** of centralised architectures.

(a)    There is one set of files. Everyone uses the same data and information.

(b)    It gives better security/control over data and files. It is easier to enforce standards.

(c)    Head office (where the computer is usually based) is able to control computing processes and developments.

(d)    An organisation might be able to afford a very large central computer, with extensive processing capabilities that smaller 'local' computers could not carry out.

(e)    There may be economies of scale available in purchasing computer equipment and supplies.

**Disadvantages** of centralised architectures.

(a)    Local offices might experience processing delays or interruptions.

(b)    Reliance on head office. Local offices rely on head office to provide information they need.

(c)    If the central computer breaks down, or the software develops a fault, the entire system goes out of operation.

## 9.2 Decentralised or distributed architectures

Key term

**Distributed architectures** spread the processing power throughout the organisation at several different locations. With modern distributed systems, the majority of processing power is held on numerous personal computers (PCs) spread throughout the organisation.

An example of a distributed architecture, with a combination of stand-alone PCs and networks spread throughout an organisation, is shown in the following diagram.

**Distributed architecture**

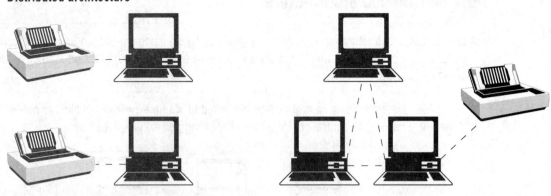

Key **features** of distributed architectures.

(a)   Many computers have their own processing capability (CPU).
(b)   Some sharing of information is possible via communication links.
(c)   The systems are usually more user-friendly than mainframe based systems.
(d)   End-users are given responsibility for, and control over, programs and data.

## 9.2.1 Advantages and disadvantages of distributed architectures

### Advantages

(a)   There is greater flexibility in system design. The system can cater for both the specific needs of each local user of an individual computer and also for the needs of the organisation as a whole, by providing communications between different local computers in the system.

(b)   Since data files can be held locally, data transmission is restricted because each computer maintains its own data files which provide most of the data it will need. This reduces the costs and security risks in data transmission.

(c)   Speed of processing.

(d)   There is a possibility of a distributed database. Data is held in a number of locations, but any user can access all of it for a global view.

(e)   The effect of breakdowns is minimised, because a fault in one computer will not affect other computers in the system.

(f)   Allows for better localised control over the physical and procedural aspects of the system.

(g)   May facilitate greater user involvement and increase familiarity with the use of computer technology.

**Disadvantages** of distributed architectures.

(a)   There may be some duplication of data on different computers, increasing the risk of data inaccuracies.

(b)   A distributed network can be more difficult to administer and to maintain, as several sites require access to staff with IT skills.

| Question | Processing methods |
|---|---|

Which of the following statements is correct?

A   With a centralised transaction processing system, batch processing is always used.
B   All database systems are updated in real time.
C   'Dumb terminals' rely on the central computer for their processing power.
D   Risks to the security of data files are higher with centralised computer systems than with decentralised systems.

C     Dumb terminals are effectively a screen and monitor plus a communications link to the central computer that enables data held on the central computer and the central computer's processing power to be used.

With a centralised transaction processing system, processing is done either by batch processing or online via remote terminals linked to the central computer.

While almost all modern databases operate using real time, some database systems process transactions in batches at the end of a day (or even at the end of the week).

Risks to the security of data files are higher with decentralised computer systems than with centralised systems, because there are more files in more, different locations.

## 9.3 Network topology

**Topology** means how a computer network is physically arranged.

**FAST FORWARD**

Three popular **network topologies** are **star**, **ring** and **tree**.

### 9.3.1 Star networks

Star networks have one central computer that acts as a service provider (server) to other computers. All communication on the network passes through the central computer.

**A star network**

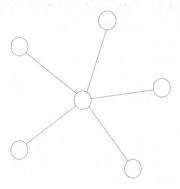

### 9.3.2 Ring networks

A ring network consists of a number of computers each linked to two others in the network. As with the star topology, any computer is able to communicate with any other in the network – although to achieve this may require data passing via other computers.

**A ring network**

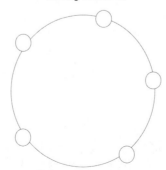

### 9.3.3 Tree networks

A tree network comprises a hierarchy of computers (or processors). The processor at the top of the tree is the most powerful – often a mainframe. Computers at lower levels are less powerful, for example microcomputers (PCs).

Communication and data transfer must follow an existing path (eg processors at the second level in the diagram below are able to transfer data between the top computer and lower level processors).

**A tree network**

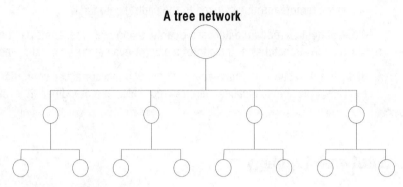

## 9.4 Client-server computing

With client-server computing each computer or process on the network is either a 'client' or a 'server'. Servers are powerful computers or processes dedicated to managing disk drives (file servers), printers (print servers), or network traffic (network servers). Clients are PCs or workstations on which users run applications. Clients rely on servers for resources, such as files, devices, and sometimes processing power.

**Key terms**

A **client** is a machine which requests a service, for example a PC running a spreadsheet application which the user wishes to print out.

A **server** is a machine which is dedicated to providing a particular function or service requested by a client. Servers include file servers (see below), print servers, e-mail servers and fax servers.

A typical client-server system includes three **hardware** elements.

- A central server (sometimes called the corporate server)
- Local servers (sometimes called departmental servers)
- Client workstations

A server computer (such as a file server) may be a powerful PC or a minicomputer. As its name implies, it **serves** the rest of the network offering a generally-accessible hard disk and sometimes offering other resources, such as a **shared printer**.

A typical client-server architecture is shown in the following illustration.

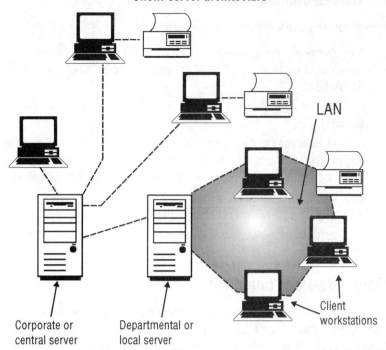

**Client-server architecture**

LAN

Corporate or central server

Departmental or local server

Client workstations

Client-server systems aim to locate software where it is most efficient – based on the number and location of users requiring access and the processing power required.

### 9.4.1 The advantages of client-server computing

| Advantage | Comment |
|---|---|
| **Greater resilience** | Processing is spread over several computers. If one server breaks down, other locations can carry on processing. |
| **Scalability** | They are highly scalable. Instead of having to buy computing power in large quantities you can buy just the amount of power you need to do the job. |
| **Shared programs and data** | Program and data files held on a file server can be shared by all the PCs in the network. With stand-alone PCs, each computer would have its own data files, and there might be unnecessary duplication of data.<br><br>A system where everyone uses the same data will help to improve data processing and decision making. |
| **Shared work-loads** | The processing capability of each computer in a network can be utilised. For example, if there were separate stand-alone PCs, A might do job 1, B might do job 2 and C might do job 3. In a network, any PC, (A, B or C) could do any job (1, 2 or 3). This is more efficient. |
| **Shared peripherals** | Peripheral equipment can be shared. For example, five PCs might share a single printer. |
| **Communication** | LANs can be linked up to the office communications network, thus adding to the processing capabilities in an office. Electronic mail, calendar and diary facilities can also be used. |
| **Compatibility** | Client/server systems are likely to include interfaces between different types of software used on the system, making it easier to move information between applications. |
| **Flexibility** | For example, if a detailed analysis of existing data is required, a copy of this data could be placed on a separate server, allowing data to be manipulated without disrupting the main system. |

### 9.4.2 The disadvantages of client-server computing

The client/server approach has some drawbacks.

(a)   A single **mainframe** may be more efficient performing some tasks, in certain circumstances. For example, where the process involves routine processing of a very large number (eg millions) of transactions.

(b)   It is easier to **control** and **maintain** a centralised system. In particular it is easier to keep data **secure**.

(c)   It may be **cheaper** to 'tweak' an existing mainframe system rather than throwing it away and starting from scratch: for example it may be possible to give it a graphical user interface and to make data exchangeable between Windows and non-Windows based applications.

(d)   Each location may need its own **network administrator** to keep things running smoothly – there may be unnecessary duplication of **skills** and staff.

(e)   Duplication of information may be a problem if individual users do not follow a disciplined approach.

## 9.5 Peer-to-peer computing

'Peer-to-peer' refers to a type of network in which each workstation has equivalent capabilities and responsibilities. This differs from client-server architectures, in which some computers are dedicated to serving the others. Peer-to-peer networks are generally simpler, but they usually do not offer the same performance under heavy workloads.

Question                                                                                   Stand-alone

Learning outcome: A(ii)

When would you expect a **stand-alone** computer to be used? Your answer should be no more than 50 words.                                                                              (4 marks)

Answer

Stand-alone computers are used when user requirements can be handled by one computer, for example for developing a personal spreadsheet model. In other cases, even organisations with large computer systems may choose to use a stand-alone computer for holding highly sensitive information.

# 10 Purchasing hardware and software

An organisation might buy hardware and software direct from a manufacturer, or through an intermediate supplier. Given that the expense is often considerable, the purchasing procedure should be carefully controlled.

## 10.1 Software sources

An organisation has a range of options when sourcing software for information systems. The four main options are described in the following table.

| Source | Comment |
| --- | --- |
| **Standard off-the-shelf package** | This is the simplest option. The organisation purchases and installs a ready-made solution. |
| **Amended standard package** | A standard package is purchased, but some customisation is undertaken so that the software meets the organisations requirements. This may require access to the source code. |

| Source | Comment |
|---|---|
| Standard package plus additions | The purchased standard package is not amended itself, but additional software that integrates with the standard package is developed. This also may require access to the source code. |
| Bespoke package | Programmers write an application to meet the specific needs of the organisation. This can be a time-consuming and expensive process. |

In this section we discuss the process and relative advantages of the two main options – purchasing an application off-the-shelf and developing a bespoke solution. The other two options include elements of both of these two main options.

**Key terms**

**Bespoke software** is designed for a specific user or situation. It may be written either 'in-house' or externally.

An **off-the-shelf package** is one that is sold to a wide range of users. The package is written to handle requirements that are common to a wide range of organisations.

## 10.2 Choosing an application package off-the shelf

**FAST FORWARD**

**Off-the-shelf software** is produced to meet requirements that are common to many organisations. The software is likely to be available **immediately** and **cost significantly less** than bespoke solutions.

Off-the-shelf packages are generally available for functions that are likely to be performed similarly across a range of organisations eg accounting. However, as the software has not been written specifically for the organisation, it may not meet all of their requirements. The following table describes some of the factors to consider when choosing an off-the-shelf application package.

| Factor | Comment |
|---|---|
| User requirements | Does the package fit the user's particular requirements? Matters to consider include data volumes, data validation routines, number of users and the reports available. |
| Processing times | Are the processing times fast enough? If response times to enquiries is slow, the user might consider the package unacceptable. |
| Documentation | Is there full and clear documentation for the user? A comprehensive user manual, a quick reference guide and on-line help should be considered. |
| Compatibility | Is the package compatible with existing hardware and software? Can data be exchanged with other related systems? |
| Controls | Access and security controls (eg passwords) should be included, as should processing controls that enable the accuracy of processing operations to be confirmed. |
| User-interface | Users are most affected by the user-interface design. The interface should be clear, logical, and consistent, and should follow standard interface conventions such as those used on most packages produced for use with the Microsoft Windows operating system. |
| Modification | Can the package be modified by the user – allowing the user to tailor it to meet their needs? |
| Support, maintenance and updates | The availability and cost of support, such as a telephone help-line, should be considered, as should the arrangements for updates and upgrades. This is particularly important if software is likely to be affected by changes in legislation eg a payroll package. |
| Cost | An organisation should aim to purchase a package that will meet its requirements. However, a package should not be purchased if the cost outweighs the value of the benefits it should bring. |

## 10.3 Developing a bespoke application

**Bespoke software** should be written so as to **match** the organisation's requirements exactly. However, the software is likely to be considerably **more expensive** than an off-the-shelf package.

Producing a bespoke software system involves the tasks shown below in the software development and testing cycle.

The process is summarised in the diagram below, and explained in the table that follows. (Many of these activities were explained in the context of systems development in Chapter 2.)

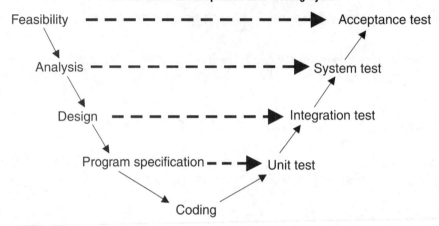

**The software development and testing cycle**

| Stages of software development | Comment |
|---|---|
| **Feasibility and analysis** | The feasibility of software solutions would have usually been covered during the overall system feasibility study. An analysis of the software requirements should therefore be available. |
| **Design and program specification** | The software requirements are used to develop a systems design specification, which in turn is used to produce a detailed program specification. The specification would be used by in-house software developers, or would be distributed to software producers (as part of the invitation to tender – covered below). |
| **Coding** | Software producers will decide how to build the package, for example identifying parts of existing programs that may be used, and establishing what will need to be coded (ie written) from scratch. Prototyping may be used to help ensure user requirements are met. |
| **Testing** Unit; Integration; System; Acceptance | Unit testing tests individual programs (or units) operating alone. Integration testing tests how two or more units of the software interact with each other. System testing tests the complete package and how it interacts with other software programs. User acceptance testing aims to ensure all user requirements included in the software specification have been met. |

# 10.4 Invitations To Tender (ITT)

**FAST FORWARD**

An organisation that requires bespoke software to be written may issue an **Invitation To Tender (ITT)** to a range of potential suppliers.

**Key term**

An **Invitation To Tender** is a document that invites suppliers to bid for the supply of specified software, or hardware, or both.

The contents of a typical ITT are outlined below. This format could be used when inviting tenders for bespoke or off-the-shelf software – although sections such as the development methodology would be shorter for off-the-shelf tenders, as this would refer only to any proposed amendments to the package.

| ITT section | Comment |
|---|---|
| **Covering letter** | An ITT will include a letter inviting the supplier to tender. The letter should specify:<br><br>• Contact names for queries relating to the tendering process and for technical queries<br><br>• The closing date for submitting tenders |
| **Instructions** | Instructions to tenderers should specify the information required in a tender. Instructions are likely to require tenderers to specify:<br><br>• Areas of their tender that do not comply with the software specification provided, and the reasons why<br><br>• The period of validity for the tender<br><br>• The basis for calculating prices, whether prices are estimates or a quote<br><br>• An indication of timescale – when work could start and an approximate completion date<br><br>• Alternative ways of approaching parts of the software design than indicated in the requirements specification |
| **Detailed software requirements** | The ITT must include a detailed requirements specification so tenderers know exactly what they are tendering for. This should include:<br><br>• The purpose of the system<br><br>• The volume of data to be processed<br><br>• Processing requirements (including details of inputs and outputs, and interfaces with other systems)<br><br>• The number of locations and users requiring access<br><br>• The speed of processing required, eg response times<br><br>• Expected life of the system<br><br>• Possible upgrades or expansion anticipated<br><br>When submitting their bids, some potential suppliers may come up with alternative specifications – these must be fully explained. |
| **Details of development model/methodology** | This section of the ITT requires tenderers to provide a description of the methodology or systems development model used to develop their software. The aim is to ensure that the supplier produces software using accepted development techniques – reducing the possibility of poor quality software. |
| **Request for details of the proposed software contract** | The ITT document should request information from potential suppliers relating to the key terms of any future software contract. We cover software contracts later in this chapter. |

## 10.5 Evaluating supplier proposals

Once vendor proposals have been obtained, they should be evaluated against what was requested within the ITT. There are many factors that should be considered when evaluating proposals. The factors to consider fit into three general categories:

- **Technical**, how well does the proposal meet the specified technical requirements?
- **Support**, what after-sales support is included?
- **Cost**, what do we get for our money?

Some of the main factors to consider when evaluating supplier proposals are described in the following table. Some of the relevant points are the same as those considered when choosing off-the-shelf software.

| Factor | Comment |
|---|---|
| Organisation needs | How well does the software meet the requirements of the organisation? If some requirements are not met, how important are they – can they be satisfied through other means? |
| Speed | Can the system cope with data volumes; is response time affected by high data volumes? |
| Documentation | Is there full and clear documentation for the user, and a technical manual that would allow further development? |
| Compatibility | Is the package compatible with existing hardware and software? Can data be exchanged with other related systems? |
| Controls | Access and security controls (eg passwords) should be included, as should processing controls that enable the accuracy of processing operations to be confirmed. |
| User-friendly | Software should be relatively easy to use and tolerant to user errors. Menu structures should be logical, the software should follow standard user-interface conventions. |
| Modification | Can the package be modified by the user – allowing the organisation to tailor it to meet its specific needs? |
| Demonstration | A demonstration version of the software may be available – this should provide a good idea of how the finished product would look, feel and operate. |
| Training provided | Training is essential for the organisation to utilise the software effectively. |
| Support, maintenance and updates | The availability and cost of support, such as a telephone help-line, should be considered, as should the arrangements for updates and upgrades. This is particularly important if software is likely to be affected by changes in legislation eg a payroll package. |
| Conditions included in the software contract | The software contract includes terms relating to the actual supply and use of the software. |
| Supplier size, reputation and customer base | Software suppliers that have been in business for a reasonable amount of time, and who have an established client base, are more likely to remain in business – and therefore be in a position to provide support. References may be available from existing customers, attesting to the quality of software and support. |
| Cost | An organisation should aim to purchase a package that will meet its requirements. However, a package should not be purchased if the cost outweighs the value of the benefits it should bring. |

## 10.6 The advantages and disadvantages of bespoke software

### 10.6.1 Advantages of bespoke software

**Advantages** of having bespoke software specially written include the following.

(a)     If it is well-written, the software should meet the organisation's specific needs.

(b)     Data and file structures may be chosen by the organisation rather than having to meet the structures required by standard software packages.

(c)     The company may be able to do things with its software that competitors cannot do with theirs. In other words it is a source of competitive advantage.

(d)     Similar organisations may wish to purchase the software.

(e)     The software should be able to be modified to meet future needs.

### 10.6.2 Disadvantages of bespoke software

Key **disadvantages** are:

(a)     As the software is being developed from scratch, there is a risk that the package may not perform as intended.

(b)     There is a greater chance of 'bugs'. Widely used off-the-shelf software is more likely to have had bugs identified and removed.

(c)     Development will take longer than purchasing ready-made software.

(d)     The cost is considerable when compared with a ready-made package.

(e)     Support costs are also likely to be higher than with off-the-shelf software.

### 10.6.3 Overcoming the risks of bespoke development

Building a bespoke software application involves much time, effort and money. The risks associated with such an undertaking are that the resulting software:

*   Does not meet user needs
*   Does not interact as intended with other systems
*   Is produced late
*   Is produced over-budget

These risks can be minimised or overcome by:

(a)     Good project management.

(b)     Involving users at all stages of development.

(c)     Ensuring in-house IT staff are able to maintain and support bespoke systems supplied from outside parties.

(d)     Ensuring the ITT document includes details of all file structures required, and details of interfaces with other systems.

## 10.7 The advantages and disadvantages of off-the-shelf packages

### 10.7.1 Advantages of off-the-shelf packages

The **advantages** of an off-the-shelf package include:

(a)     The software is likely to be available immediately.

(b)     A ready-made package will almost certainly cheaper because it is 'mass-produced'.

(c)     The software is likely to have been written by software specialists and so should be of a high quality.

(d)     A successful package will be continually updated by the software manufacturer.

(e)     Other users will have used the package already, and a well-established package should be relatively free of bugs.

(f)    Good packages are well-documented, with easy-to-follow user manuals or online help.

(g)    Some standard packages can be customised to the user's specific needs (see below).

### 10.7.2 Disadvantages of off-the-shelf packages

The **disadvantages** of ready-made packages are as follows.

(a)    The organisation is purchasing a standard solution. A standard solution may not be well suited to the organisation's particular needs.

(b)    The organisation is dependent on the supplier for maintenance of the package – ie updating the package or providing assistance in the event of problems. It is unlikely that the supplier would give access to the code that would allow organisations with the relevant expertise to amend the software themselves.

(c)    Competitors may well use the same package, removing any chance of using IS/IT for competitive advantage.

## 10.8 Customised versions of standard packages

Standard packages can be customised so that they fit an organisation's specific requirements. This can be done by purchasing the source code of the package and making modifications in-house, or by paying the producer of the package to customise it.

**Advantages** of customisation are similar to those of producing a bespoke system, with the additional advantages that:

(a)    Development time should be much quicker, given that most of the system will be written already.

(b)    If the work is done in-house the organisation gains considerable knowledge of how the software works and may be able to 'tune' it so that it works more efficiently with the company's hardware.

**Disadvantages** of customising a standard package include the following.

(a)    It may prove more costly than expected, because new versions of the standard package will also have to be customised.

(b)    Customisation may delay delivery of the software.

(c)    Customisation may introduce bugs that do not exist in the standard version.

(d)    If done in-house, the in-house team may have to learn new skills.

(e)    If done by the original manufacturer disadvantages such as those for off-the-shelf packages may arise.

**Exam focus point**

> The advantages and disadvantages of bespoke development and off-the-shelf packages are likely to be examined regularly.

## 10.9 Software contracts and licences

### 10.9.1 Software contracts

The agreement to supply bespoke software should be formally laid out in a contract. The contract to supply the software is likely to include terms relating to:

(a)    The cost, and what this figure does and does not include.

(b)    Delivery date.

(c)    Ownership of the source code, sometimes referred to as ownership rights.

(d)    Right to make copies.

(e)    Number of licensed users (the contract may include the licence agreement).

(f)    Performance criteria, such as what the software will and will not do, processing speed.

(g)    Warranty period.

(h)    Support available.

(i)    Arrangements for upgrades.

(j)    Maintenance arrangements.

## 10.9.2 Software licences

Packaged software generally has a licence, the terms of which users are deemed to have agreed to the moment the package is unwrapped or a seal is broken.

A licence typically covers matters such as:

(a)     How many users can use the software.
(b)     Whether it can be modified without the manufacturer's consent.
(c)     In what circumstances the licence is terminated.
(d)     A limitation of liability should the software contain bugs or be mis-used.

When a user purchases software they are merely buying the rights to use the software in line with the terms and conditions within the licence agreement. A breach of the licence conditions usually means the owners' copyright has been infringed.

The unauthorised copying of software is referred to as **software piracy**. If an organisation is using illegal copies of software, the organisation may face a civil suit, and corporate officers and individual employees may have criminal liability.

| Question | Software options |

Learning outcome: A (v)

(a)     What options does an organisation have if its systems software does not fit with the business processes?

(b)     What should it take into account when choosing between these options?

| Answer |

(a)     The organisation has two options.

      (i)     Change the software to match the processes.
      (ii)    Change the processes to match the software.

(b)     When making the choice, the organisation should consider:

- Costs and benefits of each option
- Their suitability, acceptability and feasibility
- The response of staff to the change
- Whether the result of either option represents industry 'best practice'
- The risk of either option causing inconsistencies or inefficient operation

## 10.10 Choosing hardware

In general terms, the choice of computer hardware will depend on the following factors.

| Factor | Comment |
| --- | --- |
| **User requirements** | The ease with which the computer configuration fits in with the user requirements (eg direct access facilities, hard-copy output in given quantities). |
| **Power** | The power of the computer must be sufficient for current and foreseeable requirements. This is measured by:<br><br>• Processor type<br>• RAM in Mb<br>• Clock speed in MHz<br>• Hard disk size in Mb or Gb |

| Factor | Comment |
|---|---|
| Reliability | There should be a low expected 'break-down' rate. There should be back-up hardware available to limit any down-time in case of hardware failure. |
| Simplicity | Systems should be as simple as possible, whilst still capable of performing the tasks required. |
| Ease of communication | The system (hardware and software) should be able to communicate well with the user. Software is referred to as 'user-friendly' or 'user-unfriendly' but similar considerations apply to hardware (eg not all terminals are of standard screen size; the number and accessibility of terminals might also have a bearing on how well the user is able to put data into the computer or extract information). |
| Flexibility | The hardware should be able to meet new requirements as they emerge. More powerful CPUs tend to be more flexible. |
| Security | Keeping out 'hackers' and other unauthorised users is easier with more powerful systems, although security can be a major problem for any computer system. |
| Cost | The cost must be justified in terms of the benefits the hardware will provide. |
| Changeover | Whether the choice of hardware will help with a smooth changeover from the old to the new system. |
| Networking | Networking capabilities. |
| Software | The hardware must be capable of running whatever software has been chosen. |

# 11 Information systems department and outsourcing

## 11.1 Information systems department or team

**FAST FORWARD**

Most organisations choose have an **information systems department**, or team responsible for the tasks and responsibilities associated with information systems.

Information systems (IS) increasingly utilise information technology (IT).

At the head of the information systems/information technology function will be either the IS/IT manager, or the IS/IT director.

An IS/IT director requires a wide range of skills. The ideal person would possess technical know-how, excellent general management ability, a keen sense of business awareness and a good understanding of the organisation's operations.

## 11.2 IS/IT steering committee

The general purpose of an IS/IT steering committee would be to make decisions relating to the future use and development of IS/IT by the organisation. The steering committee should contain representatives from all departments of the organisation.

**Common tasks of such a committee** could include:

- Ensuring IS/IT activities comply with IS/IT strategy
- Ensuring IS/IT activities compliment the overall organisation strategy
- Ensuring resources committed to IS/IT are used effectively
- Monitoring IS/IT projects
- Providing leadership and guidance on IS/IT

## 11.3 Centralisation and decentralisation

The IS/IT department or function could be **centralised** or **decentralised**.

We now look at how the IS/IT department could be structured. There are two main options – centralised or decentralised. (Note that we are now discussing IS/IT department structure, rather than system architecture which was covered earlier in this chapter.)

**Key terms**

> A **centralised** IS/IT department involves all IS/IT staff and functions being based out at a single central location, such as head office.
>
> A **decentralised** IS/IT department involves IS/IT staff and functions being spread out throughout the organisation.

There is no single 'best' structure for an IS/IT department – an organisation should consider its IS/IT requirements and the merits of each structure.

### 11.3.1 Advantages of a centralised IS/IT department

**Advantages** of a centralised IS/IT department include the following.

(a)   Assuming centralised processing is used, there is only one set of files. Everyone uses the same data and information.

(b)   It gives better security/control over data and files. It is easier to enforce standards.

(c)   Head office is in a better position to know what is going on.

(d)   There may be economies of scale available in purchasing computer equipment and supplies.

(e)   Computer staff are in a single location, and more expert staff are likely to be employed. Career paths may be more clearly defined.

### 11.3.2 Disadvantages of a centralised IS/IT department

**Disadvantages** of a centralised IS/IT department include the following.

(a)   Local offices might have to wait for IS/IT services and assistance.

(b)   Reliance on head office. Local offices are less self-sufficient.

(c)   A system fault at head office will impact across the organisation.

### 11.3.3 Advantages of a decentralised IS/IT department

**Advantages** of a decentralised IS/IT department include the following.

(a)   Each office can introduce an information system specially **tailored** for its individual needs. Local changes in business requirements can be taken into account.

(b)   Each office is more self-sufficient.

(c)   Offices are likely to have quicker access to IS/IT support/advice.

(d)   A decentralised structure is more likely to facilitate accurate IS/IT cost/overhead allocations.

### 11.3.4 Disadvantages of a decentralised IS/IT department

The **disadvantages** of a decentralised IS/IT department.

(a)   Control may be difficult – as unco-ordinated information systems may be introduced.

(b)   Self-sufficiency may encourage a lack of co-ordination between departments.

(c)   Increased risk of data duplication, with different offices holding the same data on their own separate files.

## 11.4 Outsourcing IT/IS services

Some organisations **outsource** their IT function to external organisations. Outsourcing has advantages (eg access to specialised expertise) and disadvantages (eg lack of control over a key resource).

**Key term**

**Outsourcing** is the contracting out of specified operations or services to an external vendor.

### 11.4.1 Classifications of outsourcing

There are four **broad classifications** of outsourcing.

| Classification | Comment |
|---|---|
| Ad-hoc | The organisation has a short-term requirement for increased IS/IT skills. An example would be employing programmers on a short-term contract to help with the programming of bespoke software. |
| Project management | The development and installation of a particular IS/IT project is outsourced. For example, a new accounting system. (This approach is sometimes referred to as **systems integration**.) |
| Partial | Some IT/IS services are outsourced. Examples include hardware maintenance, network management or ongoing website management. |
| Total | An external supplier provides the vast majority of an organisation's IT/IS services. For example, a third party owns or is responsible for IT equipment, software and possibly staff. |

### 11.4.2 Levels of service provision

The degree to which the provision and management of IS/IT services are transferred to the third party varies according to the situation and the skills of both organisations.

(a)  **Time-share**. The vendor charges for access to an external processing system on a time-used basis. Software ownership may be with either the vendor or the client organisation.

(b)  **Service bureaux** usually focus on a specific function. Traditionally bureaux would provide the same type of service to many organisations, eg payroll processing. As organisations have developed their own IT infrastructure, the use of bureaux has decreased.

(c)  **Facilities management (FM)**. The terms 'outsourcing' and 'facilities management' are sometimes confused. Facilities management traditionally involved contracts for premises-related services such as cleaning or site security.

In the context of IS/IT, facilities management involves an outside agency managing the organisation's IS/IT facilities. All equipment usually remains with the client, but the responsibility for providing and managing the specified services rests with the FM company. FM companies operating in the UK include Accenture, Cap Gemini, EDS and CFM.

 Case Study

The retailer Sears outsourced the management of its vast information technology and accounting functions to Accenture. First year *savings* were estimated to be £5 million per annum, growing to £14 million in the following year, and thereafter. This is clearly considerable, although re-organisation costs relating to redundancies, relocation and asset write-offs are thought to be in the region of £35 million. About 900 staff were involved: under the transfer of undertakings regulations (which protect employees when part or all of a company changes hands), Accenture was obliged to take on the existing Sears staff. This provided new opportunities for the staff who moved, while those who remained at Sears were free to concentrate on strategy development and management direction.

## 11.5 Developments in outsourcing

Outsourcing arrangements are becoming increasingly flexible to cope with the ever-changing nature of the modern business environment. Examples of outsourcing arrangements include:

(a) **Multiple sourcing**. This involves outsourcing different functions or areas of the IS/IT function to a range of suppliers. Some suppliers may form alliances to present a stronger case for selection.

(b) **Incremental approach**. Organisations progressively outsource selected areas of their IT/IS function. Possible problems with outsourced services are solved before progressing to the next stage.

(c) **Joint venture sourcing**. This term is used to describe an organisation entering into a joint venture with a supplier. The costs (risks) and possible rewards are split on an agreed basis. Such an arrangement may be suitable when developing software that could be sold to other organisations.

(d) **Application Service Providers (ASP)**. ASPs are third parties that manage and distribute software services and solutions to customers across a Wide Area Network. ASPs could be considered the modern equivalent of the traditional computer bureaux.

## 11.6 Managing outsourcing arrangements

Managing outsourcing arrangements involves deciding **what** will be outsourced, **choosing and negotiating** with suppliers and managing the supplier **relationship**.

When considering whether to outsource a particular service the following questions are relevant.

(a) Is the system of **strategic importance**? Strategic IS are generally not suited to outsourcing as they require a high degree of specific business knowledge that a third party IT specialist cannot be expected to possess.

(b) Can the system be relatively isolated? Functions that have only **limited interfaces** are most easily outsourced, eg payroll.

(c) Do we know enough about the system to manage the outsourced service agreement? If an organisation knows very little about a technology it may be difficult to know what constitutes good service and value for money. It may be necessary to recruit additional **expertise** to manage the relationship with the other party.

(d) Are our requirements likely to **change**? Organisations should avoid tying themselves into a long-term outsourcing agreement if requirements are likely to change.

A key factor when **choosing and negotiating** with external vendors is the contract offered and subsequently negotiated with the supplier. The contract is sometimes referred to as the **Service Level Contract** (SLC) or **Service Level Agreement** (SLA).

The **key elements of the contract** are described below.

| Contract element | Comment |
|---|---|
| Service level | The contract should clearly specify minimum levels of service to be provided. Penalties should be specified for failure to meet these standards. Relevant factors will vary depending on the nature of the services outsourced but could include: <br>• Response time to requests for assistance/information <br>• System 'uptime' percentage <br>• Deadlines for performing relevant tasks |
| Exit route | Arrangements for an exit route, addressing how the transfer to another supplier, or the move back in-house would be conducted. |
| Timescale | When does the contract expire? Is the timescale suitable for the organisation's needs or should it be renegotiated? |

| Contract element | Comment |
| --- | --- |
| Software ownership | Relevant factors include:<br><br>• Software licensing and security<br><br>• If the arrangement includes the development of new software who owns the copyright? |
| Dependencies | If related services are outsourced, the level of service quality agreed should group these services together. |
| Employment issues | If the arrangement includes provision for the organisation's IT staff to move to the third party, employer responsibilities must be specified clearly. |

If full facilities management is involved, and almost all management responsibility for IT/IS lies with the entity providing the service, then a close relationship between the parties is necessary (a '**partnership**'). Factors such as organisation culture need to be considered when entering into such a close and critical relationship.

On the other hand, if a relatively simple function such as payroll were outsourced, such a close relationship with the supplier would not be necessary. A 'typical' supplier – customer relationship is all that is required. (Although issues such as confidentiality need to be considered with payroll data.)

Regardless of the type of relationship, a legally binding contract is the key element in establishing the obligations and responsibilities of all parties.

 Case Study

The PA Consulting Group's annual survey of outsourcing found that 'on average the top five strategic outsourcers out-performed the FTSE by more than 100 per cent over three years; the bottom five under-performed by more than 66%'.

However, the survey revealed that of those organisations who have opted to outsource IT functions, only five per cent are truly happy with the results. A spokesman for the consultants said that this is because most people fail to adopt a proper strategic approach, taking a view that is neither long-term nor broad enough, and taking outsourcing decisions that are piecemeal and unsatisfactory.

This lack of prescience is compounded by a failure to take a sufficiently rigorous approach to selection, specification, contract drafting and contract management.

The survey found that a constant complaint among many of those interviewed is the lack of ability of outsourcing organisations to work together.

Twenty-five per cent of those asked would bring the functions they had outsourced back in-house if it were possible.

*Source: Business and Technology* magazine

## 11.7 Advantages of outsourcing arrangements

The **advantages** of outsourcing are as follows.

(a) Outsourcing can remove uncertainty about **cost**, as there is often a long-term contract where services are specified in advance for a **fixed price**. If computing services are inefficient, the costs will be borne by the outsourcing company. This is also an incentive to the third party to provide a high quality service.

(b) Long-term contracts (maybe up to ten years) encourage **planning** for the future.

(c) Outsourcing can bring the benefits of **economies of scale**. For example, an outsourcing company may conduct research into new technologies that benefits a number of their clients.

(d)    A specialist organisation is able to retain **skills and knowledge**. Many organisations would not have a sufficiently well-developed IT department to offer IT staff opportunities for career development. Talented staff would leave to pursue their careers elsewhere.

(e)    New skills and knowledge become available. A specialist company can **share** staff with **specific expertise** (such as programming in HTML to produce Web pages) between several clients. This allows the outsourcing company to take advantage of new developments without the need to recruit new people or re-train existing staff, and without the cost.

(f)    **Flexibility** (contract permitting). Resources may be able to be scaled up or down depending upon demand. For instance, during a major changeover from one system to another the number of IT staff needed may be twice as large as it will be once the new system is working satisfactorily.

An outsourcing organisation is more able to arrange its work on a **project** basis, whereby some staff will expect to be moved periodically from one project to the next.

## 11.8 Disadvantages of outsourcing arrangements

Some possible **drawbacks** are outlined below.

(a)    It is arguable that information and its provision is **an inherent part of the business and of management**. Unlike office cleaning, or catering, an organisation's IS services may be too important to be contracted out. Information is at the heart of management.

(b)    A company may have highly **confidential information** and to let outsiders handle it could be seen as **risky** in commercial and/or legal terms.

(c)    Information strategy can be used to gain **competitive advantage**. Opportunities may be missed if a third party is handling IS services, because there is no onus upon internal management to keep up with new developments and have new ideas. Any new technology or application devised by the third party is likely to be available to competitors.

(d)    An organisation may find itself **locked in** to an unsatisfactory contract. The decision may be very difficult to reverse. If the outsourcing company supplies unsatisfactory levels of service, the effort and expense the organisation would incur to rebuild its own computing function or to move to another provider could be substantial.

(e)    The use of outsourcing does not encourage awareness of the potential costs and benefits of IS/IT within the organisation. If managers cannot manage in-house IS/IT resources effectively, then it could be argued that they will not be able to manage an arrangement to outsource effectively either.

## 11.9 Information systems and broader management operations

The information systems within an organisation should complement and **support other functional areas** such as finance, human resources and marketing. For example, an intranet facilitates the sharing of information.

Effective information systems and information management **contribute towards the attainment of organisational goals**. To best achieve this, **a cohesive IS strategy** should be developed that supports the organisation's overall strategy.

As with any expenditure, the **benefits** of IS/IT systems should be **greater than their costs**.

# 12 Office technology

Common office technology includes, **e-mail**, **faxes** and **tele/videoconferencing**.

Office technology has developed massively in recent years and many systems are now **multimedia** combining data in the form of images, sound and text.

Common uses of IT in an office environment include **e-mail, fax, teleconferencing** and **videoconferencing**.

## 12.1 E-mail

Electronic mail created **near instantaneous communication** across the globe. It has reduced the need for paper-based communication and allows a 'trail' of communication to be kept. Security of emails is an important issue and care must be taken to avoid unauthorised access or damage from viruses.

## 12.2 Fax

The facsimile was the predecessor of email and it allows copies of documents to be sent through the telephone system. It is still popular where documents must be signed.

## 12.3 Tele and videoconferencing

Both systems allow participants to conduct meetings without being in the same location. Teleconferencing provides a telephone link using the Internet and satellites and permits multi-way communication. However, the lack of visible identification and recognition is a drawback.

Videoconferencing overcomes this problem through the use of a video picture, but requires special equipment and is more expensive.

Both methods provide savings in terms of time and travel costs of those involved in the meeting.

# 13 The Internet

**FAST FORWARD**

Many organisations are now utilising the **Internet** as a means of gathering and disseminating information, and conducting transactions.

**Key term**

> The **Internet** is a global network connecting millions of computers.

The Internet is the name given to the technology that allows any computer with a telecommunications link to **send and receive information** to/from any other suitably equipped computer.

The **World Wide Web** is the multimedia element which provides facilities such as full-colour graphics, sound and video. Websites are points within the network created by those who wish to provide an information point for searchers to visit and benefit by the provision of information and/or by entering into a transaction.

Most companies now have a **website** on the Internet. A site is a collection of screens providing **information in text and graphic form**, any of which can be viewed simply by clicking the appropriate button, word or image on the screen.

## 13.1 Current uses of the Internet

The scope and potential of the Internet are still developing. Its uses already embrace the following.

(a)   **Dissemination** of information and intelligence gathering.

(b)   **Product/service development** – through almost instantaneous test marketing.

(c)   **Transaction processing**  (electronic commerce or e-commerce) – both business-to-business (B2B) and business-to-consumer (B2C).

(d)   **Relationship enhancement** – between various groups of stakeholders.

(e)   **Recruitment** and job search – involving organisations worldwide.

(f)   **Entertainment** – including music, humour, art, games and some less wholesome pursuits!

The Internet provides opportunities to organise for and to automate tasks which would previously have required more costly interaction with the organisation. These have often been called low-touch or zero-touch approaches.

Tasks which a **website may automate** include:

(a) **Frequently Asked Questions (FAQs)**: carefully-structured sets of answers can deal with many customer interactions.

(b) **Status checking**: major service enquiries (Where is my order? When will the engineer arrive? What is my bank balance?) can also be automated, replacing high-cost human service processes, and also providing the opportunity to proactively offer better service and new services.

(c) **Keyword search**: the ability to search provides web users with opportunities to find information in large and complex websites.

(d) **Wizards (interview style interface)**: these can help ensure people are directed to the information most relevant to them.

(e) **E-mail and systems to route and track inbound e-mail**: the ability to route and/or to provide automatic responses will enable organisations to deal with high volumes of e-mail from actual and potential customers.

(f) **Bulletin boards**: these enable customers to interact with each other, thus facilitating self-activated customer service and also the opportunity for product/service referral. Cisco, in particular, has created communities of Cisco users who help each other – thus reducing the service costs for Cisco itself.

(g) **Call-back buttons**: these enable customers to speak to someone in order to deal with and resolve a problem; the more sophisticated systems allow the call-centre operator to know which web pages the users were consulting at the time.

(h) **Transaction processing**: usually referred to as e-commerce.

## 13.2 Problems with the Internet

To a large extent the Internet has grown organically **without any formal organisation**. There are specific communication standards, but it is not **owned** by any one body and there are no clear guidelines on how it should develop.

The **quality** of much of the information on the Internet leaves much to be desired.

Speed is a major issue. Data only downloads onto the user's PC at the speed of the slowest telecommunications link – downloading data can be a painfully **slow** procedure.

So much information and entertainment is available that employers worry that their **staff will spend too much time** browsing through non-work-related sites.

Connecting an information system to the Internet exposes the system to numerous **security issues**.

Note: We cover the security aspects of the Internet in Chapter 12 – in the context of marketing and e-commerce.

# Chapter Roundup

- In **many situations manual systems are inferior to computerised systems** in terms of productivity, speed, accessibility, quality of output, incidence of errors, 'bulk' and ease of corrections.

- The amount of **RAM** and the **processor speed** are key determinants of computer performance.

- There are a range of **input** devices available. The most efficient method will depend on the circumstances of each situation.

- The commonest methods of computer **output** are **printers** and **screen display**.

- **Hard disks**, **flash drives** and **DVDs** are common forms of **secondary storage**.

- There are five classifications of **computer software**: operating systems, utilities, programming tools, off-the-shelf applications and bespoke applications.

- The term '**database system**' is used to describe a wide range of systems that utilise a central pool of data.

- Control over the database can be facilitated by the appointment of a **database administrator** (DBA).

- Information technology can be used to **automate** and improve physical tasks in **manufacturing** organisations.

- The term **system architecture** refers to the way in which the various components of an information system are linked together, and the way they relate to each other. A **centralised** architecture involves all computer processing being carried out on a single central processor. **Distributed** architectures spread the processing power throughout the organisation at several different locations.

- Three popular network topologies are **star**, **ring** and **tree**.

- **Off-the-shelf software** is produced to meet requirements that are common to many organisations. The software is likely to be available **immediately** and **cost significantly less** than bespoke solutions.

- **Bespoke software** should be written so as to **match** the organisation's requirements exactly. However, the software is likely to be considerably **more expensive** than an off-the-shelf package.

- An organisation that requires bespoke software to be written may issue an **Invitation to Tender (ITT)** to a range of potential suppliers.

- Most organisations choose have an **information systems department**, or team responsible for the tasks and responsibilities associated with information systems.

- The IS/IT department or **function** could be **centralised** or **decentralised**.

- Some organisations **outsource** their IT function to external organisations. Outsourcing has advantages (eg access to specialised expertise) and disadvantages (eg lack of control over a key resource).

- Common office technology includes, **e-mail**, **faxes** and **tele/videoconferencing**.

- Many organisations are now utilising the **Internet** as a means of gathering and disseminating information, and conducting transactions.

# Quick Quiz

1     List four reasons why manual office systems may be less beneficial than computerised systems.

      1     ...............................................................

      2     ...............................................................

      3     ...............................................................

      4     ...............................................................

2     What is RAM?

3     List five ways an organisation could input or capture data.

      1     ...............................................................

      2     ...............................................................

      3     ...............................................................

      4     ...............................................................

      5     ...............................................................

4     Running costs of laser printers are relatively low when compared to ink-jet printers.

      True    ☐

      False    ☐

5     Computer memory is best described as:

      A     Primary storage
      B     Secondary storage
      C     Backup storage
      D     Data storage

6     State any three common computer operating systems.

7     Describe the characteristics of a database.

8     Why would an organisation issue an Invitation To Tender (ITT)?

9     What would you say is the main advantage of bespoke software?

10    What is the main disadvantage of bespoke software?

11    Identify four broad classifications of outsourcing.

12    Do you agree with the statement 'information derived from the Internet is unreliable'? Justify your answer.

1       Manual systems may be slower, more prone to error, require more labour and may be unable to handle large volumes of data. (This assumes the computerised system is operating correctly, is reliable and that staff know how to utilise it fully.)

2       RAM stands for Random Access Memory. It holds the data and programs in current use. RAM and processor speed are important indicators of processing power.

3       [Five of]

| | |
|---|---|
| Keyboard | Mouse |
| Scanner and OCR | Bar codes and scanner |
| MICR | OMR |
| EPOS | Digital cameras |
| Touch sensitive screen | Voice recognition software and a microphone |

4       True. Although they cost more to purchase, a laser printer's running cost is generally lower than an ink-jet's.

5       A       Memory is a computer's primary storage, any data held is lost when the machine is turned off.

6       Windows, UNIX, Apple Macintosh OS system and Linux.

7       A database has three major characteristics.

- It should be shared
- It should provide for the needs of different users with different requirements
- It should be capable of evolving to meet future needs

8       To invite tenders (offers to supply) for the system specified in the ITT.

9       As it is written for a specific purpose it should match user requirements very closely.

10      It's expensive when compared to off-the-shelf software.

11      Ad-hoc – a short-term requirement for increased IS/IT skills. Project management – eg an IS/IT project is outsourced. Partial – some IT/IS services are outsourced. Total – an external supplier provides the vast majority of an organisation's IT/IS services.

12      The Internet provides a means of accessing information from a wide range of organisations. Some of these organisations will provide good quality information (eg CIMA, BBC, etc), others may provide information that proves to be unreliable. Who is behind the information is a more significant indicator of reliability than the fact that the information was transmitted over the Internet.

**Now try the question below from the Exam Question Bank**

| Number | Level | Marks | Time |
|---|---|---|---|
| 3 | Examination | 30 | 54 mins |

# Operations management

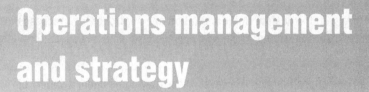

# Operations management and strategy

## Introduction

In this chapter we discuss the important roles **operations management** and **operations strategy** play in organisations.

It is tempting to think of operations as something that relates only to manufacturing organisations. However, service organisations also have 'operations'.

The service sector is playing an increasingly important role and is key creator of economic value, as well as being a vital source of employment. Hence, service operations feature as strongly as manufacturing operations in this chapter.

While working through the chapter, think about how decisions relating to the products and/or services an organisation supplies will impact upon operations.

| Topic list | Learning outcomes | Syllabus references | Ability required |
|---|---|---|---|
| 1 The scope of operations management | C(i) | C(1), C(2) | Evaluation |
| 2 The transformation process model | C(i) | C(2) | Evaluation |
| 3 Value chain analysis | C(i), C(viii) | C(1), C(17) | Evaluation |
| 4 Purchasing and supply chain management | C(i), (C(iv), C(viii) | C(13), C(16), C(17) | Evaluation |
| 5 Supply chain/network relationships | C(vii),C(viii) | C(15), C(17) | Evaluation |
| 6 Operations strategy | C(i) | C(1), C(2) | Evaluation |

# 1 The scope of operations management

Key term

> **Operations management** is concerned with the transformation of 'inputs' into 'outputs' that meet the needs of the customer.

## 1.1 The operations function

The overall objective of operations is to use a **transformation process** to add value and create **competitive advantage**. Operations involves taking input resources and transforming them into outputs of products or services for customers. Operations management involves the design, implementation and control of these processes.

FAST FORWARD

> **Operations management** is concerned with the **design**, **implementation** and **control** of the **processes** in an organisation that transform inputs (materials, labour, other resources, information and customers) into output products and services.

Organisations will invariably have an operations function. However, these may come under a variety of descriptions and the nature of operations is likely to vary from one organisation to another. The operations function might be considered as one of the three traditional 'core functions'.

(a) **Marketing and sales**. This is responsible for identifying customer needs and perhaps more significantly, for communicating information about the organisation's products or services to customers so as to procure sales orders.

(b) **Product and service development**. This is responsible for designing new products and services that will meet customer needs, to generate sales orders.

(c) **Operations**. This is responsible for fulfilling customer orders and requests through production of the goods or services, and for delivery of products or services to the customer.

There are also **support functions** within an organisation that help the core functions to operate effectively. Traditionally support functions might include accounting, HR and IT. However, what is actually a core function or a support function will depend on the particular organisation. For example, organisations that rely heavily on IT (eg the use of computer-aided manufacturing) may consider it a core function.

The functions within an organisation overlap, and for any particular task or process, input is often required from more than one core function or support function.

| The core functions: examples | | |
|---|---|---|
| | **Publishing company** | **Hotel** |
| **Marketing and sales** | Advertise through trade magazines<br>Book fairs<br>Negotiate sale of rights<br>Sell into bookshops and other outlets | Advertise across media<br>Liaise with tour operators, travel agents and booking agents |
| **Product/ service development** | Commission new titles<br>Vet submitted scripts<br>Develop new media forms, eg Internet delivery | Develop accommodation offerings, creative ambience, catering and ancillary facilities such as gym, business centre, conference facilities, entertainment etc<br>Devise new packages<br>Identify new locations |
| **Operations** | Editing<br>Printing<br>Distribution | Reservations<br>Housekeeping<br>Building maintenance<br>Catering |

At its simplest, operations management tries to ensure that organisations are run as efficiently as possible.

## 1.2 Mintzberg's operating core

Mintzberg suggested organisations are made up of five parts: **operating core**, **middle line**, **strategic apex**, **technostructure** and **support staff**.

*Henry Mintzberg* suggested one way of looking at organisations. His theory published in 1983 suggested organisations are made up of five parts.

**Five parts of an organisation (Mintzberg)**

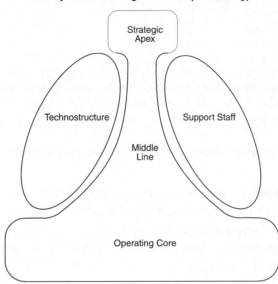

| Mintzberg's five basic parts of an organisation | |
|---|---|
| **Part** | **Comment** |
| **Operating core** | People involved producing products and services by transforming inputs such as stock using operations such as manufacturing. |
| **Middle line** | The hierarchy linking the strategic apex to the operating core. Usually comprises first line supervisors up to senior managers. |
| **Strategic apex** | Formulates and implements strategy – and if applicable links the organisation to those who own or control it. |
| **Technostructure** | Co-ordinates work through standardising processes, outputs and skills, eg HR managers includes expert advice, research and work study. |
| **Support staff** | Provide services and assistance outside the work flow, eg catering, cleaning, PR. |

# 2 The transformation process model

## 2.1 Overall process

An operation takes input resources and, through one or more processes, transforms these into outputs. Input resources are transformed in the process into a product or service that satisfies customer needs. This generalised concept of the transformation process model applies to all processes and may be depicted as follows.

**Transformation processes**

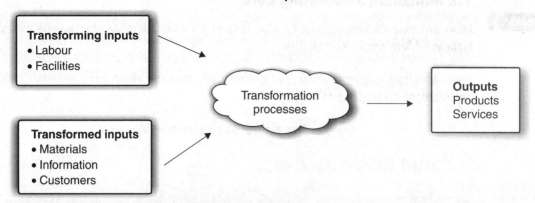

The **transformation process** could be a physical transformation, a change in nature or form (for example, a transformation of data into information), a change in location, holding an item in store, a change in ownership, or, in the case of customers, a psychological change (eg giving enjoyment).

**Inputs to the transformation process** can be categorised as either transformed resources or transforming resources.

(a) **Transformed resources** are manipulated and formed into a different condition by the process. These resources can be materials, information or customers themselves.

(b) **Transforming resources** are the resources that are used to alter the condition of the transformed resources. These consist of the work force of the organisation and facilities such as buildings, equipment and vehicles.

Here are some **practical examples of the transformation process**.

(a) In a manufacturing process, inputs of raw materials and components are manipulated by the work force, using the facilities of the organisation, into a finished product. This is then distributed to the customer. Production and distribution are stages in the transformation process. The **output** is the product.

(b) In the legal profession, a client seeks clarification about a legal problem. A lawyer holds a meeting with the client and provides the necessary advice. The **output** is an informed client.

(c) In the rail industry, rail service providers take customers, and use their work force and facilities (eg trains) to deliver the customers from one location to another. The **output** is a re-located customer.

(d) In banking, instructions from a customer (information) are processed using the facilities of the bank, and the instructions are carried out, for example by the transfer of money. The **output** is the completed transfer.

(e) In the entertainment industry, the customer might be provided with entertainment input such as a comedian telling a joke. The **output** is an entertained customer.

## 2.2 Product and service outputs

Many operations produce a **mixture** of product and service outputs. Remember also that in practice, in most countries, the service economy is as significant as the manufacturing economy. Here are some examples of the close interrelationships between service and manufacturing operations.

(a) The manufacture of machine tools is primarily concerned with the output of products. However, the organisation will also provide training and technical support services to customers.

(b) An education and training organisation might provide lectures, tutorials and workshops. The service may include the provision of products in the form of study notes or books. It might also provide an online helpline.

(c) A restaurant provides products in the form of food and drink. However, for the customer an essential ingredient of going to a restaurant is usually the overall dining experience that includes the enjoyment obtained from the service style, entertainment and general ambience.

The computer company IBM manufactures and sells hardware products and software. It has repositioned itself in recent years as a service provider, as evidenced by the purchase of the consultancy division of PricewaterhouseCoopers. In providing services it seeks the best for the client, even if this means equipment provided by another supplier.

# 3 Value chain analysis

**FAST FORWARD**

**Value chain analysis** identifies the way in which the firm organises its business's activities. It was developed by *Michael Porter* in his book *Competitive Advantage*.

*Porter* saw organisations differently to Mintzberg. Rather than a vertical hierarchy, he identified an organisation as linked functions and activities.

In Porter's analysis, **business activities** are *not* the same as **business functions**.

(a)   **Functions** are the familiar departments of a business (eg production function, the finance function) and reflect the formal organisation structure and the distribution of labour.

(b)   **Activities** are what actually goes on, and the work that is done. A single activity can be performed by a number of functions in sequence. Activities are the means by which a firm creates value in its products. (They are sometimes referred to as *value activities.*) Activities incur costs, and, in combination with other activities, provide a product or service which earns revenue.

Some examples should make this clear. An organisation needs many inputs of resources to function. It needs to secure resources from the environment. This activity can be called procurement. However, procurement will involve more departments than purchasing; accounts will certainly be involved and possibly production and quality assurance.

Firms create value for their buyers by performing these activities. The ultimate value a firm creates is measured by the amount customers are willing to pay for its products or services above the cost of carrying out value activities. A firm is profitable if the realised value to customers exceeds the collective cost of performing the activities.

There are two points to note here.

(a)   **Customers purchase value**, which they measure by comparing a firm's products and services with similar offerings by competitors.

(b)   **The business creates value** by carrying out its activities either more efficiently than other businesses, or combined in such a way as to provide a unique product or service.

## 3.1 The value chain

**Key term**

> **Value chain.** 'Sequence of business activities by which, in the perspective of the end-user, value is added to the products or services produced by an entity.'
>
> *CIMA Official Terminology*

Porter analysed the various activities of an organisation into a **value chain**. This is a model of value activities (which procure inputs, process them and add value to them in some way, to generate outputs for customers) and the relationships between them. Here is a diagram of the value chain.

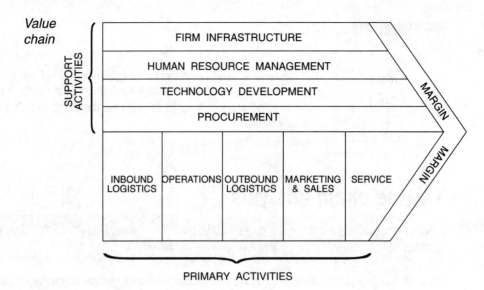

Let us examine some of these elements in turn.

## 3.2 Primary activities

The first distinction which can be made is that between **primary activities** and **support activities**.

**Primary activities** are those directly related with production, sales, marketing, delivery and services. The diagram shows five primary activities.

(a) **Inbound logistics** are those activities involved with receiving, handling and storing inputs to the production system.

(b) **Operations** are those activities which convert resource inputs into a final product. In a manufacturing firm, this is relatively easy to identify as the factory. In a service company, operations include those activities which make up the basic service.

(c) **Outbound logistics** are those activities relating to storing the product and its distribution to customers.

(d) **Marketing and sales** are those activities that relate to informing customers about the product, persuading them to buy it, and enabling them to do so.

(e) **After-sales service** includes activities such as installing products, repairing them and providing spare parts.

## 3.3 Support activities

**Support activities** are those which provide purchased inputs, human resources, technology and infrastructural functions to support the primary activities.

(a) **Procurement** consists of those activities which acquire the resource inputs to the primary activities (eg purchase of materials, subcomponents, equipment).

(b) **Technology development** (in the sense of apparatus, techniques and work organisation). These activities are related to both product design and to improving processes and/or resource utilisation.

(c) **Human resource management** is the activities of recruiting, training, developing and rewarding people.

(d) **Firm infrastructure**. The systems of planning, finance, quality control and management are activities which Porter believes are crucially important to an organisation's strategic capability in all primary activities.

## 3.4 Other elements

Furthermore, in addition to the categories described above, Porter identifies three further types of activity.

(a) **Direct activities** are concerned with adding value to inputs.

(b) **Indirect activities** enable direct activities to be performed (eg maintenance, sales force administration).

(c) **Quality assurance**. This type of activity monitors the quality of other activities, and includes: inspection, review and audit (eg the quality of the financial records).

**Linkages** connect the interdependent elements of the value chain together. They occur when one element of the value chain affects the costs or effectiveness of another. They require co-ordination.

(a) More costly product design, or better quality production, might reduce the need for after-sales service.

(b) To deliver goods on time requires smooth functioning of operations, outbound logistics and service activities such as installation.

| Question | Activities |
|---|---|

Which of the following is not a value chain primary activity?

A Inbound logistics
B Human resource management
C Marketing and sales
D Service

## Answer

B Human resource management.

## 3.5 The value system

Activities that add value do not stop at the organisation's boundaries. For example, when a restaurant serves a meal, the quality of the ingredients – although they are chosen by the cook – is determined by the grower. The grower has also added value, and the grower's success in growing produce of good quality is as important to the customer's ultimate satisfaction as the skills of the chef. Consequently, a company's value chain is connected to what *Porter* describes as a **value system**.

*Value system*

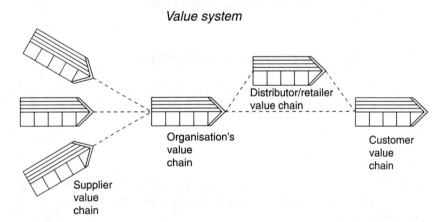

As well as managing its own value chain, a firm can secure competitive advantage by managing the linkages with its suppliers and customers. A company can create competitive advantage by making best use of these links and this means considering the value chains of these suppliers and customers. An example is a Just-in-Time system where close integration of the firm's operations with those of its suppliers is essential. We will look at supply chains in the next section.

# 4 Purchasing and supply chain management

## 4.1 Background

The nature of purchasing within organisations has changed dramatically over recent years. Historically, purchasing was viewed as a clerical function performed to buy the products and services required to carry out operations. This has changed. Purchasing today, in most organisations, is viewed as a vital function that impacts significantly on organisational performance.

Purchasing has evolved to now encompass all activities associated with the supply process. Furthermore, it is now widely recognised that the supply process has relevance for the decisions guiding the organisation's **competitive position** (*Cousins*).

**FAST FORWARD**

A **supply chain links** internal and external **suppliers** with internal and external **customers**. Effective **supply chain management** can be a source of competitive advantage.

Supply chain management is, therefore, concerned with the flow of goods and services through the organisation with the aim of making the firm more competitive (*Cousins*). Ultimately, the goal is to contribute to end-use customer satisfaction. This involves not only purchasing goods and services at competitive prices, but also focusing on cost reduction techniques, improving cycle times and reducing time-to-market.

**Key term**

**Supply chain management** is concerned with the flow of goods and services through the organisation with the aim of making the firm more competitive (*Cousins*).

**FAST FORWARD**

Many management theorists now recognise **purchasing** and **supply** as **strategic** activities.

## 4.2 Is supply a strategic process?

Purchasing has long been recognised as important mainly because the cost of raw materials and other purchases are a major **cost** for most firms and the recognition that the **quality** of input resources affects the quality of outputs.

However, to be 'strategic' an activity should be **planned** and be proactively **managed**. Key strategic issues related to supply include how to design the supply structure to meet the competitive market pressures and demands the organisation faces. To be able to validly state that supply and purchasing is treated as 'strategic', there must exist an enterprise-wide view of the firm both **internally**, with all key functions, and **externally** with supply chain partners.

## 4.3 Theorists: Reck and Long; Cousins

The changing role of purchasing and supply chain management has been the subject of much research and business writing. The syllabus for Paper P4 refers specifically to the work of *Cousins* and of *Reck and Long*.

### 4.3.1 Reck and Long

*Reck and Long* (1988) devised a model that aimed to provide an insight into the evolution of the purchasing function. Their **strategic positioning tool** identified a four-phase **development of purchasing** within organisations.

| The phases of Reck and Long's strategic positioning tool | |
|---|---|
| **Phase** | **Comment** |
| 1 Passive | • Purchasing is viewed as one of many clerical functions – similar, for example, to the payroll function.<br><br>• The focus is on efficient transaction processing. |
| 2 Independent | • There is an increasing awareness of the financial importance of the purchasing function.<br><br>• During this phase, the importance of negotiation with suppliers to securing the best prices for individual products/services purchased is recognised.<br><br>• Often includes the creation of a purchasing manager position to manage supplier negotiations.<br><br>• Cost savings achieved is the main performance indicator for assessing purchasing's overall effectiveness. |
| 3 Supportive | • The potential for purchasing to support wider organisational goals is recognised.<br><br>• This phase is often characterised by a centralised purchasing department with organisation-wide buying policies and systems.<br><br>• The emphasis is co-ordination and compliance with centrally negotiated contracts.<br><br>• The importance of careful supplier selection is recognised.<br><br>• Policies and procedures for supplier management are developed. |
| 4 Integrative | • Purchasing is now fully integrated in the major business activities of the organisation.<br><br>• Pro-active purchasing strategies are developed and followed.<br><br>• Purchasing is part of the firm's strategic planning process and purchasing strategy is aligned with corporate goals and strategy. Integrative purchasing is characterised by direct communication links with top management and a focus on long-term as well as short-term purchasing decisions (eg involvement in the product design process, cost and value analysis, involvement in the company's strategic planning process).<br><br>• The alignment of purchasing strategy with overall organisational goals and strategy often leads to new requirements in suppliers' performance and capabilities and, as a consequence, to the utilisation of supplier development practices as a tool to prevent quality deficiencies.<br><br>• Suppliers are viewed as partners and supplier management is viewed as relationship management.<br><br>• Today, closely linked or joint communication and information systems would facilitate this relationship. |

## 4.3.2 Cousins

*Cousins* (2000) conducted a 12-month research project to investigate the level of strategic maturity in the purchasing function of UK/European companies. In particular, the research aimed to establish the level of collaboration between leading UK companies (ie suppliers) and their major customers. The research looked at a range of inter-connected aspects considered important when looking at how an organisation deals with relationships relevant to overall strategy and supply strategy.

These aspects are shown in the diagram below.

**Cousin's Strategic Supply Wheel**

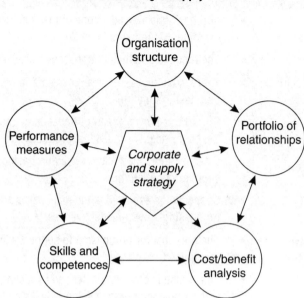

The research revealed that all of the aspects identified and shown in the Strategic Supply Wheel are inter-connected – so all need to be considered when looking at strategic supply issues. *Cousins* stated that it was clear that a focus on anyone area (eg relationship development) would be to the detriment of another area (eg performance measures). The Strategic Supply Wheel therefore shows that a firm needs to balance these resources and issues.

The research also examined the 'relationship type', using a simple classification of '**opportunistic**' (low level of co-operation with the supplier) versus '**collaborative**' (high level of co-operation).

The results showed that **the more collaborative the relationship the greater the degree of strategic alignment required** (between overall strategy and purchasing strategy).

## 4.4 Supply chain networks

Key term

A **supply chain network** is a an interconnecting group of organisations which relate to each other through linkages between the different processes and activities involved in producing products/services to the ultimate consumer.

Increasingly, organisations are recognising the need for and benefits of establishing **close links** with companies in the supply chain. Historically, businesses in the supply chain have operated relatively **independently** of one another to create value for an ultimate customer. **Independence was maintained** through holding buffer stocks, managing capacity and lead-times. This is represented in the 'Traditional' model shown below. There was very little control over other channel members, and no wider perspective on the system as a whole.

Market and competitive demands are now, however, **compressing lead times** and businesses are reducing inventories and excess capacity. Linkages between businesses in the supply chain must therefore become much tighter. This new condition is shown in the '**Integrated supply chain**' model (the second model in the following diagram).

There seems to be increasing recognition that, in the future, it will be **whole supply chains** which will compete and not just individual firms – we saw earlier how Porter's value chain achieves this.

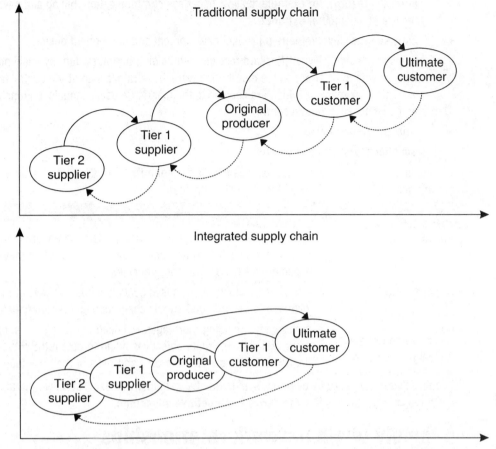

**Traditional and integrated supply chain models**

Traditional supply chain

Integrated supply chain

The aim is to co-ordinate the whole chain, from raw material suppliers to end customers. The chain should be considered as a **network** rather than a **pipeline** – a network of vendors support a network of customers, with third parties such as transport firms helping to link the companies. In marketing channels, organisations have to manage the trade-off between the desire to remain **independent and autonomous**, and the need to be **interdependent and co-operative**.

**Key terms**

> **Independence**: each channel member operates in isolation and is not affected by others, so maintaining a greater degree of control.
>
> **Interdependence**: each channel member can affect the performance of others in the channel.

If the supplier 'knows' what its customers want, it does not necessarily have to guess, or wait until the customer places an order. It will be able to better plan its own delivery systems. The potential for using the **Internet** to allow customers and suppliers to acquire up-to-date information about forecasted needs and delivery schedules is a recent development, but one which is being used by an increasing number of companies. Some supply chain relationships are strengthened and communication facilitated through the use of **extranets** (intranets accessible to authorised outsiders).

## 4.4.1 Implications for supply chain management

**Supply chain management** involves optimising the activities of companies working together to produce goods and services. The trend towards closer links with suppliers and the development of supply chain networks has implications for supply chain management.

- **Reduction in customers served**. For the sake of focus, companies might concentrate resources on customers of high potential value.
- **Price and stock co-ordination**. Firms co-ordinate their price and stock policies to avoid problems and bottlenecks caused by short-term surges in demand, such as promotions.

- **Linked computer systems**. Closer links may be facilitated through the use of Electronic Data Interchange (EDI), for example to allow paperless communication, billing and payment and through the use of a computer **extranet**.
- **Early supplier involvement** in product development and component design.
- **Logistics design**. Hewlett-Packard restructured its distribution system by enabling certain product components to be added at the distribution warehouse rather than at the central factory, for example user-manuals which are specific to the market (ie user manuals in French would be added at the French distribution centre).
- **Joint problem-solving**.
- **Supplier representative on site**.

The business case for supply chain management is the **benefits** to **all** the **participants** in terms of the performance objectives of speed, dependability and cost.

| Performance objective | Example |
|---|---|
| Speed | Plumbers need to manage their supply chains to ensure they are able to get hold of parts such as water tanks, boilers, valves etc so they can respond expeditiously to customer emergencies. |
| Dependability | A mail order business promises delivery within 10 days of receipt of order. It will need to ensure good supply chain management to fulfil its promise. |
| Cost | A company providing mortgages will need to manage its supply chain with great skill with one of its objectives being to obtain the cheapest sources of finance in keeping with the profile and risks of their mortgage lending. |

The firm that is perceived by customers and potential customers to excel at delivering the desired performance objectives is likely to derive a **competitive advantage**.

# 5 Supply chain/network relationships

Organisations are increasingly choosing to establish close relationships with others in their supply network. In this section, we look at a range of possibilities regarding how this closer relationship could be conducted.

## 5.1 Sourcing strategies

FAST FORWARD

Supply sourcing strategies include **single**, **multiple**, **delegated** and **parallel**.

There are a range of possible strategies open to an organisation when deciding who they will purchase their supplies from. The syllabus for Paper P4 refers to four options – as explained in the following table.

| Supply sourcing strategies | |
|---|---|
| Option | Comment |
| Single | **Description**<br>• The buyer chooses one source of supply.<br>**Advantages**<br>• Stronger relationship with the supplier.<br>• Possible source of superior quality due to increased opportunity for a supplier quality assurance programme.<br>• Facilitates better communication.<br>• Economies of scale.<br>• Facilitates confidentiality.<br>• Possible source of competitive advantage.<br>**Disadvantages**<br>• Vulnerable to any disruption in supply.<br>• Supplier power may increase if no alternative supplier.<br>• The supplier is vulnerable to shifts in order levels. |

| Supply sourcing strategies | |
|---|---|
| **Option** | **Comment** |
| **Multiple** | **Description** <br><br> • The buyer chooses several sources of supply. <br><br> **Advantages** <br><br> • Access to a wide range of knowledge and expertise. <br> • Competition among suppliers may drive the price down. <br> • Supply failure by one supplier will cause minimal disruption. <br><br> **Disadvantages** <br><br> • Not easy to develop an effective quality assurance programme. <br> • Suppliers may display less commitment. <br> • Neglecting economies of scale. |
| **Delegated** | **Description** <br><br> • A supplier is given responsibility for the delivery of a complete sub-assembly. For example, rather than dealing with several suppliers a 'first-tier' supplier would be appointed to deliver a complete sub-assembly (eg a PC manufacturer may delegate the production of keyboards). <br><br> **Advantages** <br><br> • Allows the utilisation of specialist external expertise. <br> • Frees-up internal staff for other tasks. <br> • The purchasing entity may be able to negotiate economies of scale. <br><br> **Disadvantages** <br><br> • First-tier supplier is in a powerful position. <br> • Competitors may utilise the same external organisation so unlikely to be a source of competitive advantage. |
| **Parallel** | **Description** <br><br> • Parallel sourcing involves mixing/combining the other three approaches to maximise the benefits of each. <br><br> **Advantage** <br><br> • If used correctly should provide an efficient/effective strategy. <br><br> **Disadvantage** <br><br> • Can be complicated to manage. |

## 5.2 Virtual companies and virtual supply chains

A relatively recent development is the so-called **virtual organisation.** This is created out of **a network of alliances and subcontracting arrangements:** it is as if most of the activities in a particular **value chain** are conducted by different firms, even though the process is loosely co-ordinated.

**FAST FORWARD**

**Virtual companies** involve all major activities being outsourced to a range of suppliers.

For example, assume a firm manufactures small toys. It could in theory outsource:

- The design to a consultancy
- Manufacturing to a subcontractor
- Delivery arrangements to a specialist logistics firm
- Debt collection to a bank (factoring)
- Filing, tax returns, bookkeeping to an accountancy firm

> A **virtual company** is a collection of separate companies, each with a specific expertise, who work together, sharing their expertise to compete for bigger contracts/projects than would be possible if they worked alone.
>
> A traditional **supply chain** is made up of the physical entities linked together to facilitate the supply of goods and services to the final consumer.
>
> A **Virtual Supply Chain (VSC)** is a supply chain that is enabled through e-business links (eg the web, extranets or EDI).

The **virtual company** concept has been around since the mid-1990s but only really became a reality when technology such as extranets came into common usage. Companies are now able to work together and exchange information online. For example, engineers from five companies could design a product together on the Internet.

Many companies have become, or are becoming, more 'virtual'. They are developing into looser affiliations of companies, organised as a supply network.

**Virtual Supply Chain** networks have two types of organisation: producers and integrators.

(a)   **Producers** produce goods and services. They have core competences in production schedule execution. Producers must focus on delivery to schedule and within cost. The sales driver within these companies is on ensuring that their capacity is fully sold through their networking with co-ordinators. Producers are often servicing multiple chains, so managing and avoiding capacity and commercial conflicts becomes key.

(b)   **Integrators** manage the supply network and effectively 'own' the end customer contact. The focus of the integrating firms is on managing the end customer relationship. Their core competence is in integrating and controlling the response of the company to customer requirements. This includes the difficult task of synchronising the responses and performance of multi-tiered networks, where the leverage of direct ownership is no longer available, and of often outsourced services such as warehousing and delivery.

Many of the most popular Internet companies are integrators in virtual companies eg Amazon.com and Lastminute.com. These organisations 'own' customer contact and manage customer relationships for a range of producers.

## 5.2.1 Advantages of virtual operations

Virtual operations have various **advantages**.

- Flexibility and speed of operation
- Low investment in assets and hence less risk involved
- Injection of market forces into all the linkages in the value chain

## 5.2.2 Disadvantages of virtual operations

But there are some **disadvantages**.

- Quality may be a problem owing to a loss of control
- The suppliers/resources may also be available to rival operations
- Customers may recognise the virtual characteristics and this might negatively affect customer perceptions of the service or product

 Case Study

First Virtual Corporation, one of the few truly virtual organisations in existence, was set up in 1993 by Ralph Ungermann. With only 50 direct employees, it generates sales of its multimedia networking equipment of about $50m. Everything except the crucial design and development work is outsourced. The company has two 'core competences' according to Ungermann: technical development and forging alliances with large companies.

The question is whether First Virtual will need to take tighter control of some functions as it grows.

## 5.3 Strategic alliances

Some firms enter long-term **strategic alliances** with others for a variety of reasons.

(a)    They share development costs of a particular technology.

(b)    The regulatory environment prohibits takeovers (eg most major airlines are in strategic alliances because in most countries – including the US – there are limits to the level of control an 'outsider' can have over an airline).

(c)    Complementary markets or technology.

Strategic alliances only go so far, as there may be disputes over control of strategic assets.

### 5.3.1 Choosing alliance partners

The following factors should be considered (*Hooley* et al. 1998) in choosing alliance partners.

| Factor | Comment |
|---|---|
| **Drivers** | What benefits are offered by collaboration? |
| **Partners** | Which partners should be chosen? |
| **Facilitators** | Does the external environment favour a partnership? |
| **Components** | Activities and processes in the network. |
| **Effectiveness** | Does the previous history of alliances generate good results? Is the alliance just a temporary blip? For example, in the airline industry, there are many strategic alliances, but these arise in part because there are legal barriers to cross-border ownership. |
| **Market-orientation** | Alliance partners are harder to control and may not have the same commitment to the end-user. |

**Alliances** have some **limitations**.

(a)    **Core competence**. Each organisation should be able to focus on its core competence. Alliances do not enable it to create new competences.

(b)    **Strategic priorities**. If a key aspect of strategic delivery is handed over to a partner, the firm loses control and flexibility.

# 6 Operations strategy

## 6.1 Brown's six items

*Brown* (2001) identified six items that should be incorporated into an organisation's operations strategy.

| Item | Comment |
|---|---|
| **Capability required** | What is it that the organisation wants to 'do' or produce? |
| **Range and location of operations** | How big does the organisation want to be – or can it be? How many sites and where should they be located? |
| **Investment in technology** | How will processes and production be performed? |
| **Strategic buyer-supplier relationships** | Who will be key strategic partners? |
| **New products/services** | What are the expected product life-cycles? |
| **Structure of operations** | How will staff be organised and managed? |

## 6.2 General points

Operations strategy theories are simply illustrations of approaches to operations strategy formulation. In broad terms, **strategy formulation** in practice will include many of the **following concepts**.

(a)     Setting **operational objectives** that are consistent with the overall business strategy of the organisation.

(b)     Translating **business strategy** or **marketing strategy** into **operations strategy**, by means of identifying key competitive factors (referred to perhaps as order-winning factors or critical success factors).

(c)     Assessing the relative importance of different **competitive factors**.

(d)     Assessing current operational performance by **comparison** with the performance of **competitors**.

(e)     Using the idea of a clean-slate or 'green-field' approach to strategy selection. Managers are asked to consider how they would ideally design operations if they could **start again from scratch**. The ideal operations design is then compared with actual operations, and important differences identified. Strategy decisions are then taken to move actual performance closer towards the ideal.

(f)     Formulating strategy could be based on other types of **gap analysis**, such as comparing what the market wants with what the operation is actually achieving, and taking decisions aimed at closing the significant gaps.

(g)     Emphasising the iterative process of strategy selection. Strategies should be **continually reviewed, refined and re-developed** through experience and in response to changes in the environment.

**Exam focus point**

The May 2007 exam offered ten-marks for an evaluation of a proposal for supplier management as part of a value system.

# Chapter Roundup

- **Operations management** is concerned with the **design**, **implementation** and **control** of the **processes** in an organisation that transform inputs (materials, labour, other resources, information and customers) into output products and services.

- Mintzberg suggested organisations are made up of five parts: **operating core**, **middle line**, **strategic apex**, **technostructure** and **support staff**.

- The **transformation process** could be a physical transformation, a change in nature or form (for example, a transformation of data into information), a change in location, holding an item in store, a change in ownership, or, in the case of customers, a psychological change (eg giving enjoyment).

- **Value chain analysis** identifies the way in which the firm organises its business's activities. It was developed by *Michael Porter* in his book *Competitive Advantage*.

- A **supply chain links** internal and external **suppliers** with internal and external **customers**. Effective **supply chain management** can be a source of competitive advantage.

- Many management theorists now recognise **purchasing** and **supply** as **strategic** activities.

- Supply sourcing strategies include **single**, **multiple**, **delegated** and **parallel**.

- **Virtual companies** involve all major activities being outsourced to a range of suppliers.

1    Which of the following are parts of an organisation according to Mintzberg?

    (i)     Strategic apex
    (ii)    Support staff
    (iii)   Middle core
    (iv)   Technostructure

    A     (i), (ii), and (iii) only
    B     (i), (ii), and (iv) only
    C     (ii) and (iv) only
    D     All of the options

2    Briefly describe the transformation process.

3    State one primary activity and one support activity as described by Porter in his value chain analysis.

4    State the four phases of Reck and Long's strategic positioning tool.

5    Which of the following are sourcing strategies?

    (i)     Single
    (ii)    Multiple
    (iii)   Delegated
    (iv)   Parallel

    A     (i) and (ii) only
    B     (i), (ii) and (iv) only
    C     (ii), (iii) and (iv) only
    D     All of the options

6    List the six items Brown identified that should be covered by an organisation's operations strategy.

# Answers to Quick Quiz

1    B     The 'middle core' is fictitious, made up from the middle line and operating core, which are parts of an organisation according to Mintzberg.

2    Transformation involves transforming and transformed inputs being processed into outputs such as products and services.

3    *Primary activities*            *Support activities*
    [One from]              [One from]

    Inbound logistics          Procurement
    Operations              Technology development
    Outbound logistics        Human resource management
    Marketing and sales      Firm infrastructure
    After-sales service

4    Passive, independent, supportive, integrative.

5    D     They are all sourcing strategies.

6    Capability required, range and location of operations, investment in technology, strategic buyer-supplier relationships, new products/services and the structure of operations.

Now try the question below from the Exam Question Bank

| Number | Level | Marks | Time |
|---|---|---|---|
| 4 | Tutorial | 15 | 27 mins |

# Managing capacity and inventory

## Introduction

In this chapter, we turn our attention to strategies for **balancing capacity with demand** and the **management of inventory**.

Capacity management is concerned with the organisation's ability to meet the demand for its products or services, in the present as well as in the future. Capacity is effectively a limiting factor on how much an organisation can produce and how much it can earn.

Today's business environment demands speed and efficiency in the delivery of products and services. This has led to increased emphasis on the need to optimise internal inventory management.

Later, we look at how the changing nature of business has led to significant changes in inventory management.

The just-in-time philosophy, covered in the final section, brings together many of the concepts discussed within the chapter.

| Topic list | Learning outcomes | Syllabus references | Ability required |
|---|---|---|---|
| 1 Capacity management | C(i), C(iv) | C(4) | Evaluation |
| 2 Balancing capacity and demand | C(i), C(iv) | C(4) | Evaluation |
| 3 Capacity planning | C(i), C(iv) | C(4) | Evaluation |
| 4 Capacity control | C(i), C(iv) | C(4), C(10) | Evaluation |
| 5 Inventory management | C(i) | C(3) | Evaluation |
| 6 Just-in-time (JIT) | C(viii) | C(10) | Evaluation |

# 1 Capacity management

FAST FORWARD

> **Capacity** is a measure of what an operation is able to produce within a specified period of time.

**Key term**

> **Capacity** has been defined as the maximum level of value added activity over a period of time that can be achieved by a process or production unit under normal working conditions.

Overcapacity or undercapacity can be detrimental to the business activities of an organisation.

## 1.1 Overcapacity

Overcapacity means **resources** available for production are **not fully utilised**.

(a) Resources are underutilised. If the costs are recovered by increasing selling prices, the products and services may become uncompetitive. The other alternative is for the costs to be written off against profits.

(b) In the service industry it could send out the wrong messages to customers eg a restaurant that is not full may give that impression that the food is not good.

## 1.2 Undercapacity

Undercapacity means **more production is being demanded than is able to be produced**.

(a) If the organisation is unable to satisfy customer demand it forgoes the profits from the products or services it missed out on selling. Moreover, the customer is likely to acquire the product or service from a rival organisation and the customer's loyalty might be lost.

(b) In the service industry, undercapacity may result in slower or less comfortable service thereby having a negative impact on customers' perceptions of the service quality delivered.

FAST FORWARD

> **Capacity management** refers to an organisation's ability to efficiently meet the demand for its products or services. Capacity planning and control is the process of **balancing** the **output capacity** and resources of an operation with the **demand from customers** for the product or service. It calls for planning the normal capacity of the operation and reacting to changes in demand.

 Case Study

The TR Morgan Motor Company produce a stylish, enthusiasts' sports car that evokes images and nostalgic feelings for a bygone era and lifestyle. The company is able to build about ten cars a week. There is a waiting list of approximately seven years to obtain a car. Many operations are done by hand, eg the body panels are painstakingly cut out by a worker using hand-held metal clippers.

The company might be able to produce more cars if it modernised and automated its production process. However, the hand-made image of Morgan cars is its unique selling proposition.

# 2 Balancing capacity and demand

One important operations management task within an organisation is **balancing** the amount they are able to produce (**capacity**) with the amount they are able to sell (**demand**).

## 2.1 Dealing with uncertainty

Uncertainties in **capacity** could be caused by a number of factors, for example the **shortage** or a delay in the supply **of a resource**. Control and re-planning measures would be necessary, for example, in a salon if clients turned up late for their appointments. For any operation, materials could be in short supply or labour supply could be disrupted by strike action, calling for **re-planning and control** measures.

Uncertainties in **demand** will also call for a **planning and control response**. The nature of planning and control will vary according to the extent to which demand is unpredictable, and a distinction is made between dependent and independent demand.

**Dependent demand** is demand that is predictable because it is based on a factor that is known. An organisation providing school meals to a number of schools can predict the demand for its meals because the size of each school population is known. Dependent demand occurs often in manufacturing, where the demand for raw materials and components can be predicted from the demand for the main product. **Materials requirement planning (MRP)** (covered later in this chapter) is a form of **dependent demand planning and control**.

Many organisations and/or operations within organisations are not able to predict demand so easily. They have to make capacity decisions based on **experience** and **judgement** about the likely **level of demand**.

### Case Study

Fast turnaround time is important for airlines because, by minimising time on the ground, an airline can maximise the productivity of its planes in the air (ie maximise capacity).

To help airlines achieve the benefits of a fast turnaround time, the Airbus A320 family aircraft has the following features.

- Larger passenger doors
- Wider aisles
- Larger overhead storage compartments
- Convenient access to underfloor baggage holds
- Wider outward-opening cargo doors

## 2.2 Planning and control activities

There are four planning and control activities associated with balancing capacity and demand.

(a) Loading
(b) Sequencing
(c) Scheduling
(d) Monitoring and controlling

### 2.2.1 Loading

Loading is the **amount of work that is allocated to an operating unit**. The term is frequently applied to the allocation of workloads to a machine or group of machines, although it has more general application than just machines. In theory, a machine can operate for 24 hours each day, seven days a week. In practice, this is not realistic. Machines cannot be in operational use if they are being cleaned, serviced or repaired. A hairdressing salon could open on a 24/7 basis but it is unlikely that customers would want their hair done at, say, 3 o'clock in the morning.

### 2.2.2 Sequencing

Decisions have to be taken when work comes in about **the order in which different jobs will be done** or different orders fulfilled. This planning and control activity is called sequencing. The sequencing of operations will be decided according to a set of rules or guidelines, which could be any of the following.

(a)    Customer priority
(b)    Due date
(c)    Last in first out
(d)    First in first out
(e)    Longest operation time first (LOT)
(f)    Shortest operation time first (SOT)

The preferred sequencing criteria should be the one that optimises operational performance in terms of:

(a)    **Dependability of delivery** (ie meeting the due dates promised to customers)
(b)    **Speed of delivery** (ie minimising the amount of time that jobs spend in the process)
(c)    **Cost**
(d)    **Minimising idle time** in work centres (which is an aspect of cost)
(e)    **Minimising inventory levels** (which is another aspect of cost)

## 2.2.3 Scheduling

Once work has been sequenced and jobs put in order for completion, it might then be necessary to prepare **a detailed timetable** for the work to be done, specifying the time that jobs should be started and when they should end. When a job goes through several stages or processes, a schedule will specify when each stage should begin and end.

Formal schedules are only needed when detailed planning is necessary to make sure that **customer demand can be met**. In operations where demand is unpredictable, scheduling is impracticable, and the operation must simply react to orders as they arrive, for example petrol stations.

For an operation that processes a large number of jobs, and each job has to go through a number of stages or machines, scheduling can be complex. There is a risk that with poor scheduling, **bottlenecks** will occur in different parts of the operation at different times.

## 2.2.4 Monitoring and control

Having loaded, sequenced and scheduled the work, management must monitor the operation to make sure that the **work is carried out as planned**. Any deviation from the plan should be identified as soon as a problem becomes apparent so that corrective measures can be taken if possible, or so that the work can be re-scheduled.

The terms 'push control' and 'pull control' refer to when control action is taken to manage the flow of work. With **push control**, the focus is on pushing work through each stage of the process, regardless of whether the next stage is ready to receive it. Push control is characterised by centralised scheduling and control. There are likely to be inventories at each stage, queues and idle time.

With **pull control**, the focus is on each stage of the process calling for work to be delivered from the previous process when it is needed. The work is not delivered from the previous process until it is needed, and the customer (internal or external) acts as the stimulus for the supplier to do the work. An example of pull control is a just-in-time purchasing and production system. With pull control, there should be less inventory in the system.

Good **communication** between management and operations levels as well as within a level are an important aspect of control. This involves informal communication amongst employees as well as holding formal meetings to both monitor progress as well as identify problems before they become serious.

Question                                           **Capacity management**

Learning outcome: C(i)

Gourmet Cuisine runs high class restaurants in high wealth areas. Each establishment can cater for approximately 150 guests at any one time, although over an evening it may well serve more guests if tables are 'recycled' (able to be booked more than once). The evening lasts from 6pm to 12pm. Over weekends some establishments might serve as many as 300 guests in an evening. Each establishment usually employs eight waiters.

Comment on the following possible ways of allocating each waiter's workload.

- Allocate certain areas to each waiter
- Allocate a spread of tables in different locations of the restaurant to each waiter
- Allocate tables in turn to a waiter as each table is occupied

## Answer

The method of distributing workloads must be efficient as well as seen to be fair.

- Allocation of tables by area is the simplest way but might be neither efficient nor fair. In most restaurants there will usually be more popular areas (corners, along the walls, by a window etc) and less popular areas (by the entrance, near the kitchen, in the middle).
- Allocating tables spread across the floor space is likely to be fairer but may be more confusing in practice for a waiter.
- Allocation in turns is again fairer, but perhaps more complex to operate. Disputes may arise owing to queue jumping by waiters to serve a generously tipping guest.

Remember in delivering service quality, flexibility is an important consideration and the rules may need to be flexed if a guest has a favourite waiter who might, according to the system, not be scheduled for that guest.

# 3 Capacity planning

## 3.1 Overview

Capacity planning and control is concerned with balancing the total **capacity** of an operation (ie the operation's resources) with the **demand** from customers for its products and services. The objective should be to achieve an **appropriate balance** between capacity provision and demand, in order to produce both **high profits** and **satisfied customers**.

Some parts of an operation will work at below full capacity due to insufficient demand. Very often, however, one or more parts of an operation will work at their capacity limit. The parts of an operation that work at their capacity limit are the **capacity constraints** for the entire operation.

**Capacity constraints** limit the total output achievable by the operation within a given period of time. This can cause **bottlenecks** in the work flow and can also result in unsatisfied demand. Management should therefore identify the constraints, and consider ways of overcoming them. For example, suppose that visitors to an out-of-town shopping centre all use the centre's car park. If the car park is limited to 1,000 spaces but the shopping centre is capable of handling many more customers, the use of the centre will be restricted by the limited available car parking space.

## 3.2 Purpose of capacity planning and control

Planning and controlling capacity involves:

(a) Planning the **normal capacity** of the operation, and
(b) Reacting to **changes** in demand.

Long-term strategic decisions have to be made about what the capacity of an operation should be, and investment decisions taken to achieve the planned capacity.

Capacity planning in the short- and medium-term has several implications for operational performance.

| Implication | Comment |
| --- | --- |
| Cost | Costs are affected by planned capacity. When the capacity of an operation exceeds demand, there will be under-utilised resources and costs will be higher than if capacity were more closely matched to demand. |
| Revenue | On the other hand, revenues could also be affected by the capacity of an operation. If demand exceeds the capacity of an operation to meet it, revenues will be forgone that could otherwise have been earned. |
| Quality | The quality of an operation could be affected by capacity planning. For example, if an operation varies its capacity by using part-time or temporary staff, the quality of the product or service might be impaired. |
| Speed of response to demand | The speed of response to demand can be improved either by building up finished goods inventories (which has a cost) or by providing sufficient capacity to avoid customers having to queue or to wait (which also has a cost). |
| Dependability of supply | The closer an operation works to its capacity limit, the less easily will it be able to cope with unexpected disruptions to the work flow. Supply will therefore be less dependable. |
| Flexibility | The flexibility of an operation, and in particular its ability to vary the volume of output it can produce, will be improved by having surplus capacity. An operation working at or close to its capacity limit is much less flexible. |

**FAST FORWARD**

The **steps in capacity planning and control** are measuring total demand, identifying alternative capacity plans that could be implemented to meet the demand, and choosing the most suitable of these alternatives.

## 3.3 Measuring demand and capacity

### 3.3.1 Forecasting demand

In most organisations, the sales and marketing department is responsible for forecasting demand. However, demand forecasts are relevant to operations management and capacity planning.

(a)   For operations management purposes, demand forecasts should be expressed in terms of **physical capacity** rather than in terms of sales revenue. It is more relevant to express demand in a manufacturing organisation in terms of standard labour hours or machine hours of capacity, for each separate process within the operation.

(b)   Forecasts should be as **accurate** as possible, because capacity will be planned on the basis of the forecasts.

(c)   Forecasts of demand should give some indication of the degree of uncertainty. Where possible, the possible **variation** in demand should be **assessed statistically**, perhaps on the basis of demand patterns from the past.

### 3.3.2 Measuring capacity

Measuring capacity is not a straightforward task, except for standardised and repetitive operations. When an operation produces a range of different products or services, measuring capacity in terms of output produced is difficult, because there isn't a standard measure of output.

Capacity might therefore be measured either in terms of **input resources available** or in terms of **output produced**.

| Operation | Capacity measure in terms of input resources | Capacity measure in terms of output produced |
| --- | --- | --- |
| Football club | Ground capacity<br>Squad size<br>Number of matches | Number of paying spectators |
| Doctors' surgery | Number of doctors<br>Number of surgery hours | Number of patients treated |
| Department store | Shelf space or volume, or floor area | Number of customers through the check-outs |
| Air travel | Number of seats available on a route | Number of passengers carried on the route each week |

Where output is non-standard, any capacity measurement based on output will have to use an **average** measure for products made or services provided. For example, a doctors' surgery might measure its capacity in terms of being able to treat 400 patients each week, this might be based on the assumption that an average time for treating each patient is ten minutes. In practice, some patients will need more than ten minutes and some less, depending on their reason for seeing the doctor.

## 3.4 Planning for capacity

FAST FORWARD

There are different ways of **planning for capacity**.

- A level capacity plan
- A chase demand plan
- A demand management plan
- A mix of the above three types of plan

### 3.4.1 Level capacity plan

A **level capacity plan** is a plan to maintain activity at a constant level over the planning period, and to ignore fluctuations in forecast demand. In a level capacity plan, staffing and other resource levels are kept constant. In a manufacturing operation, when demand is lower than capacity, the operation will produce goods for inventory. In a service operation, there will be idle resources.

Level capacity planning should result in high capacity utilisation and low unit costs.

A risk for manufacturers with level capacity planning is that a large amount of inventory could accumulate in anticipation of future demand.

If a service operation, such as a restaurant or supermarket or stock-broking business, runs a level capacity plan, it will have to accept that resources will be under-utilised for much of the time, to ensure an adequate level of service during peak demand times. Operating costs will therefore be relatively high. In periods of peak demand, the quality of service will deteriorate, since customers will have to wait or queue for service.

### 3.4.2 Chase demand plan

This type of plan is the opposite of a level capacity plan. It aims to match capacity as closely as possible to the forecast fluctuations in demand. To achieve this aim, resources must be flexible. For example, staff numbers might have to be variable and staff might be required to work overtime or shifts. Variations in equipment levels might also be necessary, perhaps by means of short-term rental arrangements.

### 3.4.3 Demand management planning

Some organisations attempt to stabilise demand and plan capacity accordingly. The aim of **demand management planning** is therefore to reduce peak demand by switching it to the off-peak periods.

The most obvious way of managing demand is through price discrimination, such as:

(a) Offering low off-peak fares on trains to encourage some customers to switch their travelling time from peak hours to off-peak, and to increase total demand for off-peak travel.

(b) Off-peak telephone charges.

(c) Off-peak holiday prices and 'weekend break' packages to build up demand out of the holiday season or at low-demand points in the week.

Producers can also use **advertising** to boost demand in off-peak periods.

### 3.4.4 Mixed plans

In practice, capacity planning is often a mixture of level capacity planning, chase demand planning and demand management planning, although possibly one of these three approaches could predominate over the other two.

### 3.4.5 Yield management

In operations with a fairly fixed short-term and medium-term capacity, such as hotels, restaurants, theatres and airlines, an objective could be to achieve as much revenue as possible from the available fixed resources. One such approach to revenue maximisation is called yield management.

A yield management approach is particularly well-suited to an operation where:

(a) Capacity is fairly fixed in the short- to medium-term.
(b) The market can be segmented, to allow some price discrimination.
(c) The service cannot be sold in advance.
(d) The marginal cost of making an additional sale is low.

Yield management techniques have been evident in airline operations, where the techniques used include:

(a) **Price discounting**. When demand is expected to be low, an airline might sell a block of tickets at a cheap price to a booking agent, who then has the task of selling on the tickets at a discount price.

(b) **Varying the capacity of different types of service**. In an airline operation, this could mean switching the space in an aircraft from first class or business seats to economy class, or *vice versa*.

(c) **Over-booking**. An airline will expect a percentage of its customers who have booked in advance to fail to arrive for their flight. Airlines therefore tend to book more passengers on to a flight than they have seats to accommodate them. If more passengers arrive than there are seats, some passengers will be offered inducements to take a later flight, or will be upgraded to first-class or business class travel.

# 4 Capacity control

Capacity control involves reacting to actual demand and influences on actual capacity as they arise.

## 4.1 Materials requirements planning (MRP I)

FAST FORWARD

**Materials requirements planning (MRP I)** is a system or technique for deciding the requirements for materials, in terms of both quantities and timing, down to the smallest material items or components.

MRP I is a technique for deciding the volume and timing of materials, in manufacturing conditions where there is dependent demand.

The purpose of an MRP I system is to:

(a)     Calculate the **quantity** of materials required, for each type of material, and
(b)     Determine **when** they will be required.

The materials requirements are calculated from:

(a)     Known future orders, ie firm orders already received from customers, plus
(b)     A forecast of other future orders that, with a reasonable degree of confidence, will be received.

The quantities of each type of materials required for the product or service will be defined in its **bill of materials**. Estimates of firm and likely demand can therefore be converted into a **materials requirements schedule**.

MRP I enables manufacturing organisations to determine when to order material, by working back from when they will be required for production, and allowing the necessary lead time for production or for purchasing from the external supplier.

## 4.2 Manufacturing resource planning (MRP II)

FAST FORWARD

**Manufacturing resource planning (MRP II)** evolved out of MRP I and is a computerised system that integrates planning information for the operations management, marketing, finance and engineering functions.

**Manufacturing resource planning**, or MRP II, evolved out of **materials requirements planning** (MRP I). It is a plan for **planning and monitoring** all the **resources** of a **manufacturing company**: manufacturing, marketing, finance and engineering.

MRP II is a computerised system that incorporates a **single database** for different functions within the organisation. Hence the engineering department, manufacturing function and finance function will all be using the same version of the bill of materials. All functions work from a **common set of data**.

MRP II is a sophisticated system that enables optimal inventory control based on the matching of supply and demand.

**Features** include:

* Production planning
* Capacity planning
* Forecasting
* Purchasing
* Order-entry
* Operations control
* Financial analysis

*Brown* (2001) believes **possible benefits** include:

* Reduced stock-outs – better customer service
* Reduced inventory holding costs
* Improved plant/facilities utilisation
* Reliable order fulfilment times
* Reduced 'crisis management' time

However, MRP II implementations are not always successful. Some potential drawbacks are illustrated in the following example.

## Case Study

A family-owned building construction company builds residential and commercial buildings. About 50% of its annual turnover comes from building large new residential estates, about 10% comes from building luxury residential homes and 40% comes from building commercial properties. The value of the properties it constructs ranges from about £80,000 to about £2 million. At any time, the company is working on about 12 projects.

The company has a sales office, an accounts and general administration section, and a production planning team. The operations department is organised around project managers, each responsible for between two and four projects at any time, and a foreman for each site. Full-time employees are organised into work groups of two, three or four individuals, and each work group has a specialist skill. The company also uses sub-contractors for many aspects of building work.

The company has recently installed a MRP II system.

One of the projects it is working on is the construction of a new residential estate of 50 houses. The houses on the estate will be of three different designs. Each design differs in terms of size, layout, window sizes, roof tile design, electricity supply features, water supply and central heating, furnishings and kitchen fittings. House buyers also have the option to pay for extra items, such as additional or more expensive bathroom fittings.

Project managers and site foremen have complained about the MRP II system. They identified the following issues.

1       The system generates a lot of figures, often using complex formulae (algorithms) to estimate the required quantities and timing of materials. The figures are produced by production planning staff, but a large number of people need to be kept informed – the foremen, project managers, possible sub-contractors and possibly also specialist work teams. This is bureaucratic.

2       The material requirements are estimated by a computer system of the production planning section. The final users of the information – and of the materials – have no sense of ownership of the figures. The figures, having been computer-produced, will be difficult to check. Project managers and foremen etc will probably have no incentive to check the figures to see whether they appear to make sense.

3       Small hold-ups or difficulties in the building work can have a significant effect on materials requirements. For example, bad weather could hold up production. Whenever scheduling has to be changed, there will be a new materials requirements schedule, and this new information will have to be distributed to all the people affected. This will add to the problems of information over-load.

4       MRP II methods work reasonably well for standardised building, but are not easily applied to one-off construction work, where materials requirements and scheduling have to be done on a one-off basis.

## 4.3 Optimised production technology (OPT)

OPT is one of several computer-based methods for scheduling production requirements to the known capacity constraints (or **bottlenecks**) of the operation. It is used to:

(a)     Identify the capacity constraints in the system.
(b)     Schedule production to these capacity constraints.
(c)     Try to identify ways of overcoming the capacity constraint, so as to increase capacity.
(d)     Having done that, identify the next capacity constraint and schedule production to this constraint.

If the activity level for an operation exceeds the limit of the known constraint, items will be produced in parts of the operation that cannot be used in other parts, due to a bottleneck around the constraining factor. OPT focuses on these bottlenecks. If the activity level is lower than the limit of the known constraint, there will be idle resources and an under-utilised operation.

## 4.4 Enterprise resource planning (ERP)

Enterprise resource planning developed out of MRP II. In an MRP II system, the consequences of any change in demand are calculated, and new instructions (eg for materials procurement) are issued accordingly. ERP performs a similar function, but on a wider basis, integrating and using databases from all parts of the organisation.

**Enterprise Resource Planning (ERP) software** attempts to integrate all departments and functions of an organisation in a computer system able to meet the needs of users from across the whole organisation. An ERP system includes a number of integrated modules designed to support all of the key activities of an enterprise. This includes managing the key elements of the supply chain such as product planning, purchasing, stock control and customer service including order tracking. ERP is now being rapidly extended to the growing number of e-business applications being developed over the Internet, connecting customer, supply chain and other activities. ERP may also include HR modules enabling control of staff scheduling and staff payments.

Features of ERP systems are:

(a)   A **client/server architecture**, that allows access to the information on the system to any person with a computer link to the system's central server.

(b)   **Decision support features**, to help with management decision-making.

(c)   Often, a **link to an external extranet system**, such as an electronic data interchange link to major supply chain partners (suppliers or customers).

One of the most popular ERP systems has been the R/3 system supplied by **SAP**. The R/3 system integrates most of an organisation's business applications, and contains sections for manufacturing and logistics, sales and distribution, financial accounting and human resource management.

ERP has been effective in some situations, for example where it has been implemented as a means of **rationalising and integrating systems** where mergers and acquisitions have led to an unco-ordinated mix of systems. ERP also provides efficiencies in supply chain management through facilitating reduced lead times.

Many ERP implementations **have failed to live up to expectations**, failing to deliver significant efficiency gains.

As they cover many areas of an organisation, ERP implementations are relatively expensive, plus they also carry significant 'hidden' costs through requiring organisations to change the way they operate. Some businesses have been restructured simply to fit the restrictions of the ERP software.

## Question                                                                                           ERP

Learning outcome: C (iv)

ERP attempts to integrate all areas and functions of an organisation in a computer system able to meet the needs of users from across the whole organisation.

(a)   What would be the potential benefits of an ERP system to a company that takes customer orders by telephone and then ships the order to the customer?

(b)   In 2004, A & P, a US grocery stores chain with an old-fashioned image, spent $250 million on an ERP system, hoping that the modernisation would help it to compete more effectively against rivals such as Wal-Mart. What might be the potential uses/benefits of ERP to a company such as A & P?

(a)   The company's basic customer service process appears to be: take an order by telephone, ship the order and then bill for it. With ERP, when a customer service operator takes a call they have all the necessary information available to deal with the customer. When the customer calls to place an order, information relating to the customer's credit rating and order history is available as is information about inventory levels. If the customer calls with a query about the progress of an order, the operator can access up-to-date order tracking information. The customer can be dealt with by one person, who has access to all the necessary information – they will not be passed from one department to another trying to find someone who can help with a request or a query.

(b)   A & P will require significant benefits from an investment of $250 million. The broad aim will be to provide as many customers as possible with goods that they want to buy. Possible benefits are:

(i)    Having access to B2B retail exchanges, where the grocery store can buy from suppliers at the keenest prices (to lower costs).

(ii)   Improving product availability through better tracking of inventory levels and customer demand patterns.

(iii)  Introducing self-checkout systems, to improve speed and reduce in-store costs.

(iv)   Improved understanding of customers and their buying preferences.

# 5 Inventory management

## 5.1 Overview

Inventories held in any organisation can generally be classified under four main headings.

- Raw materials
- Spare parts/consumables
- Work in progress
- Finished goods

For example, the raw materials of a furniture company would be wood and upholstery. Consumables would be items such as nails, screws and castors. Work in progress would be partly completed furniture. Finished goods would be tables, chairs, desks etc ready for sale. Not all organisations will have inventories of all four general categories.

**FAST FORWARD**

**Inventory control** includes the functions of inventory ordering and purchasing, receiving goods into store, storing and issuing inventory and controlling the level of inventory. Every movement of material in a business should be recorded.

### 5.1.1 Controls

There should be controls over the following functions.

- The **ordering** of inventories
- The **purchase** of inventories
- The **receipt** of goods into store
- **Storage**
- The **issue** of inventory and maintenance of inventories at the most appropriate level

Inventory controls are **required** for a number of reasons.

(a)   Holding costs of inventory may be expensive.

(b)   Production will be disrupted if the company runs out of raw materials.

(c)   If inventory with a short shelf life is not used or sold, their value may decline.

(d)   If a customer cannot be supplied immediately, customer dissatisfaction may arise.

## 5.2 Importance of keeping inventory records

Proper records should be kept of the physical procedures for ordering and receiving a consignment of goods to ensure the following.

- That enough inventory is held
- That there is no duplication of ordering
- That quality is maintained

## 5.3 Storage of inventories

Storekeeping involves storing materials to achieve the following objectives.

- Speedy **issue** and **receipt** of goods
- Full **identification** of all goods at all times
- Correct **location** of all goods at all times
- **Protection** of goods from damage and deterioration
- Provision of **secure stores** to avoid pilferage, theft and fire
- **Efficient** use of storage space
- **Maintenance** of correct stock levels
- Keeping correct and up-to-date **records** of receipts, issues and inventory levels

One of the objectives of storekeeping is to maintain accurate records of current inventory levels. This involves the accurate recording of stock movements (issues from and receipts into stores).

## 5.4 Perpetual or continuous inventory

 FAST FORWARD

**Perpetual inventory** refers to an inventory recording system whereby the records are updated for each receipt and issue of inventory as it occurs.

**Continuous** or **perpetual inventory** is the name for a **system that involves recording every receipt and issue of inventory as it occurs**. This means that there is a continuous record of the balance of each item of inventory.

'When inventory levels drop below a predetermined level a fixed amount is ordered to replace it' (Brown *et al.* 2001).

## 5.5 Periodic inventory systems

These systems involve a check of inventory levels at specific time intervals. The checks may trigger an order for new stock. The quantity ordered depends on the current inventory level.

## 5.6 ABC system

Under this system, items may be **classified as expensive, inexpensive or in a middle-cost range**. Because of the practical advantages of simplifying stores control procedures without incurring unnecessary high costs, it may be possible to segregate materials for selective stores control.

(a) Expensive and medium-cost materials are subject to careful stores control procedures to minimise cost.

(b) Inexpensive materials can be stored in large quantities because the cost savings from careful stores control do not justify the administrative effort required to implement the control.

This selective approach to stores control is sometimes called the **ABC method** whereby materials are classified A, B or C according to their **value**. A refers to **high** value inventory, B to **medium** and C to **low** value inventory. It is based upon the Pareto 80/20 rule which suggests that 20% of the items are likely to account for 80% of the overall value.

## 5.7 Obsolescence and wastage

**Obsolete inventories are those items which have become out-of-date and are no longer required.** Obsolete items are disposed of and treated as an expense in the company's financial statements.

From the perspective of operations management, proper controls should be instituted to minimise the incidence of losses arising from obsolescence or wastage.

**Slow-moving inventories are items which are likely to take a long time to be used up.**

## 5.8 Why hold inventories?

*Brown* (2001) identified the following reasons for holding inventory.

- **Protection** against supply problems
- To **meet unexpected increases** in demand
- To **improve delivery times** to customers
- To **allow bulk purchases** and associated **discounts**
- To **provide** a **buffer protecting against quality problems** in raw materials of newly finished goods
- To **improve reliability**
- To **s**moothe out production when **demand fluctuates**.

## 5.9 Holding costs

If stocks are too high, **holding costs** will be incurred unnecessarily. Such costs occur for a number of reasons.

(a)  **Costs of storage and stores operations.** Larger stocks require more storage space and possibly extra staff and equipment to control and handle them.

(b)  **Interest charges**. Holding stocks involves the tying up of capital (cash) on which interest must be paid.

(c)  **Insurance costs**. The larger the value of stocks held, the greater insurance premiums are likely to be.

(d)  **Risk of obsolescence**. The longer a stock item is held, the greater is the risk of obsolescence.

(e)  **Deterioration**. When materials in store deteriorate to the extent that they are unusable, they must be thrown away with the likelihood that disposal costs would be incurred.

## 5.10 Costs of obtaining inventories

If inventories are kept low, small quantities will have to be ordered more frequently, thereby increasing the following **ordering or procurement costs**.

(a)  **Clerical and administrative costs** associated with purchasing, accounting for and receiving goods

(b)  **Transport costs**

(c)  **Production run costs**, for stock which is manufactured internally rather than purchased from external sources

## 5.11 Inventory outage

An additional type of cost which may arise if inventories are kept too low is the type associated with running out of inventories.

- Lost contribution from lost sales
- Loss of future sales due to disgruntled customers
- Loss of customer goodwill
- Cost of production stoppages
- Labour frustration over stoppages
- Extra costs of urgent, small quantity, replenishment orders

## 5.12 Objective of inventory control

The overall objective of inventory control is, therefore, to maintain inventory levels so that the total of the following costs is minimised.

- Holding costs
- Ordering costs
- Stockout costs

## 5.13 Inventory control levels

**Inventory control levels** can be calculated in order to maintain inventory at the optimum level. The three critical control levels are **reorder level**, **minimum level** and **maximum level**. The **Economic Order Quantity (EOQ)** is the order quantity which minimises inventory costs.

Based on an analysis of past inventory usage and delivery times, a series of control levels can be calculated and used to maintain inventories at their optimum level (in other words, a level which minimises costs). These levels will determine 'when to order' and 'how many to order'.

(a) **Reorder level**. When inventories reach this level, an order should be placed to replenish stocks. The reorder level is determined by considering the rate of consumption and the lead time (lead time is the time between placing an order with a supplier and the stock becoming available for use).

(b) **Minimum level**. This is a warning level to draw management attention to the fact that inventories approaching a dangerously low level and that outages are possible.

(c) **Maximum level**. This also acts as a warning level to signal to management that stocks are reaching a potentially wasteful level.

(d) **Reorder quantity**. This is the quantity of inventory which is to be ordered when stock reaches the reorder level. If it is set so as to minimise the total costs associated with holding and ordering inventory, then it is known as the **economic order quantity**.

(e) **Average inventory**. The formula for the average inventory level assumes that inventory levels fluctuate evenly between the minimum (or safety) inventory level and the highest possible inventory level (the amount of inventory immediately after an order is received, ie safety inventory + reorder quantity).

**Exam focus point**

You won't be required to perform EOQ calculations in the P4 exam – but you do need to understand that holding inventories and ordering inventories involve costs and that these should be minimised (without risking stock-outs).

# 6 Just-in-time (JIT)

**Just-in-time** (JIT) is an approach to planning and control based on the idea that goods should be produced or services delivered **only when they are needed**, and not before. It is also known as stockless production.

## 6.1 Overview

Just-in-time is an approach to operations planning and control based on the idea that goods and services should be produced **only when they are needed** – neither too early (so that inventories build up) nor too late (so that the customer has to wait). JIT is also known as 'stockless production' and may be used as part of lean production which we cover in a later chapter.

In its extreme form, a JIT system seeks to hold zero inventories. JIT disruption at any part of the system becomes a problem for the whole operation to resolve. Supporters of JIT management argue that this will improve the likelihood that the problem will be resolved, because it is in the interest of everyone to resolve it.

## 6.2 Operational requirements of JIT

JIT requires the following characteristics in operations.

(a) **High quality**. Disruption in production due to errors in quality will reduce throughput and reduce the dependability of internal supply.

(b) **Speed**. Throughput in the operation must be fast, so that customer orders can be met by production rather than out of inventory.

(c) **Reliability**. Production must be reliable and not subject to hold-ups.

(d) **Flexibility**. To respond immediately to customer orders, production must be flexible, and in small batch sizes.

(e) **Lower costs**. As a consequence of high quality production, and with a faster throughput and the elimination of errors, costs will be reduced.

A consequence of JIT is that if there is no immediate demand for output, the operation should not produce goods for inventory.

## 6.3 The JIT philosophy

FAST FORWARD **JIT** is both a **philosophy of management** and a collection of management and operational techniques, such as work floor layout planning (to smooth and shorten the work flow), reducing set-up times and JIT purchasing.

The JIT philosophy originated in Japan in the 1970s, with companies such as the car manufacturer Toyota. At its most basic, the philosophy is thus:

(a) To do things well, and gradually do them better (continuous improvement).
(b) To squeeze waste out of the system.

The JIT philosophy has been explained in terms of high dependency theory, as follows.

'Japanese systems of production, particularly JIT and total quality control, heighten the dependency of the organisation on its agencies or 'constituents', especially employees and supplying companies. This means ... that the ability of the organisation's constituents to exert leverage in their own interests is increased. The obvious implication is that it is imperative that such organisations take steps to counterbalance this by averting the possibility of such power being used.... In the light of the vulnerability of Japanese production systems to disruption and in the light of the high dependencies of the organisation on its constituents, we suggest that such a system will only work successfully where organisations have either actively taken the appropriate measures to guard against disruption, or where social, economic and political conditions automatically provide safeguards.' (*Oliver and Wilkinson*, 1992).

A criticism of JIT, in its extreme form, is that to have no inventory between any stages in the production process ignores the fact that some stages, by their very nature, could be less reliable than others, and more prone to disruption. It could therefore be argued that some inventory should be held at these stages to provide a degree of extra protection to the rest of the operation.

### 6.3.1 Three key elements in the JIT philosophy

| Element | Comment |
|---|---|
| Elimination of waste | Waste is defined as any activity that does not add value. Examples of waste identified by Toyota were: |
| | (i) **Overproduction**, ie producing more than was immediately needed by the next stage in the process. |
| | (ii) **Waiting time**. Waiting time can be measured by labour efficiency and machine efficiency. |
| | (iii) **Transport**. Moving items around a plant does not add value. Waste can be reduced by changing the layout of the factory floor so as to minimise the movement of materials. |
| | (iv) **Waste in the process**. There could be waste in the process itself. Some activities might be carried out only because there are design defects in the product, or because of poor maintenance work. |
| | (v) **Inventory**. Inventory is wasteful. The target should be to eliminate all inventory by tackling the things that cause it to build up. |
| | (vi) **Simplification of work**. An employee does not necessarily add value by working. Simplifying work is an important way of getting rid of waste in the system (the waste of motion) because it eliminates unnecessary actions. |
| | (vii) **Defective goods** are quality waste. This is a significant cause of waste in many operations. |
| The involvement of all staff in the operation | JIT is a cultural issue, and its philosophy has to be embraced by everyone involved in the operation if it is to be applied successfully. Critics of JIT argue that management efforts to involve all staff can be patronising. |
| Continuous improvement | The goal is to meet demand immediately with perfect quality and no waste. In practice, this ideal is never achieved. However, the JIT philosophy is that an organisation should work towards the ideal, and continuous improvement is both possible and necessary. The Japanese term for continuous improvement is *kaizen*. |

## 6.4 JIT techniques

JIT is a **collection of management techniques**. Some of these relate to basic working practices.

(a)  **Work standards**. Work standards should be established and followed by everyone at all times.

(b)  **Flexibility in responsibilities**. The organisation should provide for the possibility of expanding the responsibilities of any individual to the extent of his or her capabilities, regardless of the individual's position in the organisation. Grading structures and restrictive working practices should be abolished.

(c)  **Equality of all people working in the organisation**. Equality should exist and be visible. For example, there should be a single staff canteen for everyone, without a special executive dining area; and all staff including managers might be required to wear the same uniform. An example of this is car manufacturer Honda.

(d)  **Autonomy**. Authority should be delegated to the individuals responsible directly in the activities of the operation. Management should support people on the shop floor, not direct them.

(e)  **Development of personnel**. Individual workers should be developed and trained.

(f)  **Quality of working life**. The quality of working life should be improved, through better work area facilities, job security and involvement of everyone in job-related decision-making.

(g)  **Creativity**. Employees should be encouraged to be creative in devising improvements to the way their work is done.

(h)   **Use several small, simple machines**, rather than a single large and more complex machine. Small machines can be moved around more easily, and so offer greater flexibility in shop floor layout. The risk of making a bad and costly investment decision is reduced, because relatively simple small machines usually cost much less than sophisticated large machines.

(i)   **Work floor layout and work flow**. Work can be laid out to promote the smooth flow of operations. Work flow is an important element in JIT, because the work needs to flow without interruption in order to avoid a build-up of inventory or unnecessary down-times.

(j)   **Total productive maintenance (TPM)**. Total productive maintenance seeks to eliminate unplanned breakdowns and the damage they cause to production and work flow. Staff operating on the production line are brought into the search for improvements in maintenance.

(k)   **JIT purchasing**. With JIT purchasing, an organisation establishes a close relationship with trusted suppliers, and develops an arrangement with the supplier for being able to purchase materials only when they are needed for production. The supplier is required to have a flexible production system capable of responding immediately to purchase orders from the organisation.

## 6.5 JIT planning and control

Holding inventories is one source of waste in production. Not having materials when they are needed is another. In other words, both having inventories in hand and having stock-outs is wasteful practice.

### 6.5.1 Kanban

*Kanban* is the Japanese word for card or signal. A kanban control system is a system for controlling the flow of materials between one stage in a process and the next. In its simple form, a card is used by an 'internal customer' as a signal to an 'internal supplier' that the customer now requires more parts or materials. The card will contain details of the parts or materials required.

The receipt of a card from an internal customer sets in motion the movement or production or supply of one unit of an item, or one standard container of the item.

| Question | Toyota and JIT |
| --- | --- |

Learning outcome: C (viii)

Japanese car manufacturer Toyota was the first company to develop JIT (JIT was originally called the Toyota Production System). After the end of the world war in 1945, Toyota recognised that it had much to do to catch up with the US automobile manufacturing industry. The company was making losses. In Japan, however, consumer demand for cars was weak, and consumers were very resistant to price increases. Japan also had a bad record for industrial disputes. Toyota itself suffered from major strike action in 1950.

The individual credited with devising JIT in Toyota from the 1940s was Taiichi Ohno, and JIT techniques were developed gradually over time. The *kanban* system for example, was devised by Toyota in the early 1950s, but was only finally fully implemented throughout the Japanese manufacturing operation in 1962.

Ohno identified seven wastes and worked to eliminate them from operations in Toyota. Measures that were taken by the company included the following.

(a)   The aim of reducing costs was of paramount importance in the late 1940s.

(b)   The company should aim to level the flow of production and eliminate unevenness in the work flow.

(c)   The factory layout was changed. Previously all machines, such as presses, were located in the same area of the factory. Under the new system, different types of machines were clustered together in production cells.

(d)   Machine operators were re-trained.

(e)   Employee involvement in the changes was seen as being particularly important. Team work was promoted.

(f)   The *kanban* system was eventually introduced, but a major problem with its introduction was the elimination of defects in production.

Can you explain how each of the changes became regarded as essential by Toyota's management?

(a) **Cost reduction**. Toyota was losing money, and market demand was weak, preventing price rises. The only way to move from losses into profits was to cut costs, and cost reduction was probably essential for the survival of the company.

(b) **Production levelling**. Production levelling should help to minimise idle time whilst at the same time allowing the company to achieve its objective of minimum inventories.

(c) The **change in factory layout** was to improve the work flow and eliminate the waste of moving items around the work floor from one set of machines to another. Each cell contained all the machines required to complete production, thus eliminating unnecessary materials movements.

(d) Having **cells of different machines**, workers in each work cell would have to be trained to use each different machine, whereas previously they would have specialised in just one type of machine.

(e) A **change of culture** was needed to overcome the industrial problems of the company. Employee involvement would have been an element in this change. Teamwork would have helped with the elimination of waste: mistakes or delays by one member of a team would be corrected or dealt with by others in the team. The work force moved from a sense of individual responsibility/blame to collective responsibility.

(f) The **kanban system** is a 'pull' system of production scheduling. Items are only produced when they are needed. If a part is faulty when it is produced, the production line will be held up until the fault is corrected. For a kanban system to work properly, defects must therefore be eliminated.

## 6.6 JIT in service operations

The JIT philosophy can be applied to service operations as well as to manufacturing. Whereas JIT in manufacturing seeks to eliminate inventories, JIT in service operations seeks to remove queues of customers.

Queues of customers are wasteful because:

(a) They waste customers' time.
(b) Queues require space for customers to wait in, and this space is not adding value.
(c) Queuing lowers the customer's perception of the quality of the service.

The application of JIT to a service operation calls for multiskilling, so that employees can be used more flexibly and moved from one type of work to another, in response to work flow requirements.

 Case Study

A postal delivery has specific postmen or postwomen allocated to their own routes. However, there may be scenarios where, say, Route A is overloaded while Route B has a very light load of post.

Rather than have letters for Route A piling up at the sorting office, when the person responsible for Route B has finished delivering earlier, this person might help out on Route A.

Teamwork and flexibility are difficult to introduce into an organisation because people might be more comfortable with clearly delineated boundaries in terms of their responsibilities. However, the customer is usually not interested in the company organisation structure because he or she is more interested in receiving a timely service.

In practice, service organisations are likely to use a buffer operation to minimise customer queuing times. For example, a hairdresser will get an assistant to give the client a shampoo to reduce the impact of waiting for the stylist. Restaurants may have an area where guests may have a drink if no vacant tables are available immediately; such a facility may even encourage guests to plan in a few drinks before dinner thereby increasing the restaurant's revenues.

# Chapter Roundup

- **Capacity** is a measure of what an operation is able to produce within a specified period of time.

- **Capacity management** refers to an organisation's ability to efficiently meet the demand for its products or services. Capacity planning and control is the process of **balancing** the **output capacity** and resources of an operation with the **demand from customers** for the product or service. It calls for planning the normal capacity of the operation and reacting to changes in demand.

- The **steps in capacity planning and control** are measuring total demand, identifying alternative capacity plans that could be implemented to meet the demand, and choosing the most suitable of these alternatives.

- There are different ways of **planning for capacity**.

  (a) A level capacity plan
  (b) A chase demand plan
  (c) A demand management plan
  (d) A mix of the above three types of plan

- **Materials requirements planning (MRP I)** is a system or technique for deciding the requirements for materials, in terms of both quantities and timing, down to the smallest material items or components.

- **Manufacturing resources planning (MRP II)** evolved out of MRP I and is a computerised system that integrates planning information for the operations management, marketing, finance and engineering functions.

- **Inventory control** includes the functions of inventory ordering and purchasing, receiving goods into store, storing and issuing inventory and controlling the level of inventory. Every movement of material in a business should be recorded.

- **Perpetual inventory** refers to an inventory recording system whereby the records are updated for each receipt and issue of inventory as it occurs.

- **Inventory control levels** can be calculated in order to maintain inventory at the optimum level. The three critical control levels are **reorder level**, **minimum level** and **maximum level**. The **Economic Order Quantity (EOQ)** is the order quantity which minimises inventory costs.

- **Just-in-time (JIT)** is an approach to planning and control based on the idea that goods should be produced or services delivered **only when they are needed**, and not before. It is also known as stockless production.

- **JIT** is both a **philosophy of management** and a collection of management and operational techniques, such as work floor layout planning (to smooth and shorten the work flow), reducing set-up times and JIT purchasing.

# Quick Quiz

1    An organisation is unable to produce enough output to fulfil demand. Is this an example of overcapacity or undercapacity?

2    *Fill in the gaps.* Planning and control activities associated with balancing capacity and demand are:

L ...........................        S ..........................        S ..........................

M ........................... and        C ..........................

3    'A plan to maintain activity at a constant level over the planning period.' This statement defines:

A    A chase demand plan
B    A steady capacity/plan
C    A level capacity plan
D    A demand management plan

4    Name a popular ERP software package.

5    'A perpetual inventory system may be referred to as a continuous inventory system.'

True    ☐

False    ☐

6    Briefly explain the philosophy of 'just in time'.

# Answers to Quick Quiz

1    Undercapacity

2    Loading, sequencing, scheduling, monitoring and controlling.

3    C. A level capacity plan seeks to maintain constant activity over a planning period.

4    R/3 by SAP is probably the best known ERP package.

5    True. A perpetual inventory system can also be referred to as a continuous inventory system.

6    Just-in-time aims to co-ordinate inventory procurement and production (and all associated activities) so that inventory holdings are minimised while still ensuring timely delivery to the customer.

Now try the question below from the Exam Question Bank

| Number | Level | Marks | Time |
|--------|-------|-------|------|
| 5 | Examination | 30 | 54 mins |

# 6

# Quality management

## Introduction

A significant trend in all business sectors over recent years has been an increased **emphasis on quality**. In an increasingly **competitive** environment, quality is seen as vital to success.

As with many topics in his paper, you must learn the relevant theory, but also be able to apply it to a practical situation. For example, a **theoretical** question may require you to evaluate various contemporary approaches to the management of quality – while a more **practical** question could ask you to identify and analyse problems with management of quality in an organisation described in the question.

The purposes of **external quality standards** (eg the various ISO standards appropriate to products and organisations) are also highly examinable.

We start this chapter by looking at the **concept** of quality, before moving on to the various **approaches** used to ensure quality in both the product or service produced, and the systems used by the organisation.

Later we look at business process re-engineering and one integrated approach to quality management is explained.

| Topic list | Learning outcomes | Syllabus references | Ability required |
|---|---|---|---|
| 1 The scope of quality management | C(ii) | C(11) | Analyse |
| 2 Quality control versus quality assurance | C(iii) | C(11), C(14) | Evaluation |
| 3 Quality management approaches | C(iii), C(iv), C(vi) | C(6), C(8), C(9), C(11), C(14) | Evaluation |
| 4 Benchmarking | C(v), C(ix) | C(7) | Evaluation |
| 5 International Organisation for Standardisation | C(ix) | C(11), (C12) | Analyse |
| 6 Service quality | C(vi), C(ix) | C(14) | Analyse |
| 7 Total productive maintenance (TPM) | C(v), C(ix) | C(14) | Evaluation |
| 8 Business process re-engineering (BPR) | C(ix) | C(5) | Analyse |
| 9 The TQMEX model | C(iii), C(v), C(vi) | C(7), C(8), C(11) | Evaluation |

# 1 The scope of quality management

**FAST FORWARD**

**Quality management** is concerned with ensuring that products or services are fit for their purpose, and meet specifications.

In the modern commercial environment, there has been a change in emphasis **away from quantity** (produce as much as we can) **to quality** (produce the best we can). Customers have become more sophisticated and discerning in their requirements. Poor quality products and services are no longer acceptable. **Quality** is a **base-line requirement** of any output produced by an organisation.

Quality applies to both goods and services. Whether a customer goes shopping for food or visits a dentist, he or she expects a quality experience. More importantly, quality can be the source of **competitive advantage** over the organisation's business rivals.

In an organisational context, quality is concerned with 'fitness for purpose', and **quality management** (or control) is about ensuring that products or services meet their planned level of quality, and conform to specifications.

There are several definitions of quality. Here is one.

**Key term**

> **Quality** is 'the totality of features and characteristics of a product or service which bears on its ability to meet stated or implied needs'. (*Holmes*, 1992)

Other terms related to quality are defined below.

**Key terms**

> **Quality management** is concerned with controlling activities with the aim of ensuring that products or services are fit for their purpose, and meet specifications. Quality management encompasses quality assurance and quality control.
>
> **Quality assurance** focuses on the way a product or service is produced, Procedures and standards are devised with the aim of ensuring defects are eliminated (or at least minimised) during the development/production process.
>
> **Quality control** is concerned with checking and reviewing work that has been done. Quality control therefore has a narrower focus than quality assurance.

## 1.1 Quality as a concept

Throughout this chapter, the following four themes reappear in relation to quality management.

(a)   **Commitment**. A commitment to quality is required from top management – down to the most junior level employees.

(b)   **Competence**. Employees must 'know what they are doing'. Training is important.

(c)   **Communication**. The need for quality, and the benefits of quality, must be communicated throughout the organisation.

(d)   **Continuous improvement**. Quality involves always looking to 'raise the bar'.

# 2 Quality control versus quality assurance

Traditional approaches to quality were focused on **inspection**. Modern approaches to quality focus on the **prevention** of defects through quality standards and processes.

## 2.1 Quality control

In the past, 'quality' usually meant quality control – which meant inspection. Inspection was usually carried out at three main points.

- Receiving inspection
- Floor or process inspection
- Final inspection or testing

The problem with this 'inspection' approach is that it allows for and often entails built-in waste.

(a) The inspection process itself does not add value: if it could be guaranteed that no defective items were produced, there would be no need for a separate inspection function.

(b) The inspection function itself involves the delocation of resources in terms of both people and facilities.

(c) The production of substandard products is a waste of raw materials, machine time, human efforts, and overheads (as the substandard production has to be administered).

(d) The production of defects is not compatible with newer production techniques such as just-in-time: there is no time for inspection.

(e) Working capital is tied up in stocks which cannot be sold.

(f) In a service industry, damage may already have been done to customer relations before inspection takes place.

Quality control procedures focus on the product or service produced, rather than the production processes. It involves establishing standards of quality for a product or service, implementing procedures that are expected to produce products of the required standard in most cases and monitoring output to ensure sub-standard output is rejected or corrected.

## 2.2 Quality assurance

The demand for better quality has led to the acceptance of the view that quality management should aim to **prevent** defective production rather than simply detect it.

Most modern approaches to quality have therefore tried to assure quality in the production process, (quality assurance) rather than inspecting goods or services after they have been produced.

The term 'quality assurance' is used where a supplier guarantees the quality of goods or services they supply. Quality assurance programmes usually involve a close relationship between supplier and customer, which may extend to allowing customer representatives to view and/or monitor production procedures.

Quality assurance emphasises the processes and procedures used to produce a product or service – the logic being that if these are tightly controlled and monitored the resulting product and service will be high quality. As quality has been 'built-in', the need for routine inspection of goods **after** production should be eliminated.

# 3 Quality management approaches

## 3.1 Quality management

In general terms, any quality management system should involve the activities outlined below.

Step 1    **Plan**. Establish:

    (a)    **Standards** of quality for a product (eg a software package) or service (eg performance and volume requirements).

    (b)    **Procedures** or production methods that ought to ensure that these required standards of quality are met (eg a systems development methodology).

Step 2    Devise suitable instruments and techniques to **monitor** actual quality.

Step 3    **Compare** actual quality with planned quality using quality measures.

Step 4    Take control action when actual quality falls below standard. **Quality auditing** involves a systematic inspection to establish whether quality objectives are being met. A quality audit could be carried out:

    (a)    Internally, for example by staff from internal audit or a specific quality department.

    (b)    Externally, for example by a certified agency such as an ISO review (covered later in this chapter).

    (c)    On a supplier, or on the organisation itself by a supplier – to ensure compliance with the company's quality standards.

Step 5    Review the plan and standards to ensure **continuous improvement**.

The activities and steps above describe a general approach to quality management. In the following sections, we will look at some specific methodologies or approaches associated with quality.

## 3.2 Measuring quality

### 3.2.1 Balanced scorecard

Deciding how to measure quality is an important aspect of quality management. Quality measures should cover operational, financial and customer aspects. One approach, originally developed by *Kaplan and Norton* (1990), is the use of a 'balanced scorecard' consisting of a variety of indicators both financial and non-financial. Some organisations may communicate their quality measures using means other than a balanced scorecard, but the principles on which they base their measures are generally similar. The balanced scorecard focuses on four different perspectives, as follows.

| Perspective | Question | Explanation |
| --- | --- | --- |
| **Customer** | What do existing and new customers value from us? | Gives rise to targets that matter to customers: cost, quality, delivery, inspection, handling and so on. |
| **Operational; internal operations** | What processes must we excel at to achieve our financial and customer objectives? | Aims to improve internal processes and decision making. |
| **Operational; innovation and learning** | Can we continue to improve and create future value? | Considers the business's capacity to maintain its competitive position through the acquisition of new skills and the development of new products. |
| **Financial** | How do we create value for our shareholders? | Covers traditional measures such as growth, profitability and shareholder value but set through talking to the shareholder or shareholders direct. |

The scorecard is 'balanced' in the sense that managers are required to think in terms of all four perspectives, to prevent improvements being made in one area at the expense of another.

The types of measure which may be monitored under each of the four perspectives include the following. The list is not exhaustive but it will give you an idea of the possible scope of a balanced scorecard approach. The measures selected, particularly within the internal perspective, will vary considerably with the type of organisation and its objectives. In addition, as mentioned above, targets should also be established in respect of the various measures.

| Perspective | Measures |
|---|---|
| Customer | • New customers acquired<br>• Customer complaints<br>• Telephone response times<br>• Delivery speeds |
| Operational; internal operations | • Quality control rejects<br>• Productivity levels<br>• Speed of producing management information<br>• Streamlining/systems simplification |
| Operational; innovation and learning | • Training days for employees<br>• Skills enhancement<br>• Percentage of revenue generated by new products and services<br>• Average time taken to develop new products and services |
| Financial | • Return on capital employed<br>• Revenue growth<br>• Cash flow<br>• Earnings per share |

### 3.2.2 Value for Money (VFM) audit

Originally associated with the public sector, VFM techniques are now increasingly being applied to private sector businesses. The basic approach involves identifying and **measuring key aspects of performance**, such as: money expended, inputs purchased, outputs and outcomes achieved. The relationship between money expended and inputs purchased provides a measure of **economy**. The relationship between inputs and outputs provides a measure of **efficiency**. Comparing outputs with outcomes achieved provides a measure of **effectiveness**, eg ten clients serviced (output), nine 'extremely satisfied' clients (outcome).

**Exam focus point**

In November 2006, the examiner identified the balanced scorecard and value for money audits as **strategic performance measures**.

## 3.3 Possible problems when attempting to measure quality

Measuring quality involves taking into account many variables, which can lead to problems.

| Problem | Explanation |
|---|---|
| Conflicting measures | Some measures in the scorecard such as research funding and cost reduction may naturally conflict. It is often difficult to determine the balance which will achieve the best results. |
| Selecting measures | Not only do appropriate measures have to be devised but the number of measures used must be agreed. Care must be taken that the impact of the results is not lost in a sea of information. |
| Expertise | Measurement is only useful if it initiates appropriate action. Non-financial managers may have difficulty with the usual profit measures. With more measures to consider this problem will be compounded. |
| Interpretation | Even a financially-trained manager may have difficulty in putting the figures into an overall perspective. |
| Too many measures | The ultimate objective for commercial organisations is to maximise profits or shareholder wealth. Other targets should offer a guide to achieving this objective and not become an end in themselves. |

## 3.4 Quality circles

Over the last two decades the demand for quality has permeated almost every area of business. This has led to the design of systems through which quality can be effectively controlled using **internal resources**. In this context, Americans came up with the concept of **quality circles**.

> A **quality circle** is a team of workers from within the organisation which meets at intervals to discuss issues relating to the quality of the product or service produced.

A typical quality circle comprises employees from many levels of the organisation who meet regularly. The frequency of meetings varies across organisations – every three months would normally be sufficient.

Suggestions are encouraged regarding how the product or service produced could be improved, and how processes and working practices could be improved. Members are encouraged to analyse issues in a logical way.

Wider issues may also be discussed, as it is recognised that the complete working environment will affect quality levels. In some organisations this has led to quality circles having input on issues such as health and safety, employee benefits and bonuses and training and education programmes.

### 3.4.1 Benefits of quality circles

The **benefits of quality circles** include:

(a)     Employee involvement improves morale.
(b)     Practical improvements/solutions are likely as workers know the processes involved.
(c)     Organisation unity is fostered as the circle includes all levels.
(d)     Suggestions can result in valuable savings.
(e)     A 'culture' of quality is fostered.

### 3.4.2 Drawbacks of quality circles

Possible **drawbacks** of quality circles include:

(a)     Employee 'power' is hard to control.
(b)     The scope of influence can become very wide.
(c)     Rejected suggestions may cause resentment.
(d)     Business practicalities (eg cost) may not be fully understood.

The concept of quality circles has expanded to now include groups drawn from **separate organisations** but with a common interest.

## 3.5 Total quality management (TQM)

> **Total quality management (TQM)** is a management philosophy, aimed at continuous improvement in quality standards.

> **Total quality management** (TQM) is the continuous improvement in quality, productivity and effectiveness obtained by establishing management responsibility for processes as well as output.

### 3.5.1 Writers on TQM

The principles of TQM were evolved by a number of management theorists and 'quality gurus'.

*Deming* (1982) is credited with the development of TQM in Japan. He took the view that as process variability (the amount of unpredictability in a process) decreases, quality and productivity increase. Quality can therefore be improved by reducing process variability.

His **14 points for quality improvement** stressed the need for statistical control methods, participation, education, openness and improvement.

1   Create a constancy of purpose.
2   Adopt a new quality-conscious philosophy.
3   Cease dependence on inspection.
4   Stop awarding business on price.
5   Continuous improvement in the system of production and service.
6   Institute training on the job.
7   Institute leadership.
8   Drive out fear.
9   Break down barriers between departments.
10  Eliminate slogans and exhortations.
11  Eliminate quotas or work standards.
12  Give employees pride in their job.
13  Institute education and a self-improvement programme.
14  Put everyone to work to accomplish it.

**Theory Z** was devised by *William Ouchi* in the early 1980s.

His theory Z emphasises the following elements.

- Interpersonal skills
- Group interaction and decision-making
- Participative management
- Free flow of information
- Trust
- Retention of hierarchical rules and control
- Formal procedures for planning and setting objectives

Theory Z combined aspects of US management practice (which *Ouchi* referred to as Theory A) and Japanese management practices (Theory J).

*Juran* (also known as *Duran*) (1988) argued that quality should not be seen in terms of meeting specification, but should focus on the role of the customer, both internal and external. A user-based approach to quality should focus on **fitness for use**. *Juran* emphasised the importance of management's role in quality improvement and the need to motivate the work force and involve them in quality improvement initiatives. He also emphasised that quality management should aim to ensure that the way in which work is performed (ie systems and processes) facilitated high quality output. *Juran* believed 85% of quality problems were the result of ineffective systems.

*Ishikawa* (1985) stressed the importance of people and participation in the process of solving quality problems. He devised the idea of **quality circles** to achieve participation and overcome resistance to quality control, which workers dislike because of its emphasis on statistics and the rigid specification of standards.

*Crosby* (1979) wrote about quality costs. Like other quality gurus, he argued for worker participation and the need to motivate individuals to do something about quality. His 'absolutes of quality management' were:

1   Quality is conformance to requirements.
2   Prevention is required, not an appraisal of the costs of poor quality.
3   Zero defects in production.
4   Organisations should measure the cost or price of 'non-conformance'.
5   There is no such thing as a 'quality problem'.

TQM is therefore an amalgamation of related but different ideas.

### 3.5.2 The elements of TQM

Aspects of TQM include getting things right first time, **preventing defective production** or service delivery and meeting the needs and expectations of customers or clients. TQM often involves the notion of **internal suppliers** and **internal customers** linked in **quality chains**.

TQM has been described as a natural extension of previous approaches to quality management, such as:

(a) **Inspection**, ie inspecting output in order to detect and rectify errors.

(b) **Quality control**, ie using statistical techniques to establish quality standards and monitor process performance.

(c) **Quality assurance**. This extended quality management to areas other than direct operations, and uses concepts such as quality costing, quality planning and problem solving.

The following table of principles should help you remember the key elements of TQM.

| Principle |
| --- |
| Prevention |
| Right first time |
| Eliminate waste |
| Continuous improvement |
| Everyone's concern |
| Participation |
| Teamwork and empowerment |

The mnemonic PRECEPT should help you remember them.

### 3.5.3 Internal customers and internal suppliers

In a TQM approach, all parts of the organisation are involved in quality issues, and need to work together. Every person and every activity in the organisation affects the work done by others.

TQM promotes the concept of the **internal customer** and **internal supplier**. The work done by an internal supplier for an internal customer will eventually affect the quality of the product or service to the external customer. In order to satisfy the expectations of the external customer, it is therefore also necessary to satisfy the expectations of the internal customer at each stage of the overall operation. Internal customers are therefore linked in **quality chains**. Internal customer A can satisfy internal customer B who can satisfy internal customer C who in turn can satisfy the external customer.

### 3.5.4 Service level agreements

Some organisations formalise the internal supplier-internal customer concept by requiring each internal supplier to make a **service level agreement** with its internal customer. A service level agreement is a statement of the standard of service and supply that will be provided to the internal customer and will cover issues such as the range of services supplied, response times, dependability and so on. Boundaries of responsibility and performance standards might also be included in the agreement.

Service level agreements have been criticised, however, for over-formalising the relationship between the internal supplier and internal customer, thus **creating barriers** to the development of a constructive relationship and **genuine co-operation** between them.

### 3.5.5 Quality culture within TQM

A purely procedures-driven approach is unlikely to secure a culture of quality. Interpersonal factors such as employee empowerment, teamwork and commitment are likely to be important considerations.

Every person within an organisation has an impact on quality, and it is the responsibility of everyone to get quality right. This means not just those individuals directly involved with production and dealing with customers, but also everyone in support roles and performing back office functions.

Individuals should be encouraged not just to avoid mistakes and to comply with established performance standards and procedures. However, individuals must also do something positive to improve their performance and to help improve the performance of others. The concept of **empowerment** of employees is often associated with TQM.

Teamworking skills are a key competence required of modern management. This recognises that employees are individuals with individual strengths and weaknesses. They need to work together to optimise their personal attributes for the collective benefit of the company. Allied to the notion of greater empowerment is the idea of self-managed or semi-autonomous teams. Customers can therefore relate to a team of employees who are in a position to make decisions in meeting their needs without the distraction of having to obtain authorisation from their superiors.

Commitment is also important in achieving quality. This will require management to apply their skill in persuading and motivating staff into a true commitment to quality. Ultimately it is the employees that will have to deliver the quality.

### 3.5.6 Empowerment

FAST FORWARD **TQM** includes a certain amount of procedures, but to be effective it also requires employee participation, **empowerment** and **teamwork**.

Empowerment recognises that employees themselves are often the best source of information about how (or how not) to improve quality. **Empowerment** includes two key aspects.

(a) Allowing workers to have the **freedom to decide how to do** the necessary work, using the skills they possess and acquiring new skills as necessary to be an effective team member.

(b) Making workers **responsible** for achieving production targets and for quality control.

Empowerment can be important in service organisations where formal procedures might hamper the flexibility of employees responding quickly to a customer's needs. Incidence of service personnel telling customers that other requests cannot be met because of company policy or procedures are likely to lead to dissatisfied customers.

### 3.5.7 Barriers to success

**Participation** is important in TQM, especially in the process of continuous improvement, where workforce views are valued. The management task is to encourage everybody to contribute. **Barriers to participation** include:

(a) An autocratic senior management, who believe they are the sole key to the process.

(b) A culture of individualism rather than team work. People do not share information or ideas in order to take credit for them. In practice, this might even be reinforced by the assessment and reward systems.

(c) Managers perceive their role as being to monitor and control rather than being facilitators who help this organisation meet its goals.

(d) Middle managers who feel their authority is threatened and hence make decisions to maintain their position.

Managers often find some aspects of TQM particularly hard to accept.

(a) Social and status barriers are removed with the removal of office partitions.

(b) Administrative functions must now be seen as **supporting the employees**.

(c) Managers are judged by their team building skills and contribution to team spirit, not the machismo of their behaviour.

(d) Personal skills are needed (eg the ability to listen and communicate).

(e) A manager's role is in supporting and training, not disciplining and restricting.

### 3.5.8 Continuous improvement or Kaizen

Quality management is not a one-off process, but is the **continuous** examination and improvement of existing processes. This process is sometimes referred to as '*Kaizen*'. Some authors explain Japan's competitive success in the world market place as the result of the implementation of the *Kaizen* concept in Japanese corporations.

*Kaizen* looks for uninterrupted, **ongoing incremental change**. In other words, there is always room for improvement and continuously trying to become better. Originally a Buddhist term, *Kaizen* comes from the words, 'Renew the heart and make it good'. Therefore, adaptation of the *Kaizen* concept requires changes in 'the heart of the organisation' – for example in the corporate **culture** and **structure**.

When applied to the workplace *Kaizen* means continuous improvement involving everyone – managers and workers alike. *Kaizen* can be implemented by improving every aspect of a business process in a step-by-step approach, while gradually developing employee skills through training education and increased involvement.

The **principles** of **continuous improvement/Kaizen** are:

(a) **Human resources** are the most important organisational asset.

(b) Processes should evolve by **gradual improvement** rather than radical change.

(c) Improvement should be based on statistical/quantitative evaluation of process performance.

(d) Resources, measurements, rewards, and incentives **all need to be aligned**.

(e) A philosophy of continuous improvement enables changing **customer needs** to be taken into account.

(f) A philosophy of continuous improvement enables **new technologies** to be introduced.

### 3.5.9 Quality costs

The **cost of quality** may be looked at in a number of different ways. For example, some may say that by producing higher quality output will increase costs – as more costly resources are likely to be required to achieve a higher standard. Others may focus on the idea that poor quality output will lead to customer dissatisfaction, which generates costs associated with complaint resolution.

**FAST FORWARD**

There are four types of **quality costs**; **prevention**, **appraisal/inspection**, **internal failure** and **external failure**.

| Type of cost | Definition | Examples |
|---|---|---|
| **Prevention cost** | Costs incurred prior to making the product or delivering the service – to prevent substandard quality products or services being delivered. | The cost of building quality into the product design or service design. The cost of training staff in quality improvement and error prevention. The cost of prevention devices (eg fail-safe features). |
| **Appraisal cost or inspection cost** | This is a cost incurred after a product has been made or service delivered, to ensure that the output or service performance meets the required quality standard or service performance. | The cost of inspecting finished goods or services, and other checking devices such as supplier vetting. Customer or client feedback forms (although these may be a way of keeping service staff 'on their toes'). |

| Type of cost | Definition | Examples |
|---|---|---|
| **Internal failure cost** | This is a cost arising from inadequate quality, where the problem is identified before the transfer of the item or service from the organisation to the customer or client. | Cost of materials scrapped due to inefficiencies in the procedures for goods received and stores control. Cost of materials and components lost during production or service delivery. Cost of output rejected during the inspection process. Cost of re-working faulty output. Cost of reviewing product and service specifications after failures or customer dissatisfaction. Loses due to having to sell faulty output at lower prices. Not charging for a service so as to pacify dissatisfied and angry customers or clients. |
| **External failure cost** | This is a cost arising from inadequate quality, where the problem is identified after the transfer of the item or service from the organisation to the customer. | Cost of product liability claims from customers or clients. Cost of repairing products returned by customers, including those forming part of service. Cost of replacing sub-standard products including those included with a service. Delivery costs of returned units or items. Cost of the customer services section and its operations. Loss of customer goodwill and loss of future sales. |

A **traditional approach to quality management** is that there is an optimal level of quality effort, that minimises total quality costs, and there is a point beyond which spending more on quality yields a benefit that is less than the additional cost incurred. Diminishing returns set in beyond the optimal quality level.

The TQM philosophy is different.

(a)     **Failure and poor quality are unacceptable**. It is inappropriate to think of an optimal level of quality at which some failures will occur, and the inevitability of errors is not something that an organisation should accept. The target should be zero defects. This also applies to the provision of services.

(b)     **Quality costs are difficult to measure**, and failure costs in particular are often seriously under-estimated. The real costs of failure include not just the cost of scrapped items and re-working faulty items or placating an unhappy customer or client, but also all the management time spent sorting out problems and the loss of confidence between different parts of the organisation whenever faults occur.

(c)     **A TQM approach does not accept that the prevention costs of achieving zero defects becomes unacceptably high as the quality standard improves and goes above a certain level**. In other words, diminishing returns do not necessarily set in. If everyone in the organisation is involved in improving quality, the cost of continuous improvement need not be high.

(d)     If an organisation accepts an optimal quality level that it believes will minimise total quality costs, there will be no further challenge to management to improve quality further.

The TQM quality cost model is based on the view:

(a)     **Prevention costs and appraisal** costs are subject to management influence or control. It is better to spend money on prevention, before failures occur, than on inspection to detect product or service failures after they have happened.

(b)     **Internal failure** costs and **external failure costs** are the consequences of the efforts spent on prevention and appraisal. Extra effort on prevention will reduce internal failure costs and this in turn will have a knock-on effect, reducing external failure costs as well.

In other words, higher spending on prevention will eventually lead to lower total quality costs, because appraisal costs, internal failure costs and external failure costs will all be reduced. The emphasis should be on **getting things right first time** and **designing quality** into the product or service.

### 3.5.10 Quality systems documentation

TQM is a **management philosophy**. However, implementing TQM is not simply a matter of involving employees and encouraging a quality culture. There is also a need for systems and procedures for ensuring quality. Quality systems should be documented thoroughly.

(a)    A company **quality manual** may summarise the quality management policy and system.

(b)    A **procedures manual** sets out the functions, structures and responsibilities for quality in each department.

(c)    Detailed **work instructions and specifications** for how work should be carried out show how to achieve the desired quality standards.

## Question                                                                Aims of TQM

Learning outcome: C (iv)

The UK Government department for trade promotes the adoption of a TQM approach by British companies. To compete successfully, British companies must start by eliminating the following weaknesses.

1    Doing what has always been done.
2    Not understanding competitive positioning.
3    Compartmentalising of functions.
4    Trying to control people through systems.
5    Confusing quality with grade, or grade with quality.
6    Having an acceptable quality level (AQL).
7    Fire fighting is regarded as macho.
8    The 'not my problem' syndrome.

*Required*

Explain each of these weaknesses and briefly state how a TQM approach would attempt to address each one.

## Answer

1    There is a tendency, when something doesn't work properly, to try doing it again. However, if something hasn't worked properly in the past, there is no reason to suppose that it will work in the future. TQM encourages an attitude that seeks to change how things are done.

2    Understanding competitive positioning is largely a strategic issue for management, but the Government argues that without a proper understanding of competitive positioning, and the need to have a competitive position in its markets, companies will not survive – particularly in weak or declining industries. A TQM approach includes working out ways of achieving customer satisfaction in order to compete effectively.

3    In many companies, each department or function in an organisation thinks only about its own needs and doesn't think about the needs and expectations of other departments (that might be its 'internal customers' or 'internal suppliers'). This can create problems for the other department to resolve. For example, a hospital consultant might schedule a number of surgical operations requiring varied and sophisticated nursing support for the patients, without first consulting the ward sister or matron about what support would be required and whether it could be made available. The problem would then be one for the ward sister or matron to try to sort out.

4    Management have a tendency to treat people like robots. Employees who are treated in this way will tend to act accordingly – with little concern for the work they are doing.

5    Gold-plated taps in a bath represent a high grade of materials, but if the taps have faulty washers and leak, the quality will be poor. High grade does not ensure good quality. Equally, a low grade product can provide better quality than a high-grade item. For example, uniforms worn by workers might be of a better quality ('fit for the purpose') if they are made from a cheaper, hard-wearing material, than if they are made from more expensive material that is more easily torn or more difficult to clean.

6    Having an acceptable level of quality implies that some errors are tolerable. A TQM approach is that everything should be done right the first time.

7    Managers often enjoy dealing with problems (fire-fighting) as it gives them the sense of being 'in charge'. A TQM approach is that managers waste their time if they have to deal with problems that should not have arisen in the first place.

8    There is a tendency for individuals to be unconcerned about errors they make, so long as the problem does not affect them, but someone else. With a TQM approach, employees are encouraged to think of other departments as internal customers, and accept responsibility for poor service to their customers.

### 3.5.11 Adverse feedback on TQM

TQM is susceptible to various adverse perceptions.

(a)    In practice, TQM initiatives are not introduced or implemented effectively, and the job is 'botched' by management.

(b)    After obtaining short-term benefits from introducing TQM the benefits wear off over time, due to 'quality disillusionment'.

TQM programmes can also suffer from:

(a)    A lack of top-management commitment.

(b)    A failure to understand the full range of quality issues and quality costs.

(c)    Vested interests and organisation politics.

(d)    The slow speed of introducing new initiatives in an organisation, especially a large bureaucratic organisation.

(e)    General cynicism about quality and fulfilling customer needs.

On the other hand, many organisations continue to implement TQM programmes, and some industry bodies try to encourage TQM by making annual awards to companies for quality achievements. The most well-known annual awards are probably:

(a)    The Malcolm Baldridge National Quality Award in the US.

(b)    The Deming Prize in Japan.

(c)    The EFQM Excellence Award in Western Europe.

Companies applying for an award are assessed by a team of judges on the basis of their quality standards in various areas of their operations, and are subjected to site visits. The framework for such awards can also be used by other companies for their own self-assessment purposes.

Question                                                                                    TQM and consistency

Learning outcome: C (iii)

A key word in the TQM philosophy is **consistency**.

Briefly explain what in TQM needs to be consistent, and why consistency is important.

When producing a product or service, consistency means using the same standard of resources and employing the same methods and procedures (processes). Consistency in processes should result in consistently high quality output, and a consistently satisfied customer.

## 3.6 The 5Ss

The 5Ss are **structurise**, **systemise**, **sanitise**, **standardise** and **self-discipline**.

Often associated with lean production (covered later in this chapter), the overriding idea behind the 5Ss is that there is 'a place for everything and everything goes in its place'. Every item that is used in a business process is clearly labelled and easily accessible. Discipline, simplicity, pride, standardisation and repeatability are emphasised in the 5Ss as being critical to efficiency.

| The 5Ss | | | Comment/meaning |
|---|---|---|---|
| Seiri | or | Structurise | Segregate or discard. Introduce order where possible. |
| Selton | or | Systemise | Arrange and identify for ease of use. Approach tasks systematically. |
| Seiso | or | Sanitise | Clean daily. Be tidy, avoid clutter. |
| Seiketsu | or | Standardise | Revisit each 'S' frequently. Be consistent in your approach. |
| Shitsuke | or | Self-discipline | Sustain via motivation. Do the above daily. |

## 3.7 Six Sigma

**Six Sigma** literally means six standard deviations from the mean or median value. When translated into a quality measurement and improvement programme, this equates with only 3.4 defects per million opportunities for each product or service transaction. A Six Sigma initiative involves identifying factors critical to quality (as determined by the customer), reducing process variation, increasing stability and designing systems to support the Six Sigma goal.

**Six Sigma** is a process that is designed to assist organisations to focus on developing and delivering **near-perfect products and services**.

Six Sigma ensures the progressive **elimination of defects** by:

- Identifying the root causes of error
- Confirming the critical root causes
- Implementing corrective action

By minimising defects, **customer satisfaction** should improve and this should improve **profitability**. The thinking might be summarised as follows.

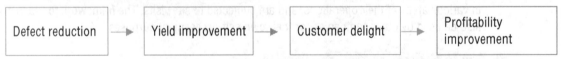

Defect reduction → Yield improvement → Customer delight → Profitability improvement

A key advantage of Six Sigma is that it can be implemented alongside other initiatives such as TQM and ISO 9000 (covered later in this chapter). However, where Six Sigma is different is that it is **customer focused**, rather than operations orientated. It looks at strategically critical outcomes that affect customer satisfaction.

The method was first devised by Motorola in the USA in 1985 to help manufacture a virtually defect free pager. It has been successfully implemented by recognised corporations such as Polaroid, Kodak, and IBM. However, it was General Electric that propelled it to current prominence and popularity.

Case Study

General Electric (GE) began key initiatives on quality in the late 1980s. According to GE company literature

'Work-Out®, the start of our journey, opened our culture to ideas from everyone, everywhere, decimated the bureaucracy and made boundaryless behaviour a reflexive, natural part of our culture, thereby creating the learning environment that led to Six Sigma.

'Now, Six Sigma, in turn, is embedding quality thinking – process thinking – across every level and in every operation of our Company around the globe.

'Work-Out® in the 1980s defined how we behave. Today, Six Sigma is defining how we work and has set the stage for making our customers feel Six Sigma.'

**There are three key elements** to GE's approach to Six Sigma.

(a)   **Delighting customers**

    (i)   The customer sets the quality standard, rather than some manager within the company.

    (ii)   There is a focus on performance, reliability, price, delivery, service and transaction processing.

(b)   **Outside-in thinking**

    (i)   The company must be seen form the customer's perspective.

    (ii)   There is a need to understand what the customer is seeing and feeling as regard the company's processes.

    (iii)   Customer knowledge is used to improve company processes and add value.

(c)   **Leadership commitment**

    (i)   GE recognises that people are key to creating quality and generating results.

    (ii)   There is a commitment to providing opportunities for employees to develop themselves in the services may provide to customers.

    (iii)   There is a focus on ensuring employee training needs are satisfied.

The expression Six Sigma is derived from the discipline of statistics. Sigma is a statistical measure of variation in output. A score of six times the Sigma within a specification means 99.999% of the manufactured items are within the specification (3.4 defects per million opportunities). A Three Sigma level of quality implies a 93.32% specification compliance (67,000 defects per million).

Case Study

**Tiffinwallah system of Mumbai**

The Tiffinwalla system in Mumbai, India, was recently singled out by Forbes Magazine as an outstanding example and awarded a Six Sigma grading.

Each day, 175,000 tiffins (lunchboxes) are delivered to offices and schools throughout Mumbai and later returned home, by approximately 5,000 people called tiffinwallahs. Each tiffin holds a variety of dishes of food. Each tiffin is collected by a tiffinwallah and taken to one of Mumbai's suburban railway stations, where they are sorted. They are collected at the destination station and taken to the building.

There is a fairly simple method of coding which manages a very low failure rate. Each tiffinwallah does not have to deal with too many tiffin boxes. The tiffinwallas make only one error in 16 million transactions. Statistically this represents 99.999% of correctness, thereby achieving Six Sigma.

BPP
LEARNING MEDIA

## 3.8 Lean production

Lean production is a manufacturing methodology developed originally for Toyota. It is also known as the Toyota Production System.

> The goal of **lean production** is 'to get the right things to the right place at the right time, the first time, while **minimising waste** and being open to change'.

**Key term**

> **Lean production** (sometimes referred to as lean manufacturing) is a philosophy of production that aims to minimise the amount of resources (including time) used in all activities of an enterprise. It involves identifying and eliminating all non-value-adding activities.

Lean production involves the systematic elimination of waste. The types of waste eliminated may be classified as follows.

- **Overproduction** and early production
- **Waiting** – time delays, idle time, any time during which value is not added to the product
- **Transportation** – multiple handling, delay in materials handling, unnecessary handling
- **Inventory** – holding or purchasing unnecessary raw materials, work in process and finished goods
- **Motion** – actions of people or equipment that do not add value to the product
- **Over-processing** – unnecessary steps or work elements/procedures (non added value work)
- **Defective units** – production of a part that is scrapped or requires rework

*Ohno* (an engineer) is generally credited with developing the principles of lean production. He argued that in addition to eliminating waste, lean production methods lead to **improved product flow** and **improved quality**. Instead of devoting resources to planning what would be required for future manufacturing, lean production focuses on reducing system response time so that the **production system is capable of rapid change to meet market demands**.

### 3.8.1 Characteristics of lean production

(a) Integrated single piece continuous workflow.

(b) Integration of the whole value chain through partnerships with suppliers and distributors.

(c) Just in time processing: a part moves to a production operation, is processed immediately, and moves immediately to the next operation.

(d) Short order-to-ship cycles times and small batch production capability synchronised to shipping schedules.

(e) Production based on orders rather than forecasts; production driven by customer demand or 'pull'.

(f) Minimal inventories at each stage of the production process.

(g) Quick changeovers of machines and equipment.

(h) Production layout based on product flow.

(i) Active involvement by workers in problem solving to improve quality and eliminate waste.

(j) Defect prevention rather than inspection and rework by building quality into the process.

(k) Team based work with multi-skilled staff empowered to make decisions.

### 3.8.2 Applications of lean techniques

During the 1980s lean production methods were adopted by many manufacturing plants in the U.S. and Europe, with varying degrees of success. Recent years have seen a renewed interest in the principles of lean production, particularly since the philosophy encourages the reduction of inventory. Dell Computers and Boeing Aircraft have embraced the philosophy of lean production with great success.

Lean techniques are applicable not only in manufacturing, but **also in a service environment**. Every system contains waste (ie something that does not provide value to the customer).

### 3.8.3 Benefits of lean production

Supporters of lean production believe it enables a company to deliver on demand, minimise inventory, maximise the use of multi-skilled employees, flatten the management structure and focus resources where they are most effective. Other benefits include:

- Waste reduction (up to 80%)
- Production cost reduction (50%)
- Manufacturing cycle times decreased (50%)
- Labour reduction (50%) while maintaining or increasing throughput
- Inventory reduction (80%) while increasing customer service levels
- Capacity increase in current facilities (50%)
- Higher quality
- Higher profits
- Higher system flexibility in reacting to changes in requirements improved
- More strategic focus
- Improved cash flow through increasing shipping and billing frequencies

## Case Study

IBM regularly compare part counts, bills of materials, standard versus custom part usage, and estimated processing costs by tearing down competitor products as soon as the latter are available. For example, during the heyday of the dot matrix printer, IBM learned that the printer made by the Epson was very complicated with more than 150 parts. IBM launched a team with a simplification goal and knocked the part count down to 62, cutting assembly from thirty minutes to only three.

## 3.9 Criticisms of lean principles

In many situations, an organisation supposedly using lean principles has not experienced the improvements in productivity and profitability expected. It is difficult to know whether this is due to **shortcomings in the lean philosophy** or whether the techniques involved are being **interpreted and applied correctly**.

For example, the 5Ss concept should be used with the aim of creating a workplace with real organisation and order which creates pride by employees in their work, improves safety and results in better quality. However, in some organisations 5S has become a cleaning and housekeeping exercise only and the important purpose of the 5S concept is lost.

Lean techniques should be seen and treated as outward signs of a more fundamental approach to operations and quality. However, many organisations seem to treat these as the end itself – they have a mistaken belief that simply putting structures and mechanisms (eg quality circles) in place will improve efficiency and quality. Sustainable differences require a change in thinking and in culture – which are difficult to achieve.

Lean production is often viewed as a simple cost-cutting exercise rather than a fundamental commitment to eliminating waste and adding value. Many companies use lean manufacturing and Six Sigma techniques to improve quality and reduce costs. But the benefits most businesses realise are only a fraction of what could be achieved if these strategies were applied over a better foundation of business plan deployment, levelling of resources and an engaged workforce.

## 3.10 World class manufacturing

In a manufacturing environment a commitment to quality (and to the customer) may be referred to as 'world class manufacturing'.

This approach involves a focus on **customer requirements** (similar to the marketing concept) and then ensuring products meet these requirements.

As customer requirements often change, **flexibility** in manufacturing operations is a key feature of world-class manufacturing.

### 3.10.1 Flexible manufacturing

Manufacturing operations designed to emphasise flexibility are sometimes referred to as '**flexible manufacturing**'.

Flexible manufacturing describes the situation where '**economies of scope**' make it economical to produce small batches of a relatively wide range of products using the same machines or production facilities.

This is a world away from traditional large-scale assembly lines with their emphasis on economies of scale.

**Exam focus point**

> It is important to be able to explain the criticisms of these lean principles – exam questions could easily require you to explain both the benefits and problems that they create.

# 4 Benchmarking

**FAST FORWARD**

> **Benchmarking** is essentially an analysis of one's own **performance compared** with that of another entity. Ideally the other entity is one that is acknowledged to be the 'best in class' at the activity in question.

**Key terms**

> **Benchmarking** is 'The establishment through data gathering, of targets and comparators, through whose use relative levels of performance (and particularly areas of underperformance) can be identified. By the adoption of identified best practices it is hoped that performance will improve. Types of benchmarking include:
>
> - **Internal benchmarking**, a method of comparing one activity with best practice elsewhere in the same organisation.
>
> - **Functional benchmarking**, in which internal functions are compared with those of the best external practitioners of those functions, regardless of the industry they are in (also known as **operational benchmarking** or **generic benchmarking**).
>
> - **Competitive benchmarking**, in which information is gathered about direct competitors, through techniques such as reverse engineering.
>
> - **Strategic benchmarking**, a type of competitive benchmarking aimed at strategic action and organisational change.' (CIMA *Official Terminology*)

The **benchmarking process** is summarised in the following diagram.

### The benchmarking process

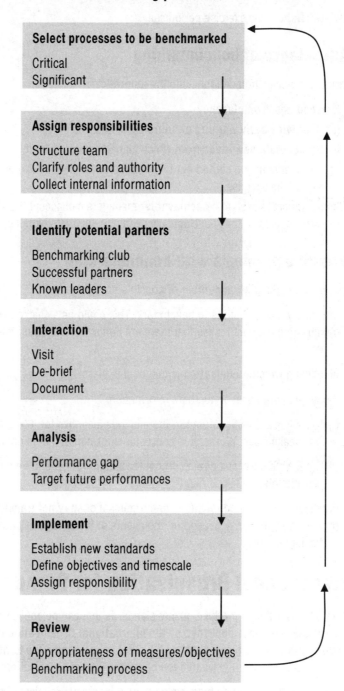

A similar **approach to benchmarking** was described by *Richard Smith* in the February 1996 edition of *CIMA Student*.

**Step 1**     Consider whether the **benefits** to be gained from a benchmarking exercise **justify the time, money and effort involved**.

**Step 2**     Make sure that **those who actually carry out the activity to be benchmarked** form part of the **benchmarking team**.

**Step 3**     **Break down the chosen activity** into specific processes or outputs that are capable of measurement. At an early stage consider how any new information collected will need to be analysed.

**Step 4**     Carry out **internal measurement**.

**Step 5**     Gather **information**, perhaps by means of a pilot survey initially.

**Step 6**     Implement **changes** that are suggested by the exercise and monitor their success.

**Step 7**     **Repeat** the exercise periodically.

## 4.1 Advantages of benchmarking

The advantages of benchmarking include the following.

(a)     It discourages **complacency**.

(b)     It can **provide early warning** of future problems.

(c)     It may **generate new ideas** from which all participants benefit.

(d)     The comparisons are carried out by the people who have to live with any **changes** implemented as a result of the exercise.

(e)     Improvement is seen to be **achievable**: managers can accept that they are not being asked to perform miracles if they have actually seen new methods working in another organisation.

## 4.2 Possible problems with benchmarking

However, benchmarking has a number of possible problems.

(a)     Deciding **which activities** to benchmark. This could be a chicken and egg problem, since the organisation may not realise that there are better ways of doing things until it has seen what others do.

(b)     Identifying **which organisation** is the 'best in class'.

(c)     Persuading organisation to share information.

  (i)     If it is a direct competitor, there is little incentive for it to give away its secrets or reveal its weaknesses. Worse, it may provide information that is not authentic.

  (ii)    Even if it is not a direct competitor a rapport needs to be built up between the organisations and this will take time.

(d)     Practices that get good results in one organisation **may not transfer successfully** to another organisation: they may depend on the talents or knowledge of particular individuals or on a particular culture.

# 5 International Organisation for Standardisation

A number of organisations produce quality standards that can be applied to  variety of organisations. The most widely used are those published by the **International Organisation for Standardisation (ISO)**. (You would reasonably assume that it ought to be IOS, but apparently, the term ISO was chosen because 'iso' in Greek means equal, and ISO wanted to convey the idea of organisations using equivalent standards.)

The ISO 9000 quality standards have been adopted by many organisations world-wide. A company registering for ISO 9000 certification is required to submit its quality standards and procedures to external inspection. If it receives a certificate, it will be subjected to continuing audit. The aim of an ISO 9000 certificate is to provide an **assurance to customers** (and suppliers) of the organisation that its products are made, or its services are delivered, in a way that meets ISO's **standards** for quality.

ISO issue standards applicable to many types of organisations and their standards are updated periodically. The ISO 9000 2000 series of standards consists of four primary standards: ISO 9000, ISO 9001, ISO 9004, and ISO 19011.

(a)     ISO 9001:2000 contains ISO's new quality management system requirements. This is the standard you need to use if you wish to become certified (registered).

(b)    ISO 9000:2000 and ISO 9004:2000 contain ISO's quality management system guidelines. These standards explain ISO's approach to quality management – ISO 9000:2000 presents definitions and discusses terminology, while ISO 9004:2000 is a set of guidelines for improving performance. These two guideline standards help organisations implement quality management, but they are not intended to be used for certification purposes.

(c)    ISO 19011 covers quality auditing standards.

(d)    ISO 14001 relates to environmental management systems. It specifies a process for controlling and improving an organisation's environmental performance. Issues covered include:

- Use and source of raw materials
- Waste
- Noise
- Energy use
- Emissions

## 5.1 ISO certified/registered or ISO compliant?

When a company claims that they are ISO 9000 certified or registered, they mean that an independent registrar has audited their quality system and certified that it meets the ISO 9001:2000 requirements (or the old ISO 9001:1994, 9002:1994, or 9003:1994 requirements). It means that a **registrar has given a written assurance** that ISO's quality management system standard has been met.

When an organisation says that they are ISO 9000 compliant, they mean that they have met ISO's quality system requirements, but have **not been formally certified** by an independent registrar. In effect, they are **self-certified**. Of course, an official Certificate does tend to carry more weight in the market place.

Organisations are granted certified or **compliant** status on the basis that their **processes** rather than their products and services meet ISO 9000 requirements. The ISO 9000 standards are **process standards**, not product standards. The logic is that high quality processes ensure high quality output.

ISO 9000 has been criticised, however, for encouraging a culture of **management by manual**. The requirement to document all procedures and to conduct internal audits of the system and its procedures, is also both time consuming and expensive.

## 5.2 Criticisms of quality accreditation

Many writers and managers have criticised formal quality schemes. These criticisms tend to emphasise the following points.

(a)    Documentation is **expensive** (in terms of time) to produce.

(b)    Rigid policies and procedures **discourage innovation** and initiative.

(c)    The schemes **encourage bureaucracy**.

(d)    The formal methods may not be consistent with ways of working in small and medium-sized organisations.

## 5.3 Other quality schemes and models

There are now many smaller self-assessment models for business/organisation improvement. In Europe, one of the most popular is the **European Quality Foundation** model.

This provides a structured methodology for organisations to measure their own performance in areas that are critical to businesses.

The model provides a basis for measurement of '**enablers**' (leadership, policies, strategies, processes and resources) and '**results**' in relation to customers, employees, society and performance indicators.

Criticisms of this and similar schemes include their **expense** (in terms of time) and the fact that scoring is largely **subjective**.

# 6 Service quality

A **market-led view of quality** is based on the idea that quality can only be defined by customers and occurs where a firm supplies products to a specification that satisfies their needs. Customer expectations serve as standards, so when the service they receive falls short of expectations, dissatisfaction occurs.

**Key term**

**Service quality** is the totality of features and characteristics of that service which bears on its ability to meet stated or implied needs.

## 6.1 Dimensions of service quality

Service quality has a number of dimensions.

(a) **Technical quality** of the service encounter (ie what is received by the customer). Was the meal edible? Was the train on time? Were the shelves fully stocked? Problems of this sort must be addressed by improving the processes of production and delivery.

(b) **Functional quality** of the service encounter (ie how the service is provided). This relates to the psychological interaction between the buyer and seller and is typically perceived in a very subjective way.

   (i) **Relationships between employees**. For instance, do these relationships appear to be professional? Do they chat to each other whilst serving the customer? Does each appear to know their role in the team and the function of their colleagues? Do they know who to refer the customer to in case of the need for more specialist advice? Are they positive about their colleagues or unduly critical?

   (ii) **Appearance and personality of service personnel**. For instance, do they seem interested in the customer and the customer's needs? Are they smartly presented? Do they convey an attractive and positive image? Do they reflect the organisation or brand (eg through uniform/livery)?

   (iii) **Service-mindedness of the personnel**. For instance, do they appear to understand and identify with the needs of the customer? Do they convey competence? Do they show willingness to help?

   (iv) **Accessibility of the service to the customer**. For instance, do the service personnel explain the service in language which the customer can understand?

   (v) **Approachability of service personnel**. For instance, do the service personnel appear alert, interested or welcoming? Or are they day-dreaming, yawning or looking at their watches?

## 6.2 Role of customer

For many service operations, the customer represents both the input and the output of a transformation process eg a patient visiting a dentist.

## 6.3 Satisfaction as a measure

Service quality therefore focuses on the extent of success achieved in creating a **transformed customer**. This can be answered in terms of customer satisfaction and might be calibrated along a 'satisfaction continuum'. *Johnston and Clark* (2001) state that customer satisfaction levels may be 'represented on a continuum from (extreme) delight to (extreme) dissatisfaction'.

| − 5 | 0 | + 5 |
| Dissatisfied | Satisfied | Delighted |

## 6.4 Customer expectations

As suggested above, quality might be measured in terms of the outcome of having a satisfied customer. Going back to the beginning of the transformation process the input is a customer with certain expectations. The organisation delivers a service that is intended to meet those customer expectations. This overall process is depicted as follows.

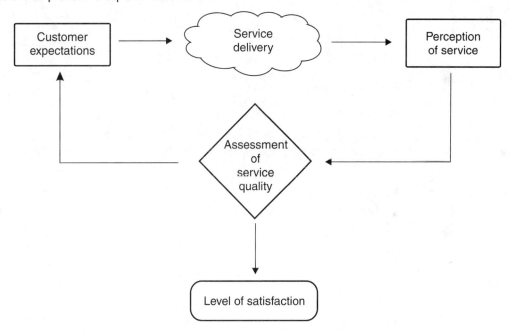

## 6.5 Level of satisfaction

From the above description of the service quality assessment process, mismatches or gaps might arise in two ways.

(a)     The service delivery does not match customer expectations.
(b)     Service delivery matches customer expectations but the customer does not perceive it to do so.

This suggests three areas that should be subject to management attention.

(a)     Influencing of customer expectations
(b)     Design and delivery of the service
(c)     Identification and influencing of customer perception of service

## 6.6 Influencing customer expectations

A prerequisite to being able to manage customers expectations or designing services to meet expectations is to accurately identify and understand them. These expectations are usually expressed in terms of 'service quality factors'.

A customer's preconceived expectations of these factors is likely to influence a customer's assessment of service quality eg a guest at an expensive hotel is likely to expect a high level of attentiveness from the hotel staff. Hence, the outcome of a satisfied or delighted customer can be affected by influencing the starting expectations of the customer.

Various authors have tried to identify generic factors that determine a customer's assessment of service quality. The following is a useful list of 18 **service quality factors**. (*Johnston and Clark*, 2001)

| | | |
|---|---|---|
| Access | Comfort | Friendliness |
| Aesthetics | Commitment | Functionality |
| Attentiveness | Communication | Integrity |
| Availability | Competence | Reliability |
| Care | Courtesy | Responsiveness |
| Cleanliness | Flexibility | Security |

The following diagram and table explain some major factors that shape customer expectations.

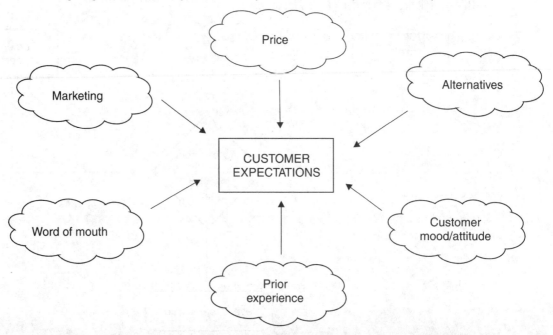

| Factor | Example |
|---|---|
| **Marketing** | Excessive claims may be difficult to deliver eg an optician advertises that no appointments are required, but a client has to actually wait 50 minutes for an eye test. |
| **Price** | Customer expectations usually increase as price increases eg if a hair salon charges high prices, clients expect a good cut and styling. |
| **Alternatives** | A good past experience at one service provider is likely to set the standard next time for an alternative service provider eg a tasty meal at one burger chain is likely to engender expectations of a similar dining experience when visiting another burger outlet. |
| **Word of mouth** | Often this is the most influential source for setting up customer expectations. |

| Factor | Example |
|---|---|
| **Previous experience** | This helps the customer develop a clearer view of what to expect. This adds to the challenge faced by the service provider but on the other hand also helps to moderate the consumers' expectations eg experience of travelling with a certain rail service may inject a certain sense of reality into what a passenger can expect. |
| **Customer's mood and attitude** | It is inevitable that a customer's mood and attitude is likely to influence his or her expectations eg a guest at a restaurant who has received some good news (got a promotion; passed an exam etc) is more likely to be tolerant of slow service. |

### 6.6.1 Service quality factors

There are various ways in which service quality factors may be classified. Four possible categories are explained below.

| Classifications | Comment |
|---|---|
| **Hygiene factors** | These are very much base line factors. If not present will tend to dissatisfy a customer, eg a hotel guest will expect proper security but it is unlikely to delight. |
| **Enhancing factors** | These may partially delight but will not be a source of dissatisfaction if absent eg a hotel guest is likely to really appreciate friendly staff but might not be dissatisfied if they are not all that cheerful. |
| **Critical factors** | These have the potential to delight as well as dissatisfy eg a hotel guest will expect staff responsiveness. |
| **Neutral factors** | These usually have little impact on satisfaction eg a hotel guest may be delighted if a hotel is aesthetically pleasing with nice wallpaper, smart fittings etc, but may well not miss them if not present. |

## Question

Service quality factors

Learning outcome: C(iv)

You have recently been appointed to manage an underground rail system for a major international city.

*Required*

Classify the 18 service quality factors (from the previous section) in terms of the four key categories; **Hygiene factors**; **Critical factors**; **Neutral factors** and **Enhancing factors**.

## Answer

| Hygiene factors | Critical factors | Neutral factors | Enhancing factors |
|---|---|---|---|
| Access | Responsiveness | Comfort | Attentiveness |
| Availability | Communication | Aesthetics | Care |
| Functionality | Competence | | Cleanliness |
| Integrity | | | Commitment |
| Reliability | | | Friendliness |
| Security | | | Courtesy |
| | | | Flexibility |

## 6.7 Dynamic expectations

Again, we are looking at a dynamic rather than a static scenario. The various influences may be stronger or weaker at different times. Hence, consumer expectations are likely to be fluid and dynamic rather than static.

## 6.8 Service delivery

FAST FORWARD

**Service delivery** refers to an entire process not just the final act at the customer or clients interface. The process starts with the initial **design** of the service.

Service delivery refers to the overall process of satisfying the customers needs and addressing the service quality factors, not only the final act of delivering the service.

This entails the entire service operation itself, the resources acquired, the service specifications, the design of the service as well as the overall service style.

### Case Study

XYZ City is a top professional football club. It was very successful in the 1960s and played winning football in an attacking and stylish way. However, the management were reluctant to disband the successful but ageing team and bring in young blood. Hence league performances dropped off, as did gate receipts.

The club's financial position deteriorated and in the 1990s it was taken over by a local self-made businessman, who was cautious with his money. By now transfer fees required to buy new players had become sky high but the new chairman was reluctant to pay what he called 'silly money'. He appointed a hard-nosed coach who emphasised the importance of defensive strength, keeping a clean sheet and winning by sneaking the odd goal, playing the so-called long-ball game. The players he required were steady, strong ball winners and he was very suspicious of 'flair players'. Results improved, however fans began to call for the manager to resign.

Here we have the scenario where the club management failed to identify, or perhaps ignored, the paying fans' expectations for stylish football. It assembled its operations resources (the players) and designed its service style (game plans and tactics) in a way that was not compatible with fans' expectations for attacking football played with flair and style.

So, the club in effect failed to deliver the service its customers expected. Hence, instead of having delighted fans, the club had frustrated and dissatisfied supporters.

This example demonstrates the importance of ensuring that **the service delivered matches customer expectations**. It also highlights the need to **manage customer expectations** to ensure that they are **realistic** and **reasonable**.

## 6.9 Perception of service

In product operations there is a physical output which is relatively easy to observe or measure in terms of quality. With service operations, the expression 'perception is reality' applies eg a training organisation employs an accountancy lecturer whom they believe has excellent presentation skills. However, appraisal forms completed by trainees give the tutor low scores for presentation skills.

Differences arise between the service delivered and the customers' perception of quality because people filter what they see and experience.

| Behaviour | Example |
|---|---|
| **Selective filtering** | A trainee blocks out factors relating to a tutor's skills he/she deems irrelevant to current needs eg a long discussion about the tutor's practical experiences. |
| **Selective distortion** | A trainee tries to reinterpret the contents of a lecture in terms of his or her own beliefs. |
| **Selective retention** | A trainee only remembers those aspects of a lecture that match his/her needs. |

# 7 Total productive maintenance (TPM)

**Total productive maintenance** or TPM originated in Japan. It is defined as 'the productive maintenance carried out by all employees through small group activities'.

'Productive maintenance' is defined as 'maintenance management which recognises the importance of reliability, maintenance and economic efficiency in plant design.' (*Nakajima*, 1988).

## 7.1 Five goals of TPM

The goals of TPM are:

(a) **Improve equipment effectiveness**. The goal should be to examine how the facilities of an operation are contributing to its effectiveness. Loss of effectiveness could be caused by defects, down-times and loss of operating speed.

(b) **Achieve autonomous maintenance**. The employees who use an item of equipment should be allowed to take on some of the responsibility for its maintenance. Specialist maintenance staff should be encouraged to take on the responsibility for improving maintenance performance.

(c) **Plan maintenance**. Maintenance should be planned, and the frequency and level of preventive maintenance and standards for condition-based maintenance should be specified.

(d) **Train all staff in maintenance skills**.

(e) **Achieve early equipment management**. This goal is linked to maintenance prevention, by which the causes of failure and the ease of maintenance of an item of equipment are considered at the design , manufacture, commissioning and installation stages, ie before the equipment is brought into operation.

One possible approach is shown in the steps below.

---

**Step 1**

**Discover** what the nature of the failure has been, its possible consequences, and the reasons why it has happened. Finding out the reason for a failure is not, at this stage, an in-depth investigation. Being aware of the reason for the failure can, however, help with making a decision about what the recovery procedure should be.

---

**Step 2**

**Act** by:

(i) Telling people involved what you propose to do about the failure, for example by keeping customers informed

(ii) Containing the failure in order to stop the consequences from spreading

(iii) Following up to make sure that the containing action has been successful.

---

**Step 3**

**Learn**. Use the failure as a learning opportunity, to find out in some depth why the failure occurred and 'engineering out' the cause to prevent it from happening again.

---

**Step 4**

**Plan**. Operations managers should incorporate the lessons learned from past failures to plan how they would deal with similar failures in the future. This involves identifying what failures might occur and their reasons and devising formal procedures to be followed if and when they occur.

---

## 7.2 Business continuity

Business continuity is a term used to describe measures to help an operation to **prevent or recover from failures**, and to continue operating in the event of a **disaster**. A disaster is a critical malfunction, that stops normal operations and might totally disrupt the business of the organisation (eg a key supplier going out of business, a major computer system failure, a bomb blast at a key location and so on).

A business continuity approach is to:

(a) Identify and assess the risks of various disasters happening.

(b) Identify core business processes, and put them into an order of priority. If the business is severely disrupted, the most urgent requirement would be to bring back into operation those processes at the top of the priority list. Make sure that employees understand these priorities.

(c) Quantify recovery times.

(d) Determine what resources will be needed to carry out the recovery, and make sure that the resources will be available if and when required.

(e) Communicate with everyone in the operation, to make sure they know what they will be required to do in the event of a disaster.

# 8 Business process re-engineering (BPR)

BPR's internal focus contrasts with benchmarking which often has a focus external to the organisation or department concerned.

The changes that may be made to processes as a result of a BPR exercise may be classified as automation, rationalisation or re-engineering.

Automation and rationalisation are relatively the most common forms of organisational change. They usually offer modest returns and little risk. **Automation** usually involves assisting employees to carry out their duties more efficiently – for example introducing a computerised accounting package.

**Rationalisation** involves not only the automation of a process but also efficient process design. For example, an automated banking system requires the standardisation of account number structure and standard rules for calculating daily account balances – in this situation automation encouraged a certain amount of rationalisation.

**Business process re-engineering** (BPR) involves fundamental changes in the way an organisation functions. *Hammer and Champy* identified the main themes of BPR as **creative use of IT**, **process re-orientation**, **ambition** and **rule breaking**. The main writing on the subject is contained in their *Reengineering the Corporation* (1993), from which the following definition is taken.

The key words here are 'fundamental', 'radical', 'dramatic' and 'process'.

(a)    'Fundamental' and radical indicate that BPR assumes nothing: it starts by asking basic questions such as 'why do we do what we do', without making any assumptions or looking back to what has always been done in the past.

(b)    'Dramatic' means that BPR should achieve 'quantum leaps in performance', not just marginal, incremental improvements.

(c)    'Process' is explained in the following paragraphs.

**Key term**

> A **process** is a collection of activities that takes one or more kinds of input and creates an output.

For **example**, order fulfilment is a process that takes an order as its input and results in the delivery of the ordered goods. Part of this process is the manufacture of the goods, but under BPR the aim of manufacturing is **not merely to make** the goods. Manufacturing should aim to **deliver the goods that were ordered,** and any aspect of the manufacturing process that hinders this aim should be re-engineered. The first question to ask might be 'Do they need to be manufactured at all; should they be purchased from another organisation?'

A re-engineered process has certain **characteristics**.

- Often several jobs are **combined** into one
- Workers often **make decisions**
- The **steps** in the process are performed in **a logical order**
- **Work** is performed where it **makes most sense**
- Checks and controls may be reduced, and **quality 'built-in'**
- One manager provides a **single point of contact**
- The advantages of **centralised and decentralised** operations are combined

## 8.1 Example: BPR

This scenario is based on a problem at Ford.

A company employs 25 staff to perform the standard accounting task of matching goods received notes with orders and then with invoices. About 80% of their time is spent trying to find out why 20% of the set of three documents do not agree.

One way of improving the situation would have been to computerise the existing process to facilitate matching. This would have helped, but BPR went further: why accept any incorrect orders at all?

> 'What if all the orders are entered onto a computerised database? When goods arrive at the goods inwards department they either agree to goods that have been ordered or they don't. It's as simple as that. Goods that agree to an order are accepted and paid for. Goods that are not agreed are *sent back* to the supplier. There are no files of unmatched items and time is not wasted trying to sort out these files.'
>
> (Alan Lewin, 'Business process re-engineering', *CIMA Student,* February 1996)

*Lewin* notes the gains for the company: less staff time wasted, quicker payment for suppliers, lower stocks, and lower investment in working capital.

## 8.2 Principles of BPR

*Hammer* presents **seven principles** for BPR.

(a)    Processes should be designed to achieve a desired **outcome** rather than focusing on existing **tasks**.

(b)    Personnel who use the **output** from a process should **perform** the process. For example, a company could set up a database of approved suppliers; this would allow personnel who actually require supplies to order them themselves, perhaps using online technology, thereby eliminating the need for a separate purchasing function.

(c)    Information processing should be **included** in the work which **produces** the information. This eliminates the differentiation between information gathering and information processing.

(d)    **Geographically-dispersed** resources should be treated as if they are **centralised.** This allows the benefits of centralisation to be obtained, for example, economies of scale through central negotiation of supply contracts, without losing the benefits of decentralisation, such as flexibility and responsiveness.

(e)    Parallel activities should be **linked** rather than **integrated**. This would involve, for example, co-ordination between teams working on different aspects of a single process.

(f)    'Doers' should be allowed to be **self-managing**. The traditional distinction between workers and managers can be abolished: decision aids such as expert systems can be provided where they are required.

(g)    Information should be captured **once** at **source**. Electronic distribution of information makes this possible.

## 8.3 Is there a BPR methodology?

*Davenport* and *Short* prescribe a **five-step approach** to BPR.

**Step 1**    Develop the **business vision and process objectives**. BPR is driven by a business vision which implies specific business objectives such as cost reduction, time reduction, output quality improvement, Total Quality Management and empowerment.

**Step 2**    **Identify the processes** to be redesigned. Most firms use the 'high impact' approach, which focuses on the most important processes or those that conflict most with the business vision. Lesser number of firms use the 'Exhaustive' approach that attempts to identify all the processes within an organisation and then prioritise them in order of redesign urgency.

**Step 3**    Understand and **measure the existing processes** – to ensure previous mistakes are not repeated and to provide a baseline for future improvements.

**Step 4**    **Identify IT levers**. Awareness of IT capabilities could prove useful when designing processes.

**Step 5**    Design and **build a prototype** of the new process. The actual design should not be viewed as the end of the BPR process – it should be viewed as a prototype, with successive alterations. The use of a prototype enables the involvement of customers.

## 8.4 Information technology and BPR

Simply computerising existing ways of doing things does not mean a process has been re-engineered. Technology may be able to add value by re-designing business processes.

IT is not the solution in itself, it is an **enabler**. BPR uses IT to allow an organisation to do things that it is not doing already. For example, teleconferencing reduces the cost of travelling to meetings – a re-engineering approach takes the view that teleconferencing allows more frequent meetings.

As *Hammer* and *Champy* put it, 'It is this disruptive power of technology, its ability to break the rules that limit how we conduct our work, that makes it critical to companies looking for competitive advantage.'

Examples of how technology has changed the way work is conducted include:

(a)    **Shared databases** allow information to be accessed simultaneously from many locations.

(b)    **Expert systems** may allow non-specialists to do work that previously required an expert.

(c)    **Telecommunications networks** mean that businesses can simultaneously reap the rewards of centralisation and decentralisation.

(d)    **Decision support tools** allow decisions to be made by a larger number of staff.

(e)    **Wireless** communication technology allows staff 'in the field' to send and receive information wherever they are.

(f)     **Interactive websites** allow personalised contact with many customers (or at least the appearance of personalised contact).

(g)     Automatic identification and **tracking technology** allows the whereabouts of objects or people to be monitored.

(h)     High performance computing allows **instant** revision of plans rather than periodic updates.

## 8.5 Problems with BPR

There are concerns that BPR has become misunderstood. According to an independent study of 100 European companies, BPR has become allied in managers' minds with narrow targets such as reductions in staff numbers and other **cost-cutting** measures.

*Champy* suggests that management itself should be re-engineered. Managers are not used to thinking in systems terms, so, instead of looking at the **whole picture** (which might affect their own jobs), they tend to **seize on individual aspects** of the organisation.

It is argued that process re-engineering is really only a part of the **wider picture**. A report in the *Financial Times* on an unnamed company suggested four sets of changes as important to the transformation from a company which **satisfies** customers, to a company that **delights** them – and from a company which is **competent** to a company which is the **best** in its industry. Extracts from the report follow.

'... **first, breaking down barriers** between its different disciplinary specialists and national units by a series of procedural and structural steps, of which the re-engineering of cross-unit processes is only one;

second, **developing an explicit set of values** and behaviour guidelines which are subscribed to (or 'shared') by everyone in the organisation;

third, **redefining the role of management** in order to foster much more empowerment, responsibility and decisiveness at every level.

All this requires the creation of the **fourth factor: an unprecedented degree of openness** and trust among managers and employees'.

### Case Study

*Workflow systems / process re-engineering*

'Work design, whether it is related to work in the factory or at the desk, is a process of arriving at the most **efficient** way of completing tasks and activities that minimises effort and reduces the possibility of mistakes. It is involved in increasing productivity and efficiency whilst maintaining or improving quality standards.

'**Today work design is often referred to as process re-engineering** and has a bad press because the perceived outcome is reduced employee numbers or downsizing. As we move increasingly to a computerised workplace the use of workflow systems is growing and changing the nature of work from one of social contact to service to the system.

'A **workflow system** is a system that organises work and allocates it to particular workstations for the attention of the person operating the workstation. The system usually also incorporates a document-management facility. There are three main forms in which workflow systems operate. These are on the **casework basis**, the **flowline basis** or an **ad hoc basis**.

'The **casework** basis functions by knowing the individual caseload of staff and directs existing cases to the appropriate caseworker and new cases or customers are allocated on the basis of equalising caseload.

'The **flowline** approach allocates a small number of tasks to each operator and the case flows along the line from screen to screen. The **ad hoc** system works on the basis of equalising workload, regardless of who may have dealt with the case previously. The choice depends on the particular circumstances of the business and the approach taken to customer service.

'**Workflow management provides supervisors with information on screen** about the workloads of individuals and information on their processing capabilities with statistics for average time taken to deal with a case, errors detected by the system as a percentage of cases, and so on. This information is intended to ensure that staff receive appropriate support and training, but can be and is used for bonus payments and league tables of performance.

'In one organisation where workflow has been used in sales-order processing, the use of the management statistics has become quite draconian and the average period of employment of sales-order staff is three months.

'The **advantages** and benefits of workflow systems come mainly from improvements in productivity and efficiency and better or speedier services to customers.

'Offset against these benefits are the **disadvantages** stemming from the way that workflow systems are implemented and managed.

'A list of the **benefits from the employer's point of view** would be:

- More efficient office procedures
- Providing workflow management
- Equalising of workloads
- Monitoring of operator performance
- Better security
- Ensuring work gets done when it should get done

'The **dangers** lie in the segmentation or specialisation in a small number of tasks before passing the work on to the next person's screen, almost like a production line. This **de-skilling** of work increases boredom and leads to high staff turnover. It also reduces social contact to a minimum and the contact that does exist takes place via the system.

'So far the casework approach, where staff deal with cases as a 'one stop shop', is the most empowering and beneficial for staff. The skills needed are high and there is a greater sense of completion and satisfaction for operators.

'In the flowline approach people are demoralised at the repetitive nature of the work. Ad hoc approaches seem to fall between two stools – there is work satisfaction to a degree and no sense of continuing customer contact.'

*Adapted from: 'Computer talk – Workflow systems Trevor Bentley – CIMA Articles database*

# 9 The TQMEX model

The **TQMEX model** shows the relationship between quality management and other aspects of operations management.

As we explained earlier, TQM focuses on the specific needs of customers in an increasingly competitive marketplace.

In order to fully understand TQM we need to understand how all elements of an organisation work towards the ultimate goal – customer satisfaction (usually achieved through superior quality).

*Ho* (1999) devised his TQMEX model to indicate the relationship between quality management and other aspects of operations management. The model demonstrates how contemporary **approaches** to quality may be **integrated** to achieve a **philosophy of quality** throughout the organisation.

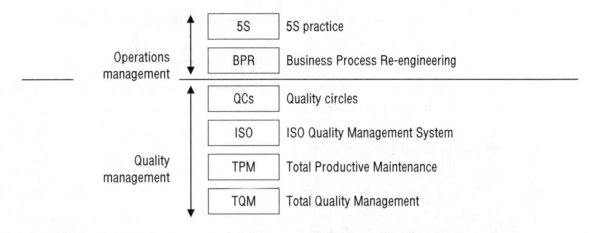

Ho's TQMEX model

**Exam focus point**

The May 2007 exam offered ten-marks for a discussion of the requirements to achieve total quality within an organisation.

# Chapter Roundup

- **Quality management** is concerned with ensuring that products or services are fit for their purpose, and meet specifications.

- Traditional approaches to quality were focused on **inspection**. Modern approaches to quality focus on the **prevention** of defects through quality standards and processes.

- **Total quality management (TQM)** is a management philosophy, aimed at continuous improvement in quality standards.

- **Aspects of TQM** include getting things right first time, **preventing defective production** or service delivery and meeting the needs and expectations of customers or clients. TQM often involves the notion of **internal suppliers** and **internal customers** linked in **quality chains**.

- **TQM** includes a certain amount of procedures, but to be effective it also requires employee participation, **empowerment** and **teamwork**.

- There are four types of **quality costs; prevention**, **appraisal/inspection**, **internal failure** and **external failure**.

- The 5Ss are **structurise**, **systemise**, **sanitise**, **standardise** and **self-discipline**.

- **Six Sigma** is a process that is designed to assist organisations to focus on developing and delivering **near-perfect products and services**.

- The goal of **lean production** is 'to get the right things to the right place at the right time, the first time, while **minimising waste** and being open to change'.

- **Benchmarking** is essentially an analysis of one's own **performance compared** with that of another entity. Ideally the other entity is one that is acknowledged to be the 'best in class' at the activity in question.

- A **market-led view of quality** is based on the idea that quality can only be defined by customers and occurs where a firm supplies products to a specification that satisfies their needs. Customers expectations serve as standards, so when the service they receive falls short of expectations, dissatisfaction occurs.

- **Service delivery** refers to an entire process not just the final act at the customer or clients interface. The process starts with the initial **design** of the service.

- **Total productive maintenance** or TPM originated in Japan. It is defined as 'the productive maintenance carried out by all employees through small group activities'.

- **Business process re-engineering (BPR)** involves focussing attention **inwards** to consider how **business processes** could be redesigned or re-engineered to improve efficiency.

- The **TQMEX model** shows the relationship between quality management and other aspects of operations management.

1  Define 'quality'.

2  What are the problems of the 'inspection' approach to quality?

3  List five principles of TQM.

   1  .............................................................
   2  .............................................................
   3  .............................................................
   4  .............................................................
   5  .............................................................

4  List four implications of TQM that could impact across the whole organisation.

   1  .............................................................
   2  .............................................................
   3  .............................................................
   4  .............................................................

5  Which of the following is not one of the 5Ss?

   A  Structurise
   B  Systemise
   C  Simplify
   D  Self-discipline

6  List five advantages of benchmarking.

   1  .............................................................
   2  .............................................................
   3  .............................................................
   4  .............................................................
   5  .............................................................

7  What is the difference between ISO compliant and ISO registered?

8  List four service quality factors.

   1  .............................................................
   2  .............................................................
   3  .............................................................
   4  .............................................................

9  State two goals of TPM.

   1  .............................................................
   2  .............................................................

10  List two possible limitations of BPR.

   1  .............................................................
   2  .............................................................

11  Who devised the TQMEX model?

   A  Kaplan and Norton
   B  Deming
   C  Ouchi
   D  Ho

1    Quality may be defined as the totality of features and characteristics of a product or service which bears on its ability to meet stated or implied needs.

2    Any three from the following.

- The inspection process itself does not add value: if it could be guaranteed that no defective items were produced, there would be no need for a separate inspection function.

- The inspection function itself involves the delocation of resources in terms of both people and facilities.

- The production of substandard products is a waste of raw materials, machine time, human efforts, and overheads (as the substandard production has to be administered).

- The production of defects is not compatible with newer production techniques such as just-in-time: there is no time for inspection.

- Working capital is tied up in inventories which cannot be sold.

- In a service industry, damage may already have been done to customer relations before inspection takes place.

3    Any five from the following: prevention, principle, right first time, zero defects, eliminate waste, everybody's concern, internal customers, quality chains, continuous improvement, employee participation and teamwork.

4    Four possible implications are: *TQM* involves giving employees a say in the processes they are involved in, and in getting them to suggest improvements. *TQM* implies a greater discipline to the process of production and the establishment of better linkages between the business functions. *TQM* involves new relationships with suppliers, which requires them to improve their output quality so that less effort is spent rectifying poor input. *TQM* requires work standardisation and employee commitment.

5    C    The other elements are sanitise and standardise.

6    Advantages include; discourages complacency, may provide early warning of problems, may generate new ideas from which all participants benefit, those involved are those who would be affected, encourages the attitude that improvement is achievable.

7    Companies who are ISO compliant have effectively self-certified themselves. ISO registered companies have been formally certified by a registrar.

8    Hygiene, enhancing, critical and neutral factors.

9    Any two of: improve equipment effectiveness, achieve autonomous maintenance, plan maintenance, train all staff in maintenance skills and achieve early equipment management.

10   Possible limitations include: BPR has become associated with narrow targets such as reductions in staff numbers and other cost-cutting measures. Managers may not look at the whole picture and focus on individual aspects of the organisation. Some believe greater emphasis should be on new processing.

11   D    *Ho* devised the TQMEX model.

Now try the question below from the Exam Question Bank

| Number | Level | Marks | Time |
|--------|-------|-------|------|
| 6 | Examination | 30 | 54 mins |

# Managing human capital

# 7

# Human resource management

## Introduction

In this chapter we start our coverage of **human resource management (HRM)**.

By way of introduction, we note that HRM is different from traditional personnel management. Human resource management takes a **strategic** approach to an organisation's recruitment, training and appraisal systems, in addition to personnel administration. The ultimate purpose of HRM is strategic success.

Any requirement for human resources revealed in the strategy-making process can be met by a mix of recruitment from outside or promotion from within (depending on the demography of the organisation and its internal labour markets).

Organisations today often require a flexible and versatile workforce, leading to a growth in part-time working, teleworking and so on. This is discussed in the context of personnel planning.

Recruitment and induction are important HRM activities. These are covered towards the end of the chapter, which concludes with a look at ethical and legal issues relevant to HRM.

| Topic list | Learning outcomes | Syllabus references | Ability required |
|---|---|---|---|
| 1 What is human resource management? | E(i), E(v) | E(1), E(2) | Comprehension |
| 2 Human resource management theories | E(i) | E(9) | Comprehension |
| 3 Assessing human resource needs: the HR plan | E(i), E(ii), E(v) | E(2), E(3), E(13) | Evaluation |
| 4 Recruitment | E(iii) | E(4) | Evaluation |
| 5 Selection | E(iii) | E(4), E(7) | Evaluation |
| 6 Induction | E(iii) | E(8) | Evaluation |
| 7 Legal and ethical issues | E(vi) | E(5), E(14) | Comprehension |

# 1 What is human resource management?

**Human resource management** (HRM) is the process of evaluating an organisation's human resource needs, finding people to fill those needs, and getting the best work from each employee by providing the right incentives and job environment – with the overall aim of helping achieve organisational goals.

## 1.1 Scope of human resource management

**Personnel management** in the past was never perceived to have a strategic role, dealing as it did with issues of hiring and firing, industrial relations and so forth. Human resource management (HRM) is concerned with the most effective use of human resources. It deals with organisation, staffing levels, motivation, employee relations and employee services.

Human resource management (HRM) is concerned with a strategic approach to people at work and their relationships as they arise in the working environment.

### 1.1.1 The objectives of HRM

It is possible to identify **four main objectives of HRM**.

(a) To develop an effective human component for the organisation which will respond effectively to change.

(b) To obtain and develop the human resources required by the organisation and to use and motivate them effectively.

(c) To create and maintain a co-operative climate of relationships within the organisation and to this end to perform a 'firefighting' role dealing with disputes as they arise.

(d) To meet the organisation's social and legal responsibilities relating to the human resource.

### 1.1.2 Why is HRM important?

Effective human resource management and employee development are strategically necessary for the following reasons.

(a) To **increase productivity**. Developing employee skills might make employees more productive, hence the recent emphasis on public debate on the value of training.

(b) To **enhance group learning**. Employees work more and more in multi-skilled teams. Each employee has to be competent at several tasks. Some employees have to be trained to work together (ie in teamworking skills).

(c) To **reduce staff turnover**. Reducing staff turnover, apart from cutting recruitment costs, can also increase the effectiveness of operations. In service businesses, such as hotels, or retail outlets, reductions in staff turnover can be linked with repeat visits by customers. As it is cheaper to keep existing customers than to find new ones, this can have a significant effect on profitability.

(d) To **encourage initiative.** Organisations can gain significant advantage from encouraging and exploiting the present and potential abilities of the people within them.

## 1.2 Views of human resource management

### 1.2.1 Personnel management: the old view

The **traditional view** of personnel management has involved:

- Setting general and specific management policy for employment relationships
- Collective bargaining with employees
- Finding, getting and holding prescribed types and numbers of employees

- Providing opportunities for personal development and growth as well as requisite skills and experience
- Incentivising: developing and maintaining the motivation in work
- Reviewing employee performance

### 1.2.2 Human resource management

FAST FORWARD

> **Human resource management (HRM)** is based on the assumption that the management and deployment of staff is a key **strategic** factor in an organisation's competitive performance. HRM requires top management involvement and the promotion of culture and **values,** so that employees' **commitment**, as opposed merely to their consent, is obtained.

Human resource management (HRM) reflects a wider view than traditional personnel management.

*Armstrong* (2003) defined HRM as 'a strategic approach to the acquisition, motivation, development and management of the organisation's human resources.'

*Bratton and Gold* (1999) gave a more detailed definition. 'HRM emphasises that employees are crucial to achieving sustainable competitive advantage, that human resources practices need to be integrated with the corporate strategy, and that human resource specialists help organisational controllers to meet both efficiency and equity objectives.'

A precise interpretation of HRM centres on the following notions.

(a)    The personnel function has become centrally concerned with issues of broader relevance to the business and its objectives, such as change management, the introduction of technology, and the implications of falling birth rates and skill shortages for the resourcing of the business.

(b)    HRM should be **integrated with strategic planning**, that is, with management at the broadest and highest level. The objectives of the HR function should be directly related to achieving the organisation's goals for growth, competitive gain and improvement of 'bottom line' performance.

(c)    HRM managers should be professionals.

*S Tyson* and *A Fell* (*Evaluating the Personnel Function*) suggest **four major roles** for human resource management which illustrate the shift in emphasis to the strategic viewpoint.

(a)    To represent the organisation's **central value system** (or culture).
(b)    To **maintain the boundaries of the organisation** (its identity and the flow of people in and out of it).
(c)    To provide **stability and continuity** (through planned succession, flexibility and so on).
(d)    To adapt the organisation to **change**.

Some companies will have a separate human resource function with staff authority over other departments. Smaller companies may not be able to afford the luxury of such a function.

HRM is thus a **set of activities** that may or may not have a separate department to manage it.

**Exam focus point**

> The November 2005 paper had 10 marks available for explaining the role of a newly named 'HR' division (the division was previously named 'personnel').

## 1.3 The human resource cycle

A relatively simple model that provides a framework for explaining the nature and significance of HRM is the human resource cycle (*Devanna* 1984).

The model is shown below.

**Human resource cycle**

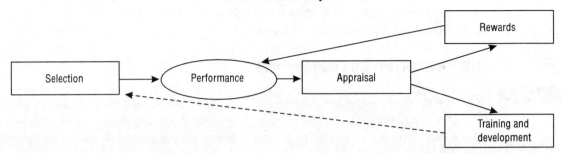

**Selection** is important to ensure the organisation obtains people with the qualities and skills required.

**Appraisal** enables targets to be set that contribute to the achievement of the overall strategic objectives of the organisation. It also identifies skills and performance gaps, and provides information relevant to reward levels.

**Training and development** ensure skills remain up-to-date, relevant, and comparable with (or better than) the best in the industry.

The **reward system** should motivate and ensure valued staff are retained.

**Performance** depends upon each of the four components and how they are co-ordinated.

## 1.4 The Guest model of HRM

*David Guest* (1997) developed a model to show the relationship between an organisation's HRM strategy and HRM activities.

| Guest's six components | | | | | |
|---|---|---|---|---|---|
| ① HRM strategy | ② HRM practices | ③ HRM outcomes | ④ Behavioural outcomes | ⑤ Performance outcomes | ⑥ Financial outcomes |
| Differentiation (innovation)<br><br><br>Focus (quality)<br><br><br>Cost (cost reduction) | Selection<br>Training<br>Appraisal<br>Rewards<br>Job redesign<br>Involvement<br>Status and security | Commitment<br>Quality<br>Flexibility | Effort<br>Motivation<br>Co-operation<br>Involvement<br>Organisational citizenship | *High:*<br>Productivity<br>Quality<br>Innovation<br>*Low:*<br>Absenteeism<br>Employee turnover<br>Conflict<br>Customer complaints | Profits<br>Return on investment |

The model proposes that HRM practices should aim to result in high staff commitment and high quality, flexible employees. Achieving these three HRM outcomes will facilitate the achievement of the behavioural, performance and financial outcomes shown in the table.

## 1.5 Limitations of HRM models

Models of HRM practices (such as *Devanna's* and *Guest's*) tend to underestimate the influence of external opportunities or threats and internal strengths and weaknesses.

External factors such as competition, technology, political/legal factors, economic factors and social/cultural factors will all impact upon HRM.

Internal factors such as the organisational structure and culture will also impact upon HRM.

In addition, the way people are managed often depends upon the approach favoured by their line manager. Some managers favour the 'hard' or rational approach – others believe in a 'softer' approach that emphasises individual and organisational development.

Cultural, economic and legal traditions within a country will also shape HR policies. For example, in Japan and the USA there is little state intervention in business and therefore organisations are free to form their own practices. However, in communist and former communist states such as China and Eastern European countries there is a high degree of state intervention and little choice for individual organisations. In Western Europe, strong education and welfare systems create indirect state intervention that has substantial influence on the labour market.

## Case Study

**London bus drivers**

The pressures faced by recruiters and, indeed, human resources managers in general is exemplified by recruiting for the bus industry. Here, problems of staff turnover, reward, recruitment catchment areas and pools, labour market trends and key stakeholder pressures are thrown into sharp focus.

London bus drivers tend to stay in a job for less than a year. The capital's bus companies are facing the highest levels of staff turnover since the 1950s. A combination of the reviving economy and the expanding London bus network means that some bus companies are having to replace up to 40 per cent of drivers a year.

Pay is one issue, shift work is another. But the bus companies, competing in a deregulated market, are under pressure to match their services to commuter needs, rather than the body clocks of their drivers.

The squeeze on numbers is now so acute that some bus companies are looking outside London for staff. Other bus companies in London believe that recruiting drivers from outside their local area spells trouble. Instead, it has broadened its recruitment policy to include significantly older and younger drivers, as well as more women.

# 2 Human resource management theories

**FAST FORWARD**

*Taylor, Mayo, Schein, Weber, Lawrence* and *Lorsch* propose some important HRM theories.

In this section we look at some of the most significant theories related to the management of people. Note that we cover the related area of motivational theories in Chapter 8.

## 2.1 Taylor: scientific management

We start back around the year 1900, when *Frederick W Taylor* pioneered the **scientific management** movement. He argued that management should be based on 'well-recognised, clearly defined and fixed principles, instead of depending on more or less hazy ideas.' Taylor was an engineer and mostly concerned with **engineering** management. His aim was increased **efficiency** in production, that is, increased productivity. His methods were later applied to many other types of work.

### 2.1.1 Principles of scientific management

The **principles of scientific management** are outlined below.

(a)  **The development of a true science of work**. 'All knowledge which had hitherto been kept in the heads of workmen should be gathered and recorded by **management**. Every single subject, large and small, becomes the question for scientific investigation, for reduction to law.'

(b)  **The scientific selection and progressive development of workers:** workers should be carefully trained and given jobs to which they are best suited.

(c)  **The bringing together of the science and the scientifically selected and trained men**. The application of techniques to decide what should be done and how, using workers who are both properly trained and willing to maximise output, should result in maximum productivity.

(d)    **The constant and intimate co-operation between management and workers:** 'the relations between employers and men form without question the most important part of this art.' There is much that is relevant today in this approach and the pursuit of productivity is still a major preoccupation for management at all levels. 'Business Process Re-engineering' is lineally descended from Scientific Management.

### 2.1.2 Examples of Scientific Management

The following are **examples of Scientific Management** in practice.

(a)    **Work study techniques** established the 'one best way' to do any job. No discretion was allowed to the worker. Subsequently, *Henry Ford's* approach to mass production broke each job down into its smallest and simplest component parts: these single elements became the newly-designed job.

(b)    **Planning the work and doing the work were separated.** Workers did what they were told - they did not have any control over how they completed a task.

(c)    **Workers were paid incentives** on the basis of acceptance of the new methods and output norms as the new methods greatly increased productivity and profits.

(d)    All aspects of the work environment were **tightly controlled** in order to attain maximum productivity.

 Case Study

It is useful to consider an application of Taylor's principles. In testimony to the House of Representatives Committee in 1912, Taylor used as an example the application of scientific management methods to shovelling work at the Bethlehem Steel Works.

(a)    Facts were first gathered by management as to the number of shovel loads handled by each man each day, with particular attention paid to the relationship between weight of the average shovel load and the total load shifted per day. From these facts, management was able to decide on the ideal shovel size for each type of material handled in order to optimise the speed of shovelling work done. Thus, scientific technique was applied to deciding how work should be organised.

(b)    By organising work a day in advance, it was possible to minimise the idle time and the moving of men from one place in the shovelling yard to another. Once again, scientific method replaces 'seat-of-the-pants' decisions by supervisors.

(c)    Workers were paid for accepting the new methods and 'norms' and received 60% higher wages than those given to similar workers in other companies in the area.

(d)    Workers were carefully selected and trained in the art of shovelling properly; anyone consistently falling below the required norms was given special teaching to improve his performance.

(e)    'The new way is to teach and help your men as you would a brother; to try to teach him the best way and to show him the easiest way to do his work. This is the new mental attitude of the management towards the men....'

(f)    At the Bethlehem Steel Works, Taylor said, the costs of implementing this method were more than repaid by the benefits. The labour force required fell from 500 men to 140 men for the same work.

## 2.2 Mayo, Schein: Human relations

In the 1930s, a critical perception of scientific management emerged. *Elton Mayo* was pioneered a new approach called **human relations**. This concentrated mainly on the concept of 'Social Man' *(Schein)*: **people are motivated by 'social' or 'belonging' needs**, which are satisfied by the social relationships they form at work.

Attention shifted towards people's higher psychological needs for growth, challenge, responsibility and self-fulfilment. *Herzberg* (see later) suggested that only these things could positively motivate employees to improved performance.

The human relations approaches contributed an important awareness of the influence of the human factor at work on organisational performance.

(a)     Most theorists offered guidelines to enable practising managers to satisfy and motivate employees and so (theoretically) to obtain improved productivity.

(b)     However, as far as the practising manager is concerned there is still **no simple link between job satisfaction and productivity** or the achievement of organisational goals.

### 2.3 Weber: Bureaucracy, rational form

In the 1940's, *Max Weber* a German sociologist developed a theory of **bureaucracy**. Under bureaucracy, authority is bestowed by dividing an organisation into jurisdictional areas (production, marketing, sales and so on) each with specified duties. Authority to carry them out is given to the officials in charge, and rules and regulations are established in order to ensure their achievement. Managers get things done because their orders are accepted as legitimate and justified. *Weber* suggested that organisations naturally evolved toward this **rational** form.

### 2.4 Lawrence and Lorsch: Contingency theory

Another very important development in the study of organisations is **contingency theory**, a concept based upon the idea that the organisation structure and the management approach must be tailored to the situation. They argued there is no one best way to manage.

One form of contingency theory was developed by *Lawrence and Lorsch* (1967). They concluded that organisations in a stable environment are more effective if they have more detailed procedures and a more centralised decision-making process while organisations in an unstable environment should have decentralisation, employee participation, and less emphasis on rules and standard procedures to be effective.

# 3 Assessing human resource needs: the HR plan

**FAST FORWARD**

**HRM planning** should be based on the **organisation's strategic planning processes**, with relation to analysis of the labour market, forecasting of the external supply and internal demand for labour, job analysis and plan implementation.

**Key term**

**Planning** '(the) establishment of objectives, and the formulation, evaluation and selection of the policies, strategies, tactics and action required to achieve them'.

Human resource planning concerns the acquisition, utilisation, improvement and return of an enterprise's human resources. Human resource planning deals with:

*   Budgeting and cost control
*   Recruitment
*   Retention (company loyalty, to retain skills and reduce staff turnover)
*   Downsizing (reducing staff numbers)
*   Training and retraining to enhance the skills base
*   Dealing with changing circumstances

**The process of human resources planning**

```
┌─────────────────────────────────────────────┐
│ 1. STRATEGIC ANALYSIS                         │
│   •   of the environment                      │
│   •   of the organisation's manpower strengths and │
│       weaknesses, opportunities and threats   │
│   •   of the organisation's use of employees  │
│   •   of the organisation's objectives        │
└─────────────────────────────────────────────┘
                      ↓
┌─────────────────────────────────────────────┐
│ 2. FORECASTING                                │
│   •   of internal demand and supply           │
│   •   of external supply                      │
└─────────────────────────────────────────────┘
                      ↓
┌─────────────────────────────────────────────┐
│ 3. JOB ANALYSIS                               │
│   •   investigating the task performed in each job │
│   •   identifying the skills required         │
└─────────────────────────────────────────────┘
                      ↓
┌─────────────────────────────────────────────┐
│ 4. RECRUITMENT AND TRAINING                   │
│   •   recruiting and selecting required staff │
│   •   training and developing existing staff  │
└─────────────────────────────────────────────┘
```

## 3.1 Strategic analysis

The current and future position should constantly be kept under review.

(a) **The environment**: population and education trends, policies on the employment of women and on pension ages and trends generally in the employment market must be monitored.

(b) The organisation's HR **strengths, weaknesses, opportunities and threats** need to be analysed so as to identify skills and competence gaps and the level of innovation. Threats may involve competitors 'poaching' staff.

(c) **Human resource utilisation**. An assessment should be made of how effectively the organisation is currently utilising its staff.

(d) **Objectives**. Core and subsidiary corporate objectives should be analysed to identify the manpower implications. New products, technology, 'culture' and structure will all make demands on staff.

**Timescales** are very important. An immediate gap may prompt instant recruitment while long-term corporate objectives allow planned staff development, providing them with the skills required.

Human resources are hard to predict and control.

(a) **Demand**. Environmental factors (eg the economy) create uncertainties in the demand for labour.

(b) **Supply**. Factors such as education or the demands of competitors for labour create uncertainties in the supply of labour.

(c) **Goals**. Employees have their own personal goals, and make their own decisions about whether to undertake further training. When large numbers of individuals are involved, the pattern of behaviour which emerges in response to any change in strategy may be hard to predict.

(d) **Constraints**. Legislation as well as social and ethical values constrain the ways in which human resources are used, controlled, replaced and paid.

## 3.2 Forecasting

**Estimating demand**. Planning future HR needs requires accurate forecasts of turnover and productivity (eg if fewer staff are required for the same output). The demand can be estimated from:

- New venture details
- New markets (need new staff)
- New products/services
- New technology (new skills)

- Divestments
- Organisational restructuring (eg relocation)
- Cost reduction plans

**Estimating supply**

(a)   **Current workers. A stocks and flows analysis** will define the **internal labour market**. It describes, not just aggregate quantities, but movements in and out of certain grades, by occupation and grade and according to length and service. This can be used in **modelling**.

(b)   The **external labour market**. Labour **market research** does four things.

    (i)     It measures potential employees' awareness of the organisation.
    (ii)    It discerns attitudes of potential employees towards the organisation.
    (iii)   It suggests possible segments for advertising purposes.
    (iv)   It provides analysis of population trends for long-term forecasting.

A **position survey** compares demand and supply. Differences in the numbers required/available, their grade, skills or location can be removed by applying an integrated manpower strategy.

## 3.3 Closing the gap between demand and supply: the HR plan

At the business unit level, the human resources plan will arise out of the strategic HR plan.

(a)   The **work required to be done** will largely result **from the business plan**. Production management might determine **how** the work will be done. If, for example, the company is introducing new machinery, then the human resource requirements (eg training, possible redundancy, safety measures) need to be considered.

(b)   **The skills base** includes technical skills, interpersonal skills, and management skills. The need for **technical** and **management** skills are obvious enough. **Interpersonal skills** are important, as they deal with the service offered to customers and affect teamwork.

The HR plan is prepared on the basis of staffing requirements and the implications for productivity and costs. It should include budgets, targets and standards, and should also allocate responsibilities for implementation and control (reporting, monitoring achievement against plan).

The HR plan can be broken down into **subsidiary plans** as shown in the following table.

| Plan | Comment |
|---|---|
| **Recruitment plan** | Numbers; types of people; when required; recruitment programme. |
| **Training plan** | Numbers of trainees required and/or existing staff needing training; training programme. |
| **Redevelopment plan** | Programmes for transferring, retraining employees. |
| **Productivity plan** | Programmes for improving productivity, or reducing manpower costs; setting productivity targets. |
| **Redundancy plan** | Where and when redundancies are to occur; policies for selection and declaration of redundancies; re-development, re-training or re-location of redundant employees; policy on redundancy payments, union consultation etc. |
| **Retention plan** | Actions to reduce avoidable labour wastage. |

### 3.3.1 Tactical plans

**Tactical plans** can then be made, within this integrated framework, to cover all aspects of the HRM task.

- Pay and productivity bargaining
- Physical conditions of employment
- Management and technical development and career development
- Organisation and job specifications
- Recruitment and redundancies
- Training and retraining
- Staffing costs

### 3.3.2 Staffing shortages or surpluses

Shortages or surpluses of labour which emerge in the process of formulating the position survey must be dealt with.

(a) Dealing with a **shortage**

    (i)      Internal transfers and promotions, training etc
    (ii)     External recruitment
    (iii)    Reducing labour turnover, by reviewing possible causes
    (iv)    Overtime
    (v)     New equipment and training to improve productivity so reducing the need for more people

(b) Dealing with a **surplus**

    (i)      Allowing employee numbers to reduce through natural wastage
    (ii)     Restricting recruitment
    (iii)    Introduce part-time working for previously full-time employees
    (iv)    Redundancies – as a last resort, and with careful planning

**Exam focus point**

> Candidates in May 2005 were required to describe the main issues and stages in devising a human resource plan.

## 3.4 Stages in human resources planning

*Laurie Mullins* (2002) devised a model of the different elements involved in HRM planning. *Mullins'* model covers many of the areas covered in this section – it is shown below.

**Stages in human resources planning**

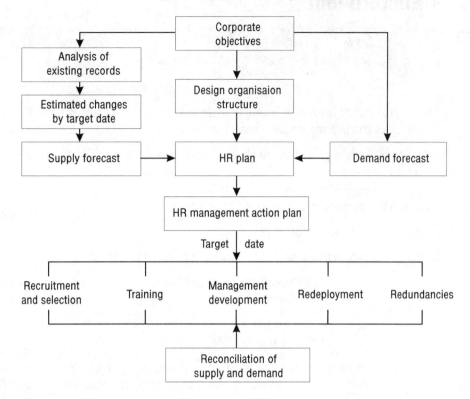

## 3.5 Control over the HR plan

Once the HR plan has been established, regular **control reports** should be produced.

(a)   **Actual** numbers recruited, leaving and promoted should be compared with **planned** numbers. Action may be required to correct any imbalance – depending upon the cause.

(b)   Actual pay, conditions of employment and training should be compared with assumptions in the HR plan. Do divergences explain any excessive staff turnover?

(c)   Periodically, the HR plan itself should be reviewed and brought up to date.

Question                                                    **Employee enthusiasm/commitment**

Learning outcome: E (v)

Enthusiastic and committed employees ensure business success. Do you agree?

Answer

Although enthusiastic and committed employees are often the driving force behind business success, they do not guarantee or ensure success.

(a)   No matter how good, loyal, committed and enthusiastic the people are, if the basic commercial strategy is wrong, the company will fail.

(b)   A strong culture of enthusiasm for all initiatives can inhibit people who have genuine valid concerns from voicing these – which may led to expensive mistakes.

# 4 Recruitment

FAST FORWARD

**Recruitment** is a means by which people from outside the organisation are brought in. **Selection** is the process of choosing who is offered the job.

**Key terms**

**Recruitment** is concerned with finding applicants: going out into the labour market, communicating opportunities and information and generating interest.

**Selection** consists of procedures to choose the successful candidate from among those made available by the recruitment effort.

## A systematic approach to recruitment and selection

**Step 1**  Detailed personnel **planning**.

**Step 2**  **Job analysis**, so that for any given job there are two things.

    (a)    A statement of the component tasks, duties, objectives and standards (**a job description**).

    (b)    A definition of the kind of person needed to perform the job (**a person specification**).

**Step 3**  Identification of vacancies, by way of the personnel plan (if vacancies are created by demand for new labour) or requisitions for replacement staff by a department which has 'lost' a current job-holder.

**Step 4**  Evaluation of the sources of labour, again by way of the personnel plan, which should outline personnel supply and availability, at macro- and micro-levels. Internal and external sources, and media for reaching both, will be considered.

**Step 5**  Review of applications, assessing the relative merits of broadly suitable candidates.

**Step 6**  Notifying applicants of the results of the selection process.

**Step 7**  Preparing employment contracts, induction, training programmes and so on.

In the remainder of this section we look at processes related to recruitment and the actual job or role. Selection issues are covered in the next section.

## 4.1 Job analysis, competences and job design

FAST FORWARD

**Job analysis** determines the requirements for a job. The job's tasks are set out in a job description. A job specification describes the skills or competences required for the job. A **person specification** describes the sort of person suitable for a job.

Procedures for recruitment should only be carried out in the context of a recruitment policy, which might cover issues such as internal/external applications of post, non-discrimination and so forth, courteous processing of applicants, the type of tests favoured.

**Key term**

**Job analysis** is: 'the process of collecting, analysing and setting out information about the content of jobs in order to provide the basis for a job description and data for recruitment, training, job evaluation and performance management. Job analysis concentrates on what job holders are expected to do.'

(*Armstrong*)

## 4.1.1 Job analysis

The management of the organisation needs to analyse the sort of work needed to be done in order to recruit effectively. The type of information needed is outlined below.

| Type of information | Comments |
|---|---|
| **Purpose of the job** | This might seem obvious. As an accountant, you will be expected to analyse, prepare or provide financial information; but this has to be set in the context of the organisation as a whole. |
| **Content of the job** | The tasks you are expected to do. If the purpose of the job is to ensure, for example, that people get paid on time, the tasks involve include many activities related to payroll. |
| **Accountabilities** | These are the results for which you are responsible. In practice they might be phrased in the same way as a description of a task. |
| **Performance criteria** | These are the criteria which measure how good you are at the job. These are largely task related. |
| **Responsibility** | This denotes the importance of the job. For example, a person running a department and taking decisions involving large amounts of money is more responsible that someone who only does what he or she is told. |
| **Organisational factors** | Who does the jobholder report to directly (line manager)? |
| **Developmental factors** | Likely promotion paths, if any, career prospects and so forth. Some jobs are 'dead-end' if they lead nowhere. |
| **Environmental factors** | Working conditions, security and safety issues, equipment and so on. |

## Case Study

Chase Manhattan Bank has clear procedures.

The competence definition and the scale are used to assess to what extent the individual has developed the competence, through seven points ranging from 'minimal knowledge' to 'recognisable ability' (representing a firm professional standard) and up to 'advisory level' (related to the best in the external market). This range is positioned as an external, absolute scale, not an internal relative measure. As such, it is used for individuals (always starting with self-analysis) to agree with their manager their individual competence profile, or for managers to specify the competence demands of given roles or specific job vacancies, or for the business to profile the differing requirements of customers.

It reaches the strategic needs of the organisation at its most macro level, but equally – and vitally, as a prerequisite for a successful corporate agenda – it supports a stream of products which get to the individual's agenda of professional development, career opportunity and performance-related reward.

## 4.1.2 Competences

A current approach to job design is the development and outlining of **competences**.

**Key term**

A person's **competence** is 'a capacity that leads to behaviour that meets the job demands within the parameters of the organisational environment and that, in turn, brings about desired results'. (*Boyzatis*)

Some take this further and suggest that a competence embodies the ability to **transfer** skills and knowledge to new situations within the occupational area.

**Different sorts of competences**

(a) **Behavioural/personal** competences are underlying personal characteristics and behaviour required for successful performance, for example, 'ability to relate well to others'. Most jobs require people to be good communicators.

(b) **Work-based/occupational competences** are 'expectations of workplace performance and the outputs and standards people in specific roles are expected to obtain'. This approach is used in NVQ systems. They cover what people have to do to achieve the results of the job. For example, a competence for a Chartered Management Accountant might be to 'produce financial and other statements and report to management'.

(c) **Generic competences** can apply to all people in an occupation.

**Some competences for managers** are shown in the following table.

| Competence area | Competence | |
|---|---|---|
| **Intellectual** | • Strategic perspective<br>• Analytical judgement<br>• Planning and organising | |
| **Interpersonal** | • Managing staff<br>• Persuasiveness<br>• Assertiveness and decisiveness | • Interpersonal sensitivity<br>• Oral communication |
| **Adaptability** | • Flexibility<br>• Coping with change | |
| **Results** | • Initiative<br>• Motivation to achievement<br>• Business sense | |

These competences can be elaborated by identifying **positive** and **negative** indicators.

## 4.1.3 Job design

Parameters of job design (*Mintzberg*).

(a) Job specialisation

    (i) **How many different tasks** are contained in the jobs and how broad and narrow are these tasks? **The task may be determined by operations management**. Until recently, there has been a trend towards narrow specialisation, reinforced, perhaps by demarcations laid down by trade unions. On the production line, a worker did the same task all the time. Modern techniques, however, require workers to be **multi-skilled**.

    (ii) **To what extent does the worker have control over the work?** At one extreme ('Scientific Management') the worker has little control over the work. At the other extreme (eg an electrician) the worker controls the task.

(b) **Regulation of behaviour**. Co-ordination requires that organisations formalise behaviour so as to predict and control it.

(c) **Training** in **skills** and indoctrination in **organisational values**.

*Belbin* (1997) described a way of **tailoring job design** to delayered, team based structures and flexible working systems.

(a) Flattened delayered hierarchies lead to greater flexibility but also to uncertainty and sometimes to a **loss of control**.

(b) Old hierarchies tended to be **clearer** in establishing responsibilities.

## 4.2 Job description

Key term

> A **job description** sets out the purpose of the job, where it fits in the organisation structure, the context of the job, the accountabilities of the job and the main tasks the holder carries out.

### 4.2.1 Purposes of job descriptions

| Purpose | Comment |
|---|---|
| Organisational | Defines the job's place in the organisational structure |
| Recruitment | Provides information for identifying the sort of person needed (person specification) |
| Legal | Provides the basis for a contract of employment |
| Performance | Performance objectives can be set around the job description |

### 4.2.2 Contents of a job description

(a) **Job title** (eg Assistant Financial Controller). This indicates the function/department in which the job is performed, and the level of job within that function.

(b) **Reporting to** (eg the Assistant Financial controller reports to the Financial Controller), in other words the person's immediate boss. (No other relationships are suggested here.)

(c) **Subordinates** directly reporting to the job holder.

(d) **Overall purpose** of the job, distinguishing it from other jobs.

(e) **Principal accountabilities or main tasks**

    (i) Group the main activities into a number of broad areas.

    (ii) Define each activity as a statement of accountability: what the job holder is expected to achieve (eg **tests** new system to ensure they meet agreed systems specifications).

(f) The current fashion for multi-skilling means that **flexibility** is expected.

Exam focus point

> The November 2005 paper included a question (in Section C) requiring candidates to produce a job description for a driver (based on information contained in the scenario).

## 4.3 Alternatives to job descriptions

**Detailed** job descriptions are perhaps only suited for jobs where the work is largely repetitive and therefore performed by low-grade employees: once the element of **judgement** comes into a job description it becomes a straitjacket. Many of the difficulties that arise where people adhere strictly to the contents of the job description, rather than responding flexibly to task or organisational requirements.

Perhaps job descriptions should be written in terms of the **outputs and performance levels** expected. Some firms are moving towards **accountability profiles** in which outputs and performance are identified explicitly.

### 4.3.1 Role definitions

Whereas a **job** is a group of tasks, a role is more than this. A **role** is a part played by people in meeting their objectives by working competently and flexibly within the context of the organisation's objectives, structures and processes. A **role definition** is wider than a job description. It is less concerned with the details of the job content, but how people interpret the job.

### 4.3.2 Person specification

Possible areas the specification may cover include:

- Personal skills
- Qualifications
- Motivation
- Personality and disposition
- Innate ability (aptitude)
- Intelligence

### 4.3.3 Seven-point plan

*Alec Rodgers* devised a framework for the selection process that includes seven points. It can be remembered using the mnemonic **BADPIGS**

| Point | Examples |
|---|---|
| **Background/Circumstances** | Location, car owner |
| **Attainments** | Qualifications, career achievements |
| **Disposition** | Calm, independent |
| **Physical make-up** | Strength, appearance, health |
| **Interests** | Mechanical, people-related |
| **General Intelligence** | Average, above average |
| **Special aptitudes** | Manual dexterity, mental sharpness |

 Question        Job description

Do you have a job description? How well do you think it describes what you actually do on a day-to-day basis? If you do not have a job description, draw one up, and then draw up a job and person specification. How well do *you* match?

## 4.4 Advertising job vacancies

After a job description and a personnel specification have been prepared, the organisation should advertise the job vacancy.

The job description and personnel specification can be used as guidelines for the wording of any advertisement or careers prospectus pamphlet.

The choice of advertising medium will depend on **cost, frequency,** the frequency with which the organisation wants to advertise the job vacancy and its **suitability** to the target audience.

### 4.4.1 Advertising media for recruitment

A range of options are available when advertising a position.

- In-house magazines
- Professional journals
- National newspapers
- Local newspapers
- Local radio
- Job centres
- Recruitment agencies
- Schools careers officers
- University careers officers
- Careers/job fairs
- Open days
- The Internet

### 4.4.2 Agencies

Employment agencies may be used to ease the effort involved in both recruitment and selection. More junior posts can often be filled from among an agency's pool of registered candidates. Recruitment and selection of more senior staff may be outsourced to **executive search agencies**, who will manage the whole process. This may include preparing the job definition and person specification; advertising and less formal, word-of-mouth communication; and the initial interview process. One or two candidates will then be presented for assessment.

### 4.4.3 Initial screening

The final process in the recruitment phase (before moving on to 'Selection') is the initial screening of candidates (usually by reviewing CVs and selecting some candidates for interview).

**Exam focus point**

The November 2005 exam offered candidates 10 marks for explaining the aspects of the HR strategy that would change significantly due to a set of circumstances.

# 5 Selection

**FAST FORWARD**

**Selection** involves a filtering process, by reviewing application forms, interviewing and testing. **Interviews** are a widely used selection method. **Tests** can assess intelligence, personality etc. An **assessment centre** approach may be used.

A variety of techniques may be used in selection, those chosen in a particular circumstance must be:

- **Reliable** – generate consistent results
- **Valid** – accurately predict performance of employees
- **Fair** – non-discriminating
- **Cost-effective** – the benefits of obtaining good quality staff must justify the costs of selecting them

An ineffective selection process may result in the

- Employment of unsuitable applicants
- Rejection of suitable applicants

Both errors may be costly to put right.

## 5.1 Application forms

Job advertisements usually ask for a CV (résumé) or require an application form to be completed. The CV is more usual in applications for executive posts, except in the public sector. Application forms are usual for jobs below executive level, and at all levels in the public sector.

The application form should therefore help those making the selection to **sift through the applicants**, and to reject some at once so as to avoid the time and costs of unnecessary interviews. It should therefore:

(a) **Obtain relevant information** about the applicant which can be compared with the requirements of the job.

(b) Give applicants the opportunity to write about themselves, such as their career ambitions or why they want the job.

## 5.2 The interview

**Aims of the interview** (often the deciding factor)

- Finding the best person for the job, through direct assessment
- Giving the applicant the chance to learn about the firm

### 5.2.1 Preparation

The interviewer should study three things.

(a) The **job description** (and specification if separate), to review the major demands of the job.

(b)   The **personnel specification**, to make an assessment of the applicant's character and qualifications.

(c)   The **application form**, to decide on questions or question areas for each applicant.

## 5.3 Conduct of the interview

The following factors should be taken into account.

(a)   The **layout** of the room and the number of interviewers should be planned carefully.

(b)   The **manner** of the interviewers, their tone of voice, and the way their early questions are phrased can all be significant in establishing the tone of the interview.

(c)   **Questions** should be put **carefully**. The interviewers should not be trying to confuse the candidate, but should be trying to obtain the information they need.

(d)   The **candidate should be encouraged** to **talk**.

(e)   The **candidate** should be **given** the **opportunity** to **ask questions**.

## 5.4 Limitations of interviews

Interviews have the following limitations

(a)   **Unreliable assessments**. Interviewers may disagree. A suitable candidate might be rejected or an unsuitable candidate offered a job.

(b)   **They fail to provide accurate predictions** of how a person will perform in the job. Research has shown this time and again.

(c)   The **interviewers are likely to make errors** of judgement even when they agree about a candidate.

(i)   A **halo effect**: a **general** judgement based on a **single** attribute.

(ii)  **Contagious bias**. Interviewers might change the behaviour of the applicant by suggestion. The wording of questions or non-verbal clues might lead the applicant to tell the interviewers more of what they wanted to hear.

(iii) Interviewers sometimes **stereotype** candidates on the basis of insufficient evidence, eg on the basis of dress, hair style, accent of voice etc.

(iv)  **Incorrect assessment** of qualitative factors such as motivation, honesty or integrity. Abstract qualities are very difficult to assess in an interview.

(v)   **Logical error**. An interviewer might draw conclusions about a candidate from what he or she says without logical justification for those conclusions.

(vi)  **Incorrectly used rating scales**. For example, if interviewers are required to rate a candidate on a scale of 1-5 for a number of different attributes, there might be a tendency to mark candidates inconsistently.

Interviewers should be **trained** to conduct and assess interviews.

## Question

Interviews

Learning outcome: E (iii)

Some courses offer tuition in interview technique to candidates looking for jobs. Do you think this means interviews are likely to be less reliable as a means of candidate selection?

## Answer

If interview techniques are taught, it might imply that success at interview will have more to do with a candidate's ability to present themself in an interview situation rather than their ability to do the job. On the other hand, an interview is a test of how well a person performs under pressure, in an unfamiliar environment and with strangers. The interview might therefore reflect some of the interpersonal skills required for a job.

## 5.5 Testing of candidates

Tests are used supplement interviews or select applicants for interview. The following types of test may be used.

(a) **Psychological tests and personality tests.** An individual may be required to answer a long series of questions or score a variety of statements which indicate basic attitude profiles.

(b) **Intelligence tests** measure the applicant's general intellectual ability.

(c) **Proficiency tests** are perhaps the most closely related to an assessor's objectives, because they measure ability to do the **work involved.**

(d) **Aptitude tests** aim to provide information about the candidate's abilities. Aptitude tests can test mental ability (IQ tests, tests in mathematics, general knowledge or use of English) and physical dexterity.

(e) **Psychometric tests** contain features of all of the above. They are selection tests that seek to **quantify** psychological dimensions of job applicants, for example intelligence, personality and motivation. Candidates might be required to answer a list of questions. Those answers are then marked and the candidate is given a score.

Case Study

The *Myers-Briggs Type Indicator* is used to categorise people as to whether they are introvert/extrovert, objective/intuitive, logical/emotional, decisive/ hesitant, and so forth. These tests may be used:

(a) In the initial selection of new recruits.
(b) In the allocation of new entrants to different branches of work.
(c) As part of the process of transfer or promotion.

### 5.5.1 Advantages and disadvantages of tests

Tests have the following advantages and disadvantages.

| Advantages | Disadvantages |
|---|---|
| A test can be a sensitive measuring instrument. | They may over-simplify complex issues. |
| Tests are standardised, so that all candidates are assessed by the same yardstick. | They are culturally-specific. Many tests for managers were developed in the US. The cultures in other countries may differ. |
| Tests always measure the same thing (eg IQ). | |

## 5.6 Group selection methods

**Group selection methods** might be used by an organisation as the final stage of a selection process for management jobs. They are not generally used for lower level staff due to their cost. They consist of a series of tests, interviews and group situations over a period of two days or so, involving a small number (eg six to eight) of candidates for a job. After an introductory chat to make the candidates feel at home, they will be given one or two tests, one or two individual interviews, and several group situations in which the candidates are invited to discuss problems together and arrive at solutions as a management team.

Advantages and disadvantages of group selection methods include:

| Advantages | Disadvantages |
|---|---|
| Selectors have more time to study the candidates. | Time and cost. |
| They test interpersonal skills. | The lack of experience of interviewers/selectors. |
| They reveal more about the candidates' personalities. | Candidates might behave atypically in a contrived situation. |
| They are suitable for selection of potential managers. | |

## 5.7 Assessment centres

A relatively recent development in the attempt to ensure good recruitment and selection decisions are made is the **assessment centre approach**.

An assessment centre may or may not be a particular permanent location – the term refers more the process of selection rather than to any specific building. The approach involves candidate or employee **behaviour being observed and judged** by more than one assessor, using specifically developed **simulations**. This approach is generally used for senior positions, as it is time consuming (in terms of combined people hours) and therefore relatively expensive.

Trained assessors observe and evaluate candidates on their managerial qualities while candidates are performing a variety of situational exercises. Video is frequently used to help the assessors gather information.

### 5.7.1 Assessment centre exercises

Assessment centre exercises are intended to measure dimensions such as:

- Planning and organising skills
- Leadership
- Analytical skills
- Problem solving

- Decision-making
- Creativity
- Sociability and sensitivity
- Delegation

Assessor opinions are pooled and ratings discussed with fellow assessors. The exercises should allow **key job success behaviours** to be directly observed and measured. Findings are often presented in formal reports.

### 5.7.2 Are assessment centres effective?

Assessment centres are most often used as part of a **selection process**, but may also be used to identify training and development needs or to enhance skills (through simulations).

Studies reveal that if assessment techniques are robust, targeted, well-designed and properly implemented, the assessment centre approach produces **reliable outcomes** when compared to single-method approaches such as interviews and questionnaires.

However, the approach can be costly and will only produce good results if the assessors have the required skills to make **meaningful judgements** based on the behaviour of candidates. For example, assessors should be able to organise their behavioural observations by job-related dimensions.

## 5.8 References

It is common to obtain references from the candidate's previous employers and other people the candidate is acquainted with. A reference enables an employer to check the **basic accuracy** of the candidate's CV – but little more than this.

**Exam focus point**

In November 2006, candidates were required to produce selection process guidelines for an organisation presented with a shortlist of candidates.

## 5.9 Negotiation

A job represents an **economic exchange**: the employer obtains the **services of the employee**, who receives **benefits** such as pay and paid holiday in return. There are also less tangible features to employment. An employer is entitled to a reasonable degree of **loyalty** and **commitment**, while most employees will seek **job satisfaction**, **security of employment** and **personal development**.

It is important that both employer and employee feel that the exchange they have contracted is a **fair** one. If they do not their relationship will be strained from the outset. An employee who feels undervalued will seek alternative employment. An employer who feels exploited will seek to cut pay, benefits and number employed at every opportunity.

For these reasons it is important that there should be a process of **negotiation** at the time an offer of employment is made. This need only be very brief, and in many junior positions may be very limited in scope. For more senior posts, negotiation may be more extensive.

## 5.10 Realistic job previews (RJP)

One method (suggested by *Herriot*) sometimes used to ensure both parties 'know what they are letting themselves in for' is a realistic job preview.

This usually involves a prospective employee spending some time 'shadowing' an existing employee in a similar role.

RJPs have been found to lower expectations about the job and the organisation – sometimes resulting in candidates withdrawing from contention. Candidates that do complete a RJP and accept the role are more likely to be committed to the job and the organisation.

# 6 Induction

New recruits need time to learn the job and settle in. Many organisations have formal procedures for **induction** designed to **integrate** new recruits as quickly as possible.

All new staff should go through a proper process of induction. The context of induction programmes may vary, depending on the role being undertaken, but it is unlikely that anyone can make a satisfactory start without at least some basic orientation. Induction may be carried out by the recruit's supervisor, by a departmental trainer or mentor, by HR staff or by a combination of all three.

## 6.1 Induction elements

An induction programme typically would include the following elements.

(a)     A **welcome**

(b)     **Introductions** to immediate colleagues, colleagues and supervisor

(c)     Explanation of the **nature of the job**: a written job description will make this process easier. Some detailed technical matters may be identified as suitable for deferment to a later date.

(d)     **Safety** rules and procedures

(e)     **Terms and conditions of employment**: a booklet is often provided giving full details, but essential matters such as hours of work; authorisation of absence and overtime; and any important legal obligations should be explained in full.

(f)     Orientation to the wider **mission** of the department and the organisation. This is particularly important in organisations that provide services, because of the importance of **staff attitude and motivation** in the provision of high quality service.

(g)     Explanation of any systems of continuing **training**, **coaching** or **mentoring**. Many recruits are expected (and indeed, themselves expect) to undertake significant amounts of training. Rules relating to attendance, qualification and failure to progress must be explained.

Induction should enable the newcomer to make a quick start as a productive member of staff. It also gives the recruit and the organisation a chance to become acquainted. From the point of view of the organisation this can be helpful in such matters as deciding how best to make use of the recruit's particular set of abilities and competences and how to deal with any problems. The recruit benefits by obtaining a fuller picture of the new work environment. This can be particularly useful when inaccurate or incomplete impressions have been formed at the recruitment stage.

## 6.2 'Dialogic learning'

One element of induction emphasised by *Harrison* (1992) is integrating recruits into how the organisation operates including the overall culture, beliefs and mission. *Harrison* referred to this is 'dialogic learning'.

# 7 Legal and ethical issues

HRM incorporates a number of **legal and ethical issues**, particularly in relation to individual conduct, recruitment, selection, dismissal and redundancy.

In this section we look at some of the ethical and legal issues relevant to organisations in general, with a particular emphasis on issues related to Human Resource Management (HRM). The legal issues covered are done so from a practical standpoint, rather than covering the precise legal position and legal penalties.

## 7.1 Legal issues

In most countries employment is a widely regulated area with legislation and regulations covering the recruitment, selection, work-practices, and dismissal of employees. In this section, reflecting the emphasis of the Paper 4 syllabus, we don't cover regulations and legislation in detail. We focus instead on general principles that are often included in employment-related regulations and legislation. These are discussed where appropriate throughout this chapter.

## 7.2 Ethics

**Key term**

**Ethics**: a set of moral principles to guide behaviour.

Ethical concepts such as fairness and equality play an important part in HRM.

## 7.3 Issues relevant to employee recruitment and selection

From an ethical standpoint, employee selection should be made on the basis of who can best perform the role on offer. Other issues, such as a candidate's sex, race/ethnicity, religion, sexual orientation and physical status should not play a part in the decision (unless the inclusion of one of these factors such as physical ability can be shown to be fundamental to the job).

Practical steps that can be taken in the employee recruitment process include the following.

(a) **Advertising**

(i) Any wording that suggests preference for a particular group should be avoided (except for genuine occupational qualifications).

(ii) Employers must not indicate or imply any 'intention to discriminate'.

(iii) Recruitment literature should state that the organisation is an Equal Opportunities employer.

(iv) The placing of advertisements only where the readership is predominantly of one race or sex is construed as indirect discrimination. This includes word-of-mouth recruiting from the existing workforce, if it is not broadly representative.

(b) **Recruitment agencies**. Instructions to an agency should not suggest any preference.

(c) **Application forms**. These should avoid questions which are not work-related (such as domestic details) or which only one or some groups are asked to complete.

(d) **Interviews.** Any non-work-related question should be asked of all subjects, if at all, and even then, some types of question may be construed as discriminatory. (You should not, for example, ask only women about plans to have a family or care of dependants.) Some organisations protect themselves by having a witness at interviews, or by taking detailed notes, in the event that a claim of discrimination is made.

(e) **Selection tests**. These must be wholly relevant, and should not favour any particular group. Even personality tests have been shown to favour white male applicants.

(f) **Records**. Reasons for rejection, and interview notes, should be carefully recorded, so that in the event of investigation the details will be available.

## 7.4 Disciplinary procedures and dismissal

The grounds and procedures for dismissing an employee should be stated clearly in the organisation's disciplinary procedures policy. Except for instances of exceptional misconduct, dismissal should be the final step in the disciplinary process.

Many minor cases of poor performance or misconduct are best dealt with by **informal advice, coaching or counselling**. An informal oral warning may be issued. None of this forms part of the formal disciplinary procedure, but workers should be informed clearly what is expected and what action will be taken if they fail to improve.

If the problem persists, it may be decided that formal disciplinary action is needed. Three stages are often recommended. These are usually thought of as consecutive, reflecting a progressive response. However, it may be appropriate to miss out one of the earlier stages when there have been serious infringements.

**First warning**. A first formal warning could be either oral or written depending on the seriousness of the case.

(a) An **oral warning** should include the reason for issuing it, notice that it constitutes the first step of the disciplinary procedure and details of the right of appeal. A note of the warning should be kept on file but disregarded after a specified period, such as six months.

(b) A **first written warning** is appropriate in more serious cases. It should inform the worker of the improvement required and state that a final written warning may be considered if there is no satisfactory improvement. A copy of the first written warning should be kept on file but disregarded after a specified period, such as 12 months.

**Final written warning**. If an earlier warning is still current and there is no satisfactory improvement, a final written warning may be appropriate.

### 7.4.1 Disciplinary sanctions

The final stage in the disciplinary process is the imposition of sanctions.

(a) **Suspension without pay**

This course of action would be next in order if the employee has committed repeated offences and previous steps were of no avail. Disciplinary lay-offs usually extend over several days or weeks. Some employees may not be very impressed with oral or written warnings, but they will find a disciplinary lay-off without pay a rude awakening. This penalty is only available if it is provided for in the contract of employment.

(b) **Dismissal**

Dismissal is **termination of employment** (either with or without notice) by the employer. Dismissal without notice is only allowed in circumstances acceptable under statute.

If an employee resigns because the conduct of the employer is deemed to have terminated the employment contract, this may be treated as '**constructive dismissal**'.

Termination of an employee's employment contract must be done in a way which follows correct procedures, otherwise a claim for unfair dismissal may follow.

| Acceptable reasons for dismissal | |
|---|---|
| Conduct | • Unacceptable conduct continuing after warnings/counselling |
| Capability | • The employee is not capable of the role (after appropriate guidance, training etc) |
| Breach of statutory duty | • If continuing the employment relationship would mean the employer breaching a statutory duty |
| Other 'substantial reason' | • Dishonesty<br>• Loss of trust |
| Redundancy | • Cessation of business<br>• Relocation of business<br>• Cessation of work employed for |

Dismissal is a drastic form of disciplinary action, and should be reserved for the most serious offences. For the organisation, it involves waste of a labour resource, the expense of training a new employee, and disruption caused by changing the make-up of the work team.

### 7.4.2 Unfair dismissal

In many countries some reasons are classed **automatically** as grounds for **unfair dismissal**. The main grounds applicable in the UK are set out below.

- Dismissal on grounds of race, sex or disability discrimination
- Pregnancy or other maternity-related grounds
- Due to a request for flexible working practices
- Trade union membership or activities
- Taking steps to avert danger to health and safety at work
- Seeking to enforce rights relating to the national minimum wage
- Refusing or opting out of Sunday working (in the retail sector)

### 7.4.3 Redundancy

True redundancy arises when **the role an employee performs is no longer required**, perhaps due to restructuring or different working methods. Some (unethical) organisations use redundancy as an excuse to terminate the employment of employees who are no longer wanted, but who could not justifiably be dismissed on disciplinary grounds.

Organisations that act ethically have **policies governing redundancy**. These tend to cover areas such as pre-redundancy **consultation** with employees and post redundancy **support**. Selecting which employees will be made redundant must be fair and in accordance with established policies. Outplacement consultants may be provided to help redundant employees find suitable jobs and to provide training. Other issues could relate to the use of voluntary redundancy and early retirement measures where possible.

In the UK, the legal position is that an employee dismissed on the grounds of **redundancy** (that is that their position is no longer required) may claim remedies for unfair dismissal if in fact the position was not redundant.

Alternatives to enforced redundancies could include:

- Reduced overtime
- Recruitment limits (or a 'freeze')
- Enforced retirement (of those over retirement age)
- Voluntary early retirement (of those close to retirement age)
- Shorter hours
- Job shares (eg two employees working shorter hours)
- Voluntary redundancy

Redundancy is likely to be an unpleasant experience, particularly for those employees made redundant. Even if a generous redundancy payment is made, this is unlikely to provide the means to support previous expenditure levels for very long.

Managers also need to ensure remaining employees remain motivated, and morale is as high as can be expected in the circumstances.

## 7.5 Relationship management in disciplinary situations

Even if the manager uses sensitivity and judgement, imposing disciplinary action tends to generate **resentment**. The challenge is to apply the necessary disciplinary action as constructively as possible.

(a)     **Immediacy** means that after noticing the offence, the manager proceeds to take disciplinary action as speedily as possible, subject to investigations, while at the same time avoiding haste and on-the-spot emotions which might lead to unwarranted actions.

(b)     **Advance warning.** Employees should know in advance (eg in a Staff Handbook) what is expected of them and what the rules and regulations are.

(c)     **Consistency.** Consistency of discipline means that each time an infraction occurs appropriate disciplinary action is taken. Inconsistency in application of discipline lowers the morale of employees and diminishes their respect for the manager.

(d)     **Impersonality.** Penalties should be connected with the act and not based upon the personality involved, and once disciplinary action has been taken, no grudges should be borne.

(e)     **Privacy.** As a general rule disciplinary action should be taken in private, to avoid the spread of conflict and the humiliation or martyrdom of the employee concerned.

**Exam focus point**

Candidates in May 2005 were asked to discuss how a 'good employer' could achieve required job reductions – including supporting those individuals affected.

## 7.6 Ethics in business dealings

Ethics refer to a code of moral principles that people follow with respect to what is right or wrong. Ethical principles are not necessarily enforced by law, although the law incorporates moral judgements (eg theft is wrong ethically, and is also punishable legally).

Companies have to follow legal standards, or else they will be subject to fines and their officers might face similar charges. Ethics in organisations relates to **social responsibility** and **business practice.** Increasingly, consumers and businesses prefer to purchase from and do business with organisations with high ethical standards.

One issue related to personal business ethics that crops-up fairly regularly is the issue of employees going public about the unethical or illegal conduct of their employer. **Whistle-blowing** is the disclosure by an employee of illegal, immoral or illegitimate practices on the part of the organisation. However, as employees have a duty of confidentiality to their employer, the issue is rarely a simple one. It is often impractical for whistle-blowers to carry on working for that employer as both sides have lost trust in the other.

In the UK, the Public Interest Disclosure Act 1999 offers some protection to whistle-blowers, but both the subject of the disclosure and the way in which it is made must satisfy the requirements of the Act.

### 7.6.1 CIMA's Ethical Guidelines

All CIMA members and registered students are subject to **CIMA's Ethical Guidelines, which you should download from the CIMA website**. These guidelines make it clear that members must:

- Observe the highest standards of conduct and integrity
- Uphold the good standing and reputation of the profession
- Refrain from any conduct which might discredit the profession

In particular, you should pay attention to the fundamental principles given in the Introduction and the discussion of objectivity and the resolution of ethical conflicts that appear in Part A. These matters are discussed briefly below.

The **fundamental principles of CIMA's Ethical Guidelines** are:

(a)    **Integrity** is more than not telling lies; professional accountants must not be party to anything which is deceptive or misleading.

(b)    **Objectivity** is founded on fairness and avoiding all forms of bias, prejudice and partiality. There is more on objectivity in Part A of the code.

(c)    **Professional competence and due care**

(d)    **Confidentiality**. Employers and clients are entitled to expect that confidential information will not be revealed without specific permission or unless there is a legal or professional right or duty to do so.

(e)    **Professional behaviour** protects the reputation of the professional and the professional body.

(f)    **Professional and technical standards** must be complied with.

**Objectivity** is further discussed in the code, including guidance on factors that may tend to prejudice objectivity, such as personal relationships, the influence of more senior staff and conflicts of interest.

Resolution of **ethical conflicts** is also covered. The possibility of such conflicts arising is discussed. Possible situations could include:

- Pressure from an overbearing supervisor
- Pressure from a friend or relation
- Divided loyalties

A CIMA member or student should act responsibly, honour any legal contract of employment and confirm to employment legislation.

In cases where the CIMA member/student is encouraged or required to act illegally, resignation may be the only option (if discussion fails to resolve the situation).

**Exam focus points**

> CIMA's ethical guidelines are examinable. You must download a copy from the CIMA website (www.cimaglobal.com).
>
> The May 2007 exam offered ten-marks for a discussion around the necessary changes to HR practices and employee attitudes for a change to be successful. Note how this ties in two later chapters as well as this one. Do not view all chapters as separate topics.

# Chapter Roundup

- **Personnel management** in the past was never perceived to have a strategic role, dealing as it did with issues of hiring and firing, industrial relations and so forth. Human resource management (HRM) is concerned with the most effective use of human resources. It deals with organisation, staffing levels, motivation, employee relations and employee services.

- **Human resource management (HRM)** is based on the assumption that the management and deployment of staff is a key **strategic** factor in an organisation's competitive performance. HRM requires top management involvement and the promotion of culture and **values,** so that employees' **commitment**, as opposed merely to their consent, is obtained.

- *Taylor*, *Mayo*, *Schein*, *Weber*, *Lawrence* and *Lorsch* propose some important **HRM theories**.

- **HRM planning** should be based on the **organisation's strategic planning processes**, with relation to analysis of the labour market, forecasting of the external supply and internal demand for labour, job analysis and plan implementation.

- **Recruitment** is a means by which people from outside the organisation are brought in. **Selection** is the process of choosing who is offered the job.

- **Job analysis** determines the requirements for a job. The job's tasks are set out in a job description. A job specification describes the skills or competences required for the job. A **person specification** describes the sort of person suitable for a job.

- **Selection** involves a filtering process, by reviewing application forms, interviewing and testing. **Interviews** are a widely used selection method. **Tests** can assess intelligence, personality etc. An **assessment centre** approach may be used.

- New recruits need time to learn the job and settle in. Many organisations have formal procedures for **induction** designed to **integrate** new recruits as quickly as possible.

- HRM incorporates a number of **legal and ethical issues**, particularly in relation to individual conduct, recruitment, selection, dismissal and redundancy.

# Quick Quiz

1   What are the objectives of human resource management?

2   Who developed a version of contingency theory?

    A    Mayo and Schein
    B    Weber
    C    Lawrence and Lorsch
    D    Taylor

3   What are the contents of the HR plan?

4   What are the three parameters of job design?

5   Distinguish between recruitment and selection.

6   What is a job description?

7   Which of the following are likely to be involved in the induction process?

    A    A supervisor
    B    A departmental mentor
    C    HR staff
    D    All of the above

8   *Fill in the missing words.*

    Ethics are a set of .......................... that ....................................... .

# Answers to Quick Quiz

1   To develop an effective human component for the organisation, which will respond well to change; to obtain, develop and motivate the human resources needed by the organisation; to create and maintain a co-operative climate of relationships within the organisation to satisfy the social and legal responsibilities relating to the human resource.

2   C    Lawrence and Lorsch developed a form of contingency theory.

3   The HR plan breaks down into subsidiary plans for recruitment, training, redundancy, retention, productivity and redevelopment.

4   Mintzberg suggests: job specialisation; regulation of behaviour; and training in skills and indoctrination in organisational values.

5   Recruitment is about finding applicants while selection is about choosing the right applicants.

6   A job description sets out the purpose of the job, where it fits into the organisation, its context, accountabilities and main tasks.

7   D    All are likely to play some part in a recruit's induction.

8   Ethics are a set of **moral principles** that **guide behaviour**.

Now try the question below from the Exam Question Bank

| Number | Level | Marks | Time |
|---|---|---|---|
| 7 | Examination | 30 | 54 mins |

# Motivation and performance

## Introduction

This chapter concentrates on the interaction and relationship between **the individual and the organisation**, particularly in relation to personality and related psychological factors.

Areas covered include individual needs and wants on the one hand, motivation and incentives on the other, and the resultant behaviour patterns displayed by individuals at work.

We also analyse and appraise the relevance of some of the major theories of motivation.

Finally, we outline some relatively recent developments in working arrangements.

| Topic list | Learning outcomes | Syllabus references | Ability required |
|---|---|---|---|
| 1 The organisation's interest in employee motivation | E(iv) | E(9) | Evaluation |
| 2 Motivation | E(iv) | E(9) | Evaluation |
| 3 Motivation theories | E(iv) | E(9) | Evaluation |
| 4 Money and job satisfaction | E(iv) | E(6) | Evaluation |
| 5 Working arrangements and types of organisation | E(ii), E(v) | E(10), E(13) | Evaluation |

# 1 The organisation's interest in employee motivation

Frustration, conflict, feelings of failure and low prospects tend to show themselves in such effects as high labour turnover, absenteeism or preoccupation with financial rewards (in compensation for lack of other satisfactions) – which can be as self-defeating for the organisation as they are unhealthy for the individual.

We should also note that there are a great many other work and non-work variables in the equation. A happy workforce will not necessarily make the organisation profitable (if the market is unfavourable): they will not necessarily be more productive (if the task itself is badly designed or resources scarce) nor even more highly motivated.

Therefore, to ensure employee performance benefits the organisation, organisations should take into account all factors that influence employee motivation.

# 2 Motivation

FAST FORWARD

**Motivating employees** to work hard and perform well is a perennial problem for managers. Some management practices are based on quite crude assumptions of how people are motivated.

It is in an organisation's interests to know the reasons or motives behind people's behaviour. In particular, if the organisation finds reasons why people might perform well at work, it can utilise that knowledge to encourage them.

## 2.1 Mullins' classifications of motivation

According to *Mullins* (2005) **motivation** is 'the driving force within individuals by which they attempt to achieve to achieve some goal in order to fulfil some need or expectation.'

*Mullins* also identified three classifications for understanding motivation.

| Classification | Examples |
|---|---|
| Economic reward | Pay and benefits |
| Intrinsic satisfaction | Enjoyment of the job and personal development |
| Social relationships | Team working and forming friendships with colleagues |

Question

Motivation

Think about the factors in yourself or your organisation that motivate you:

(a)     To turn up to work at all?
(b)     To do an average day's work?
(c)     To work particularly hard?

# 3 Motivation theories

FAST FORWARD

Motivation directs **individual behaviour**. It is in the interests of an employer to know how to motivate employees' behaviour for the employer's benefit.

(a)     **Money**. This is often thought of as the key motivating factor. This theory is advocated by *Taylor*, *Schein* and *McGregor*.

(b)     **Content theories** assume that human beings have a package of motives which they pursue: they have a set of needs or desired outcomes. *Maslow's* need hierarchy theory and *Herzberg's* two-factor theory are two of the most important approaches of this type.

(c)    **Process theories** explore the process through which outcomes become desirable and are pursued by individuals. This approach assumes that man is able to select his goals and choose the paths towards them, by a conscious or unconscious process of calculation. Expectancy theory is an example of this type.

## 3.1 Taylor, maximising prosperity

In the late nineteenth and early twentieth centuries, *Taylor* established four principles to achieve the maximum prosperity for employers and employees.

(a)    **Science** should be used to **determine fair pay** for a **day's work**.

(b)    **Scientific methods** should be used in the **recruitment** and **selection** of staff who should be developed to ensure they are capable of **meeting output** and **quality targets**.

(c)    '**Mental revolution**'. Staff should be encouraged to fulfil their potential.

(d)    There should be **constant** and **intimate co-operation** between **management** and **staff**.

*Taylor* appreciated how productivity would improve if staff were specialised and equipped with the knowledge and skills required to perform their role. Jobs should be broken down into functions that would each be performed by an individual. However, this view resulted in over-staffing in some organisations as a relatively large number of middle managers controlled the other workers.

*Taylor* also held the view that as **workers were rational** and would be **motivated** by the **highest remuneration** that was possible.

## 3.2 Schein, common behavioural traits

*Schein* identified four groups of 'man' with common behavioural traits.

(a)    **Rational economic man**

This group is motivated by the maximisation of economic gain and by following their own self-interest.

(b)    **Social man**

Performance of this group is improved by raising morale, through socialisation at work. Rather than acting as a controller, managers should be seen as facilitators.

(c)    **Self-actualising man**

This group is motivated through self-fulfilment (see *Maslow* below). In terms of work they are motivated by challenge and responsibility.

(d)    **Complex man**

Motivation is based on a 'psychological contract' between employers and employees. Each has their own expectations of the 'contract' and motivation depends on their fulfilment.

## 3.3 McGregor's Theory X and Theory Y

*Douglas McGregor* categorises **managers' assumptions** into two types.

**Key term**

> **Theory X and Theory Y:** Two contrasting managerial approaches to motivation described by *McGregor*.

(a)    **Theory X. This is the theory that most people dislike work and responsibility and will avoid both if possible**. Therefore, most people must be coerced, controlled, and threatened with punishment to get them to make an adequate effort towards the achievement of the organisation's objectives.

(b) **Theory Y. This theory holds that individuals want to satisfy their individual needs through work and wish to make a contribution towards goals that they have helped to establish.** Therefore managers who take a Theory Y approach seek to allow their staff to follow their own path and satisfy their own needs.

When deciding which approach to take, the following issues are important.

(i) **Strict controls** and **close supervision** may be a source of **conflict**.

(ii) **Self-motivation** and **commitment** maybe more **effective** and **less confrontational**.

(iii) **Treating individuals** in a **Theory X manner** may **prevent** the use of **initiative** and **encourage** doing the **minimum required**.

(iv) **Theory X is ineffective** when managing individuals who are **not financially motivated** or who are **not afraid of punishment**.

## 3.4 Maslow's hierarchy of needs

Key term

> **Hierarchy of needs**: a ranked structure of behavioural stimuli within the individual, which explain motivation.

Apart from 'biogenic needs' or 'drives', that is, biological determinants of behaviour, activated by deprivation, there are **psychogenic needs** - emotional or psychological needs. The American psychologist *Abraham Maslow* argued that man has seven innate needs, and put forward certain propositions about the motivating power of these needs.

He described two higher order needs.

(a) The need for freedom of inquiry and expression: for social conditions permitting free speech and encouraging justice, fairness and honesty.

(b) The need for knowledge and understanding: to gain and order knowledge of the environment, to explore, learn, experiment. These are essential pre-requisites for the satisfaction of the remainder.

The other five needs can be arranged in a 'hierarchy of relative pre-potency'. Each level of need is **dominant until satisfied**; only then does the next level of need become a motivating factor. A need which has been satisfied no longer motivates an individual's behaviour. The need for self-actualisation can never be satisfied.

There is a certain intuitive appeal to Maslow's theory. After all, you are unlikely to be concerned with status or recognition while you are hungry or thirsty because **primary survival needs** will take precedence. Likewise, once your hunger is satisfied, the need for food is unlikely to be a motivating factor.

It is also worth noting that Maslow did *not* intend his views to be applied to the specific context of behaviour at work: needs can be satisfied by aspects of a person's life outside work. However, since work provides a livelihood and takes up such a large part of a person's life, it is obviously going to play an important part in the satisfaction of their needs.

There are **various problems** associated with **Maslow's theory**.

(a) **Empirical verification** for the hierarchy is hard to come by. Physiological and safety needs are not always uppermost in the determination of human behaviour.

(b) **Research** does not bear out the proposition that needs become less powerful as they are satisfied, except at the very primitive level of primary needs like hunger and thirst.

(c) It is **difficult to predict** behaviour using the hierarchy: the theory is too vague.

(d) **Application** of the theory in work contexts presents various difficulties. For example, the role of money or pay is problematic, since it arguably represents other rewards like status, recognition or independence.

(e) The **ethnocentricity** of Maslow's hierarchy has also been noted – it does seem broadly applicable to Western English-speaking cultures, but it is less relevant elsewhere.

## 3.5 Herzberg's two-factor content theory

The American psychologist *Frederick Herzberg* interviewed 203 Pittsburgh engineers and accountants. The subjects were asked to recall **events which had made them feel good about their work, and others which made them feel bad about it**. Analysis revealed that the factors which created satisfaction were different from those which created dissatisfaction.

*Herzberg* identified two groups of work related factors which caused satisfaction and dissatisfaction respectively. He called these factors **motivators** and **hygiene factors**.

**Key terms**

> **Motivators** produced satisfaction when present and were capable of motivating the individual.
>
> **Hygiene factors** (or **maintenance factors**) could not give satisfaction or provide motivation when present. Their absence, however, caused dissatisfaction.

In his book *Work and the Nature of Man*, *Herzberg* distinguished between **hygiene factors** and **motivator factors**, based on what he saw as two separate 'need systems' of individuals.

(a) There is a **need to avoid unpleasantness**. This need is satisfied at work by hygiene factors. Hygiene satisfactions are short-lived: individuals come back for more, in the nature of drug addicts.

(b) There is a **need for personal growth**, which is satisfied by motivator factors, and not by hygiene factors.

**A lack of motivators at work will encourage employees to focus on poor hygiene** (real or imagined) and to demand more pay for example. Some individuals do not seek personal growth: these are 'hygiene seekers' who may be able to be satisfied by hygiene factors.

**Hygiene factors** are essentially **preventative**. They prevent or **minimise dissatisfaction** but do not give satisfaction, in the same way that sanitation minimises threats to health, but does not give 'good' health. They are called 'maintenance' factors because they have to be continually renewed to avoid dissatisfaction.

**Motivator factors create job satisfaction** and are effective in motivating an individual to superior performance and effort. These factors give the individual a sense of self-fulfilment or personal growth.

The following table contains examples of hygiene and motivation factors.

| Hygiene factors | Motivation factors |
| --- | --- |
| Company policy and administration | Advancement |
| Salary | Gaining recognition |
| Quality of supervision | Responsibility |
| Interpersonal relationships | Challenge |
| Working conditions | Achievement |
| Job security | Growth in role |
| Status (may also be a motivation factor) | |

*Herzberg* suggested that if there is sufficient **challenge**, **scope** and **interest** in the job, there will be a lasting **increase in satisfaction** and the employee will work well; productivity will be above normal levels.

The extent to which a job must be challenging or creative to a motivator-seeker will depend on each individual's ability and their tolerance for **delayed success**.

In the following section we look at how employers may adjust the nature or conditions of a job/role in an attempt to enhance employee **motivation**.

**Exam focus point**

In May 2006, candidates had to explain the thinking behind a new strategy put forward by a chief executive using *Herzberg's* theory as a framework.

## 3.6 Job restructuring or redesign

**Job redesign** aims to improve performance through increasing the understanding and motivation of employees. Job redesign also aims to ensure that an individual's job suits them in terms of what motivates them and their need for personal growth and development.

**Job rotation** allows for a little variety by moving a person from one task to another. Work people often do this spontaneously. Job rotation permits the development of extra **skills**, but does not develop **depth of skill**.

**Job enlargement** increases the *width* of the job by adding extra, usually related, tasks. It is not particularly popular with workers, many of whom prefer undemanding jobs that allow them to chat and daydream.

**Job enrichment** increase the *depth* of responsibility by adding elements of **planning** and **control** to the job, thus increasing its meaning and challenge. The worker achieves greater autonomy and growth in the role.

## 3.7 Job characteristics model

*Hackman and Oldham* developed the job characteristics model that sets out the links between employee motivation, satisfaction and performance (including personal growth) and the characteristics of their job or role.

*Hackman and Oldham's* **motivating potential score (MPS)** is an attempt to measure a job's potential to produce motivation and satisfaction. The NPS is computed from scores in questionnaires designed to diagnose the extent to which the job displays **five core characteristics**.

(a)  **Skill variety**: the breadth of job activities and skills required
(b)  **Task identity**: whether the job is a whole piece of work with a visible outcome
(c)  **Task significance**: the impact of the job on other people
(d)  **Autonomy**: the degree of freedom allowed in planning and executing the work
(e)  **Feedback**: the amount of information provided about the worker's job performance

*Hackman and Oldham* suggest that the first three characteristics above contribute to the 'experienced meaningfulness of the work' and this is borne out by empirical research. The extent to which a job's autonomy and feedback, as measured by *Hackman and Oldham*, contribute to job satisfaction is less clear-cut.

## 3.8 Expectancy theory: a process theory

The expectancy theory of motivation is a process theory, based on the assumptions of cognitive psychology that human beings are rational and are aware of their goals and behaviour.

Essentially, the theory states that **the strength of an individual's motivation to do something will depend on the extent the expected results of this effort will contribute towards personal needs or goals**.

In 1964 *Victor Vroom*, another American psychologist, worked out a formula by which human motivation could actually be assessed and measured, based on an expectancy theory of work motivation. *Vroom* suggested that the strength of an individual's motivation is the product of two factors.

(a)   The strength of his preference for a certain outcome. *Vroom* called this **valence**. It may be represented as a positive or negative number, or zero – since outcomes may be desired, avoided or considered with indifference.

(b)   The individual's expectation that the outcome will result from a certain behaviour. *Vroom* called this **subjective probability**: it is only the individual's 'expectation', and depends on his perception of the probable relationship between behaviour and outcome. As a probability, it may be represented by any number between 0 (no chance) and 1 (certainty). It is also called **expectancy**.

In its simplest form, the expectancy equation therefore looks like this.

| Force or strength of motivation to do something | = | Valence ie strength of his preference for a certain outcome | × | Expectation that behaviour will result in desired outcome |

This is what you would expect: if either valence or expectation have a value of zero, there will be no motivation.

(a)   If an employee has a high expectation that productivity will result in a certain outcome (say, promotion), but he is indifferent to that outcome (doesn't want the responsibility), $V = 0$, and he will not be motivated to productive behaviour.

(b)   If the employee has a great desire for promotion – but does not believe that productive behaviour will secure it for him, $E = 0$, and he will still not be highly motivated.

(c)   If $V = -1$, (perhaps because the employee fears responsibility and does not want to leave his work group), the value for motivation will be negative, and the employee may deliberately under-produce.

Are human beings really so predictable, however? Are we as **rational** as expectancy theory implies?

Expectancy theory has been useful in organisational practice because it does make room for the subjectivity of human perceptions. In its most complex form, where a number of alternative expected outcomes are taken into account, the expectancy equation can be a fair reflection of the various influences on behaviour.

The value attached to an **outcome** will partly reflect what is valued generally (and especially by the individual's colleagues or career models) in a particular organisation.

The **expectancy** will reflect the individual's **experience** of what can be achieved in the organisation, what rewards have been received in the past for certain behaviours.

Expectancy theories suggest the following stages to improve employee motivation.

**Stage 1**   Determine what an **individual values**.

**Stage 2**   Identify desired **managerial behaviour**.

**Stage 3**   Set performance levels which are **perceived** to be **achievable**.

**Stage 4**   Determine methods to **link managerial behaviour** to **individual performance**.

**Stage 5**   Ensure adequate rewards are in place to **encourage performance**.

**Stage 6**   Ensure reward system is **fair** and **equitable**.

## 3.9 Other process theories

### 3.9.1 Equity theory

Equity theory deals with issues of fairness, in other words that people seek a fair return for their efforts, not necessarily the maximum reward. *Adams* makes these suggestions.

(a)     People compare what they receive with what others receive, for a perceived level of effort.
(b)     **Inequity** exists if another person gets more for a given level of input.
(c)     People get more upset the more inequity there is.
(d)     The more upset someone is, the harder he or she will work to restore 'equity'.

Equity theory was backed up in the laboratory but hard to apply in the real world.

### 3.9.2 Goal-setting theory

Goal-setting theory suggests that **goals** can motivate.

(a)     Challenging goals, providing they have been accepted, lead to better performance than easy goals.
(b)     The best goals are specific as they focus people's attention.
(c)     Knowledge of results is essential.

Goal theory has the most empirical support of any motivation theory, but there are some limits to how it applies.

(a)     Research has concentrated on quantity not quality of output.
(b)     At work, people pursue several goals consecutively; achieving one may mean neglecting another. This is particularly a problem for organisations where trade offs have to be made.

## 3.10 Psychological contracts

FAST FORWARD

> There is a set of **expectations** which can **form a psychological contract** between an organisation and employees.

A **psychological contract** exists between individuals in an organisation and the organisation itself.

(a)     The individual expects to derive certain benefits from membership of the organisation and is prepared to expend a certain amount of effort in return.
(b)     The organisation expects the individual to fulfil certain requirements and is prepared to offer certain rewards in return.

Three types of psychological contract can be identified.

(a)     **Coercive contract**. This is a contract in which the individual considers that he or she is being forced to contribute his efforts and energies involuntarily, and that the rewards they receive in return are inadequate compensation.

(b)     **Calculative contract**. This is a contract, accepted **voluntarily** by the individual, in which he expects to do his job in exchange for a readily identifiable set of rewards. With such psychological contracts, motivation can only be increased if the rewards to the individual are improved. If the organisation attempts to demand greater efforts without increasing the rewards, the psychological contract will revert to a coercive one, and motivation may become negative.

(c)     **Co-operative contract**. This is a contract in which the individual identifies himself with the organisation and its goals, so that they actively seek to contribute further to the achievement of those goals. Motivation comes out of success at work, a sense of achievement, and self-fulfilment.

The individual will probably want to share in the planning and control decisions which affect his work, and **co-operative contracts are therefore likely to occur where employees participate in decision-making**.

Motivation happens when the psychological contract, within which the individual's motivation calculus operates for new decisions, is viewed in the same way by the organisation and by the individual, and when both parties are able to fulfil their side of the bargain – the individual agrees to work, or work well, in return for whatever rewards or satisfactions are understood as the terms of the 'contract'.

## Question

Douglas McGregor suggested that managers have one of two views or theories about subordinates.

*View 1*   Individuals want to satisfy their needs through work and wish to make a contribution to the goals they have helped to establish.

*View 2*   Most people dislike work and responsibility, and so have to be coerced, controlled, and threatened with punishment, to get them to do their job adequately.

A    View 1 is called Theory X and view 2 is called Theory Y, and McGregor suggested that the most effective managers hold view 1

B    View 1 is called Theory Y and view 2 is called Theory X, and McGregor suggested that the most effective managers hold view 2

C    View 1 is called Theory X and view 2 is called Theory Y, and McGregor suggested that the most effective managers hold view 2

D    View 1 is called Theory Y and view 2 is called Theory X, and McGregor suggested that the view held by the most effective managers depends on the circumstances

## Answer

D    The more effective view of managers depends on the circumstances of the work. If a manager is in charge of a large number of people doing repetitive, routine work, a Theory X approach is likely to be more effective. At other times, a Theory Y approach will be more effective, for example in dealing with subordinates who are managers or professionals.

# 4 Money and job satisfaction

**FAST FORWARD**

Pay (money) can be a motivator in certain circumstances. However, these depend on the value individuals ascribe to pay and the way in which incentive schemes are implemented. **Pay is usually considered a hygiene factor**.

You may have noticed that none of the well-known catalogues of human needs mentions money - yet it is often assumed to be a means of satisfying any or all of the other needs. The value of money as a motivator will therefore depend on its **perceived value** for the individual, but, on the other hand, it can usefully be offered as an incentive because it is instrumental in satisfying so many different needs.

We must remember, however, that an employee needs income to live. Employees probably have two basic concerns: to earn **enough** money and that their pay should be **fair**. This can be assessed in two ways.

(a)    **Equity** – a fair rate for the job
(b)    **Relativity**, or fair differentials, that is, justified differences between the pay of different individuals

## 4.1 Payment systems

*Armstrong* and *Murlis* (1998) suggested that payments to employees have two elements.

- **Pay** with scope to reward **progression** and **promotion**
- **Benefits** such as pensions, company cars and medical insurance

### 4.1.1 Organisational aims for payment systems

At the organisational (strategic) level, payment systems have the following goals.

- Aid **recruitment**
- **Retain** employees
- **Reward** employees for performance

### 4.1.2 Managerial aims for payment systems

At the managerial level, payment systems are used to:

- Reward and motivate employees fairly and consistently
- Further the organisation's objectives by providing competitive rewards
- Encourage performance and progression through development
- Recognise non-performance factors such as skill and competence
- Ensure salary costs are controlled

## 4.2 Pay structures

Common types of pay structure include:

- **Graded**. A pay range is attached to particular levels of job grades.

- **Broad-banded structures** usually encompass the whole workforce from the clerk to the senior manager. The range of pay in this structure is typically higher than in graded structures.

- **Individual**. Pay is allocated to individuals rather than 'bands'. It is most commonly used for senior management positions and avoids the problem of over/under payment which can result from grading.

- **Job family structures**. Jobs in specific functions such as accounts or HR are grouped into families. The jobs differ in terms of skill levels or responsibility (such as accounts technician and management accountant) and pay is determined accordingly.

- **Pay** or **profession/maturity curves**. These recognise that in certain roles, pay must be progressive to allocate pay fairly. Especially where knowledge or experience is key to the role.

- **Spot rates**. Allocate a rate of pay for a specific job often linked to the market price.

- **Rate for age**. Allocates a rate of pay or pay bracket for employees based on age.

- **Pay spines** are often used by government organisations where it is important for pay to be relative across a range of roles. They are a series of incremental points from the lowest to the highest paid jobs. Pay scales for specific jobs are superimposed onto the spine to ensure pay is relative.

- **Manual worker pay structures** recognise the difference in status between those who work in manual roles against those in other parts of the organisation. Real differentials are incorporated that reflect differences in skill and responsibility but otherwise they are similar to other pay structures.

- **Integrated structures** incorporate one grading system for all employees except senior management. They are often used where employees were paid historically under separate agreements.

The assumption behind most payment systems is that money is the prime motivating factor. As *Herzberg*, among others, suggested, however, it is more likely to be a cause of dissatisfaction.

*Herzberg* himself admitted that pay is the most important of all the hygiene factors. *Goldthorpe, Lockwood et al*, in their *Affluent Worker* study of the Luton car industry, suggested that workers may have a purely **instrumental** orientation to work – deriving satisfaction not from the work itself but from the rewards obtainable with the money earned by working. The Luton workers experienced their work as routine and dead-end, but had made a rational decision to enter employment which offered high monetary reward rather than intrinsic interest.

As expectancy theory indicates, pay is only likely to motivate a worker to improved performance if there is a clear and consistent link between performance and monetary reward and if monetary reward is valued.

Salary structures do not always allow enough leeway to reward individual performance in a job (since fairness usually dictates a rate for the job itself, in relation to others): **incentive schemes**, however, are often used to re-establish the link between effort and reward.

## 4.3 Pay differentials

As mentioned above, pay differentials are often key to determining salaries for employees. To calculate pay differentials an organisation should refer to market rates for the roles and decide a policy of how its pay levels will reflect the market rate. The following methods may be used in determining pay rates.

### 4.3.1 Points-factor evaluation scheme

**Stage 1**  Evaluate the roles and calculate evaluation job scores based on the level or category of employee.

**Stage 2**  Plot job scores on a scatter diagram and draw a line of 'best fit'.

**Stage 3**  Plot the upper, median and lower market pay rates from the available information.

**Stage 4**  Plot a desired pay policy line based on the market data.

**Stage 5**  Decide on the overall shape of the pay structure based on the pay policy.

**Stage 6**  Define pay ranges for each level taking into account flexibility for pay-progression.

### 4.3.2 Ranking/market method

**Stage 1**  Rank the existing jobs and plot actual pay rates to show current pay policy.

**Stage 2**  Plot market data and derive a 'best fit' policy.

**Stage 3**  Decide on a pay range policy and plot upper and lower pay rates using the 'best fit' policy as the mid-range.

**Stage 4**  Develop a grade structure and pay rates for each grade.

## 4.4 Incentive schemes

The purpose of incentive schemes is to **improve performance by linking it to reward**. It is believed that performance incentives take effect in several ways.

(a)  Staff members' effort and attention are **directed to where they are most needed**; the need for performance is emphasised.

(b)  **Commitment and motivation are enhanced**. This is particularly important when there are cultural obstacles to improvement.

(c)  **Achievement** can be rewarded separately from **effort**, with advantages for the recruitment and retention of high quality employees.

A further advantage is that labour costs are linked to organisational performance.

Schemes may be based on individual performance or on group performance. Individual schemes are common when the work is essentially individualistic and the output of a single person is easy to specify and measure. However, much work is performed by teams and it is impossible to identify each person's output. Such work calls for a group incentive scheme. The main problem with team incentive payments is that there is unlikely to be a single consistent standard of effort or achievement within the group. Inevitably there will be those who perform better than others and they are likely to be aggrieved if all group members are rewarded equally.

The ultimate group incentive scheme is the organisation wide scheme, in which all employees are rewarded in accordance with overall performance, usually as measured by profit . This tends to be very popular in good times and the cause of disappointment and resentment when the firm is doing badly. The value of such schemes is questionable.

### 4.4.1 Types of incentive scheme

There are three main types of incentive scheme:

- Performance related pay (PRP)
- Bonus schemes
- Profit-sharing

### 4.4.2 Performance related pay

The most common individual PRP scheme for wage earners is straight **piecework**: payment of a fixed amount per unit produced, or operation completed.

For managerial and other salaried jobs, however, a form of **management by objectives** will probably be applied.

(a) Key results will be identified and specified, for which merit awards (on top of basic salary) will be paid.

(b) There will be a clear model for evaluating performance and knowing when, or if, targets have been reached and payments earned.

(c) The exact conditions and amounts of awards can be made clear to the employee, to avoid uncertainty and later resentment.

For service and other departments, a PRP scheme may involve bonuses for achievement of key results, or points schemes, where points are awarded for performance on various criteria (efficiency, cost savings, quality of service and so on). Certain points totals (or the highest points total in the unit, if a competitive system is used) then win cash or other awards.

However, *Otley* (1987) discovered that employees become demotivated if they fail to meet targets, resulting in a high degree of performance reduction.

### 4.4.3 Bonus schemes

**Bonus schemes** are supplementary to basic salary, and have been found to be popular with entrepreneurial types, usually in marketing and sales. Bonuses are both incentives and rewards.

**Group incentive schemes** typically offer a bonus for a group (equally, or proportionately to the earnings or status of individuals) which achieves or exceeds specified targets. Typically, bonuses would be calculated monthly on the basis of improvements in output per man per hour against standard, or value added (to the cost of raw materials and parts by the production process).

**Value added schemes** work on the basis that improvements in productivity increases value added, and the benefit can be shared between employers and employees on an agreed formula. So if sales revenue increases and labour costs stay the same, or sales revenue remains constant but labour costs decrease, the balance becomes available. There has been an increase in such schemes in recent years.

### 4.4.4 Profit sharing schemes and employee shareholders

**Profit sharing schemes** offer employees (or selected groups of them) bonuses, perhaps in the form of shares in the company, related directly to profits. The formula for determining the amounts may vary, but in recent years a straightforward distribution of a percentage of profits above a given target has given way to a value added related concept.

Profit sharing is in general based on the belief that all employees can contribute to profitability, and that that contribution should be recognised. If it is, the argument runs, the effects may include profit-consciousness and motivation in employees, commitment to the future prosperity of the organisation and so on.

The actual incentive value and effect on productivity may be wasted, however, if the scheme is badly designed.

(a)   A **perceivably significant sum** should be made available to employees – once shareholders have received appropriate return on their investment – say, 10% of basic pay.

(b)   There should be a clear, and not overly delayed, **link between performance and reward**. Profit shares should be distributed as frequently as possible – consistent with the need for reliable information on profit forecasts and targets and the need to amass a significant pool for distribution.

(c)   The scheme should only be introduced if profit forecasts indicate a reasonable chance of achieving the target: profit sharing is welcome when profits are high, but the potential for disappointment is great.

(d)   The greatest effect on productivity arising from the scheme may in fact arise from its use as a focal point for discussion with employees, about the relationship between their performance and results, and areas and targets for improvement. Management must be seen to be committed to the principle.

<table>
<tr><td>Exam focus point</td><td>While reading through this chapter, consider what factors should be taken into account when designing reward and remuneration packages, as this was a requirement in the May 2006 exam.<br><br>The November 2007 exam offered ten-marks for a discussion of the difficulties of designing and operating a reward scheme for performance.</td></tr>
</table>

## 4.5 Difficulties associated with incentive schemes

Incentive schemes have the following potential difficulties.

(a)   Increased earnings simply may not be an incentive to some individuals. An individual who already enjoys a good income may be more concerned with increasing his leisure time, for example.

(b)   Workers are unlikely to be in complete control of results. External factors, such as the general economic climate, interest rates and exchange rates may play a part in **profitability** in particular. In these cases, the relationship between an individual's efforts and his reward may be indistinct.

(c)   Greater specialisation in production processes means that particular employees cannot be specifically credited with the success of particular products. This may lead to frustration amongst employees who think their own profitable work is being adversely affected by inefficiencies elsewhere in the organisation.

(d)   Even if employees are motivated by money, the effects may not be altogether desirable. An instrumental orientation may encourage self-interested performance at the expense of teamwork: it may encourage attention to output at the expense of quality, and the lowering of standards and targets (in order to make bonuses more accessible).

(e)   It is often all too easy to manipulate the rules of the incentive scheme, especially where there are allowances for waiting time, when production is held up by factors beyond the control of the people concerned. Special allowances, guaranteed earnings and changes in methods also undermine incentive schemes.

(f)   Poorly designed schemes can produce labour cost increases out of proportion to output improvements.

The results of research into the benefits and problems of performance-related pay (carried out in the 1990s) are shown below.

| | Black & Decker | Komatsu UK | Birds Eye Walls | Co. A | Co. B | Co. C | Co. D | Co. E |
|---|---|---|---|---|---|---|---|---|
| **1 Benefits of PRP cited** | | | | | | | | |
| Improves commitment and capability | Yes | Yes | Yes | Yes | Yes | Yes | Yes | Yes |
| Complements other HR initiatives | Yes | Yes | Yes | Yes | Yes | Yes | | Yes |
| Improves business awareness | Yes | Yes | Yes | | Yes | Yes | | |
| Better two-way communications | Yes | Yes | Yes | | Yes | Yes | | Yes |
| Greater supervisory responsibility | | Yes | Yes | Yes | Yes | | | Yes |
| **2 Potential problems cited** | | | | | | | | |
| Subjectivity | | | Yes | | | Yes | Yes | Yes |
| Supervisors' commitment and ability | Yes | Yes | Yes | | Yes | Yes | Yes | Yes |
| Translating appraisals into pay | Yes | Yes | Yes | Yes | | Yes | | Yes |
| Divisive/against team working | | | Yes | Yes | | Yes | Yes | Yes |
| Union acceptance/employee attitudes | | | Yes | Yes | Yes | | Yes | Yes |

The research concluded that in the wrong hands, PRP can do more harm than good, so organisations considering PRP should consider carefully whether it is appropriate for them. Other payment systems which do not seek to directly link individual performance and reward may be more suited to the aims of the business.

---

All such schemes are based on the principle that people are willing to work harder to obtain more money. However, the work of *Elton Mayo* and *Tom Lupton* has shown that there are several constraints which prevent most people from seeking to maximise their earnings.

(a)   Workers are generally capable of influencing the timings and control systems used by management.

(b)   Workers remain suspicious that if they achieve high levels of output and earnings then management will alter the basis of the incentive rates to reduce future earnings. Work groups therefore tend to restrict output to a level that they feel is **fair** and **safe**.

(c)   Generally, the workers conform to a group output norm. The need to have the approval of their fellow workers by conforming to that norm is more important than the money urge.

In the *Affluent Worker* study referred to above, *Goldthorpe* and *Lockwood* recognised that people do not, by and large, seek to maximise their earnings. Instead, a person will work as hard as necessary to earn the money they want – but not past the point at which the deprivations demanded of him (in terms of long hours or danger or antisocial conditions) are greater than they feel are worthwhile.

## 4.6 Total reward schemes

**Key term**

A **total reward scheme** (or package) is a bundle of cash and non-cash motivators offered to staff.

**Total reward schemes** recognise that individuals are all different and may not all be motivated by money. The fact that an individual can supplement their remuneration package may in itself be an attraction for prospective employees.

*Carrington* (2004) identified the drivers for the development of total reward package. The key driver was the skills shortage in the 1990s that caused '**talent wars**' where organisations had to **attract staff** in a more **competitive manner**. Around the same time many organisations were **developing** a **vision** and **culture** – these schemes helped further this development.

**Flexible benefits** are another method of rewarding staff. Certain incentives have become more or less popular over time and *Prickett* (2006) identified which are growing, static and declining in popularity.

| Growing | Static | Declining |
|---|---|---|
| Bicycles | Personal shopping and dry cleaning (city firms mainly) | Golden parachutes |
| Childcare | Shopping vouchers | Bonus schemes |
| Computers | Health and dental insurance | Share schemes |
| Flexible pension schemes (tax efficient) | Gym membership | Final salary pension schemes |

Examples of other **non-cash benefits** that may be offered include:

- **Training**
- **Flexible working hours**
- **Working at home**
- **Career progression**
- The **pursuit** of **green** or **ethical policies** by the company

*Carrington* (2004) identified a number of **advantages** of such schemes. In particular they make a **positive statement** about the culture of the organisation, the **creation** of a **more inclusive** rather than a 'them and us' attitude and **improved recruitment** and retention as a result of **employer branding**.

# 5 Working arrangements and types of organisation

**FAST FORWARD**

The ways in which people are **allowed and encouraged to work** will affect their motivation and performance.

For example, allowing employees flexibility in when they complete their weekly hours (flexitime) may allow them to deal with domestic issues when they arise, meaning the time they actually spend working is more productive.

## 5.1 Attitudes and values

Working methods and arrangements cover much more then the nuts and bolts of hours and pay. For example, modern management theorists emphasise values such as the following.

(a)  **Multi-skilling**. Multi-skilled teams involve individuals who are able to perform a variety of team tasks, as required. This enables tasks to be performed more flexibly, using labour more efficiently.

(b)  **Flexibility**. Flexibility is about being able to respond and adapt quickly to rapidly-changing customer demands, or to other changes such as technological change and different working methods. This has created the following.

   (i)   Smaller, **multi-skilled**, temporary structures, such as project or task-force teams.

   (ii)  Multi-functional units, facilitating communication and co-ordination across departmental boundaries. This is sometimes referred to as a **matrix structure**, since an employee may report both to a line manager *and* to a project or product manager.

   (iii) Flexible deployment of the labour resource, for example through part-time and temporary working, outsourcing, flexitime and so on (see later in this section).

(c)  **Empowerment**. Empowerment involves giving employees the freedom to take responsibility for their goals and actions. This may release hidden resources (creativity, initiative, leadership, innovation), which would otherwise remain inaccessible. People are allowed to use their own judgement.

The extent to which these values are incorporated into an organisation's **HR plan and policies** will depend upon the type of organisation, the role of the employees and the philosophy of top management. Some different types of organisation that have implications for working methods are covered later in this section.

## 5.2 Flexible working arrangements

When establishing policies and procedures on **flexible work arrangements**, organisations seek to provide employees with a means to achieve a **balance** between professional and personal responsibilities in a manner that **benefits both the employee and the employer**.

A well-structured policy should be developed that provides a clear understanding of the expectations and responsibilities of all parties involved in the flexible work arrangement, and ensures that the same criteria for making decisions on flexible work arrangements are applied to all employees.

The key to successful flexible work arrangements is to tailor the arrangement to the particular needs of the individual and the organisation. When considering which flexible work arrangements to offer employees, organisations should consider the arrangement's practicality, fairness, and flexibility within the environment of the organisation.

**Typical flexible work arrangements** include:

(a)  **Flexitime**. Flexitime is an arrangement where employees work the standard number of hours in a workday (or in some arrangements within a work week), but are given some flexibility as to when they work these hours. Most organisations establish 'core working hours', meaning there are certain hours during the day in which it is mandatory for the employee to be at the workplace. For example, an employee on flexitime may have to work 7.5 hours per day, but be able to start their day anytime between 7 and 10 a.m. and finish between 3 and 6 p.m.

(b)  **Compressed week**. A compressed week is an arrangement where an employee works the standard number of hours in a one-or two-week period, but compresses those hours into fewer work days (thus working longer hours on the days the employee is at work). For example, in a 40-hour work week an employee on a compressed work week may work four 10-hour days in a week with one day off, or nine 9-hour days with one day off every two weeks.

(c)  **Job sharing**. Job sharing is an arrangement where two employees share one position. There are many combinations of work hours that are used for job sharing. For example, one employee might work Monday to Wednesday and the other employee Thursday and Friday, or one employee might work mornings and the other afternoons.

(d)  **Part-time/Reduced hours**. Part-time or reduced hours are arrangements where an employee works less than the standard work week hours (and are paid only for those hours).

(e)  **Telecommuting or homeworking**. Telecommuting is an arrangement where an employee works either part or all of their workweek from a location other than the standard place of work (office). Typically employees in such an arrangement work from their homes. For example, an employee may work three days a week at the office and two days a week from home.

### 5.2.1 Implementing flexible work arrangements

Organisations introducing flexible working should compile a formal flexible work agreement to be completed and signed by the employer and the employee. The agreement should include the specific details of the arrangement.

Often there is an unreasonable requirement that individuals who work a compressed work week should be required to be available or on-call on their day off, or, on the other hand, the probably reasonable expectation that employees with the right to work at home should come into work for a meeting held on their work-at-home day. These issues should be covered by the flexible work arrangement agreement.

### 5.2.2 Types of flexibility

Three types of flexibility organisations look to achieve in the context of HRM are numerical flexibility, financial flexibility and task flexibility.

**Numerical flexibility** can be achieved through the use of temporary workers – both contractors and agency staff. *Atkinson* (1984) distinguished between 'core employees' (high status, job security) and 'periphery workers' on temporary or flexible hour contracts.

**Financial flexibility** is achieved through variable systems of reward (eg bonuses, performance-related pay).

**Task flexibility** (sometimes referred to as functional flexibility) involves having employees able to undertake a wider range of tasks. Introducing task flexibility could involve employees undertaking a wider range of tasks at the same 'level' (horizontally) or undertaking tasks previously carried out by employees at higher or lower levels (vertically).

**Exam focus point**

The May 2005 exam offered eight marks for discussing how the organisation in the scenario could achieve workforce flexibility.

### 5.2.3 Advantages and disadvantages of flexible work arrangements

The **potential benefits to the employer** are increased employee motivation and productivity; increased employee commitment to the organisation; ability to attract high performing individuals; and reduced absenteeism and staff turnover.

Possible **disadvantages to the employer** include increased difficulty co-ordinating work (which has implications for job design), a loss of direct control and possibly the dilution of organisation culture as employees see less of each other.

The potential **benefits to the employee** are: reduction in stress due to conflicting personal and professional priorities; and increased job satisfaction, energy and creativity.

Potential **disadvantages to employees** include the loss of the distinction between home and office life and the increased possibility of being distracted from work tasks.

## 5.3 Human Resource Management in different types of organisation

The need to work in different ways has been brought about partly by the changing nature of business and the evolvement of different types and forms of organisations.

### 5.3.1 Project-based teams

There is a general trend in organisation structures (particularly in service organisations) away from traditional hierarchies towards flatter structures with reporting lines that cross functional boundaries. Instead of traditional departments, some organisations operate using multi-skilled employees organised into various work teams based around factors such as customer groups or particular projects.

This has implications for the HR plan and policies. For example, if a general pool of multi-skilled employees is required, recruitment policy should reflect that fact – rather than recruiting large numbers of specialists. Extensive training programmes are also likely to be required.

The **advantages and disadvantages of project-based organisations** can be summarised as follows.

| Advantages | Disadvantages |
|---|---|
| **Greater flexibility** of:<br>(i) **People**. Employees develop an attitude geared to accepting change.<br>(ii) **Workflow and decision-making**. Direct contact between staff encourages problem solving and big picture thinking.<br>(iii) **Tasks and structure**. The matrix structure may be readily amended, where projects are completed. | **Dual authority** threatens a conflict between functional managers and product/project area managers. |
| **Inter-disciplinary co-operation** and a mixing of skills and expertise, along with improved communication and co-ordination. | An individual with two or more bosses may suffer stress from **conflicting demands or ambiguous roles**. |
| **Motivation and employee development**: providing employees with greater participation in planning and control decisions. | **Cost**: product management posts are added, more consultation is required eg meetings. |
| **Market awareness**: the organisation tends to become more customer/quality focused. | **Slower decision making** |
| **Horizontal workflow**: Bureaucratic obstacles are removed. | Possible lack of accountability |

### 5.3.2 The 'new organisation'

Some recent trends (identified by writers such as *Blyton* and *Peters*) have emerged from the focus on **flexibility** as a key organisational value.

(a) **Flat structures**. The flattening of hierarchies does away with levels of organisation which lengthened lines of communication and decision-making and encouraged ever-increasing specialisation. Flat structures are more responsive, because there is a more direct relationship between the organisation's strategic centre and the operational units serving the customer.

(b) **'Horizontal structures'**. What *Peters (Liberation Management)* calls 'going horizontal' is a recognition that functional versatility (through multi-functional project teams and multi-skilling, for example) is the key to flexibility. In the words (quoted by *Peters*) of a Motorola executive: 'The traditional job descriptions were barriers. We needed an organisation soft enough between the organisational disciplines so that … people would run freely across functional barriers or organisational barriers with the common goal of getting the job done, rather than just making certain that their specific part of the job was completed.'

(c) **'Chunked' and 'unglued' structures**. So far, this has meant teamworking and decentralisation, or empowerment, creating smaller and more flexible units within the overall structure. *Charles Handy's* **'shamrock organisation'** (with a three-leafed structured of core, subcontractor and flexible part-time labour) is gaining ground as a workable model for a leaner and more flexible workforce, within a controlled framework.

(d) **Output-focused structures**. The key to all the above trends is the focus on results, and on the customer, instead of internal processes and functions for their own sake. A **project management** orientation and structure, for example, is being applied to the supply of services within the organisation (to internal customers) as well as to the external market, in order to facilitate listening and responding to customer demands.

(e) **'Jobless' structures**. Meanwhile, the employee becomes not a job-holder but the vendor of a portfolio of demonstrated outputs and competences (*Bridges*). This is a concrete expression of the concept of **employability**, which says that a person needs to have a portfolio of skills which are valuable on the open labour market: employees need to be mobile, moving between organisations rather than settling in to a particular job.

### 5.3.3 Virtual organisations

The global explosion of Information and Communication Technology (ICT) has also had a major impact on work organisation. In particular, it has created the concept of **virtual teams** and even **virtual organisations**. Virtual teams are interconnected groups of people who may not be present in the same office or organisation (and may even be in different areas of the world) but who:

- Share information and tasks (eg technical support provided by a supplier),
- Make joint decisions (eg on quality assurance or staff training), and
- Fulfil the collaborative (working together) function of a team.

ICT has facilitated this kind of collaboration, simulating team working via teleconferencing, video-conferencing, networked computers and the World Wide Web.

(a) Dispersed individuals and units can use such technology to access and share up-to-date research, product, customer, inventory and delivery information (eg using Web-based databases and data tracking systems).

(b) Electronic meeting management systems allow virtual meeting participants to talk and listen to each other on teleconference lines, while sharing data and using electronic 'white boards' on their PCs.

This has enabled organisations to:

(a) **Outsource** areas of organisational activity to other organisations and freelance workers (even 'off-shore' in countries where skilled labour is cheaper), without losing control or co-ordination.

(b) **Organise 'territorially'** without the overhead costs of local offices, and without the difficulties of supervision, communication and control. Dispersed centres are linked to a 'virtual office' by communications technology and can share data freely.

(c) **Centralise** shared functions and services (such as data storage and retrieval, technical support or secretarial services) without the disadvantages of 'geographical' centralisation, and with the advantages of decentralised authority. Databases and communication (eg via e-mail) create genuine interactive sharing of, and access to, common data.

(d) **Adopt flexible cross-functional and multi-skilled working**, by making expertise available across the organisation. A 'virtual team' co-opts the best people for the task – regardless of location.

## Chapter Roundup

- **Motivating employees** to work hard and perform well is a perennial problem for managers. Some management practices are based on quite crude assumptions of how people are motivated.

- Motivation directs **individual behaviour**. It is in the interests of an employer to know how to motivate employees' behaviour for the employer's benefit.

- Pay (money) can be a motivator in certain circumstances. However, these depend on the value individuals ascribe to pay and the way in which incentive schemes are implemented. **Pay is usually considered a hygiene factor**.

- The ways in which people are **allowed and encouraged to work** will affect their motivation and performance.

- When establishing policies and procedures on **flexible work arrangements**, organisations seek to provide employees with a means to achieve a balance between professional and personal responsibilities in a manner that **benefits both the employee and the employer**.

# Quick Quiz

1    Why should an organisation take an interest in an individual's personal development?

2    According to Mullins, which three are classifications for understanding motivation?

    (i)     Economic reward
    (ii)    Intrinsic satisfaction
    (iii)   Extrinsic goals
    (iv)   Social relationships

    A     (i), (ii) and (iii)
    B     (i), (ii) and (iv)
    C     (i), (iii) and (iv)
    D     (ii), (iii) and (iv)

3    Distinguish between hygiene factors and motivator factors.

4    Which type of pay structure is described below? 'Allocate a rate of pay for a specific job often linked to the market price'.

    A     Graded
    B     Rate for age
    C     Pay spine
    D     Spot rate

5    List four examples of flexible working arrangements.

    1     .............................................................
    2     .............................................................
    3     .............................................................
    4     .............................................................

# Answers to Quick Quiz

1   Poor personal development can cause high labour turnover, absenteeism or preoccupation with financial rewards – self-defeating for the organisation and unhealthy for the individual.

2   B   According to Mullins three classifications for understanding motivation are economic reward, intrinsic satisfaction and social relationships.

3   Hygiene factors satisfy the need to avoid unpleasantness, while motivators satisfy the need for personal growth.

4   D   The description is of a spot rate pay structure.

5   Any four from flexitime, job sharing, part-time, homeworking, compressed week, reduced hours or telecommuting.

## Now try the question below from the Exam Question Bank

| Number | Level | Marks | Time |
|---|---|---|---|
| 8 | Tutorial | 20 | 36 mins |

# Training, appraisal and career management

## Introduction

**Training** aims to improve employee efficiency and productivity. The strategic purpose of training is to raise the overall skills level of the organisation.

**Appraisal** is an important tool in monitoring employee performance and planning for the future. It forms an important channel of two-way communication. Appraisal can be used for a number of purposes.

- Setting targets for improvement
- Determining training needs
- Considering potential for promotion
- Reviewing remuneration

Both the organisation and the individual should gain benefits from an effective appraisal system integrated into organisational planning and control strategy.

Formal **career management** policies and procedures are now found in many larger organisations. This reflects an increased emphasis on promoting from within, enabling individuals to develop their careers and organisations to retain the knowledge held by employees.

| Topic list | Learning outcomes | Syllabus references | Ability required |
|---|---|---|---|
| 1 Human resource development | E(ii), E(iii) | E(2), E(4) | Evaluation |
| 2 Training and development needs | E(ii), E(iii) | E(2), E(4) | Evaluation |
| 3 Methods of development and training | E(ii), E(iii) | E(2), E(4), E(11) | Evaluation |
| 4 Evaluating training | E(ii), E(iii) | E(2), E(4) | Evaluation |
| 5 Appraisal | E(ii), E(iii) | E(12) | Evaluation |
| 6 Career management | E(ii), E(iii) | E(3), E(11) | Evaluation |

# 1 Human resource development

FAST FORWARD

> **Human resource development (HRD)** involves training, education and development.

Resourcing an organisation (in HRM jargon) is about building and maintaining the **skills and knowledge base** of the organisation.

**Key term**

> **Human resource development** (HRD) is the process of extending personal abilities and qualities by means of education, training and other learning experiences.

## 1.1 What is development?

**Key terms**

> **Development** is 'the growth or realisation of a person's ability and potential through the provision of learning and educational experiences'.
>
> **Training** is 'the planned and systematic modification of behaviour through learning events, programmes and instruction which enable individuals to achieve the level of knowledge, skills and competence to carry out their work effectively'.
>
> *(Armstrong, Handbook of Personnel Management Practice)*

The overall purpose of employee and management development includes:

- **Ensure** the firm meets current and future performance objectives by...
- **Continuous improvement** of the performance of individuals and teams, and by...
- **Maximising people's** potential for growth (and promotion).

### 1.1.1 Training and development strategy

Organisations often have a **training and development strategy**, based on the overall strategy for the business. We can list the following steps.

**Step 1**     Identify the skills and competences are needed by the **business plan.**

**Step 2**     Draw up the **development strategy** to show how training and development activities will assist in meeting the targets of the corporate plan.

**Step 3**     **Implement** the training and development strategy.

This approach produces training with the right qualities.

- Relevance
- Problem-based (ie corrects a real lack of skills)
- Action-oriented
- Performance-related

### 1.1.2 Effective learning programmes

The following principles are key to effective learning programmes:

| Principle | Explanation |
|---|---|
| **Participants** | Must have the ability, skills, knowledge and motivation to learn. |
| **Overview** | An overview of what is to be learnt should be provided before focusing of specific tasks. |
| **Feedback** | Participants should receive, accurate and timely feedback on their progress. |

| Principle | Explanation |
|---|---|
| Rewards | Progress should be rewarded by positive re-enforcement such as praise or tangible items such as certificates. |
| Active involvement | Successful learning involves taking part rather than listening or reading. |
| Learning curve | Training must reflect the fact that some skills are picked up quickly whereas some will take time to develop. Progress is not always at the same pace. |
| Job specific | Training should be as realistic as possible to the job concerned to minimise problems of applying the new skill of knowledge. |

## 1.2 HRD and the organisation

The **benefits for the organisation** of training and development programmes are outlined in the following table.

| Benefit | Comment |
|---|---|
| **Minimise the learning costs** of obtaining the skills the organisation needs | Training supports the business strategy. |
| Lower costs and **increased productivity**, thereby improving performance | Some people suggest that higher levels of training explain the higher productivity of German as opposed to many British manufacturers. |
| **Fewer accidents**, and better health and safety | EU health and safety directives require a certain level of training. Employees can take employers to court if accidents occur or if unhealthy work practices persist. |
| **Less need for detailed supervision** | If people are trained they can get on with the job, and managers can concentrate on other things. Training is an aspect of **empowerment**. |
| **Flexibility** | Training ensures that people have the **variety** of skills needed – multi-skilling is only possible if people are properly trained. |
| **Recruitment and succession planning** | Training and development attracts new recruits and ensures that the organisation has a supply of suitable managerial and technical staff to take over when people retire. |
| **Change management** | Training helps organisations manage change by letting people know why the change is happening and giving them the skills to cope with it. |
| **Corporate culture** | Training programmes can be used to build the corporate culture or to direct it in certain ways, by indicating that certain **values** are espoused. |
| | Training programmes can **build relationships** between staff and managers in different areas of the business. |
| **Motivation** | Training programmes can increase commitment to the organisation's goals. |

## 1.3 Training and the employee

For the individual employee, the benefits of training and development are more clear-cut, and few refuse it if it is offered.

| Benefit | Comment |
|---|---|
| Enhances portfolio of **skills** | Even if not specifically related to the current job, training can be useful in other contexts, and the employee becomes more attractive to employers and more promotable. |

| Benefit | Comment |
|---|---|
| Psychological benefits | The trainee might feel reassured that he/she is of continuing value to the organisation. |
| Social benefit | People's social needs can be met by training courses – they can also develop networks of contacts. |
| The job | Training can help people do their job better, thereby increasing job satisfaction. |

## 1.4 Possible shortcomings of training

Training is not always the answer to performance related problems.

(a) It is irrelevant to problems caused by faulty organisation, layout, methods, equipment, employee selection and placement and so on.

(b) Cost, time, inconvenience, apathy and an unrealistic expectations of training in the past may restrict its effectiveness.

(c) Limitations imposed by intelligence, poor motivation and the psychological restrictions of the learning process also restrict its effectiveness.

Question

Human resource development

Which of the following are aspects of human resource development (HRD)?

(i) Providing formal training courses
(ii) On-the-job training
(iii) Succession and career planning
(iv) Job re-design

A    (i) only
B    (i) and (ii) only
C    (i), (ii) and (iii) only
D    All of the above.

Answer

D    HRD covers all aspects of personal and management development, including formal training and on-the-job training, planning the succession into senior management positions, and career planning for individuals (particularly management recruits). Job re-design is also related to development, because the content of a job can be altered to provide better or different learning experiences.

# 2 Training and development needs

FAST FORWARD

The management of training and development is an iterative, rational process that includes several different aspects.

- Identification of training **needs**
- Definition of training **objectives**
- **Planning** of training
- **Delivery** of training
- **Evaluation** of training

## 2.1 The training process

In order to ensure that training meets the real needs of the organisation, large firms adopt a planned approach to training. This has the following steps.

**Step 1**  **Identify and define the organisation's training needs**. It may be the case that recruitment might be a better solution to a problem than training.

**Step 2**  **Define the learning required** – in other words, specify the knowledge, skills or competences that have to be acquired. For technical training, this is not difficult: for example, all finance department staff will have to become conversant with the new accounting system.

**Step 3**  **Define training objectives** – what must be learnt and what trainees must be able to do after the training exercise.

**Step 4**  **Plan training programmes** – training and development can be planned in a number of ways, employing a number of techniques, as we shall learn about in Section 3. (Also, people have different approaches to learning, which have to be considered.) This covers three things.

- Who provides the training
- Where the training takes place
- Divisions of responsibilities between trainers, line managers or team leaders and the individual personally.

**Step 5**  **Implement the training**.

**Step 6**  **Evaluate the training**: has it been successful in achieving learning objectives?

**Step 7**  Go back to Step 2 if more training is needed.

## 2.2 Training needs analysis

## Case Study

**Training for quality**

The British Standards for Quality Systems (BS EN ISO 9000) identifies training needs for those organisations registering for assessment, and also shows the importance of a systematic approach to ensure adequate control.

The training, both by specific training to perform assigned tasks and general training to heighten quality awareness and to mould attitudes of all personnel in an organisation, is central to the achievement of quality.

The comprehensiveness of such training varies with the complexity of the organisation.

The following steps should be taken:

1  Identifying the way tasks and operations influence quality in total.

2  Identifying individuals; training needs against those required for satisfactory performance of the task.

3  Planning and carrying out appropriate specific training.

4  Planning and organising general quality awareness programmes.

5  Recording training and achievement in an easily retrievable form so that records can be updated and gaps in training can be readily identified.

As the example above demonstrates, **training needs analysis covers three issues**.

| | Current state | Desired state |
|---|---|---|
| 1 | Organisation's current results | Desired results, standards |
| 2 | Existing knowledge and skill | Knowledge and skill needed |
| 3 | Individual performance | Required standards |

The difference between the two columns is the **training gap**. Training programmes are designed to improve individual performance, thereby improving the performance of the organisation.

**Training surveys** combine information from a variety of sources to discern what the training needs of the organisation actually are.

(a) The **business strategy** at corporate level.

(b) **Appraisal and performance reviews:** the purpose of a performance management system is to improve performance, and training maybe recommended as a remedy.

(c) **Attitude surveys** of employees, asking them what training they think they need.

(d) **Evaluation** of existing training programmes.

(e) **Job analysis,** which deals with three things:

- Reported difficulties people have in meeting the skills requirement of the job
- Existing performance weaknesses that could be remedied by training
- Future changes in the job

The job analysis can be used to generate a training specification covering the knowledge needed for the job, the skills required to achieve the result, attitudinal changes required.

## 2.3 Setting training objectives

The **training manager** will have to make an initial investigation into the problem of the gap between job or competence requirements and current performance of competence.

If training would improve work performance, training **objectives** can then be defined. They should be clear, specific and related to observable, measurable targets.

- Behaviour – what the trainee should be able to do
- Standard – to what level of performance
- Environment – under what conditions (so that the performance level is realistic)

### 2.3.1 Example

'At the end of the course the trainee should be able to describe … or identify … or distinguish x from y … or calculate … or assemble …' and so on. It is insufficient to define the objectives of training as 'to give trainees a grounding in …' or 'to encourage trainees in a better appreciation of …': this offers no target achievement which can be quantifiably measured.

Training objectives link the identification of training needs with the content and methods of training.

| Training needs | Learning objectives |
|---|---|
| To know more about the Data Protection Act | The employee will be able to answer four out of every five queries about the Data Protection Act without having to search for details. |
| To establish a better rapport with customers | The employee will immediately attend to a customer unless already engaged with another customer. |
| | The employee will greet each customer using the customer's name where known. |
| | The employee will apologise to every customer who has had to wait to be attended to. |
| To assemble clocks faster | The employee will be able to assemble each clock within thirty minutes. |

Having identified training needs and objectives, the manager will have to decide on the best way to approach training: there are a number of types and techniques of training, which we will discuss below.

# 3 Methods of development and training

**Training** can be **on-the-job** or at a different site. **Formal** training courses are useful if the subject is relevant to the job, and if the course involves interaction with other members of the company. Background knowledge is then imparted through on-the-job training. The learning organisation values training as a source of desirable improvement and uses it as a means to encourage innovation.

## 3.1 Incorporating training needs into an individual development programme

**Key term**

A **personal development plan** is a 'clear developmental action plan for an individual which incorporates a wide set of developmental opportunities including formal training'.

The purpose of a personal development plan will vary.

- Improving performance in the existing job
- Developing skills for future career moves within and outside the organisation.

**Key term**

**Skills:** what the individual needs to be able to do if results are to be achieved. Skills are built up progressively by repeated training. They may be manual, intellectual or mental, perceptual or social.

Preparing a personal development plan involves these steps.

**Step 1** Analyse the current position. You could do a personal SWOT analysis. The supervisor can have an input into this by categorising the skills use of employees on a grid as follows, in a **skills analysis**.

|  |  | Performance | |
|--|--|------|------|
|  |  | High | Low |
| Liking of skills | High | Likes and does well | Likes but doesn't do well |
|  | Low | Dislikes but does well | Dislikes and doesn't do well |

The aim is to try to incorporate more of the employees' interests into their actual roles.

**Step 2** **Set goals to cover performance in the existing job**, future changes in the current role, moving elsewhere in the organisations, developing specialist expertise. Naturally, such goals should have the characteristic, as far as possible of **SMART objectives** (ie **S**pecific, **M**easurable, **A**chievable, **R**ealistic and **T**ime-bound).

**Step 3** **Draw up action plan** to achieve the goals.

## 3.2 Formal training

### 3.2.1 Formal training methods

**Formal training** methods include the following.

(a) **Internal courses** run by the organisation's training department or other employees.

(b) **External courses** (held either on or off-site) run by an outside organisation.

(c)    There are a wide range of training course types.

      (i)    **Day release**: the employee works in the organisation and on one day per week attends a local college or training centre for theoretical learning.

      (ii)    **Distance learning**, **evening classes and correspondence courses**, which make demands on the individual's time outside work. This is commonly used, for example, by typists wishing to develop or 'refresh' shorthand skills.

      (iii)    **Revision courses** for examinations of professional bodies.

      (iv)    **Block release** courses which may involve four weeks at a college or training centre followed by a period back at work.

      (v)    **Sandwich courses**, usually involve six months at college then six months at work, in rotation, for two or three years.

      (vi)    A **sponsored full-time course** at a university for one or two years.

(d)    **Techniques** used in training delivery might include:

- Lectures
- Seminars, in which participation is encouraged
- Simulations

(e)    **Computer-based training** involves interactive training via PC. This could involve the use of CD-ROMs or online delivery via the Internet.

### 3.2.2 Methods used on courses

**Common course training methods** include the following.

(a)    **Lectures**. Lectures are suitable for large audiences and can be an efficient way of putting across information. However lack of participation may lead to lack of interest from, and failure to understand by most of the audience.

(b)    **Discussions.** Discussions aim to impart information but allow much greater opportunities to audience participation. They are often suitable for groups up to 20 and can be a good means of maintaining interest.

(c)    **Exercises**. An exercise involves a particular task being undertaken with pre-set results following guidance laid down. They are a very active form of learning and are a good means of checking whether trainees have assimilated information.

(d)    **Role plays.** Trainees act out roles in a typical work situation. They are useful practice for face-to-face situations. However, they may embarrass and may not be taken seriously.

(e)    **Case studies.** Case studies identify causes and/or suggest solutions. They are a good means of exchanging ideas and thinking out solutions. However trainees may see the case study as divorced from their real work experience.

## 3.3 Disadvantages of formal training

(a)    An individual will not benefit from formal training unless he or she **wants to learn**. The individual's superior may need to provide encouragement in this respect.

(b)    If the **subject matter** of the training course does not **relate to an individual's job**, the learning will quickly be forgotten.

(c)    Individuals may not be able to carry over what they have learnt to their own particular job.

## 3.4 On the job training

On the job training can include a wide range of activities.

One employee shadowing another is one common method; being assigned a 'mentor' is another.

*Pedler* (1986) pointed out that at management level learning and development are often accidental or unconscious. Any activity that results in a manager being more willing or capable to control events has a developmental aspect to it.

More specific or structured on the job training schemes typically have the following characteristics.

(a) The assignments should have a **specific purpose** from which the trainee can learn and gain experience.

(b) The organisation must **tolerate any mistakes** which the trainee makes. Mistakes are an inevitable part of on the job learning.

(c) The work should **not be too complex**.

Methods of on the job training include the following.

(a) **Demonstration/instruction**: show the trainee how to do the job and let them get on with it. It should combine **telling** a person what to do and **showing** them how, using appropriate media. The trainee imitates the instructor, and asks questions.

(b) **Coaching**: the trainee is put under the guidance of an experienced employee who shows the trainee how to do the job. The coach should:

  • Establish learning targets.
  • Plan a systematic learning and development programme.
  • Identify opportunities for broadening the trainee's knowledge and experience.
  • Take into account the strengths and limitations of the trainee.
  • Exchange feedback.

(c) **Job rotation**: the trainee is given several jobs in succession, to gain experience of a wide range of activities.

(d) **Temporary promotion**: an individual is promoted into his/her superior's position whilst the superior is absent.

(e) **'Assistant to' positions**: a junior manager with good potential may be appointed as assistant to the managing director or another executive director.

(f) **Action learning**: a group of managers are brought together to solve a real problem with the help of an advisor who explains the management process that actually happens.

(g) **Committees**: trainees might be included in the membership of committees, in order to obtain an understanding of inter-departmental relationships.

(h) **Project work**: Work on a project with other people can expose the trainee to other parts of the organisation.

## 3.5 The learning cycle (Kolb)

*Kolb* suggested that **formal classroom-type learning** is 'a specialist activity **cut off** from the real world and unrelated to one's life': a teacher or trainer directs the learning process on behalf of a **passive** learner.

**Experiential learning**, on the other hand, involves **doing** and puts the learners in an **active** problem-solving role.

**Self-learning** encourages learners to formulate and commit themselves to their own learning objectives.

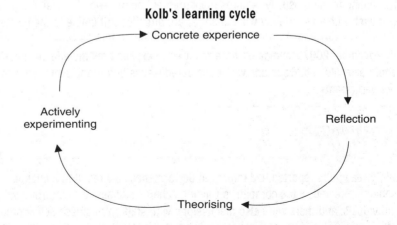

**Kolb's learning cycle**

The implication of Kolb's theory is that to be effective, learning must be **reinforced by experience**.

### 3.6 Training in different industries or sectors

Training and development activities vary in both approach and frequency/quantity across different sectors and employee groups. *Hendry* (1995) attributes these differences to different types of labour markets.

*Hendry* points out that service sectors tend to rely on retraining and training employees (an **internal** labour market).

Manufacturing industries have instead tended to rely on the apprenticeship system, which provides a more 'portable' qualification resulting in an **external**, occupational labour market.

# 4 Evaluating training

There are a number of ways of **validating** and **evaluating** a training scheme.

> **Validation of training** means observing the results of the course and measuring whether the training objectives have been achieved.
>
> **Evaluation of training** means comparing the actual costs of the scheme against the assessed benefits which are being obtained. If the costs exceed the benefits, the scheme will need to be redesigned or withdrawn.

(a) **Trainees' reactions to the experience:** asking the trainees whether they thought the training programme was relevant to their work, and whether they found it useful.

(b) **Trainee learning:** measuring what the trainees have learned on the course by means of a test at the end of it.

(c) **Changes in job behaviour following training.** This is relevant where the aim of the training was to learn a skill.

(d) **Organisational change as a result of training:** finding out whether the training has affected the work or behaviour of other employees not on the course.

(e) **Impact of training on the achievement of organisational goals:** seeing whether the training scheme has contributed to the achievement of the overall objectives of the organisation.

## 4.1 Levels of evaluation

*Kirkpatrick* (1998) identified four levels at which **training can be evaluated**.

- **Reaction** – how the trainees act, enjoyment level
- **Learning** – has the knowledge been absorbed?
- **Behaviour** – have required behavioural changes taken place?
- **Results** – what benefits have resulted from the training (eg better quality, reduced costs)?

Evaluating training usually requires measurement before and after training. It is difficult however to establish with any certainty what changes are directly attributable to the training alone.

> In November 2007, candidates were required to explain how the effectiveness of a staff training event could be evaluated. Good answers considered issues before the event, after the event and the reaction of the participants.

 Case Study

Whitbread pubs reported had improved performance as a result of a change in the company's training scheme. Previously the company's training scheme had aimed to improve the service standards of individuals, and there were also discussions with staff on business developments. It was felt however that other companies in the same sector had overtaken Whitbread in these respects.

Whitbread therefore introduced an integrated approach to assessment of the performance of pubs. Assessment is by four criteria; training (a certain percentage of staff have to have achieved a training award), standards (suggested by working parties of staff), team meetings and customer satisfaction. Managers are trained in training skills and they in turn train staff, using a set of structured notes to ensure a consistent training process.

Pubs that fulfil all the criteria win a team hospitality award, consisting of a plaque, a visit from a senior executive, and a party or points for goods scheme. To retain the award and achieve further points, pubs have then to pass further assessments which take place every six months.

The scheme seemed to improve standards. Significantly staff turnover was down and a survey suggested morale had improved, with a greater sense of belonging particularly by part-time staff. A major cause of these improvements may well be the involvement of staff and management in the design process.

# 5 Appraisal

Appraisal **reviews** and **rewards** performance and potential. It is part of performance management and can be used to establish areas for improvement and training needs.

**Key term**

**Appraisal**: the systematic review and assessment of an employee's performance, potential and training needs.

## 5.1 Why are appraisals needed?

Employee appraisal can be viewed as a control tool as it aims to influence employee behaviour and maximise utilisation of the organisation's human resource. The process of appraisal is designed to review performance over the past period and improve it in the future.

Appraisals are needed for a number of reasons.

(a)     Managers and supervisors may obtain **random impressions** of employees' performance (perhaps from their more noticeable successes and failures), but **rarely form a coherent, complete and objective picture**.

(b)     They may have a fair idea of their employees' **shortcomings** – but may not have devoted time and attention to the matter of **improvement and development**.

(c)     **Judgements are easy to make, but less easy to justify** in detail, in writing, or to the subject's face.

(d)     **Different assessors may be applying a different set of criteria, and varying standards of objectivity and judgement**. This undermines the value of appraisal for comparison, as well as its credibility in the eyes of the appraisees.

(e)     Unless stimulated to do so, **managers rarely give their staff adequate feedback on their performance**.

## 5.2 The purpose of appraisal

The general purpose of any appraisal system is to improve efficiency. Personnel appraisal aims to ensure individuals are performing to the best of their ability, are developing their potential and that the organisation is best utilising their abilities. It may include:

(a)     **Reward review**. Measuring the extent to which an employee is deserving of a bonus or pay increase as compared with his or her peers.

(b)     **Performance review**, for planning and following-up training and development programmes, ie identifying training needs, validating training methods and so on.

(c)     **Potential review**, as an aid to planning career development and succession, by attempting to predict the level and type of work the individual will be capable of in the future.

The **objectives of appraisals** include the following.

(a) Establishing the **key deliverables** an individual has to produce to enable the organisation to achieve its objectives.

(b) Comparing the individual's **level of performance against a standard**, as a means of quality control.

(c) Identifying the individual's **training and development needs** in the light of actual performance.

(d) Identifying areas that **require improvement**.

(e) Monitoring the organisation's **initial selection procedures** against subsequent performance.

(f) **Improving communication** between different levels in the hierarchy.

## 5.3 An appraisal system

A **typical appraisal system** is outlined below.

**Step 1** **Identification of criteria for assessment**, perhaps based on job analysis, performance standards, person specifications and so on.

**Step 2** The **preparation by the subordinate's manager of an appraisal report**. In some systems both the appraisee and appraiser prepare a report. These reports are then compared.

**Step 3** An **appraisal interview**, for an exchange of views about the appraisal report, targets for improvement, solutions to problems and so on.

**Step 4** **Review of the assessment by the assessor's own superior**, so that the appraisee does not feel subject to one person's prejudices. Formal appeals may be allowed, if necessary to establish the fairness of the procedure.

**Step 5** The **preparation and implementation of action plans** to achieve improvements and changes agreed.

**Step 6** **Follow-up** monitoring the progress of the action plan.

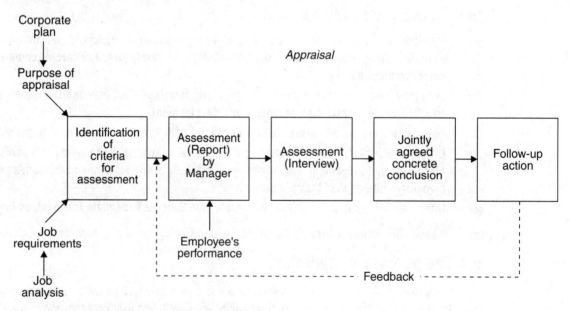

## 5.4 Three difficulties with appraisal

Effective appraisals can be difficult to implement. Three particular difficulties are:

(a) The **formulation of desired traits and standards** against which individuals can be consistently and objectively assessed.

(b) **Recording assessments**. Managers should be encouraged to utilise a standard and understood framework, but still allowed to express what they consider important, and without too much form-filling.

(c) **Getting the appraiser and appraisee together**, so that both contribute to the assessment and plans for improvement and/or development.

## 5.5 Appraisal techniques

The following techniques are often used in an appraisal system.

(a) **Overall assessment**. Managers write in narrative form their judgements about the appraisees. There will be no guaranteed consistency of the criteria and areas of assessment, however, and managers may not be able to convey clear, effective judgements in writing.

(b) **Guided assessment**. Assessors are required to comment on a number of specified characteristics and performance elements, with guidelines as to how terms such as 'application', 'integrity' and 'adaptability' are to be interpreted in the work context. This is more precise, but still rather vague.

(c) **Grading**. Grading adds a comparative frame of reference to the general guidelines, whereby managers are asked to select one of a number of levels or degrees to which the individual in question displays the given characteristic. These are also known as **rating scales**. Numerical values may be added to ratings to give rating scores. Alternatively a less precise **graphic scale** may be used to indicate general position on a plus/minus scale.

*Factor: job knowledge*

High __✓__ Average ____ Low

(d) **Behavioural incident methods**. These concentrate on **employee behaviour**, which is measured against typical behaviour in each job, as defined by common **critical incidents** of successful and unsuccessful job behaviour reported by managers.

(e) **Objectives and results-orientated schemes**. This reviews performance against specific targets and standards of performance agreed in advance. The manager becomes a counsellor. Learning and motivation theories suggest that clear and known targets are important in modifying and determining behaviour. The objectives set as part of an appraisal process should be agreed – and (again) these should be **SMART** (**S**pecific, **M**easurable, **A**chievable, **R**ealistic and **T**ime-bound).

(f) Assessments must be related to a common standard (the appraisal standard), in order for comparisons to be made between individuals: on the other hand, they should be related to meaningful performance criteria, which take account of the critical variables in each different job.

## 5.6 Self-appraisal

Individuals may carry out their own self-evaluation as a major input into the appraisal process. This has the advantage that the system is clearly aimed at the needs of the individual. Such a scheme has several **advantages**.

(a) It **saves the manager time** as the employee identifies the areas of competence which are relevant to the job and his/her relative strengths in these competences.

(b) It offers **increased responsibility** to the individual which may improve motivation.

(c) This may be a way of reconciling the goals of both the individual and the organisation.

(d) It may overcome the problem of needing skilled appraisers, thus cutting training costs and reducing the managerial role in appraisal.

(e) In giving the responsibility to an individual, the scheme may offer more **flexibility** in terms of timing, with individuals undertaking ongoing self-evaluation.

**However,** people are often not the best judges of their own performance. Many schemes combine the two – manager and subordinate fill out a report and compare notes.

## 5.7 The appraisal report

Most appraisal systems provide for appraisals to be recorded. The form of the appraisal report will vary between organisations and the role involved – report forms of various lengths and complexity may be designed.

The layout of the report and factors to be included in the report should be established before the interview. The report is likely to focus on key performance issues that relate to the **job description**.

The report is likely to cover key competences. A **competence** is an observable skill or ability to complete a particular task successfully. It can include the ability to transfer skills and knowledge to new situations.

## 5.8 Interviews and counselling

The extent to which any discussion or counselling interview is based on the written appraisal report varies in practice.

*Maier* (*The Appraisal Interview*) identifies three types of approach to appraisal interviews.

(a)   **The tell and sell method**. The manager tells the subordinate how he or she has been assessed, and then tries to sell (gain acceptance of) the evaluation and the improvement plan. This requires unusual human relations skills in order to convey constructive criticism in an acceptable manner, and to motivate the appraisee.

(b)   **The tell and listen method**. The manager tells the subordinate how he or she has been assessed, and then invites the subordinate to respond. Moreover, this method does not assume that a change in the employee will be the sole key to improvement: the manager may receive helpful feedback about how job design, methods, environment or supervision might be improved.

(c)   **The problem-solving approach**. The manager abandons the role of critic altogether, and becomes a counsellor and helper. The discussion is centred not on the assessment, but on the employee's work problems. The employee is encouraged to think solutions through, and to make a commitment to personal improvement.

## 5.9 Follow-up

After the appraisal interview, the manager may complete the report, with an overall assessment, assessment of potential and/or the jointly-reached conclusion of the interview, with recommendations for follow-up action. The manager should then discuss the report with the counter-signing manager (usually his or her own superior), resolving any problems that have arisen in making the appraisal or report, and agreeing on action to be taken. The report form may then go to the management development adviser, training officer or other relevant people as appropriate for follow-up.

Follow-up procedures typically include the following.

(a)   Informing appraisees of the results of the appraisal, if this has not been central to the review interview.

(b)   Carrying out agreed actions on training, promotion and so on.

(c)   Monitoring the appraisee's progress and checking that he has carried out agreed actions or improvements.

(d)   Taking necessary steps to help the appraisee to attain improvement objectives, by guidance, providing feedback, upgrading equipment, altering work methods or whatever.

If appraisal systems operate **successfully** as feedback control systems (in other words, if they do alter employees' performance) and identify behaviours to be encouraged, then, assuming organisational success is to some measure based on individual performance, they will influence the success of strategy.

## 5.10 Improving the appraisal system

In theory, such appraisal schemes may seem very fair to the individual and very worthwhile for the organisation, but **in practice the appraisal system often goes wrong**.

There are **disadvantages to appraisal schemes**. It can be a very **bureaucratic** process and may be treated as an **annual ritual**. It is easy for appraisal to become **confrontational**, with the manager taking a judgmental line, or for it to degenerate into a **purposeless** chat.

### 5.10.1 Barriers to effective appraisal

*Lockett* (in *Effective Performance Management*) suggests that **appraisal barriers** can be identified as follows.

| Appraisal barriers | Comment |
|---|---|
| **Appraisal as confrontation** | Many people dread appraisals, or use them 'as a sort of show down, a good sorting out or a clearing of the air.'<br><br>(a) There is a lack of agreement on performance levels.<br><br>(b) The feedback is subjective – in other words the manager is biased, allows personality differences to get in the way of actual performance etc.<br><br>(c) The feedback is badly delivered.<br><br>(d) Appraisals are 'based on yesterday's performance not on the whole year'.<br><br>(e) Disagreement on long-term prospects. |
| **Appraisal as judgement** | The appraisal 'is seen as a one-sided process in which the manager acts as judge, jury and counsel for the prosecution'. However, the process of performance management 'needs to be jointly operated in order to retain the commitment and develop the self-awareness of the individual.' |
| **Appraisal as chat** | The other extreme is that the appraisal is a friendly chat 'without … purpose or outcome … Many managers, embarrassed by the need to give feedback and set stretching targets, reduce the appraisal to a few mumbled "well dones!" and leave the interview with a briefcase of unresolved issues.' |
| **Appraisal as bureaucracy** | Appraisal is a form-filling exercise, to satisfy the personnel department. Its underlying purpose, improving individual and organisational performance, is forgotten. |
| **Appraisal as unfinished business** | Appraisal should be part of a continuing process of performance management. |
| **Appraisal as annual event** | Many targets set at annual appraisal meetings become irrelevant or out-of-date. |

A problem with many appraisal schemes in practice is that they **reinforce hierarchy**, and are perhaps unsuitable to organisations where the relationship between management and workers is **fluid** or participatory. Upward, customer and 360° appraisals address this, but they are not widely adopted. (These are covered later.)

Appraisal systems, because they target the individual's performance, concentrate on the **lowest level of performance feedback.** They ignore the organisational and systems context of that performance. (For example, if any army is badly led, no matter how brave the troops, it will be defeated.) Appraisal schemes seem to regard most **organisation problems** as a function of the **personal characteristics** of its members.

### 5.10.2 Appraisal and pay

Another issue is the extent to which the **appraisal system** is **related to** the pay and **reward system**.

Many employees consider that the appraisal system should be linked with the reward system, on the grounds that extra effort or excellent performance should be rewarded.

Although this appears to be a fair view, there are **drawbacks** to it.

(a) **Funds available** for pay rises rarely depend on one individual's performance alone – the whole company has to do well.

(b) **Continuous improvement** is always necessary – many firms have 'to run to stand still'. Continuous improvement should perhaps be expected of employees as part of their work, not rewarded as extra.

(c) In low-inflation environments, **cash pay rises are fairly small**.

(d) **Comparisons between individuals** are hard to make, as many smaller firms cannot afford the rigour of a job evaluation scheme.

(e) Performance management is about a lot more than pay for *past* performance – it is often **forward looking** with regard to future performance.

**Performance Related Pay (PRP)** is often introduced when other organisational or HR changes are made such as:

- The **introduction** of an **appraisal scheme**
- The **development** of **flexible working arrangements**
- The **decentralisation** of **HR** or the **responsibility** of **pay determination**
- The **harmonisation** of **working arrangements** through the organisation

Payment systems are often modified as a result of the introduction of PRP.

- PRP may form the **basis** of all **general pay increases**
- PRP may **replace pay increases for length of service** or **qualifications**
- PRP may be used as **additional payments above the maximum** for the grade where performance is very high.

All organisations can introduce PRP but it is often best **implemented gradually**.

By **initially introducing** it to **senior management**, they will **experience it first hand** before they apply it to their staff.

The use of PRP could be **restricted** to **specific groups** of workers to allow **adequate testing** and to **ensure sufficient safeguards are in place** before it is introduced to other workers.

### 5.10.3 Management expertise and employee empowerment

There can be **problems conducting appraisals** in organisations where **empowerment** is practised and employees are given more responsibility.

(a) Many managers **may not know enough** about the performance of individual workers to make a fair judgement.

(b) In some jobs, managers do not have the **technical expertise** to judge an employee's output.

(c) **Employees depend on other people** in the workplace/organisation to be effective – in other words, **an individual's results may not be entirely under his/her control**.

A person's performance is often indirectly or directly influenced by the **management style** of their line manager, who will also usually be the person conducting the appraisal.

However, given the seniority of the manager over the appraisee, the appraisee may be reluctant to raise issues related to their manager's management style.

Even the best objective and systematic appraisal scheme is subject to **personal** and **interpersonal problems**.

(a) Appraisal is often **defensive on the part of the appraisee**, who believes that criticism may mean a low bonus or pay rise, or a lost promotion opportunity.

(b) Appraisal is often **defensive on the part of the superior**, who cannot reconcile the role of judge and critic with the human relations aspect of interviewing and management. Managers may in any case feel uncomfortable about 'playing God' with employee's futures.

(c) The superior might show **conscious or unconscious bias** in the appraisal or may be influenced by rapport (or lack of it) with the interviewee. Systems without clearly defined standard criteria will be particular prone to the subjectivity of the assessor's judgement.

(d) The manager and subordinate may both **be reluctant to devote time and attention to appraisal**. Their experience in the organisation may indicate that the exercise is a waste of time (especially if there is a lot of form-filling) with no relevance to the job, and no reliable follow-up action.

(e) The organisational culture may **simply not take appraisal seriously**: Interviewers are not trained or given time to prepare, appraisees are not encouraged to contribute, or the exercise is perceived as a 'nod' to Human Relations with no practical results.

### 5.10.4 Making improvements

The appraisal scheme should itself be assessed (and regularly re-assessed) according to the following general criteria for evaluating appraisal schemes.

| Criteria | Comment |
| --- | --- |
| **Relevance** | • Does the system have a useful purpose, relevant to the needs of the organisation and the individual?<br>• Is the purpose clearly expressed and widely understood by all concerned, both appraisers and appraisees?<br>• Are the appraisal criteria relevant to the purposes of the system? |
| **Fairness** | • Is there reasonable standardisation of criteria and objectivity throughout the organisation?<br>• Is it reasonably objective? |
| **Serious intent** | • Are the managers concerned committed to the system – or is it just something the personnel department thrusts upon them?<br>• Who does the interviewing, and are they properly trained in interviewing and assessment techniques?<br>• Is reasonable time and attention given to the interviews – or is it a question of 'getting them over with'?<br>• Is there a genuine demonstrable link between performance and reward or opportunity for development? |
| **Co-operation** | • Is the appraisal a participative, problem-solving activity – or a tool of management control?<br>• Is the appraisee given time and encouragement to prepare for the appraisal, so that he can make a constructive contribution?<br>• Does a jointly-agreed, concrete conclusion emerge from the process?<br>• Are appraisals held regularly? |
| **Efficiency** | • Does the system seem overly time-consuming compared to the value of its outcome?<br>• Is it difficult and costly to administer? |

### 5.10.5 Upward appraisal

FAST FORWARD

**Upward appraisal** obtains a new perspective on managers by using information from their subordinates. **360° appraisal** extends this process to co-workers, customers and suppliers.

A notable modern trend, adopted in the UK by companies such as BP and British Airways and others, is **upward appraisal**, whereby employees are not rated by their superiors but by their subordinates. The followers appraise the leader.

**Advantages of upward appraisal** include the following.

(a) Subordinates tend to know their superior better than superiors know their subordinates.

(b)     As all subordinates rate their managers statistically, these ratings tend to be more reliable – the more subordinates the better. Instead of the biases of individual managers' ratings, the various ratings of the employees can be converted into a representative view.

(c)     Subordinates' ratings have more impact because it is more unusual to receive ratings from subordinates. It is also surprising to bosses because, despite protestations to the contrary, information often flows down organisations more smoothly and comfortably than it flows up. When it flows up it is qualitatively and quantitatively different. It is this difference that makes it valuable.

**Problems with the method** include fear of reprisals, vindictiveness, and extra form processing. Some bosses in strong positions might refuse to act, even if a consensus of staff suggested that they should change their ways.

### 5.10.6 Customer appraisal

In some companies part of the employee's appraisal process must take the form of **feedback from 'customers' (whether internal or external)**. This may be taken further into an influence on remuneration (at *Rank-Xerox*, 30% of a manager's annual bonus is conditional upon satisfactory levels of 'customer' feedback). This is a valuable development in that customers are the best judges of customer service, which the appraisee's boss may not see.

### 5.10.7 360 degree appraisal

Taking downwards, upwards and customer appraisals together, some firms have instituted **360 degree appraisal** (or multi-source appraisal) by collecting feedback on an individual's performance from the following sources.

(a)     The person's immediate manager.

(b)     People who report to the appraisee, perhaps divided into groups.

(c)     Peers and co-workers: most people interact with others within an organisation, either as members of a team or as the receivers or providers of services. They can offer useful feedback.

(d)     Customers: if sales people know what customers thought of them, they might be able to improve their technique.

(e)     The manager personally: all forms of 360 degree appraisal require people to rate themselves. Those 'who see themselves as others see them will get fewer surprises'.

Sometimes the appraisal results in a counselling session, especially when the result of the appraisals are conflicting. For example, an appraisee's manager may have a quite different view of the appraisee's skills than subordinates.

Question                                                                      Performance appraisal

Most large organisations have a performance appraisal process.

*Required*

(a)     Briefly describe the most common objectives of a performance appraisal system.          6 marks

(b)     Explain why appraisal systems are often less effective in practice than they might be, and advise what management can do to try and ensure their effectiveness.          14 marks

(Total = 20 marks)

Answer

(a)     The general purpose of any assessment or appraisal is to improve the efficiency of the organisation by ensuring that the individual employees are performing to the best of their ability – and developing their potential for improvement. Objectives of a formal performance appraisal system include the following:

- To enable a picture to be drawn up of overall staff levels and skills, strengths and weaknesses. This enables more effective personnel planning
- To monitor the undertaking's initial selection procedures against the subsequent performance of recruits
- To establish what the individual has to do in a job in order that the objectives for the section or department are realised
- To assess an individual's performance including strengths and any weaknesses. This helps identify training needs
- To assess appropriate rewards (pay, bonuses etc)
- To assess potential. At the organisational level this permits career and succession planning. At the individual level it facilitates an individual development plan

(b) A problem with many appraisal schemes in practice is that they reinforce hierarchy, and are perhaps unsuitable to organisations where the relationship between management and their subordinates is fluid or participatory.

Appraisal systems target the individual's performance in isolation, often ignoring the organisational and systems context of that performance. For example, if an employee is not given sufficient time or other resources to produce high quality output, the system or way of working is at fault rather than the employee.

Appraisal schemes also often imply most organisation problems are a result of the personal characteristics of its members, rather than as symptomatic of wider dysfunction.

A performance appraisal system's effectiveness depends to a great extent on the ability, effort, and integrity of line managers. The effectiveness of any appraisal system relies heavily on the quality and reliability of assessment. Variations in the consistency of reporting standards can quickly lead to a feeling of dissatisfaction and injustice.

However well designed the appraisal system it is not possible to apply a completely objective approach to every unique situation. The system should therefore always allow for at least a degree of discretion and personal judgement. The reporting system should give the appraiser an opportunity to record formally any necessary qualifications to the given ratings.

The appraisal may tend to concentrate too much on feedback on past performance and especially on the recent past. The lapse of time between events which occurred early in the reporting period and completing the appraisal may lead to a distortion in the overall flavour of the report. Sometimes too limited attention is paid to changes required to bring about an improvement in future performance.

In some organisations the problems associated with performance appraisal have been recognised and management have taken steps taken to limit their detrimental effect. Examples include:

- Upward appraisal and 360 degree appraisal to reduce the hierarchical nature of the process and present a wider view.
- Competence-based frameworks have been introduced that focus on the performance rather than on the qualities of the appraisee. This can increase the objectivity of the appraisal.
- Appraisal is becoming more recognised by senior management as a benefit to the organisation. This has been driven to some extent by employment protection legislation requiring a less arbitrary approach to such matters as reward, promotion, discipline and dismissal. This has led to increased emphasis on ensuring equitable appraisal systems are in place.
- Schemes of integrated performance management have been introduced, incorporating appraisal within a wider, structured approach to the management of the human resource.

# 6 Career management

**Career management** affects both the individual and the organisation. It is particularly relevant to managers and professionals. It provides the organisation with a pool of promotable managers and the individual with appropriate training and experience.

**Career management**, sometimes referred to as career planning or career development, is an aspect of HRM. It is a technique whereby the progress of individuals within an organisation from job to job is planned with organisational needs and individual capacity in mind.

Career management is both an individual and an organisational issue.

(a) It ensures that the organisation has a reserve of managers-in-waiting. In flat or delayered organisations this is particularly important, as the jump in responsibility from junior to senior positions is much wider than in organisations with extensive hierarchies.

(b) It ensures people get the right training to enable them to develop the right abilities for the job.

For the organisation, career management also determines whether, as a matter of policy, the organisation will promote from **within when possible**, as opposed to hiring **outsiders**.

## 6.1 Succession planning

Large organisations are able to plan (to some extent) a **logical progression** for individuals through its hierarchy over time. The objective is to ensure suitable replacements (in terms of experience and ability) are available to take over positions above them as they become available.

### 6.1.1 Advantages of succession planning

The following are advantages of succession planning.

- Can be **cheaper** than advertising or using agencies
- Develops **career structures**
- **Motivates employees** as rewards are visible (ie promotions are seen by all)
- **Maintains** the organisation's **culture** as long-serving employees are promoted
- It is **logical** and **rational**

### 6.1.2 Disadvantages of succession planning

The following are disadvantages of succession planning.

- Large 'talent pools' make it **hard to decide** who to promote
- **Reduces 'fresh blood'** at higher levels in the organisation
- Vacancies may occur **before** suitable replacements are ready for promotion
- **Better candidates** may be available **outside** the business
- **Planning requires** resources to manage it
- **Job-for-life** is increasingly becoming an **outdated concept** and the best staff may leave before vacancies become available

## 6.2 Barriers to career planning/succession planning

Flatter organisation structures, the growth of cross-functional teams and generally shorter periods of employment with a particular organisation have led to reduced potential for succession planning. Individuals now tend to take increased responsibility for their own career progression, and are more likely to accept that this may involve working for a number of organisations (and/or for themselves) throughout their career.

## Question

Career management

Learning outcome: E(iii)

Identify the type of career management system operated in the following cases.

(a) 'People join us at Trainee level. Within two years they are promoted to Assistant Accountant. Their titles denote the sort of skills and experience they are expected to have. After qualification, they are promoted to Senior Accountant, then Supervisor. Promotion above Supervisor level is not guaranteed, but some may go on to reach Manager grade, dealing with larger clients, and overseeing more staff. Exceptional candidates could one day become Partners of the firm'.

(b) 'We're a fashion design firm. We recruit directly from art schools. Recruitment levels vary each year – we have to be flexible. People who work with us are required to show a willingness to get involved and a flair for ideas which combine cutting edge fashion design with a real-world understanding of the people that buy our clothes. Career progression? – the sky's the limit for the talented'.

## Answer

(a) Long-range, structured planning at the lower levels which tapers off at the higher levels.

(b) The fashion firm combines a policy of recruitment as and when it is needed, with an assumption that people can create their own career structure. People can get on, but this cannot be planned.

## 6.3 Management development

FAST FORWARD

**Management development** includes general education, specific learning and wider experience. It is essential if managers are to make the leap from functional to general management.

Key term

**Management development** is the process of improving the effectiveness of an individual manager by developing the necessary skills and understanding of organisational goals.

*Pedlar et al.* considered the **development of management** should be down to the individual concerned and that the organisation should provide a system that increases managers' capacity and willingness to take control and responsibility for their own learning.

**Self-development** is now emphasised by many professional organisations such as **CIMA**. The modern view is that membership of an organisation does not ensure competence in the future. New knowledge must be learnt and skills must be maintained and developed.

*Pedlar et al* found several possibilities for learning. It can be **planned** (conscious), **accidental** (unconscious) and take place **at or away from work**.

Although management development is in some respects a natural process, the term is generally used to refer to **a conscious policy** within an organisation to provide a programme of individual development. A variety of techniques could be used, either on or off the job.

- Formal education and training
- On-the-job training
- Group learning sessions
- Job rotation
- Career planning
- Counselling

**Accidental** learning is unplanned. For example, situations at work or socially may develop personal attributes of a manager.

The principle behind management development is that by giving an individual time to study the techniques of being a good manager, and by counselling them about their achievements in these respects, the individual will realise their full potential. The time required to bring a manager to this potential is *possibly* fairly short.

Part C Managing human capital | **9: Training, appraisal and career management** 237

## 6.4 The transition from functional to general management

There is one particular aspect of management development and training that organisations should look at closely – **the transition from functional to general management**.

The change in a manager's work caused by moving from a functional to a general management position can be seen by highlighting some of the important differences in the two types of role.

To help with the transition from technical to general management, an organisation should have a **planned management development programme**. This could have several aspects.

(a) Individuals should be encouraged to acquire suitable **educational qualifications** for senior management. 'High-fliers' for example might be encouraged to study for an MBA early on in their career. Senior finance managers ought to have an accountancy qualification.

(b) **In-house training programmes** might be provided for senior managers and individuals who are being groomed for senior management. Formal training in general management skills can be very helpful.

(c) **Careful promotion procedures** should aim to ensure that only managers with the potential to do well are promoted into senior management positions.

(d) There should be a system of **regular performance appraisal**, in which individuals are interviewed and counselled by their managers on what they have done well, what they have not done so well, how to improve their performance in their current job and how to develop their skills for a more senior job.

(e) **Opportunities to gain suitable experience** should be provided to managers who are candidates for more senior positions. There are several possibilities.

　　(i)　Allowing subordinates to stand in for their boss whenever the boss is away

　　(ii)　Using staff officer positions to groom future high fliers

　　(iii)　Using a divisionalised organisation structure to delegate general management responsibilities further down the management hierarchy.

**Exam focus point**

The May 2007 exam offered three ten-mark questions on training and development. Candidates were required to:
(a)　Explain the stages of systematic training and development.
(b)　Describe the advantages and (c) the disadvantages of individual career coaching.

# Chapter Roundup

- **Human resource development (HRD)** involves training, education and development.

- The management of training and development is an iterative, rational process that includes several different aspects.
    - Identification of training **needs**
    - Definition of training **objectives**
    - **Planning** of training
    - **Delivery** of training
    - **Evaluation** of training

- **Training** can be **on-the-job** or at a different site. **Formal** training courses are useful if the subject is relevant to the job, and if the course involves interaction with other members of the company. Background knowledge is then imparted through on-the-job training. The learning organisation values training as a source of desirable improvement and uses it as a means to encourage innovation.

- There are a number of ways of **validating** and **evaluating** a training scheme.

- Appraisal **reviews** and **rewards** performance and potential. It is part of performance management and can be used to establish areas for improvement and training needs.

- There are **disadvantages to appraisal schemes**. It can be a very **bureaucratic** process and may be treated an **annual ritual**. It is easy for appraisal to become **confrontational**, with the manager taking a judgmental line, or for it to degenerate into a **purposeless chat**.

- **Upward appraisal** obtains a new perspective on managers by using information from their subordinates. **360° appraisal** extends this process to co-workers, customers and suppliers.

- **Career management** affects both the individual and the organisation. It is particularly relevant to managers and professionals. It provides the organisation with a pool of promotable managers and the individual with appropriate training and experience.

- **Management development** includes general education, specific learning and wider experience. It is essential if managers are to make the leap from functional to general management.

# Quick Quiz

1   Define human resource development.

2   What are the advantages of training to an organisation?

3   What are the steps in a training programme?

4   What are the steps in a personal development plan?

5   Who identified reaction, learning, behaviour and results as levels at which training can be evaluated?

    A    Kirkpatrick
    B    Hendry
    C    Kolb
    D    Pedlar

6   State three purposes of appraisal.

7   What is guided assessment?

8   What is career management?

# Answers to Quick Quiz

1   The process of extending personal abilities and qualities by means of education, training and other learning experiences.

2   Less need for supervision; personal flexibility; recruitment and succession planning; change management; development of corporate culture; improved motivation.

3   Identify training needs; define learning requirements; define training objectives; plan training programmes; implement the training; evaluate the training.

4   A personal SWOT analysis; goal setting; plan formulation.

5   Kirkpatrick

6   Reward review; performance review; potential review

7   Grading using rating scales

8   The planning and control of individual progression with individual and organisational requirements in mind.

Now try the question below from the Exam Question Bank

| Number | Level | Marks | Time |
|---|---|---|---|
| 9 | Examination | 30 | 54 mins |

P
A
R
T

D

# Marketing

# Marketing and marketing management

## Introduction

In Part D of this Text we cover the marketing area of the syllabus.

We start this chapter with an explanation of marketing, the **marketing concept** and the **marketing mix**. The syllabus refers to the marketing concept as a business philosophy. This shows that the examiner wants you to understand that 'marketing' means much more than the traditional view of 'advertising' and 'public relations'. Bear this in mind as you work through the chapter.

Later in the chapter we look at how **marketing activities** are **organised** and **managed** – and the role of marketing within an organisation. There are a number of key areas covered including marketing strategies, service marketing and social responsibility.

This is a fairly long chapter – you may prefer to work through it in two or three 'sessions'.

| Topic list | Learning outcomes | Syllabus references | Ability required |
|---|---|---|---|
| 1　The development of markets and marketing | D(i) | D(1) | Comprehension |
| 2　The marketing mix | D(i), D(ii), D(iii) | D(1) | Evaluation |
| 3　The marketing concept and a marketing orientation | D(i), D(ii) | D(1), D(8) | Evaluation |
| 4　The marketing department | D(ii) | D(1), D(12) | Evaluation |
| 5　The marketing environment | D(iv) | D(2) | Comprehension |
| 6　Marketing and strategy | D(vi) | D(12) | Analysis |
| 7　Marketing strategies | D(vi) | D(12) | Analysis |
| 8　Marketing communications | D(i), D(ii) | D(1), D(8) | Evaluation |
| 9　Pricing | D(iii), D(vi) | D(9) | Analysis |
| 10　Services and service marketing | D(iv) | D(8) | Comprehension |
| 11　Social responsibility and ethics | D(ii), D(vi) | D(16) | Evaluation |

# 1 The development of markets and marketing

FAST FORWARD

**Marketing** is the management of **exchange relationships** between a supplier and a customer. The traditional 4Ps of marketing product, price, place (distribution) and promotion are important concepts.

## 1.1 Background

Markets existed as soon as goods started to be **exchanged**. In pre-industrial societies, each family might have bred its own animals for food and clothes (made from skins). Soon, however, people found that they were able to produce more food than they needed for themselves: they had surpluses. One person might then offer to exchange his spare food for someone else's spare clothes, or his own spare beef for another's spare vegetables. This is known as **bartering**. As time went on, people became more **specialised**: one person might not produce any food himself, but might get food from other people in exchange for labour.

The next stage was to avoid the need to exchange goods directly for other goods or services by inventing **money**: a vet who liked mutton could then get cash from one farmer, who only had cows, and spend it with another farmer, who could offer sheep for sale. By this stage, there was a fully fledged **market**: indeed, once there were lots of different farmers and lots of vets, there were several markets: a beef market, a mutton market, a market for veterinary services and so on.

The growth of markets received a big boost during the Industrial Revolution in the eighteenth and nineteenth centuries. **Production** became concentrated in big factories, towns grew bigger and **trade** increased as people became more likely to buy goods rather than produce them themselves. Industries had a **production orientation** – this means that they would concentrate on making things efficiently, and assume that someone would buy whatever they made.

**Mass production techniques** increased the number and types of goods on the market and reduced unit costs. With cheaper products on offer, **demand** was such that until very recently many business problems centred on production and selling rather than marketing, since it was more important to **produce enough** of a product to satisfy strong demand than to think about **customer needs**.

Production is no longer the main problem facing business concerns. Indeed, for most products and services, it is **excess supply** rather than excess demand which is the problem. In these circumstances, the focus has switched from 'how to produce enough' (**supply factor**) to 'how to increase demand' (**demand factor**). Today, the driving force behind marketing is satisfying customer demands.

## 1.2 Definitions of marketing

**Key term**

> **Marketing** is the process of planning and executing the concepts of pricing, promotion and distribution of ideas, goods and services in order to create exchanges that satisfy individual and organisational objectives.

Another definition is given by the UK's Chartered Institute of Marketing.

> 'Marketing is the management process which identifies, anticipates and supplies customer requirements efficiently and profitably.'

This definition emphasises the wide scope of marketing, ranging from initial identification of customer needs by means of research, right through to eventual, profitable satisfaction of those needs. This definition is important because it stresses the importance of the customer and, more particularly, customer satisfaction.

*Kotler* on the other hand emphasised the importance of getting 'the right product or service to the customer, at the right price, at the right time'.

## 1.3 Products, goods and services: a note on terminology

A **product** is something that is offered to a market.

(a)  Soap powder is an example of a **fast moving consumer good** (FMCG). It is a physical product that is bought often. Other tangible products include motor cars, personal computers and so on.

(b)  **Durable goods** are purchased less often and tend to be more expensive than FMCGs. Televisions, cars and computers are examples of durable goods.

(c)  A haircut is also a type of product: it is an example of a **service** product.

Broadly speaking, the word **product** can refer to physical **goods** or **services**. FMCGs and durable goods combined are sometimes referred to as consumer goods.

## 1.4 Strategic and tactical marketing

Marketing involves several types of activity and many types of decision. For many firms, the products they provide are fundamental to their existence.

(a)  **Strategic marketing** is tied is with the corporate strategy, by identifying which products and markets the firm wishes to operate in.

(b)  **Tactical marketing** is focused more on the short term and on particular elements of the marketing mix.

| Example: retail | |
| --- | --- |
| **Strategic marketing** | A fashion retailer decides to open in the capital city of a country it had not operated in before as it believes there are new, wealthy customers |
| **Tactical marketing** | End of season sale to make way for new stock. |

 Case Study

There are many different types of bank account available. Customers of banking services generally have expectations that their accounts will be updated efficiently and effectively, over a period of time, so that they have access to funds.

(a)  **Traditional 'western' banking**

Banks like to offer other products to their customers, so that a customer with a current account may also open a savings account. The bank is able to use the money to lend, at higher interest rates, to other customers, thereby earning a profit. Increased competition in the UK banking sector has led to many new bank accounts being set up offering different benefits. The newcomers, offering more attractive rates of interest, want to persuade customers in other banks to switch.

(b)  **'Islamic' banking**

The classic banking model is held by some Muslims to contradict certain tenets of Islam. However, Muslims, like anybody, need banking services. Crucially the difference involves the payment of interest, which is frowned upon. Many banks are now able to structure lending transactions in a fashion that is acceptable to Islam.

In both cases (a) and (b) the bank is providing a service and, over the long term, engaging in a relationship with its customers.

## 1.5 Exchanges

The role of marketing is to identify, anticipate and supply satisfactions to customers, to facilitate mutually beneficial exchanges.

**Exchange and marketing**

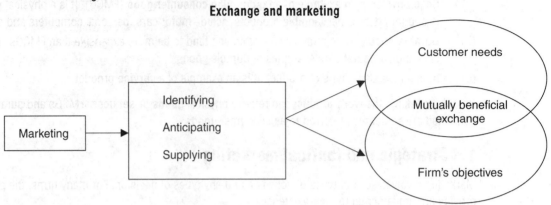

## 2 The marketing mix

**FAST FORWARD**

*Kotler and Keller* (2006) define the **marking mix** as 'the set of controllable variables and their levels that the firm uses to influence the target market'.

Most of us have experience of being marketed 'to' in a variety of different ways. In developed countries and, increasingly, in developing ones, people are subjected to a variety of different marketing activities.

Media and public spaces are full of advertisements: posters, TV ads, pop-up ads on websites, even text messages on mobile phones: in marketing terminology these are known as **promotion** (or marketing communications).

Many of these messages aim, ultimately, to persuade people to want to purchase certain **products** or services. **People** are trained to produce and deliver these products or services to **places** where we can buy them. Sophisticated **processes** might be involved in production and managing the sale. Delivery is also designed and managed. For a service (which by its nature is intangible), sometimes we require **physical evidence** that the service is to be provided: for example, a letter or guarantee for building work or testimonials or references to reassure potential customers. The **price** we pay is not arbitrary: it has been thought through. Phrases such as 'that was good value for money' suggest that price and value are important in buying decisions.

In the paragraphs above, seven words or phrases beginning with 'p' have been emboldened. These form what is known as the extended marketing mix. Traditionally, the marketing mix was the 'four Ps', which were referred to in relation to consumer goods, such as soap powder (**product**: soap, **price**, **place**: shops, **promotion**: advertisements). The three extra 'P's have been added to describe the issues in service industries (eg restaurant: waiters, the cooking process, the physical environment) of the restaurant.

| The extended marketing mix the 7 Ps | |
|---|---|
| **The traditional marketing mix** | **You can add . . . (3 Ps)** |
| Product | People (the '5th P') |
| Price | Processes |
| Place (distribution) | Physical evidence |
| Promotion | |

## 2.1 Product

A **product** (goods or services) is anything that satisfies a need or want. It is not a 'thing' with 'features' but a package of benefits.

From the firm's point of view the product element of the marketing mix is what is being sold, whether it be widgets, power stations, haircuts, holidays or financial advice. From the customer's point of view, a **product is a solution to a problem or a package of benefits.** Many products might satisfy the same customer need. On what basis might a customer choose?

(a) **Customer value** is the customer's estimate of how far a product or service goes towards satisfying his or her need(s).

(b) Every product has a price, and so the customer makes a **trade-off** between the **expenditure** and **the value offered**.

(c) According to *Kotler* a customer must feel he or she gets a better deal from buying an item than by any of the alternatives.

**The nature of the product**

(a) The **core product** is the most basic description of the product – a car is a means of personal transport. The **actual product** is the car itself, with all its physical features such as a powerful engine, comfortable seats and a sun roof. The **augmented product** is the car plus the benefits which come with it, such as delivery, servicing, warranties and credit facilities for buyers.

(b) The **product range** consists of two dimensions.

   (i) **Width**. A car maker may have products in all parts, known as segments, of the market: luxury cars, family cars, small cheap cars, and so on.

   (ii) **Depth**. It may then offer a wide variety of options within each segment – a choice of engines, colours, accessories and so on.

(c) **Benefits offered to the customer.** Customers differ in their attitudes towards new products and the benefits they offer.

Product issues in the marketing mix will include such factors as:

- Design (size, shape)
- Features
- Quality and reliability

- After-sales service (if necessary)
- Packaging

## 2.1.1 The product life cycle

**FAST FORWARD**

The product life cycle includes four main stages: **introduction**, **growth**, **maturity** and **decline**. Some writers also include **shakeout** between growth and maturity.

The classic pattern of a product life cycle is in four-stages, an introduction to the market, a growth, market maturity and then decline. However, products can be rejuvenated so that their life cycle continues. The priorities for performance objectives will change as a product goes through the different phases of its life cycle.

(a) **Introduction stage**. The product or service offers something new to customers. There are unlikely to be any competing products, but heavy advertising costs may be incurred to raise customer awareness. **Design changes** may be required, as customer needs become better understood. A business needs to establish an **operational capability** that allows it to be flexible and capable of adapting and changing.

(b) **Growth stage**. The volume of demand for the product increases, and there are likely to be more competitors in the market. **Product features** may become important between different suppliers. The main objective for the operations function could be to keep up with the growing demand. Speed of response to customer orders and reliability of supply could also be significant. **Quality standards** will have to be maintained or improved in response to the growing competition, and cost and price are likely to be much more significant.

(c)     **Market maturity**. Demand levels off. Some early competitors are likely to have left the market, which might now be shared by a small number of firms. Product design will be largely **standardised**, although firms might try to develop new varieties of the product to extend its life cycle. Firms in the market are likely to compete on price and/or on value for money (product differentiation). To remain competitive, it will be important to achieve low costs through **productivity** improvements, whilst still providing reliability of supply.

(d)     **Decline stage**. Total demand declines and competitors will start to withdraw from the market. There will nevertheless be excess capacity in the industry, and the remaining firms will compete on price. Cost targets will remain the key operational objective. The company may also decide to stop making and selling the product, and to focus its energies instead on another developing/growing product.

Some writers refer to an additional phase between market growth and market maturity. Often at this time, some of the weaker players in the market (initially attracted by market growth) are 'shaken out' of the market by the stronger organisations. This is referred to as a '**shakeout**'.

**The Product Life Cycle**

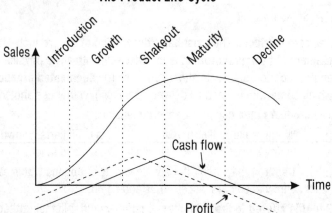

## 2.2 Place

Place deals with how the product is distributed, and how it reaches its customers.

(a)     **Channel**. Where are products sold? In supermarkets, corner shops? Which sales outlets will be chosen?

(b)     **Logistics.** The location of warehouses and efficiency of the distribution system is also important. A customer might have to wait a long time if the warehouse is far away. Arguably, the **speed of delivery** is an important issue in **place**.

A firm can distribute the product itself (direct distribution) or distribute it through intermediary organisations such as retailers.

## 2.3 Promotion

Many of the practical activities of the marketing department are related to **promotion**. Promotion is the element of the mix over which the marketing department generally has most control. A useful mnemonic is AIDA which summarises the aims of promotion.

- Arouse **Attention**
- Generate **Interest**
- Inspire **Desire**
- Initiate **Action** (ie buy the product)

Promotion in the marketing mix includes all marketing communications which let the public know of the product or service.

- Advertising (newspapers, billboards, TV, radio, direct mail, Internet)
- Sales promotion (discounts, coupons, special displays in particular stores)

- Direct selling by sales personnel.
- Public relations

### 2.3.1 Advertising

There are two schools of thought concerning the **effectiveness** of **advertising**. The average European has several thousand advertising encounters each day. This can be from posters to TV adverts or Internet pop ups.

Several brands view high levels of advertising as **ineffective** in terms of number of 'encounters' needed to achieve a sale. Brands including **Red Bull** and the **Body Shop** do not rely on advertising as their main source of promotion. Instead they look to create **positive feelings** towards them using other methods.

Other brands such as **Orange**, **Walkers Crisps** and **Tango** view advertising as so **effective** that it is essential. Not advertising would put them at a serious disadvantage to their competitors.

*Lancaster and Withey* (2005) identified the following elements of successful advertising. It must be

- **Well planned** and **executed**
- **Effective** as a method of communication
- Part of an **overall effective promotional mix**
- **Aligned** with the overall **values** and **mission** of the **company**

## 2.4 Price

The price element of the marketing mix is the only one which brings in revenue. Price is influenced by many factors.

(a) **Economic influences**: supply and demand; price and income elasticities
(b) **Competitors' prices**. Competitors include other firms selling the same type of product, as well as firms selling substitute products. Generally, firms like to avoid price wars.
(c) **Quality connotations**. High price is often taken as being synonymous with quality, so pricing will reflect the a product's image.
(d) **Discounts**. These can make the product attractive to distributors.
(e) **Payment terms** (eg offering a period of interest free credit)
(f) **Trade-in allowances**
(g) The stage in the **product life cycle**.
    (i) **Penetration pricing** is charging a low price to achieve early market share advantages
    (ii) **Skimming pricing** charging high prices early on to reap the maximum profits.

## 2.5 The extended marketing mix

This is also known as the service marketing mix because it is specifically relevant to the marketing of **services** rather than **physical products**. The intangible nature of services makes these extra three Ps particularly important.

### 2.5.1 People

The role of employees in the marketing mix is particularly important in **service marketing**, because of the **inseparability** of the service from the service provider: the creation and consumption of the service generally happen at the same moment, at the interface between the server and the served. Front-line staff must be selected, trained and motivated with particular attention to customer care and public relations.

In the case of some services, the **physical presence** of people performing the service is a vital aspect of customer satisfaction. The staff involved are performing or producing a service, selling the service and also liaising with the customer to promote the service, gather information and respond to customer needs.

### 2.5.2 Processes

Efficient **processes** can become a marketing advantage in their own right. If an airline, for example, develops a sophisticated ticketing system, it can offer shorter waits at check-in or wider choice of flights through allied airlines. Efficient order processing not only increases customer satisfaction, but cuts down on the time it takes the organisation to complete a sale.

Issues to be considered include the following.

* Policies, particularly with regard to ethical dealings (a key issue for many consumers)
* Procedures, for efficiency and standardisation
* Automation and computerisation of processes
* Queuing and waiting times
* Information gathering, processing and communication times
* Capacity management, matching supply to demand in a timely and cost effective way
* Accessibility of facilities, premises, personnel and services

Such issues are particularly important in service marketing; because of the range of factors and people involved, it is difficult to standardise the service offered. Quality in particular specifications will vary with the circumstances and individuals.

Services are also innately **perishable**: their purchase may be put off, but they cannot be stored.

This creates a need for process planning to ensure efficient work.

### 2.5.3 Physical evidence

Services are **intangible**: there is no physical substance to them. This means that even when money has been spent on them the customer has no **evidence of ownership**. These factors make it difficult for consumers to perceive, evaluate and compare the qualities of service provision, and may therefore dampen the incentive to consume.

Issues of intangibility and ownership can be tackled by making available a physical symbol or representation of the service product or of ownership, and the benefits it confers. For example, tickets and programs relating to entertainment; and certificates of attainment in training are symbolic of the service received and a history of past positive experiences.

Physical evidence of service may also be incorporated into the design and specification of the service environment by designing premises to reflect the quality and type of service aspired to. Such environmental factors include finishing, decor, colour scheme, noise levels, background music, fragrance and general ambience.

We shall look at the seven Ps later as we consider marketing in more detail.

**Exam focus point**

> If a question refers to **four** elements of the marketing mix the examiner is referring to the traditional elements of product, price, place and promotion – the 4Ps. If **five** elements are referred to, add 'people' to the traditional four. The other additional Ps referred to above could be referred to in longer written answers.

# 3 The marketing concept and a marketing orientation

**FAST FORWARD**

> Marketing considerations can, in fact, **influence all activities** undertaken by an organisation. The value chain and internal customer concept show how ideas related to customer satisfaction and customer value can be implemented through the organisation.

The marketing concept and marketing orientation are two interrelated terms. The definitions that follow are from *Brassington and Pettit* (2000).

| Marketing concept | Marketing orientation |
|---|---|
| A philosophy of business, permeating the whole organisation, that holds that they key to organisational success is meeting customers' needs more effectively and more closely than competitors. | An approach to business that centres its activities on satisfying the needs and wants of its customers. |
| = A BELIEF SYSTEM | = ACTUAL PRACTICES |

## 3.1 The marketing concept

The marketing **concept** is a belief system. A belief system can be incorporated in the culture of the organisation: the culture involves the beliefs and patterns of behaviour of people in the organisation. The belief can be espoused consciously or people may feel that way anyway without having to learn the belief.

The organisation as a whole can claim to be 'customer orientated': slogans, such as 'We put the customer first' abound. Many organisations put customer satisfaction in their statements of corporate purpose (mission statements). But official claims to be customer orientated are often just claims – rhetorical statements – with little basis in fact.

### 3.1.1 The marketing concept in practice

Even though the marketing concept, with its attempt to match goods to consumer needs, is widely accepted, there will **always be a need for a persuasive sales force**.

The sales force's effort will be more successful if products and services **meet market needs**. A market-led approach will make what is on sale more acceptable to customers. Salespeople are no longer left trying to persuade potential buyers to change their perceptions of what they need. More productive activities such as developing leads, providing better customer service and identifying changes in customer requirements (to which the organisation needs to respond) can be pursued.

All good sales presentations are customer orientated. Instead of merely cataloguing a series of product features, the salesperson concentrates **on promoting the benefits that will be derived from the company's product or service**.

## 3.2 A marketing orientation

FAST FORWARD

Typically, marketing has focused on **persuading consumers** to buy products or services. A **production orientation** assumed that consumers would buy whatever the firm produced. Firms with a **sales orientation**, again, are **focused on the needs of the seller** rather than the buyer.

The marketing concept and marketing orientation are often compared to other 'orientations' that supposedly existed beforehand.  These are briefly described below.

### 3.2.1 Production orientation

A **production orientation** may be defined as the management view that success is achieved through producing goods or services of optimum quality and cost. The major task of management is to pursue improved production and distribution efficiency. It assumes that customers will **always be around to buy the product**.

The comparison between a marketing orientation built around the customer and an orientation built around the product is illustrated in the following diagram.

**Comparison of marketing orientation with production orientation**

| Marketing orientation | Production orientation |
|---|---|
| Determine customer needs | Determine whether goods can be made/ service delivered |
| Invest resources | Invest resources |
| Make product/service | Make product/service |
| Market the product/service (profit via customer satisfaction) | Sell the product (profit via increased turnover) |
| Market feedback | |

Perhaps the most well-known example of production orientation was the Model T Ford, one of the earliest motor cars to be produced for the mass market. *Henry Ford* famously said that Ford's customers could have the (mass-produced) Model T in any colour, so long as it was black.

### 3.2.2 Sales orientation

Under **a sales orientation the tendency is to make the product and then actively and aggressively sell it**. Underlying this philosophy is a belief that a good sales force can sell just about anything to anybody. A sales orientation is the management view that effective selling and communications are the keys to business success.

Selling is preoccupied with the seller's need to convert his product into cash; marketing with the idea of satisfying the needs of the customer by means of the product and the whole cluster of things associated with creating, delivering and finally consuming it.

### 3.2.3 Product orientation

Product orientated organisations focus on product development, for example the introduction of new product features. This approach is based upon the belief that a more advanced product or one with more features will be perceived as superior.

### 3.2.4 The potential impact of a marketing orientation

The marketing concept suggests that companies should focus their operations on their customers' needs rather than be driven solely by the organisation's **technical competence** or **resource capability** to produce a particular range of products or services, or by a belief in the sales force.

If the organisation has got its marketing right, it will have produced products and services that meet customers' requirements at a price that customers accept. In theory, at least, little sales effort will be needed.

 Case Study

Many of the UK's banks have spent fortunes on hiring marketing people, often from fast-moving consumer goods (FMCG) companies, producing expensive television commercials and creating a multiplicity of products, brochures and leaflets. But most customers still cannot distinguish between the major players, so what competitive advantage have any of these organisations gained?

Is this marketing in the sense of understanding and meeting customers' needs better than the competition, or is it old-fashioned selling with the name changed?

This is an interesting question, with points that could be made in support of and in opposition to the question raised. Marketing people could point to the following as examples of successful product differentiation.

(1) The successful development by Barclays of a multi-channel banking service to customers including Internet banking. Later, other major banks 'caught up' by implementing their own Internet operations.

(2) The advertising campaign by Nationwide, focusing on their policy of offering special 'deals' to existing customers as well as new customers.

(3) The positioning of the Co-operative Bank in the UK as a bank with an ethical, environmental and socially-responsible attitude to banking.

### 3.2.5 Push v Pull

Traditionally, marketing activities focused on **pushing** goods out to resellers and consumers.

A **'pull' approach** on the other hand, aims to produce a product that consumer demand will **pull** into retail outlets.

## 3.3 The marketing concept: summary

To conclude, marketing has three dimensions.

(a) It is a **culture**. The marketing concept is to put the consumer first.

(b) It involves **strategy**. A company must select the markets it intends to sell to and the products or services it will sell. These selections are strategic decisions.

(c) It involves **tactics**. Marketing tactics can be considered as the 7Ps of the marketing mix.

Case Study

**Volkswagen**

Volkswagen (VW) is one of the world's largest car makers, based in Wolfsburg, Germany, and part-owned by the state. Here is what the *Financial Times* had to say when their autocratic leader, Ferdinand Piech, was replaced.

'Mr Piech's influence on the company runs deep. In nine years he rescued it from the disastrous recession of the 1990s. He oversaw a successful strategy of building multiple vehicles off the same underlying platform and had engineers invent the world's best air conditioning system.

'However, Mr Piech, an accomplished engineer, indulged his technical department. Engineering took priority over sales and marketing and investors regarded it has having let its research and development (R&D) spending run out of control. Internal competition between brands, designed to drive the engineers to greater successes, led to overlapping models being sold by different marques, damaging their image.

'Changes since Mr Piech's resignation have shifted power in the organisation away from engineering. The biggest change was the appointment of a product manager to oversee the development of a car from concept through to production line. This made development more responsive to customer demand and less susceptible to engineering preferences – such as the long-standing resistance to providing proper cupholders, something overcome only recently at VW and other German, engineering-led car-makers.

The past lack of attention to customer desires was illustrated by the VW's relatively late entry in to the sport utility vehicle and small people carrier markets.

# 4 The marketing department

**FAST FORWARD**

Because marketing is chiefly concerned with customers, markets and products, it is in many ways linked to **corporate strategy**. Marketing considerations influence corporate strategy. However, marketing is also one way by which corporate strategy is implemented.

We have already briefly described how marketing orientation can permeate the activities of the organisation by orientating it round the customer. We will now look at the activities traditionally associated with marketing and marketing staff. In larger organisations these may be carried out by a department – in smaller organisations specific marketing staff may only number one or two.

The marketing department plays a key role in **co-ordinating marketing activities**. The **marketing manager** has to take responsibility for planning, resource allocation, monitoring and controlling the marketing effort.

In order to ensure that marketing activities are as effective as they can be, co-ordination of marketing efforts for different products in different markets is essential. Individual marketing campaigns themselves should also be co-ordinated and consistent.

Marketing typically involves the following **types of activity**.

| Marketing activities | |
|---|---|
| **Researching** markets and customers | • Research new and existing markets and competitors.<br>• Identify market segments: groups of customers with similar needs.<br>• Investigate behaviour of individual and organisational buyers. |
| Contributing to overall corporate **strategy** | Marketing people can offer key insights to the strategy-making process. |
| Generating **demand** | Marketing people aim to generate demand for the company's products by ensuring it is presented, priced and distributed appropriately. |
| Marketing communications: **promotion**; brand building | • The 'classic' marketing activities include advertising, public relations, building an image of the organisation to customers, corporate identity and so on.<br>• A brand offers a unique way of identifying a product or group of products. How the brand is designed, and how it is 'positioned' in the market place can really help.<br>• Choice of media (eg advertising, Internet) |
| **Product** design and planning | Marketing people try to specify the customer benefits that are built into the product, and can help in product design and so on. Marketers will liaise with product designers to identify launch dates, key features and so on. |
| **Pricing** | Pricing is one of the tougher decisions, given its impact on profit and relation to costs. In competitive markets, marketers try to reduce the impact of price on buying decisions. However, marketers have to balance what the market will want with what the company can afford. Discount policy can also be included here. |
| Distribution (**place**) | How to reach the customer<br><br>Channels of distribution<br><br>*Campbell* (1997) identified four common distribution channels:<br><br>• Producer to consumer<br>• Producer to retailer to consumer<br>• Producer to wholesaler to retailer to consumer<br>• Producer to agent to wholesaler to retailer to consumer |

| Marketing activities | |
|---|---|
| **People** | Marketing is sometimes considered very different to HRM, however in services especially, how people behave to customers is very important. |
| | For manufactured goods, after-sales service, and how complaints are handled, are very significant. |
| **Processes** and operations | Here is the link to operations management. Services and products are generated by processes, all of which can impact on the customer (eg booking an airline ticket, buying a holiday over the Internet). Marketing people need to convey to process designers what are the key expectations. |
| Client relationship management | In most organisations, marketing people are those who manage the day-to-day relationship with the client and keep the client informed about products and services, endeavouring to build a relationship. |
| Selling | Some marketers, for example those selling financial services, might sell directly to the customer. |

# 5 The marketing environment

 **FAST FORWARD**

All organisations exist in, interact with and are **influenced** by their environment.

## 5.1 PESTEL factors

One way of classifying environmental factors is shown below.

| PESTEL factors | | | | | |
|---|---|---|---|---|---|
| Political | Economic | Social/Cultural | Technological | Ecological | Legal |

These factors influence the organisation in many ways. However in marketing, we are particularly interested in how they impact on **markets** and **customers.**

**Environment and markets**

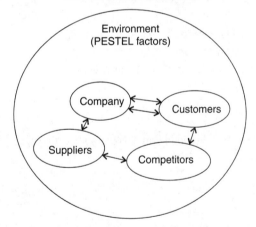

For example, political factors may influence the market for financial services by encouraging customers to take out certain types of investment. Economic factors may influence customers' buying power. The following table shows the type of impact on customers.

| Factor | Impact on customers |
|---|---|
| **Political factors**<br><br>• Changes in government and/or changes in government policy.<br>• Political instability could lead to warfare or civil unrest. | This can affect consumers' confidence in the future, their spending power or their rights. Clearly this fundamentally affects normal business. Government policy could give consumers more rights in relation to business. |
| **Economic factors**<br><br>These include overall rate of economic growth, inflation, interest rates, exchange rates, consumers propensity to save. | Ultimately, this determines consumers effective demand for products and services. Uncertainty about the future may lead to more saving and less spending. General prosperity may lead to more spending on luxury items. |
| **Social/cultural factors**<br><br>Demography relates to the composition of the population, where people live, social classification.<br><br>Culture relates to people's values and beliefs. There may be many subgroups (subcultures) within a culture. | Demographic factors suggest the size and purchasing power of customer groups. Some products may indicate high status. Different groups may be suitable for segmentation.<br><br>Culture has significant consequences for the acceptability of marketing communications messages, attitudes to products (eg alcoholic drinks), attitudes towards purchasing, and so on. |
| **Technological factors**<br><br>• New products<br>• New processes<br>• New working methods<br>• New communication methods<br>• New ways of distribution | Companies may be able to change the products or services they offer, but they can also communicate in different ways. Customers may have different attitudes to innovation, some preferring to stay with tried and trusted products or patterns of behaviour. |
| **Ecological factors**<br><br>• Long-term trends in the global physical environment, such as climate change.<br>• Natural climatic impacts, such as flooding, earthquakes and so on.<br>• As well as considering the physical environment, we should consider customers attitudes to it, as a developing cultural factor with an influence on political decision-making. | The effect on customers is two-fold. Changing attitudes enable businesses to satisfy new needs with new products, for example organic vegetables. Natural disasters are a business opportunity for insurance companies, but also those supplying aid and construction companies. |
| **Legal factors**<br><br>• The law affects ways of doing business.<br>• Specific laws exist for particular areas of economic activity. | • Do legislation and judicial decisions increase the customer's rights?<br>• Particular classes of customer may be protected in some cases (eg funeral services)<br>• Are customers increasingly willing and able to take legal action? |

Note that you may sometimes see legal factors grouped with political, and ecological factors either excluded or combined with social and cultural factors. The framework is then referred to as **PEST** rather than **PESTEL**.

**Exam focus point**

The November 2006 exam offered candidates 10 marks for evaluating an organisation's situation regarding marketing and ethical issues (ethics are discussed later this chapter). It offered a further 10 marks for explaining how the organisation could develop a marketing strategic plan.

The November 2007 exam required an explanation of the importance of understanding an organisation's external and internal environment.

# 6 Marketing and strategy

Marketing strategy should complement and be **consistent** with a firm's overall corporate strategy.

## 6.1 Corporate and marketing strategies

The process of corporate planning and the relationship with marketing strategy is shown in the following table.

| | Corporate | Marketing |
|---|---|---|
| **Set objectives** | For the firm as a whole: eg increase profits by X%. | For products and market: eg increase market share by X%; increase turnover. |
| **Internal appraisal** (*strengths and weaknesses*) | Review the effectiveness of the different aspects of the organisation. | Conduct a marketing audit: a review of marketing activities. Does the firm have a marketing orientation? |
| **External appraisal** (*opportunities and threats*) | Review political, economic, social, technological, ecological factors impacting on the whole firm. | Review environmental factors as they affect customers, products and markets. |
| **Gaps** | There may be a gap between desired objectives and forecast objectives. How to close the gap. | The company may be doing less well in particular markets than it ought to. Marketing will be focused on growth. |
| **Strategy** | Develop strategies to fill the gap: eg diversifying, entering new markets. | A marketing strategy is a plan to achieve the organisation's objectives by specifying: <br><br>• Resources to be allocated to marketing <br>• How those resources should be used <br><br>In the context of applying the marketing concept, a marketing strategy would: <br><br>• Identify target markets and customer needs in those markets <br>• Plan products which will satisfy the needs of those markets <br>• Organise marketing resources, so as to match products with customers |
| **Implementation** | Implementation is delegated to departments of the business. | The plans must be put into action, eg advertising space must be bought. |
| **Control** | Results are reviewed and the planning process starts again. | Has the firm achieved its market share objectives? |

## 6.2 The marketing plan

In more detail, the **marketing plan** might take the following form (based on *Kotler*, 1994).

| Section | Content |
|---|---|
| **The executive summary** | This is the finalised planning document with a summary of the main goals and recommendations in the plan. |
| **Situation analysis** | This consists of the SWOT (strengths, weaknesses, opportunities and threats) analysis and forecasts. |
| **Objectives and goals** | What the organisation is hoping to achieve, or needs to achieve, perhaps in terms of market share or 'bottom line' profits and returns. |
| **Marketing strategy** | This considers the selection of target markets, the marketing mix and marketing expenditure levels, as described in the preceding table. |
| **Strategic marketing plan** | <ul><li>Three to five or more years long</li><li>Defines scope of product and market activities</li><li>Aims to match the activities of the firm to its distinctive competences</li></ul> |
| **Tactical marketing plan** | <ul><li>One year time horizon</li><li>Generally based on existing products and markets</li><li>Concerned with marketing mix issues</li></ul> |
| **Action plan** | This sets out how the strategies are to be achieved.<br><br>(a) Marketing mix strategy<br><br><ul><li>The product</li><li>The price</li><li>Place (distribution)</li><li>Promotion (advertising etc)</li><li>People</li><li>Processes</li><li>Physical evidence</li></ul><br>(b) The mix strategy may vary for each segment. |
| **Budgets** | These are developed from the action programme. |
| **Controls** | These will be set up to monitor the progress of the plan and the budget. |

**Exam focus point**

In November 2005, candidates were required to identify the main issues that the company in the scenario should include in a marketing action plan. Good answers would use the 'Ps' (Product, Price, Place, Promotion, People, Processes and Physical evidence) as a framework and identify related issues in the scenario for discussion.

To summarise then, the following diagram shows how marketing planning fits into the corporate plan.

**Marketing and corporate planning**

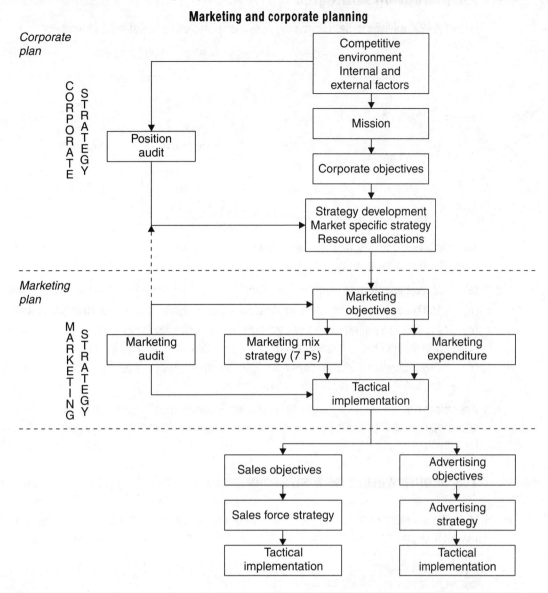

The examiner has stressed that a true marketing orientation is a philosophy that impacts upon all areas of an organisation. As such, it should permeate throughout the organisation. Try to avoid thinking of marketing only as advertising or PR – from what you have read in this chapter you should understand that such a narrow view is outdated.

# 7 Marketing strategies

## 7.1 Marketing objectives

**FAST FORWARD**

Marketing objectives should be **SMART**: **S**pecific; **M**easurable; **A**chievable; **R**elevant and **T**ime-bound.

Marketing objectives should be clear statements of where the organisation wants to be in marketing terms. They describe what the organisation expects to achieve as a result of its planned marketing actions. Marketing objectives should be **SMART**: **S**pecific; **M**easurable; **A**chievable; **R**elevant and **T**ime-bound. Examples of marketing objectives could include:

'To increase market share from the current X% to Y% by 20XX.'
'To achieve a sales revenue of £X million at a cost of sales not exceeding 80% in 20X1.'

These are developed from corporate objectives.

## 7.2 Marketing strategies

*Ansoff* (1987) devised a matrix showing possible strategies for products and markets.

*Ansoff's competitive strategies (Ansoff matrix)*

Products

|  |  | Existing | New |
|---|---|---|---|
| Markets | Existing | Market Penetration 1 | Product Development 4 |
|  | New | Market Development 2 | Diversification 16 |

The numbers in the quadrants are an approximate indication of the **risk** attached to each strategy. Diversification is the riskiest.

(a) **Market penetration** involves increasing sales of the **existing products in existing markets**.

(b) **Market development** entails **expansion into new markets using existing products**.

(c) **Product development** involves the redesign or repositioning of existing products or the introduction of completely new ones in order to appeal to existing markets.

(d) **Diversification** is much more risky than the other three because the organisation is moving into areas in which it has little or no experience.

*Ansoff's* matrix then leads naturally to **marketing** activities such as research to identify new markets and new products, and the deployment of the **marketing mix** in exploiting these product/market opportunities for growth.

## 7.3 Segmentation as a strategy

**Key term**

**Market segmentation** is the subdividing of a market into distinct subsets of customers, where any subset may conceivably be selected as a target market to be reached with a distinct marketing mix.

| Mass market approach | Segmentation |
|---|---|
| Mass or total market approach does not distinguish between customers. It assumes that majority needs can be satisfied with a single marketing mix. This approach is still relevant for marketing commodities. Many industrial products, such as steel, oil and metals are commodities and marketed as such. Commodities are less common in consumer markets, but we might identify gas, electricity, sugar and mains water supply. | Marketing activity is more effective if groups can be identified and targeted. This is done by market segmentation which groups potential customers according to identifiable characteristics relevant to their purchasing behaviour. |

We cover segmentation in detail in the next chapter.

## 7.4 Targeting as a strategy

Limited resources, competition and large markets make it ineffective and inappropriate for companies to sell to the entire market; that is, every market segment. For the sake of efficiency they must select target markets. Marketing managers may choose one of the following policy options.

(a)   **Undifferentiated marketing** aims to produce a single product and get as many customers as possible to buy it. Segmentation is ignored.

(b)   **Concentrated marketing** attempts to produce the ideal product for a single segment of the market (eg Rolls Royce for the very wealthy).

(c)   **Differentiated marketing** attempts to introduce several versions of a product, each aimed at a different market segment (for example, the manufacture of several different brands of washing powder).

## 7.5 Positioning as a strategy

Positioning is a marketing strategy which accepts that a product cannot be 'all things to all people', but will always be compared to other products, as we have seen. A company can develop or build a position for a market.

**Strategic positioning map**

# 8 Marketing communications

## 8.1 The marketing communications mix

FAST FORWARD When conducting a marketing campaign, there are a range of possible **communication methods and channels** the campaign could utilise.

The following diagram shows a range of methods and that can be used to influence a customer or potential customer.

*Promotional influences on the customer*

These tools represent the deployment of deliberate and intentional methods calculated to bring about a **favourable response in the customer's behaviour**.

The diagram represents the most obvious promotion methods, though other parts of the marketing mix, including the product itself, pricing, policy and distribution channels are also important.

Choosing the correct tools for a particular promotions task is not easy. The process is still very much an art, though it is becoming more scientific because of the access to consumer and media databases. Computer systems may be utilised to match consumer characteristics with promotional tools.

In reality, an experienced marketing manager may be able to reach sensible conclusions almost intuitively, based on what has been successful in the past and on knowledge of both customers and competitors.

### 8.1.1 Consumer and business-to-business markets

The comment above about experience of a particular market can be generalised in the case of the two broad categories of consumer and business-to-business markets. **Consumer markets** (or business-to-consumer markets **B2C**) are categorised as consisting of mass audiences which are cost-effectively accessible by television or national newspaper advertising. Supermarkets allow customers to serve themselves and there is little or no personal selling.

**Business-to-business markets (B2B)**, by contrast, involve a great deal of personal selling at different levels in the organisation. The needs of individual companies are different and therefore mass advertising would be most wasteful. Building on these generalised comments it is possible to present the mix of appropriate tools in the following diagram.

**Variation of promotion tools with type of market**

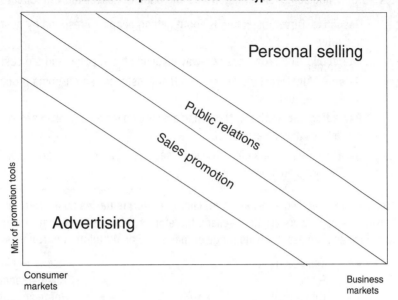

## 8.1.2 Integrated marketing communications

It is necessary to integrate all the promotional elements to achieve the maximum influence on the customer. **Integrated marketing communications** represents all the elements of an organisation's marketing mix that favourably influence its customers or clients. It goes beyond the right choice of promotion tools to the correct choice of the marketing mix. This is illustrated in the diagram below.

*The integrated marketing communication process*

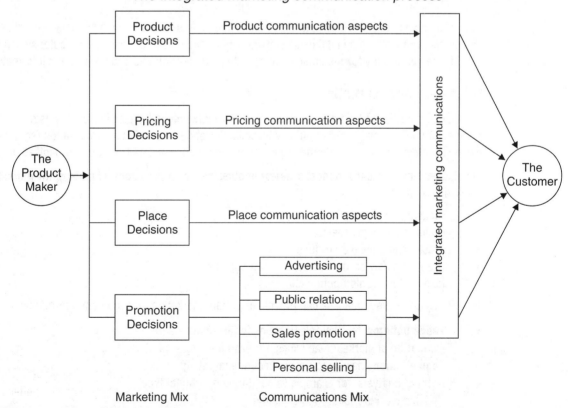

## 8.2 Direct marketing

> The Institute of Direct Marketing in the UK defines **direct marketing** as 'The planned recording, analysis and tracking of customer behaviour to develop relational marketing strategies'.
>
> It is worth noting some further key words and phrases associated with direct marketing.
>
> (a) **Response**. Direct marketing is about getting people to respond by post or telephone to invitations and offers.
>
> (b) **Interactive**. The process is two-way involving the supplier and the customer.
>
> (c) **Relationship**. Direct marketing is in many instances an on-going process of selling again and again to the same customer.
>
> (d) **Recording and analysis**. Response data are collected and analysed so that the most cost-effective procedures may be arrived at.
>
> (e) **Strategy**. Direct marketing should be seen as a part of a comprehensive plan stemming from clearly formulated objectives.

Because direct marketing **removes all channel intermediaries** apart from the advertising medium and the delivery medium, there are no resellers, therefore avoiding loss of control and loss of revenue. Direct marketing encompasses a wide range of media and distribution opportunities, such as:

- Television
- Radio
- Direct mail

- Inserts (eg in newspapers)
- Telemarketing
- Home shopping using the Internet

 Case Study

Direct Line, the insurance company, turned the motor insurance industry on its head through its ability to by-pass the traditional brokers and offer the average consumer not only a cheaper form of insurance, but a high degree of service.

Above all, the power of the **computer** has transformed the processes by which marketers relate to their customers. Improvements in database software and reductions in the cost of computer systems, now provide the opportunity for the smallest of operations to develop and benefit from the information era.

### 8.2.1 Database marketing

The type of information held on a database used for marketing will typically include customer, market and competitor information. Information may be collated from both inside the organisation (eg the firm's existing customers) and outside the organisation (eg purchased data from other organisations).

The database may be used to meet a variety of objectives with numerous advantages over traditional marketing methods.

- Focusing on prime prospects
- Evaluating new prospects
- Cross-selling related products
- Launching new products to potential prospects
- Identifying new distribution channels

An effective marketing database can provide important marketing management information.

- **Usage patterns**, for example, reasons for account closures
- **Evaluation** of marketing activities, for example response rates
- **Segmentation** analysis to ensure accurate targeting
- **Account analysis**, for example value, duration, product type
- Updated **market research** information

The information held on the database enables the effective tailoring of future offer messages to existing and potential customers.

### 8.2.2 Fulfilment

Direct marketing aims to solicit a response. **Fulfilment** is the act of servicing the customer's response. The act of fulfilment may take on a number of different activities including handling customer complaints, taking orders, offering advice and providing service and despatching goods. In all of these cases, it is safe to assume that the customer requires a prompt, courteous and effective response. Typical fulfilment activities include:

- Processing requests
- Picking, packaging and despatch
- Credit card validation and processing
- Analysing and reporting response data

### 8.2.3 Telemarketing

**Key term**

> **Telemarketing** is the planned and controlled use of the telephone for sales and marketing opportunities.

Unlike all other forms of direct marketing, telemarketing allows for **immediate two-way communication**. Telemarketing is a quick, accurate and flexible tool for gathering, maintaining and helping to exploit relevant up-to-date information about customers and prospects.

**Characteristics of telemarketing**

(a)    **Targeted**. The message is appropriately tailored to the recipient.

(b)    **Personal**. Telemarketers can determine and respond immediately to the specific needs of individuals, building long-term personal and profitable relationships.

(c)    **Interactive**. Since the dialogue is live, the conversation can be guided to achieve the desired results; the representative is in control.

(d)    **Immediate**. Every outbound call achieves an immediate result, even if it is a wrong number or 'not interested'. Customers and prospects can be given 24 hour constant access to the company.

(e)    **High quality**. Minimum amounts of information can be gathered accurately, kept up-to-date and used to select and prioritise leads for follow up calls.

(f)    **Flexible**. Conversations can be tailored spontaneously as the representative responds to the contact's needs. There are no geographical constraints on calls and they can be timed to suit the contact.

(g)    **Accountable**. Results and effectiveness can be checked continuously.

(h)    **Experimental**. Campaign variables can be tested quickly, and changes made whilst the campaign is in progress.

**Telemarketing** may be used for a range of **purposes**.

(a)    **Building, maintaining, cleaning** and **updating databases** to be used in marketing initiatives.

(b)    Market **evaluation** and **test marketing**. Almost any feature of a market can be measured and tested by telephone. Feedback is immediate so responses can be targeted quickly to exploit market knowledge.

(c)    **Dealer support**. Leads can be passed on to the nearest dealer.

(d)    **Traffic generation**. The telephone, combined with postal invitations, is the most cost effective way of screening leads and encouraging attendance at promotional events.

(e)    **Direct sales and account servicing**. The telephone can be used at all stages of the relationship with the prospects and customers. This includes lead generation, establishing buying potential and defining the decision-making process.

(f)    **Customer care and loyalty building**. Every telephone contact opportunity can demonstrate to customers that they are valued.

(g)    **Crisis management**. If, for example, there is a consumer scare, immediate action is essential to minimise commercial damage. A dedicated hotline number can be advertised to provide information and advice.

**Problems with telemarketing**

Telemarketing can be costly. There are few economies of scale, and techniques such as direct mail and media advertising can work out to be cheaper. Labour overheads are potentially high, although this can be counterbalanced by operating the business from a central point.

A telemarketer can only contact around 30 to 40 customers in a day, whereas media advertising can reach a mass audience in a single strike. However, media advertising married with a telephone contact number can be a very powerful combination.

If poorly handled, telemarketing may be interpreted as intrusive. This may alienate the customer and lead to lost sales opportunities.

## 8.3 The Internet

The Internet has huge potential wherever data and communication are important. It can enhance **customer service** and thus promote stronger marketing relationships. (We covered some basic aspects of the Internet in Chapter 3.)

Two good example of this are software fixes that can be downloaded from IT manufacturers' websites and the publication of flight schedules. Manufacturers' websites can be used to provide information on new uses for old products; this very simple type of **market development** can mean increased sales. They are also very useful as an ancillary to advertisements in other media: 'See our website for full catalogue'.

Websites can be used for **direct sales**. Sometimes this amounts to little more than a modern version of catalogue selling, but the 'Add to shopping cart' approach can help the customer by making it unnecessary to complete and add up an order form. There are a number of useful techniques.

(a)     Give something away, charge for something else. For example, give the trial version of a software package, sell the full featured version.

(b)     Precede the free download with a commercial for something else.

(c)     Use 'today only' offers; a website can be changed extremely quickly.

**Fulfilment** is crucial to the success of any e-commerce venture. Some goods can themselves be delivered over the Internet, for example software, music and documents. However, where material goods must be physically delivered, back-office systems and procedures must be in place to ensure the product reaches the purchaser.

Media companies can use their websites to provide a new dimension of information and entertainment, which leads to increased product involvement and hence enhanced perceived value. Examples are newspaper web editions and home pages for movies.

**Information** can be obtained from site visits since the Internet is interactive and visitors can be asked questions. One popular approach is to run competitions; filling in the entry form can glean significant information. Such information is invaluable for database marketing purposes.

### 8.3.1 Rules for Internet success

- Web surfers tend to move quickly; if a site is to succeed it must seize attention **immediately**.
- Sophisticated graphics and video may look good, but few people will wait for them
- Anything new about the site should be emphasised on the Home page.
- Selling should offer **price savings** over normal shopping; surfers need an incentive to buy online.
- The Internet is unlike traditional direct mail methods in that it does not intrude into the potential customer's life: the customer comes looking for the website. It is therefore essential that a site is **registered** with the major search engines such as Google.

## Case Study

### Spam

'Scott Richter does not like to be disturbed. He has little patience for the telemarketers who bother him at home and laments the drop-in salespeople who ignore the 'no soliciting' sign outside his office. But Mr Richter does a bit of soliciting himself. In fact, anti-spam activists claim he is one of the top 200 spammers, responsible for about 90 per cent of the junk e-mails circulating in cyberspace, a branding that could make him one of the most reviled men in America.

''People have to understand, we're a legitimate business. We are not the basement spammer,'' he says of his company, OptInRealBig.com.

'Spam works on the principle that there is 'a sucker born every minute'. And it thrives on the fact that it costs virtually nothing to produce.

'It is, in short, a numbers game in which a spammer's odds of success increase with every additional e-mail sent. By firing out millions of e-mails at a time, spammers say they can turn a profit if just 0.2 per cent of recipients purchase the products offered for sale. This infinitesimal response rate would bankrupt normal direct marketers, who must pay postage fees much higher than the costs of sending spam.

'Mr Richter readily acknowledges that he fires off more than 10m commercial e-mails every day – but only to recipients who have at one time or another agreed to receive bulk e-mail.

'Moreover, his e-mails contain an 'unsubscribe' button that enables recipients to opt out of future mailings. And this, he says, indicates that his e-mails are not spam.

'Mr Richter began his career in cyberspace when he tried selling pagers over the Internet, a business that flopped about three years ago. Saddled with left-over hardware, he cast about for a new online venture. He came up with bulk e-mail.

*Financial Times,* 29 April 2003

# 9 Pricing

## 9.1 Price setting

> **FAST FORWARD**
>
> There are three main types of influence on price setting in practice: **costs, competition** and **demand**.

### 9.1.1 Costs

In practice, cost is the most important influence on price. Many firms base price on simple **cost-plus** rules: in other words, costs are estimated and then a profit margin is added in order to set the price. This method is fairly easy to apply and ensures that costs are covered. Costs are usually available from accounting records.

A common example occurs with the use of **mark-up** pricing. This is used by retailers and involves a fixed margin being added to the buying-in price of goods for resale.

Because the cost-plus approach leads to price stability, with price changing only being used to reflect cost changes, it can lead to a marketing strategy which is **reactive** rather then **proactive**. In addition, there is very limited consideration of **demand** in cost-based pricing strategies. From a marketing perspective, cost-based pricing may lead to **missed opportunities** as little or no account is taken, particularly in the short run, of the price consumers are **willing** to pay for the brand, which may actually be higher than the cost-based price.

### 9.1.2 Competition

In some markets, **going rate pricing** in which some form of average level of price becomes the norm, perhaps, in the case of a high level of branding in the market, including standard price differentials between brands.

In some market structures **price competition may be avoided by informal agreement** leading to concentration on non-price competition; the markets for cigarettes and petrol are examples of this. Note that explicit agreement to fix prices is illegal. Price-setting here is influenced by the need to **avoid retaliatory responses by competitors**.

### 9.1.3 Demand

Rather than cost or competition as the prime determinants of price, a firm may base pricing strategy on the **intensity** and **elasticity** of demand. **Strong demand may lead to a high price, and a weak demand to a low price**: much depends on the ability of the firm to segment the market price in terms of elasticity.

For products or services with a typical downward sloping demand curve, fewer purchasers will buy at a **higher price**. If a supplier can identify those purchasers still willing to pay the higher price the supplier could benefit through charging them a higher price. This is called **price discrimination** or **differential pricing**.

In practice, measurement of price elasticity and, implementing differential pricing can be very difficult. There are a number of bases on which discriminating prices can be set.

(a)   **By market segment.** A cross-channel ferry company would market its services at different prices in England, Belgium and France, for example. Services such as cinemas and hairdressers are often available at lower prices to old age pensioners and juveniles.

(b)   **By product version.** Many car models have 'add on' extras which enable one brand to appeal to a wider cross-section of customers. Final price need not reflect the cost price of the add on extras directly: usually the top of the range model would carry a price much in excess of the cost of provision of the extras, as a prestige appeal.

(c)   **By place.** Theatre seats are usually sold according to their location so that patrons pay different prices for the same performance according to the seat type they occupy.

(d)   **By time.** This is perhaps **the most popular type of price discrimination**.

 Case Study

Off-peak travel bargains, hotel prices, telephone and electricity charges are all attempts to increase sales revenue by covering variable but not necessarily average cost of provision. UK rail operators are successful price discriminators, charging more to rush hour rail commuters whose demand is inelastic at certain times of the day.

Price sensitivity will vary amongst purchasers. **Those who can pass on the cost of purchases will be least sensitive** and will respond more to other elements of the marketing mix.

**Pricing research is notoriously difficult**, especially if respondents try to give rational rather than their 'real' response. As the respondent is not actually faced with the situation they may give a hypothetical answer that is not going to be translated into actual purchasing behaviour. Nevertheless, pricing research is increasingly common as firms struggle to assess the perceived value customers attribute to a brand to provide an input to their pricing decisions.

## 9.2 Competitors' actions and reactions

An organisation, in setting prices, **sends out signals to rivals**. **These rivals are likely to react** in some way. In some industries (such as petrol retailing) pricing moves in unison; in others, price changes by one supplier may initiate a price war, with each supplier undercutting the others.

In established industries dominated by a few major firms, it is generally accepted that a **price initiative by one firm** will be countered by a **price reaction** by competitors. Here, prices tend to be fairly stable, unless pushed upwards by inflation or strong growth in demand.

In the event that a **rival cuts prices** expecting to increase market share, a firm has several options.

(a)   It will **maintain its existing prices** if the expectation is that only a small market share would be lost, so that it is more profitable to keep prices at their existing level. Eventually, the rival firm may drop out of the market or be forced to raise its prices.

(b)   It may **maintain its prices** but respond with a **non-price counter-attack**. This is a more positive response, because the firm will be securing or justifying its current prices.

(c)   It may **reduce its prices**. This should protect the firm's market share at the expense of profitability. The main beneficiary from the price reduction will be the consumer.

(d)   It may **raise its prices** and respond with a **non-price counter-attack**. The extra revenue from the higher prices might be used to finance promotion on product changes. A price increase would be based on a campaign to emphasise the quality difference between the firm's own product and the rival's product.

## 9.3 Quality connotations

In the absence of other information, some customers tend to **judge quality by price**. Thus a price change may send signals to customers concerning the quality of the product. A rise may be taken to indicate improvements, a reduction may signal reduced quality, for example, through the use of inferior components or a poorer quality of raw material. Thus any change in price needs to take such factors into account.

## 9.4 New product pricing

Most pricing decisions for existing products relate to price changes. Such changes have a **reference point** from which to move (the existing price). But **when a new product is introduced for the first time there may be no such reference points**; pricing decisions are most difficult to make in such circumstances. It may be possible to seek alternative reference points, such as the price in another market where the new product has already been launched, or the price set by a competitor.

## 9.5 Multiple products

Most organisations market not just one product but a **range of products**. These products are commonly interrelated, perhaps being complements or substitutes. The pricing strategy is likely to focus on the profit from the whole range rather than that on each single product. Take, for example, the use of loss leaders: a very low price for one product is intended to make consumers buy other products in the range which carry higher profit margins. Another example is selling razors at very low prices whilst selling the blades for them at a higher profit margin. People will buy many of the high profit items but only one of the low profit items – yet they are 'locked in' to the former by the latter. Loss leaders also attract customers into retail stores where they will usually buy normally priced products as well as the loss leaders.

## 9.6 Price setting strategies summary

After considering the issues in Sections 9.1 to 9.5, the following price setting strategies can be developed.

### 9.6.1 Market penetration

**Market penetration objective**: here the organisation sets a **relatively low price** for the product or service in order to **stimulate growth of the market and/or to obtain a large share** of it. This strategy was used by Japanese motor cycle manufacturers to enter the UK market. It worked famously: UK productive capacity was virtually eliminated and the imported Japanese machines could then be sold at a much higher price and still dominate the market.

Such sales maximisation is appropriate under three conditions.

- Unit costs will fall with increased output (economies of scale)
- The market is price sensitive and relatively low prices will attract additional sales
- Low prices will discourage new competitors

### 9.6.2 Market skimming

**Market skimming objective:** Skimming involves **setting a high initial price for a new product in order to take advantage of those buyers who are ready to pay a much higher price for a product.** A typical strategy would be initially to set a premium price and then gradually to reduce the price to attract more price sensitive segments of the market. This strategy is really an example of **price discrimination over time**. It may encourage competition, and growth will initially be slow.

This strategy is appropriate under three conditions.

- There is insufficient production capacity and competitors cannot increase capacity
- Some buyers are relatively insensitive to high prices
- High price is perceived as high quality

### 9.6.3 Early cash recovery

**Early cash recovery objective**: an alternative pricing objective is to recover the investment in a new product or service as quickly as possible, to achieve a minimum payback period. The price is set to facilitate this objective. This objective would tend to be used in three circumstances.

- The business is high risk
- Rapid changes in fashion or technology are expected
- The innovator is short of cash

### 9.6.4 Product line promotion

**Product line promotion objective**: here, management of the pricing function is likely to focus on **profit from the range of products** which the organisation produces **rather than to treat each product as a separate entity**. The product line promotion objective will look at the whole range from two points of view.

- The interaction of the marketing mix
- Monitoring returns to ensure that net contribution is worthwhile

### 9.6.5 Cost-plus pricing

A firm may set its initial price by marking up its unit costs by a certain percentage or fixed amount, as already discussed.

### 9.6.6 Target pricing

A variant on cost-plus where the company tries to determine the price that gives a specified rate of return for a given output.

### 9.6.7 Price discrimination / selective pricing

In its pure form this involves **setting different prices** for **the same product** when it is **sold in different markets**. Three sub-categories have evolved.

(a)    **Category**

The product is cosmetically modified to justify a price differential. For example a 'budget' version of a product is modified into a 'premium' version.

(b)    **Consumer group**

The price differential is justified by **targeting different consumer groups** for example, OAP or student prices. They are often used by leisure facilities such as leisure centres or galleries.

(c)    **Peak**

The **price** is **set in accordance** with **demand**. For example, the price of train ticket is often more expensive in the morning when most people travel to work.

The danger is that price cuts to one buyer may be used as a **negotiating lever** by another buyer. This can be countered in three ways.

(a)    Buyers can be split into clearly defined segments, such as overseas and home, or students' concessionary fares.

(b)    Own branding, where packaging is changed for that of a supermarket, is a variation on this.

(c)    Bulk buying discounts and aggregated rebate schemes can favour large buyers.

## 9.6.8 Going rate / competitive prices

**Going rate pricing** involves trying to keep in line with industry norm for prices, this is also known as **competitive pricing** where prices are set with reference to competitors' pricing.

## 9.6.9 Price leadership / predatory pricing

In some markets a **price leader** (often a large corporation) emerges. A price leader dominates price levels for a class of products; increases or decreases by the price leader are followed by the market. The price dominant firm may lead without moving at all. The price leader generally has a large market share and will usually be an efficient producer with a reputation for technical competence.

The role of price leader is based on a track record of having initiated price moves that have been accepted by both competitors and customers. Any dramatic changes in industry competition, (a new entrant, or changes in the board room) may endanger the price leadership role.

**Predatory pricing** is a similar strategy but the reason for setting a low price is to damage the competition.

 Case Study

### Credit cards

The price of a credit card may include an annual fee and an interest rate. The interest rate may be influenced by the actual rate and any period of free credit.

Interest rates vary

- Some customers who are low risk can get low rates.
- Others are charged high rates.

Price discrimination is thus used for different groups of customers.

To capture business, card companies offer:

- Interest free or low interest periods
- Free balance transfers
- Reward points

In other words, price is consciously used to attract new customers – but doesn't appear to be used to reward customer loyalty.

# 10 Services and service marketing

## 10.1 The rise of the service economy

In terms of employment, in the UK and many other countries more people now work in the service sector than in all other sectors of the economy. In terms of output, the major contributors to national output are the public and private service sectors.

**Key term**

> **Services** include:
>
> '... those separately identifiable but intangible activities that provide want-satisfaction, and that are not, of necessity, tied to, or inextricable from, the sale of a product or another service. To produce a service may or may not require the use of tangible goods or assets. However, where such use is required, there is no transfer of title (permanent ownership) to these tangible goods.'                    *(Cowell, 1995)*
>
> '... any activity of benefit that one party can offer to another that is essentially intangible and does not result in the ownership of anything. Its production may or may not be tied to a physical product.'     (Kotler *et al.* 2002)

**FAST FORWARD**

> The **marketing of services** presents a number of different challenges. As a consequence, particular marketing practices have been developed.

There are many service industries which are highly market-oriented (for instance, in retailing, transport hire, cleaning and hotel groups), but there are many which remain relatively unaffected by marketing ideas and practices, or which have only just begun to adopt them (for example, legal services). Marketing ideas are likely to become much more important as competition within the service sector intensifies.

## 10.2 Marketing characteristics of services

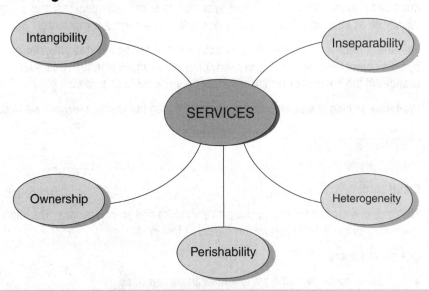

**FAST FORWARD**

> The following characteristics of services distinguish them from goods, and have marketing implications.
>
> - **Intangibility**: services cannot be touched or tasted
> - **Inseparability**: services cannot be separated from the provider
> - **Heterogeneity** (or lack of 'sameness'): the standard of service will vary with each delivery
> - **Perishability**: services cannot be stored for provision 'later'
> - **Ownership**: service purchase does not transfer ownership of property

We will look at each characteristic in detail, along with its marketing implications.

## 10.2.1 Intangibility

'Intangibility' refers to the lack of substance which is involved with service delivery. Unlike goods, there are no substantial material or physical aspects to a service: no taste, feel, visible presence and so on. This creates difficulties and can inhibit the desire to consume a service, since customers are not sure what they will receive.

Marketers and consumers need to try to overcome this problem. The marketer wishes to make the choice of the product 'safer' and make the consumer feel more comfortable about paying for something they do not then own and which has no physical form. **Dealing with intangibility** may involve the following.

(a) **Increasing the level of tangibility**. Use physical or conceptual representations/illustrations to make the customer feel more confident as to what it is that the service is delivering: the 'physical evidences' component of the extended marketing mix.

(b) **Focusing the attention of the customer on the principal benefits of consumption**. Communicating the benefits of purchasing the service so that the customer visualises its use. Promotion and sales material could provide images or records of previous customers' experience.

(c) **Differentiating the service and reputation-building**. Enhancing perceptions of customer service and customer value by offering excellence in the delivery of the service. This reputation can be attached to brands, which must then be managed to secure and enhance their market position, (for example, the Virgin brand).

## 10.2.2 Inseparability

Services often cannot be separated off from the provider, for example having dental treatment or taking a journey. Neither exists until they are actually being experienced/consumed by the person who has bought them. The 'creation' of many services is simultaneous with consumption, where the service is

- Made available
- Produced
- Sold        } all at the same time
- Consumed

Provision of the service may not be separable from the person or personality of the seller. Consequently, increasing importance is attached to the need to instil values of quality, reliability and to generate a service ethic in customer-facing staff. This points up the need for excellence and customer orientation and the need to invest in high quality people and high quality training: the 'people' component of the extended marketing mix.

## 10.2.3 Heterogeneity (lack of 'sameness' or consistency)

Many services face the problem of maintaining consistency in the standard of output. Variability of quality occurs because of the large number of variables involved. The quality of the service may depend heavily on who it is that delivers the service. For example, booking a holiday using standard procedures may well be quite different on a quiet winter afternoon and on a hectic spring weekend, and may well vary according to the person dealing with your case.

In terms of marketing policy, heterogeneity highlights the need to develop and maintain processes for:

- Consistency of quality control, with clear and objective quality measures
- Consistency of customer service and customer care, standardising as far as possible
- Effective staff selection, training and motivation in customer care
- Monitoring service levels and customer perceptions of service delivery

These measures correspond to both the 'processes' and 'people' elements of the extended marketing mix.

## 10.2.4 Perishability

Services cannot be stored: they are innately perishable. Seats on a bus or the services of a doctor exist only for periods of time. If they are not consumed, they 'perish'. They cannot be used later. They cannot be 'produced' in advance, to allow for peaks in demand.

This presents specific marketing problems. Meeting customer needs depends on staff being available as and when they are needed. This must be balanced against the need for a firm to minimise unnecessary expenditure on staff wages. **Anticipating and responding to levels of demand** is, therefore, a key planning priority.

Policies must seek to smooth out fluctuations in supply/demand relationship, or allow for contingencies. Examples include:

- Using price variations to encourage off-peak demand (eg on travel services)
- Using promotions to stimulate off-peak demand (eg free mobile calls between certain hours)
- Using flexible staffing methods to cover fluctuations in demand (eg part-time and temporary working, outsourcing to call centres)

### 10.2.5 Ownership

Services do not result in the transfer of property. The purchase of a service only gives the customer access to or the right to use a facility, not ownership. This may lessen the perceived customer value of a service – particularly if the benefit does not accrue until some time in the future (like a pension, or a voucher for future use).

There are two basic approaches to addressing this problem.

(a) **Promote the advantages of non-ownership**. This can be done by emphasising the benefits of paid-for maintenance, or a periodic upgrading of the product. Radio Rentals have used this as a major selling point with great success.

(b) **Make available a tangible symbol or representation of ownership** such as a certificate, voucher, merchandise item or simple receipt. This can come to embody the benefits enjoyed.

 Case Study

**Railways and airlines**

In the UK, in the nineteenth century, railway passengers could buy tickets for first, second and third classes. Now they buy first and 'standard' classes. The UK was a society heavily stratified by wealth, and so offering three classes of tickets would seem a natural way of targeting a market segmented by wealth.

In India today, again there are first, second and third classes (with permutations based on air conditioned compartments, sleepers etc). In China there exist 'hard' and 'soft' classes.

Airlines offer a useful contrast. Segmentation is partly based on purpose of visit and time of booking. Business class was directed to people travelling on business expense accounts (who would travel economy on their own account). Some airlines offer 'premium' economy seats to those who would want more legroom. The 'low-cost' airlines flying in the US and Europe designed for the 'no-frills' consumer, are increasingly frequented by business travellers, for short haul trips.

# 11 Social responsibility and ethics

 FAST FORWARD

**Social responsibility** requires that organisations will not act in a way which harms the general public or which is thought to be irresponsible. In this section we look at social responsibility in a marketing context.

## 11.1 The well-being of individuals and society

Critics of marketing argue that it is often dedicated to selling products which are potentially damaging to the health and well-being of the **individual** or **society**. Examples include tobacco, alcohol, automobiles, detergents and even electronic goods such as computers.

 BPP
LEARNING MEDIA

It has been argued that even seemingly harmless, products, such as soft drinks, can damage individuals and societies. In traditional societies, new products can disrupt social order by introducing new aspirations, or changing a long established way of life.

How should organisations react to these problems? There may be conflict between what is profitable for a business organisation and the interests of the customer, or of society.

Advocates of **social responsibility** feel that **the concerns of the community ought to be the concerns of business** since businesses exist within society, and depend on it for continued existence. Business has a moral obligation to assist in the solution of those problems which it causes.

Many organisations and businesses now accept that it is necessary for organisations to develop a sense of responsibility for the consequences of their actions within society at large, rather than simply setting out to provide consumer satisfaction and maximise profits.

**FAST FORWARD**

**Social responsibility** involves accepting that the organisation is part of society and, as such, is accountable to that society for the consequences of the actions which it takes.

Some businesses 'put something back' into society through sponsorship of events, community projects or charitable donations. This may also have a positive effect on how the organisation is viewed – it may be good **Public Relations** (PR).

## 11.2 Ethics and the law

Social responsibility is closely related to ethics. Ethics deal with personal moral principles and values, whereas laws are the rules that can actually be enforced in court. Behaviour which is not subject to legal penalties may still be unethical and socially irresponsible.

Case Study

Think about this example. The US-based RJ Reynolds Tobacco Company considered targeting Afro-Americans for a new brand of cigarette, while public health statistics show that this group has a high incidence of lung cancer and smoking related illnesses. This is perfectly legal, but is it ethical?

We can classify marketing decisions according to ethics and legality in four different ways.

- **Ethical and legal** (eg paying above the minimum wage)
- **Unethical and legal** (eg 'gazumping')
- **Ethical but illegal** (eg publishing stolen but revealing documents about government mismanagement)
- **Unethical and illegal** (eg employing child labour)

## 11.3 Ethics in marketing

**FAST FORWARD**

**Ethical issues** usually revolve around **safety**, **quality**, and **value** and frequently arise from failure to provide adequate **information** in marketing communications to the customer.

### 11.3.1 Product issues

This may range from omission of uncomfortable facts in product literature to deliberate deception. A typical problem arises when a product specification is changed to reduce cost. Clearly, it is essential to ensure that product function is not compromised in any important way, but a decision must be taken as to just what emphasis, if any, it is necessary to place on the changes in product literature. Another, more serious, problem occurs when product safety is compromised. **Product recall** is the issue here.

When the French company Perrier discovered that its mineral water was in danger of contamination, they immediately withdrew all supplies, suffering huge losses. By acting ethically, the company's reputation was enhanced. On the other hand, when Coca Cola experienced similar problems with its launch of a new bottled water in the UK, it dithered and suffered a huge blow to its image.

## 11.3.2 Promotion issues

Ethical considerations are particularly relevant to **promotional practices**. Advertising and personal selling are areas in which the temptation to select, exaggerate, slant, conceal, distort and falsify information is potentially great. Questionable practices here are likely to create **cynicism in the customer** and ultimately to preclude any degree of trust or respect for the supplier. Many people think that persuading people to buy something they don't really want is intrinsically unethical, especially if hard sell tactics are used.

Also relevant to this area is the problem of **corrupt selling practices**. It is widely accepted that a small gift such as a mouse mat or a diary is a useful way of keeping a supplier's name in front of an industrial purchaser. Most business people would however condemn the payment of substantial bribes to purchasing officers to induce them to favour a particular supplier. But where does the dividing line lie between these two extremes?

### Marketing ethics

'GSK markets its medicines to doctors, hospitals and governments. In some countries, such as the US, we also advertise medicines directly to consumers.

'Our specialist sales representatives meet regularly with doctors and pharmacists to inform them about our medicines and their approved uses.

'We believe that sales representatives play an important role in providing up-to-date information to doctors on our products and their benefits to patients. However, we recognise that the marketing of pharmaceutical products raises some challenging issues.

'In particular, some people are concerned that marketing by pharmaceutical companies exerts undue influence on doctors, that sales representatives do not always give doctors full information about potential side effects, or that promotion for unapproved uses may be common despite increased training, monitoring and oversight.

'The promotion of pharmaceutical products is highly regulated and several governments are extending legislation in this area. For instance, six US states require pharmaceutical companies to restrict or report their interactions with doctors. Requirements vary from prohibiting companies from providing meals to setting annual spending limits or requiring transparent reporting. Similar legislation is being considered in many other states. The American Medical Association now enables doctors to request that their prescribing activity is not shared with pharmaceutical companies.

'Our approach to addressing these issues includes the following:

*   All GSK employees must comply with our marketing codes of practice – revised and strengthened in 2006 – and our policies governing consumer advertising
*   Sales and marketing employees receive training to ensure they have a good understanding of our marketing policies and the legal framework governing their sales activities
*   We have programmes to monitor compliance including, in some regions, feedback from doctors on our sales practices ...

**Europe**

'We updated the GSK European Promotion of Medicines Code of Practice in March 2006 to ensure alignment with the updated EFPIA Code. The major changes include:

- New sections on distributing product information to healthcare professionals via email or the internet
- Prohibiting the use of competitions with prizes to promote our medicines ...

**Consumer advertising**

'This section explains our approach to advertising our prescription medicines in the US and our consumer healthcare products in other markets.

**Direct-to-consumer advertising**

'In the US we advertise our prescription medicines to consumers through TV and print advertisements. This is known as direct-to-consumer (DTC) advertising. New Zealand, Bangladesh and Korea also allow limited DTC advertising. DTC advertising of prescription medicines is not permitted in other markets. ...

'All DTC television advertisements (including audio and visual components) are submitted to the US Food and Drug Administration (FDA) for review at least 30 days in advance. No problems with GSK DTC advertising were identified by the FDA during 2006.

'Members of the public and healthcare professionals can send comments on DTC advertising to PhRMA's Office of Accountability established in 2006. These are forwarded to the relevant company. The Office of Accountability reports periodically on the comments and the companies' response to the FDA. In 2006, GSK did not receive any comments from the Office of Accountability regarding its DTC advertising.

'In 2006, our employees involved in DTC marketing attended training on our new policy and the PhRMA Principles. We also developed a DTC e-Learning module for future training. ...

**Advertising to children**

'Our guidelines for advertising to children meet or exceed local laws and codes of practice. They prohibit advertising designed to appeal to, or targeted at, children below the legally mandated minimum age. For example, in the UK we do not buy advertising space in children's media and we do not supply vending machines to primary schools.

'Sports star sponsorship is important to brands such as Lucozade Sport. Our guidelines state that only people who set an appropriate example should be used for sponsorship, and they should have an appeal that is not solely to children below the age of 13. '

Taken from GlaxoSmithKline's *Corporate Responsibility Report of 2006*

# Chapter Roundup

- **Marketing** is the management of **exchange relationships** between a supplier and a customer. The traditional 4Ps of marketing product, price, place (distribution) and promotion are important concepts.

- *Kotler and Keller* (2006) define the **marking mix** as 'the set of controllable variables and their levels that the firm uses to influence the target market'.

- The product life cycle includes four main stages: **introduction**, **growth**, **maturity** and **decline**. Some writers also include **shakeout** between growth and maturity.

- Marketing considerations can, in fact, **influence all activities** undertaken by an organisation. The value chain and internal customer concept show how ideas related to customer satisfaction and customer value can be implemented through the organisation.

- Typically, marketing has focused on **persuading consumers** to buy products or services. A **production orientation** assumed that consumers would buy whatever the firm produced. Firms with a **sales orientation,** again are **focused on the needs of the seller** rather than the buyer.

- Because marketing is chiefly concerned with customers, markets and products, it is in many ways linked to **corporate strategy**. Marketing considerations **influence corporate strategy**. However, marketing is also one way by which corporate strategy is implemented.

- All organisations exist in, interact with and are **influenced** by their environment.

- Marketing strategy should complement and be **consistent** with a firm's overall corporate strategy

- Marketing objectives should be **SMART**: **S**pecific; **M**easurable; **A**chievable; **R**elevant and **T**ime-bound.

- When conducting a marketing campaign, there are a range of possible **communication methods and channels** the campaign could utilise.

- There are three main types of influence on price setting in practice: **costs, competition** and **demand**.

- The **marketing of services** presents a number of different challenges. As a consequence, particular marketing practices have been developed.

- The following characteristics of services distinguish them from goods, and have marketing implications.

    - **Intangibility**: services cannot be touched or tasted
    - **Inseparability**: services cannot be separated from the provider
    - **Heterogeneity** (or lack of 'sameness'): the standard of service will vary with each delivery
    - **Perishability**: services cannot be stored for provision 'later'
    - **Ownership**: service purchase does not transfer ownership of property

- **Social responsibility** involves accepting that the organisation is part of society and, as such, will be accountable to that society for the consequences of the actions which it takes.

- **Social responsibility** requires that organisations will not act in a way which harms the general public or which is thought to be irresponsible.

- **Ethical issues** usually revolve around **safety**, **quality**, and **value** and frequently arise from failure to provide adequate **information** in marketing communications to the customer.

1    Which of the following is a fast moving consumer good (FMCG)?

    A     Haircuts

    B     Soap powder

    C     Cars

    D     Televisions

2    Processes are one of the four 'traditional' elements of the marketing mix.

    True   ☐

    False   ☐

3    A marketing orientation means that a company will centre its activities on satisfying the needs and wants of:

    A     Shareholders

    B     Management

    C     Employees

    D     Customers

4    What does the abbreviation 'PESTEL' stand for?

5    State the contents of a marketing plan.

6    Why do marketers segment the market?

7    'Business-to-business markets should make use of mass marketing as much as possible'

    True   ☐

    False   ☐

8    Identify the three main types of influences on price setting.

9    List five characteristics of services often used to distinguish them from goods.

    1     ...............................................................

    2     ...............................................................

    3     ...............................................................

    4     ...............................................................

    5     ...............................................................

10   Explain the concept of social responsibility.

1   B   Soap powder is an example of a FMCG.

2   Product, Price, Place (distribution), Promotion are the four 'traditional' elements of the marketing mix.

3   D   Marketing orientation approaches seek to satisfy the needs and wants of consumers.

4   Political, Economic, Social/cultural, Technological, Ecological/Environmental and Legal factors.

5   Executive summary, situation analysis, objectives and goals, marketing strategy, strategic marketing plan, tactical marketing plan, action plan, budgets, controls.

6   Because marketing activity should be more effective if potential customers are able to be grouped (segmented) according to characteristics relevant to their purchasing behaviour.

7   False. In business-to-business markets, mass marketing is wasteful, as the needs of individual companies are different. Mass marketing is only effective in markets where the needs of all customers are broadly the same.

8   Costs, competition and demand.

9   Intangibility, Inseparability, Heterogeneity, Perishability, Ownership.

10  Social responsibility involves an acceptance that the organisation has a responsibility to (and is accountable to) society for the actions it takes.

Now try the question below from the Exam Question Bank

| Number | Level | Marks | Time |
|--------|-------|-------|------|
| 10 | Tutorial | 20 | 36 mins |

# 11

# Buyer behaviour and market research

## Introduction

In Chapter 10 we described the marketing orientation as being focused on the customer, and explained that the relationship marketing approach holds that firms should try to establish long-term relationships with clients, not simply chase the next transaction.

However, all this presupposed that the 'customer' is a relatively simple concept. This is not necessarily the case. In this chapter we look more closely at **customers** (or **buyers**).

We attempt to explain some aspects of **customer behaviour**, and also look at the activities undertaken by marketers to better understand their market.

| Topic list | Learning outcomes | Syllabus references | Ability required |
|---|---|---|---|
| 1  The customer | D(ii), D(iv) | D(3) | Evaluation |
| 2  Buyer behaviour | D(ii), D(iv) | D(3), D(6) | Evaluation |
| 3  Organisations as buyers | D(ii), D(iv) | D(6) | Evaluation |
| 4  Market segmentation, target markets and positioning | D(ii), D(iv) | D(7) | Evaluation |
| 5  Forecasting demand | D(ii), D(vi) | D(14) | Evaluation |
| 6  Market research | D(ii), D(iv) | D(4), D(5) | Evaluation |

# 1 The customer

FAST FORWARD 'The customer' in a transaction can involve a number of different roles

We mentioned in Chapter 10 that marketing deals fundamentally with exchange relationships, that is, normally, that money is given by a customer for products and/or services provided by a supplier. 'The customer' in a transaction can involve a number of different roles as shown below.

| 'Customer' | | Household example: a family pet animal needing vaccination | Business example: ordering of office stationery |
|---|---|---|---|
| **Buyer** | The person who selects a product or service | A veterinary surgeon, on the pet owner's behalf, recommends and orders a vaccine. | The office manager may order stationery for other departments. |
| **Payer** | The person who finances the purchase | The pet-owner pays for the vaccination – or perhaps an insurance company pays in the end. | The payer is the company, via the accounts department. |
| **User** | Receives the benefit of the product or service | The pet receives the benefit of the vaccination (but the owner receives emotional benefits, too, perhaps). | Users are those with access to the stationery. |

The value of this distinction is that it enables marketing efforts and activities to be correctly focused on the people involved in the transaction. In the business example above, an office supplies company would direct most of its marketing efforts to the office manager buying the stationery. The approach to the accounts department would be slightly different: a relationship might have to be built up to ensure speedy payment.

 Case Study

**Bajaj Auto**

'If you want to sell goods to grown-ups, target the real decision-makers – their pre-teen kids.

'Indian motorcycle maker Bajaj Auto is one company that's caught on to that trick. Its latest series of television advertisements feature a boy who's rescued from a spate of minor childhood tragedies, like missing a school outing or being late for a party, by his dad astride the Bajaj motorcycle.

''Kids have far more computer– and gizmo-savvy than their parents. "They surf the net, they surf TV," says R L Ravichandran, Bajaj Auto's vice-president of marketing. "They now wield enormous influence on the purchase decisions of the household".

'Like their counterparts in the United States, kids in Asia aged 8 to 13, dubbed 'tweens' are gaining rapid influence over the household items their parents buy. The difference is that in the US, pre-teens influence decisions by begging their parents to buy stuff; in Asia, parents often ask their kids for advice. Increasingly, companies in Asia are getting wise to this and targeting tweens, who are emerging as in-house brand experts.

'That's particularly so in developing countries, where there's a wide knowledge gap between parents, many of whom were the first generation to enter the middle class, and their kids, who grew up exposed to cable TV and the Internet.

'This is happening at a time when societal shifts are already giving Asian kids a stronger voice in the home. Across Asia, couples are having fewer children. At the same time, extended family households, once dominated by the father, grandfather and even uncles, are giving way to nuclear families, a move that's further shifting the balance of power in the family home.

From the *Far Eastern Economic Review,* 14th August 2003.

# 2 Buyer behaviour

**Buyer behaviour** describes the activities and decision processes relating to buying. **The process** describes a sequence of steps, from need recognition, through information search, evaluation of alternatives, purchase decision and post-purchase evaluation.

Treating buying behaviour as a process also enables us to distinguish between the different buying roles that customers sometimes assume. Typically, marketers make a distinction between:

- Consumers as buyers
- Organisations as buyers

## 2.1 Consumer buying

Consumer decision making can be broken down into five stages or steps as shown in the table below (based upon *Lancaster and Withey* 2003).

| | Element | Comment |
|---|---|---|
| Step 1 | **Need/problem recognition** | The customer recognises a need or a problem to solve. This is a motive to search for a solution. |
| Step 2 | **Pre-purchase/ information search** | Marketers can provide product information, tailored to need. The customer might come up with alternatives. |
| Step 3 | **Evaluation of alternatives** | Marketers can make products available for evaluation and provide comparative information about competing products: the important thing, though, is to get the product onto the short-list of options. |
| Step 4 | **The purchase decision** | Selection and purchase. |
| Step 5 | **Post-purchase evaluation** | Experience 'feeds back' to the beginning of the process, providing positive or negative reinforcement of the purchase decision. If the consumer is dissatisfied, he will be back at the problem recognition stage again. If the consumer is satisfied, the next decision process for the product may be cut short and skip straight to the decision, on the basis of loyalty. |

Such a model provides a useful descriptive **framework** for marketers.

## 2.2 Influences on consumer buying

Overall, factors affecting customer behaviour are **social** (such as reference groups, roles and status), **cultural**, **personal** (eg age, economic status, lifestyle) and **psychological** (eg attitudes).

Transactions involving an organisation or business selling to a consumer are sometimes referred to as Business-to-Consumer or **B2C** transactions.

Some of the main influences on consumer buying are shown in the following diagram (based upon *Lancaster and Withey*). We explain the factors shown later in this section.

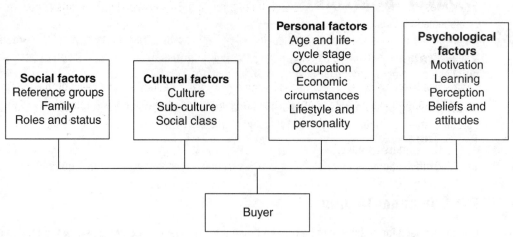

**Influences on buyers**

**2.2.1 Social factors**

Social factors relate to the social groupings a consumer belongs to or aspires to, and trends in society which influence buying patterns. The learning of gender-related, consumer and occupational roles are examples of socialisation.

**2.2.2 Reference groups**

A **reference group** is an actual or imaginary individual or group that influences an individual's evaluations, aspirations or behaviour.

Reference groups influence a buying decision by making the individual **aware** of a product or brand, allowing the individual to **compare** his attitude with that of the group, encouraging the individual to **adopt an attitude consistent** with the group, and then **reinforcing and legitimising** the individual's decision to conform.

 Case Study

Group membership has entered cyberspace as 'netizens' around the world rapidly form virtual communities. Members are linked to one another via their computers, and all of their interactions are digital. This electronic anonymity opens up exciting new opportunities for many, especially those who have difficulty interacting in face-to-face settings (eg the Internet has made a dramatic difference to the lives of many disabled people who can now interact with others around the world without having to leave home). New technologies allow people to chat about their mutual interests, to help one another with enquiries and suggestions, and to get suggestions for new products and services.

**2.2.3 Roles**

A 'role' is the sum or 'system' of expectations which other people have of an individual.

An example may help to explain what is meant by 'roles'. A male may consider himself to be a **father** and **husband**, a good **neighbour** and an active member of the **local community**, a **supporter** of his sports club, an amateur **golfer**, a conscientious **church-goer**, a man of certain **political** views, a **professional** and a **marketer**.

The other individuals who relate to him when he is in a particular role are called his **role set**. At work, he will have one role set made up of colleagues, superiors and subordinates, and any other contacts in the course of business: at home, he will have another role set consisting of family members.

Knowledge of roles can help with **market segmentation** and product positioning: categories such as executives, or young mothers, carry with them a range of role expectations, norms and signs which can be appealed to or catered for.

### 2.2.4 Status

**Status** has been called 'a kind of social identification tag': as such, it is the basis of the determination of social class, or social stratification. It also forms part of the individual's self-image.

### 2.2.5 The family

Families differ in many ways, not only in broad issue of socio-economic status but in buyer behaviour and consumption patterns.

## Case Study

**'What is the family?'**

- 'Western' nuclear family': husband, wife, children living together.
- Multi-generational family. Rather than set up a new home, a recently-married son may bring his wife to live with his parents. Such a family unit may contain parents, children, the children's spouses, grandchildren and so on.
- Extended family: carers and grandparents, in a close network of support. In the West, with the increase in divorce levels, some children effectively live in their father's 'family' some of the time and their mother's at other times. They may live with step-brothers and step-sisters.
- Single parent households: these are families headed by a lone parent, rather than two.

### 2.2.6 Cultural factors

Culture comprises the values, attitudes and beliefs in the pattern of life adopted by people, that help them integrate and communicate as members of society. Culture comprises cultural artefacts, lifestyles, and so on. For example, alcohol consumption is part of the culture of many countries in Western Europe, whereas it is frowned on in Muslim and some other countries.

### 2.2.7 Personal factors

'Personal' factors include such things as age, stage of family and life cycle, occupation, economic circumstances and lifestyle.

Individuals will buy different types of product depending on their **age**. This is particularly relevant to such products as clothes, furniture and recreation.

The **family life cycle** is used in the West to model purchase behaviour patterns. For example, couples at the early stages of their marriage before having children will have different needs and consumption patterns from those, say, after their children have left home. In the UK, where house purchase is the norm, this has particular implications for sellers of financial services.

A person's **occupation** will influence consumption and the task for marketers is to identify the occupational groups that have an above average interest in their products and services.

Buying patterns are also heavily influenced by an individual's **economic circumstances**. An individual's economic circumstances consist of:

- Spendable income: its level, stability and time pattern
- Savings and assets, including the percentage that is liquid
- Borrowing power
- Attitude toward spending versus saving

A **lifestyle** is an individual's way of living as identified by his or her activities, interests and opinions. Marketers will search for relationships between their products and lifestyle groups. There are many different lifestyle classifications.

## 2.2.8 Psychological factors

The process of buyer behaviour is also influenced by four psychological factors:

- Motivation
- Perception
- Learning
- Beliefs and attitudes

**Motivation** is an inner state that energises, activates, or moves, that directs or channels.

(a) *Maslow's* (1954) theory of motivation seeks to explain why people are driven by particular needs at particular times. Maslow argues that human needs are arranged in **a hierarchy** comprising, in their order of importance: physiological needs, safety needs, social needs, esteem needs and self-actualisation needs.

(b) *Herzberg* (1968) developed a 'two-factor theory' of motivation that distinguishes between **factors that cause dissatisfaction and factors that cause satisfaction**. The task for the marketer is, therefore, to avoid 'dissatisfiers' such as, for example, poor after-sales service, as these things will not sell the product but may well unsell it. In addition the marketer should identify the major satisfiers or motivators of purchase and make sure that they are supplied to the customer.

These theories were covered from the point of view of employee motivation in Chapter 8.

**Perception** is the process whereby people select, organise and interpret sensory stimuli into a meaningful and coherent picture. The way consumers view an object (for example, their mental picture of a brand or the traits they attribute to a brand) may vary according to their past experience, expectation, needs, interests, attitudes and beliefs.

**Learning** concerns the process whereby an individual's behaviour changes as a result of their experience.

## 2.2.9 Beliefs and attitudes

A **belief** is a descriptive thought that a person holds about something. Beliefs are important to marketers as the **brand beliefs** that people have about products make up the brand images of those products.

An **attitude** describes a person's enduring favourable or unfavourable cognitive evaluations, emotional feelings, and action tendencies toward some object or idea. **Attitudes** lead people to behave in a fairly **consistent** way towards similar objects. Attitudes tend to settle into a consistent pattern – to change one attitude may entail major changes to other attitudes.

 Case Study

For example, some people believe that Japanese-manufactured cars are more reliable than British-manufactured cars.

# 3 Organisations as buyers

> Organisations are viewed as more rational than individuals. The buying **decision making process** is likely to be **formal**.

## 3.1 Differences between organisational and consumer buying

**Organisational (or industrial) buying** is the process organisations use to establish the need for purchased products and services and how these products and services are selected and purchased.

Transactions between organisations or businesses are sometimes referred to as Business-to-Business or **B2B**. (Transactions involving an organisation or business and a consumer are sometimes referred to as Business-to-Consumer or **B2C**.)

When considering **organisational markets** the following factors should be taken into account:

(a) Organisational markets normally comprise **fewer buyers**, with a few buyers responsible for the majority of sales.

(b) Because of this smaller customer base and the importance and power of larger customers there is generally a **close relationship between buyer and seller**.

(c) **Demand** for industrial goods is ultimately derived from the demand for consumer goods. In addition, the total demand for many industrial products is **inelastic**, in other words, it is not much affected by price changes.

(d) The purchase decision is usually made by **consensus** in an organisational setting, rather than being the responsibility of one person.

**Exam focus point**

> The syllabus specifically refers to how Business to Business (B2B) marketing differs from Business-to-Consumer marketing (B2C). The factors explained above could be relevant in that context.

## 3.2 Process of organisational buying behaviour

A typical organisational buying process is summarised in the following table.

| Stage in behaviour | Comment |
|---|---|
| **Stage 1.** **Recognise the problem** | The stimulus may come from within or outside the firm. |
| **Stage 2.** **Develop product specifications or service requirements to solve the problem.** | People participating in the buying decision assess the problem or need and determine what will be required to resolve or satisfy it. This may take the form of detailed specifications. |
| **Stage 3.** **Search for products and suppliers.** | The third stage of the process is similar to that of information search, utilising trade shows, trade publications, supplier catalogues, and soliciting proposals from known suppliers. This should result in a list of several alternative products. |
| **Stage 4.** **Evaluate products relative to specifications.** | These are evaluated in order to ascertain whether they meet the product specifications developed in the second stage. Suppliers may also be evaluated according to criteria such as price, service and ability to deliver. |
| **Stage 5.** **Select and order the most appropriate product.** | The most appropriate product and supplier is then selected. In some cases an organisational buyer may select a number of suppliers in order to reduce the possibility of disruption caused by strikes, shortages or bankruptcy of suppliers. The order will then be made, often with specific details regarding terms, credit arrangements, delivery dates and technical assistance or after-sales service. |

| Stage in behaviour | Comment |
| --- | --- |
| Stage 6.<br>Evaluate the product and supplier performance. | The product and supplier will then be evaluated by comparing with specifications regarding product quality and so on, and the performance of the supplier over the terms of the contract for the sale. |

## 3.3 The Decision Making Unit (DMU) in the organisation

A major difference between consumer and organisational buying behaviour is the fact that **organisational purchase decisions are rarely made by a single individual**. Normally, purchasing decisions are made by a number of people from different functional areas, possibly at different levels within the organisation.

*Webster and Wind* (1972) suggested six **groups within the Decision Making Unit** (DMU).

| Groups within the DMU | |
| --- | --- |
| Users | Initiate the buying process and help define purchase specifications. |
| Influencers | Help define the specification and also provide an input into the process of evaluating the available alternatives. |
| Deciders | Have the responsibility for deciding on product requirements and suppliers. |
| Approvers | Authorise the proposals of deciders and buyers. |
| Buyers | Have the formal authority for the selection of suppliers and negotiating purchase terms. |
| Gatekeepers | By controlling the flow of information, may be able to stop sellers from reaching individuals within the buying centre. |

The size, structure and formality of the DMU will vary depending on the specific situation. Key considerations include:

- **Who** are the principal participants in the buying process?
- In what areas do they exert the **greatest influence**?
- What is their **level of influence**?
- What **evaluative criteria** do each of the participants make use of and how **professional** is the buying process?
- To what extent is **buying centralised** in large organisations?

The **people** involved in the buying process must be convinced that the purchase will be safe for them, for example, there was an advertising slogan to the effect that 'nobody gets sacked for buying IBM'.

## 3.4 Selection criteria

The consideration of this area so far has concentrated on the factors influencing the organisational buying decision. The issue of precisely how organisational buyers make the purchase decision, in terms of the selection criteria determining the choice of supplier, has been the subject of various pieces of research. Important selection criteria could be as follows.

- Delivery capability
- Quality
- Price
- Repair and after-sales service
- Technical capability
- Performance history
- Production facilities
- Help and advice
- Control systems
- Reputation

- Financial position
- Attitude toward the buyer
- Compliance with bidding procedures
- Training support
- Communications on the progress of the order
- Management and organisation
- Packaging
- Moral/legal issues
- Location
- Labour relations

# 4 Market segmentation, target markets and positioning

A **segment** is a group of customers with similar characteristics who can be **targeted** with the same marketing mix. Segmentation bases can include objective classifications (eg age) as well as more subjective approaches such as lifestyle or attitudes.

## 4.1 What is segmentation?

A market is not a mass, homogeneous group of customers, each wanting an identical product. Every market consists of potential buyers with different needs, and different buying behaviour.

**Key term**

> **Market segmentation** may be defined as the subdividing of a market into distinct and increasingly homogeneous subgroups of customers, where any subgroup can conceivably be selected as a target market to be met with a distinct marketing mix.

Although the total market consists of widely different groups of consumers, each group consists of people (or organisations) with **common needs and preferences**, who perhaps react to 'market stimuli' in much the same way.

Each market segment can become a **target market for a firm**, and would require a unique marketing mix if the firm is to exploit it successfully.

The firm can then **position its offer** to account for the roles of each segment.

## 4.2 Identifying segments

(a)  **One basis will not be appropriate in every market**, and sometimes **two or more bases might be valid** at the same time.

(b)  One basis or 'segmentation variable' might be 'superior' to another in a hierarchy of variables. Here are thus **primary and secondary segmentation variables**.

(c)  Segmentation variables include geography, population, demographics and behaviour.

 Case Study

Consider an airport café. You could identify a number of possible segments.

- Business travellers
- Airport employees
- Groups
- Single tourists

However, further analysis could reveal that running through each of these categories is the same fault line.

- Those 'in a hurry'
- Those with time to spare

For marketing purposes, this latter segmentation exercise may be more useful, and the café can develop an 'express menu' for those in a hurry.

## 4.3 Market segmentation and marketing planning

**Segmentation** enables firms to **differentiate** their product to meet customer needs. It enables alternatives to mass marketing, by targeting particular groups of buyers.

Market segmentation is based on the recognition of the diverse needs of potential buyers. Different customer attitudes may be grouped into segments. A different marketing approach is needed for each market segment. The important elements in any definition of market segmentation are as follows.

(a) Each segment consists of people (or organisations) with common needs and preferences, who may react to 'market stimuli' in much the same way.

(b) Each segment can become a target market with a unique marketing mix.

A total market may occasionally be homogeneous but this is rare. A segmentation approach to marketing succeeds when there are identifiable 'clusters' of consumer wants in the market.

## 4.4 Benefits of market segmentation

(a) The organisation may be able to identify **new marketing opportunities**, because it will have a better understanding of customer needs in each segment, with the possibility of spotting further sub groups.

(b) **Specialists can be used for each of the organisation's major segments.** For example, small business counsellors can be employed by banks to deal effectively with small firms. A computer consultancy can have specialist sales staff for, say, shops, manufacturers, service industries and local government authorities. This builds competences and establishes effective marketing systems.

(c) The **total marketing budget** can be allocated proportionately to each segment and the likely return from each segment. This optimises return on investment.

(d) The organisation can **make small adjustments** to the product and service offerings and to the promotional aspects for each segment. This again promotes efficient use of resources.

(e) The organisation can try to **dominate particular segments**, thus gaining competitive advantage. Advantages accrued function synergistically to promote improved competitive ability; in other words, the outcome is more than the sum of its parts.

(f) The **product range** can more closely reflect differences in customer needs. Marketing relies on responsiveness to the consumer. When this is improved, benefits can flow.

Question                                                          Market segmentation

Learning outcome: D(ii)

Identify and briefly explain five benefits that a company may obtain through market segmentation.

Answer

| Benefit | Brief explanation |
|---|---|
| **Better satisfaction of customer needs** | One solution will not satisfy *all* customers. |
| **Revenue growth** | Segmentation means that more customers may be attracted by, and pay more for, what is on offer, in preference to competing products. |
| **Customer retention** | By targeting customers, their needs are more likely to be met leading to repeat purchase. |
| **Targeted communications** | Segmentation enables clear communications as people in the target audience share common needs. |
| **Innovation** | By identifying un-met needs, companies can innovate to satisfy them. |

## 4.5 The bases for segmentation

There are many different bases for segmentation; one basis will not be appropriate in every market, and sometimes two or more bases might be valid at the same time. One segmentation variable might be 'superior' to another in a hierarchy of variables.

Simple segmentation could be on one of the bases below.

- Geographical area
- Age
- End use (eg work or leisure)
- Gender
- Level of income
- Occupation
- Education
- Religion
- Ethnicity
- Nationality
- Social class
- Buyer behaviour
- Lifestyle (see below)

**Lifestyle segmentation** deals with the **person** as opposed to the **product** and attempts to discover the particular **lifestyle patterns of customers**. Lifestyle refers to 'distinctive ways of living adopted by particular communities or subsections of society'. It involves combining a number of behavioural factors, such as motivation, personality and culture.

One simple example generalises lifestyle in terms of four categories, as follows.

| Lifestyle categories | |
|---|---|
| **Upwardly mobile, ambitious** | These individuals seek a better and more affluent lifestyle, principally through better paid and more interesting work, and a higher material standard of living. A customer with such a lifestyle will be prepared to try new products. |
| **Traditional and sociable** | Here, compliance and conformity to group norms bring social approval and reassurance to the individual. Purchasing patterns will therefore be 'conformist'. |
| **Security and status seeking** | This group stresses 'safety' and 'ego-defensive' needs. This lifestyle links status, income and security. It encourages the purchase of strong and well known products and brands, and emphasises those products and services which confer status and make life as secure and predictable as possible. Products that are well established and familiar inspire more confidence than new products, which will be resisted. |
| **Hedonistic preference** | This lifestyle places emphasis on 'enjoying life now' and the immediate satisfaction of wants and needs. Little thought is given to the future. |

This lifestyle analysis is clearly much more relevant to advanced Western economies, the US in particular and has no value for analysing markets in emerging economies.

## 4.6 Current aspects of market segmentation and product positioning

Approaches to market segmentation and product positioning are continually changing. Here are a few developments in recent years.

| Development | Comment |
|---|---|
| There is a growing awareness that consumers should be segmented according to the purpose of the segmentation. | For example, the same customers of a retail bank can be segmented by their account profile, for the purpose of product cross-selling, by their attitudes to risk-taking for the purpose of delivering advertising messages and by socio-economic type for the purpose of selecting a marketing medium. |
| There is growing interest in customer database analysis, and the idea of 'letting the data speak for itself'. | Customer information on a database is analysed in order to identify segments or patterns of behaviour. This technique, known as 'data mining' is likely to increase in significance as e-commerce grows in popularity. |

| Development | Comment |
|---|---|
| There is growing emphasis on segmentation by 'soft' data. | Consumer attitudes and needs and lifestyles (as distinct from 'hard data' such as age, lifestyle, socio-economic grouping, and so on). |
| There is a growing use of sub-segmentation or 'hybrid segmentation' methods. | Consumers within a particular segment can be sub-divided into different segments, and each sub-segment is targeted in a different way. |
| Computer models are used. | These will discover suitable additions to a product line, that will appeal to a separately-distinguished market segment. |

## 4.7 Validity and attractiveness of the current served segments

### 4.7.1 Segment validity

A market segment will only **be valid if it is worth designing and developing a unique marketing mix** for that specific segment. A general rule is that a valid segment must be **substantial**, **measurable** and **accessible**. The following questions are commonly asked to decide whether or not the segment can be used for developing marketing plans.

| Criteria | Comment |
|---|---|
| **Can the segment be measured?** | It might be possible to conceive of a market segment, but it is not necessarily easy to measure it. For example, with a segment based on people with a conservative outlook to life, can conservatism of outlook be measured by market research? |
| **Is the segment big enough?** | There has to be a large enough potential market to be profitable. |
| **Can the segment be reached?** | There has to be a way of getting to the potential customers via the organisation's promotion and distribution channels. |
| **Do segments respond differently?** | If two or more segments are identified by planners, but each segment responds in the same way to a marketing mix, the segments are effectively one and the same, therefore there is no point in distinguishing them from each other. |
| **Can the segment be reached profitably?** | Do the identified customer needs, cost less to satisfy than the revenue they earn? |
| **Is the segment suitably stable?** | The stability of the segment is important, if the organisation is to commit huge production and marketing resources to serve it. The firm does not want the segment to 'disappear' next year. Of course, this may not matter in some industries. |

### 4.7.2 Segment attractiveness

A segment might be valid and potentially profitable, but is it potentially **attractive?** Segments which are most attractive will be those whose needs can be met by building on the company's strengths and where forecasts for demand, sales profitability and **growth** are favourable.

## 4.8 Target markets

Having analysed the attractiveness of a segment, the firm will now choose one or more **target markets**. A **target market** is a market or segment selected for special attention by an organisation (possibly served with a distinct marketing mix). The management of a company may choose one of the following policy options.

| Marketing strategy | Comment | Alignment to competitive strategy |
|---|---|---|
| **Mass (or undifferentiated) marketing** | This policy is to produce a single product and hope to get as many customers as possible to buy it; segmentation is ignored entirely. | The mass (or undifferentiated) marketing approach can be pursued by cost leaders or companies pursuing a differentiation strategy with a single market. |
| **Concentrated marketing** | The company attempts to produce the ideal product for a single segment of the market (for example, Rolls Royce cars). The disadvantage of concentrated marketing is the business risk of relying on a single segment of a single market. | Concentrated marketing is effectively a focus strategy, whether by cost or differentiation. |
| **Differentiated marketing** | The company markets several product versions, each aimed at a different market segment. The disadvantage of differentiated marketing is the additional costs of marketing and production. When the costs of further differentiation of the market exceed the benefits from further segmentation and target marketing, a firm is said to have 'over-differentiated'. | Differentiated marketing is effectively a multi-focus strategy, with a company pursing different opportunities in different segments. |

 Case Study

**Reaching Out to an Older Crowd**

For decades, marketing has been youth-focused. But the fact is, 90 million Americans are 50 and over – that's 42% of the adult population of the U.S. And during the next decade that number will grow by 22 million.

''Small-business owners who start recognising **the needs and preferences of middle-aged and older consumers** have the chance to gain an advantage over larger firms'', says Dick Stroud. Stroud is the founder of 20plus30, a London-based marketing consultancy. He spoke recently with columnist Karen E. Klein, edited excerpts of their conversation follow.

'When talking about older people, the U.S. media and marketing industry uses the term 'boomers.' Europe has adopted the term '50-plus.' These groups represent **a very large number of potential customers**. During the next decade, their numbers will increase six times faster than their children and grandchildren's age group of 15- to 34-year-olds.

'The other reason why the over-50s are so important relates to their **purchasing power**. The 2001 Consumer Expenditure Survey revealed that older consumers are the primary purchasers of transportation, healthcare, housing, food, pensions, and personal insurance. More than half of all cars purchased by an average American household occur after the head of the household turns 50; and they are big spenders on vacations and travel.

To market to this group effectively, business owners should decide **what segment** of the over-50 population is appropriate to his or her product or service. This could be done on the basis of geography, income, lifestyle, gender, or any number of other factors. Then, **research** is needed to understand what the target customers really want.

The most dangerous stereotype is to view all over 50s as a single group. The next mistake is to believe any of the nonsense about older people being averse to trying new brands, not wanting to use technology, or not seeking new life experiences. None of these assumptions is substantiated by research.

I think **the Internet** could be a really important marketing tool for this group. The physiological effects of aging need to be considered here – image size, colour, contrast and Website structure are all important. I think the bottom line is that smaller companies are already leading the way in marketing to this demographic and they're going to continue to do so. For example, there are an awful lot of small travel companies that focus almost exclusively on 50-plus customers because they do spend a lot on travel. They have found, maybe by accident, that this is a growth market for them, and they've become very successful at it.

I've also seen this in the insurance industry. Real estate, with the amount of people who sell their property and move as they reach this age group, is another huge sector. But there are lots of other ways to think about it, if business owners get creative and pay attention.

Adapted from an article by Karen E. Klein, *Business week online*, April 3, 2006

## 4.9 Positioning

**Positioning** is the act of designing the company's offer and image so that it occupies a **distinct** and valued place in the target customer's mind.

(a)     Many products are, in fact, very similar, and the key issue is to make them distinct in the customer's mind.

(b)     Few products occupy a market space on their own. Inevitably they will be positioned **in relation** to competing products and companies.

(c)     People remember 'number 1', so the product should be positioned as 'number 1' in relation to a positioning variable.

- Attributes (eg size)
- Benefits (eg convenience)
- Use/application (ease of use; accessibility)
- User (the sort of person the product is meant to appeal to)
- Product category (consciously differentiated from competition)
- Image
- Quality/price (premium price)

# 5 Forecasting demand

FAST FORWARD

> **Sales forecasting** can involve complex relationships. It's debatable whether demand forecasting is a science or an art – as it involves methods that derive from judgmental sources and from statistical sources it is probably a bit of both.

Businesses are forced to look well ahead in order to plan their investments, launch new products, decide when to close or withdraw products and so on. By forecasting costs and using the sales forecast, organisations are able to forecast profits and other financial outcomes. The sales forecasting process is therefore a critical one for most businesses.

Market research information can help forecast future sales levels. This often involves the use of statistical techniques which are outside the syllabus for Paper P4.

The forecast data used includes information relating to both the present and the future.

## 5.1 Current demand

'Current demand' could involve considering a number of factors, such as:

- Total market potential
- Area market potential (geographic)
- Total industry sales
- Relative market shares

## 5.2 Forecasting future demand

Very few products or services lend themselves to easy forecasting. Those that do usually involve a product with a constant level of sales and a market with either no competition (monopolies) or predictable competition (oligopolies).

Preparing a sales or demand forecast usually involves three stages:

**Step 1** Prepare a macroeconomic forecast – what will happen to overall economic activity in the relevant economies in which a product is to be sold.

**Step 2** Prepare an industry sales forecast – what will happen to overall sales in an industry based on the issues that influence the macroeconomic forecast.

**Step 3** Prepare a company sales forecast – based on what management expect to happen to the company's market share.

Demand forecasts are based on three types of information:

- What customers are currently doing in the market (Industry sales data, Company sales data)
- Customer intentions in relation to buying products (Survey of Buyers' Intentions, **Market Tests, Sales Force Opinions, Expert Opinions)**
- What customers have done in the past in the market (Past-Sales Analysis)

### 5.2.1 Survey of Buyers' intentions

There are many market research businesses that undertake surveys of customer intentions – and sell this information to businesses that need the data for sales forecasting purposes. The value of a customer intention survey increases when there are a relatively small number of customers, the cost of reaching them is small, and they have clear intentions.

### 5.2.2 Market tests

Instead of simply asking customers about their intentions, marketers may conduct market tests. Tests are particularly appropriate when finalising product design (eg 'Would you buy this product at this price?'). Several alternative designs for a new product may be evaluated, for example, various features of a laptop personal computer, such as price, weight, battery life, screen clarity and processing power could be varied and the customer asked to reveal their most valued features by making trade-offs among various features.

### 5.2.3 Sales force opinions

Another option is to use opinions from members of the sales force to forecast sales. This may be difficult if the product is new, although salespeople may be able to get a feel for the market by talking with clients and potential clients.

Unfortunately, sales people may try to forecast low sales if these forecasts will form the basis of their future sales targets. On the other hand, marketing executives may provide over-optimistic forecasts to help gain approval for the project or motivate the sales force.

### 5.2.4 Expert opinions

Expert opinion studies are widely used for forecasting of marketing problems. For example, forecasts may be obtained from industry experts, distributors or consultancies. Sometimes independent forecasts from more than one expert source may be combined to produce what should be a more realistic forecast.

### 5.2.5 Past-sales analysis

Many businesses prepare their sales forecast on the basis of past sales. Time series analysis involves breaking past sales down into four components:

- The trend: are sales growing, remaining steady ('flat-lining') or in decline?
- Seasonal or cyclical factors that occur in a regular pattern.
- Erratic events; these include fashion fads, terrorist strikes and other disturbances to the market which should be ignored when identifying normal sales patterns.
- Responses: the results of particular measures that have been taken to increase sales (eg a major new advertising campaign).

# 6 Market research

**FAST FORWARD**

**Market research** is needed to obtain the type of data about customers and their needs that is necessary for marketing plans. Both **quantitative** and **qualitative** data have an important role.

**Key term**

**Market research** is the process of gathering, recording, analysing and reporting data and information relating to the company's market, customers and competitors.

Typically, market research is used to determine the characteristics of markets, suggest opportunities for products and selling approaches and to suggest segments.

The research can relate to:

(a)    Existing products and services (for example, service received at a garage)

(b)    New products and services (although customers are most sincere when spending!)

## 6.1 A typical research programme

Most research problems can be analysed into five steps.

| Step | | Example |
|------|--|---------|
| **Step 1** | Defining the problem | <ul><li>Explaining a fall in sales</li><li>Investigating potential demand for a new product</li><li>Investigating attitudes to the brand</li><li>Investigating what matters most to consumers</li></ul> |
| **Step 2** | Developing the hypotheses to be tested, and the purpose of the research | In some studies, the researchers have a particular question they want to test. The purpose of some research may be to see if it is worth doing further research. |
| **Step 3** | Collecting data | A variety of approaches is used. |
| **Step 4** | Analyse and interpret the data | The type of analysis depends on the type of research. Not all research is quantitative with statistical validity. The emphasis on statistical assumptions is important: statistics can be misunderstood and misused. |
| **Step 5** | Report the findings | The results of the research are written up and presented in a report to the client. |

### 6.1.1 Quantitative vs qualitative data

**Quantitative data** enables measurement. The purpose is to measure the response of a sample of consumers, on the assumption that the measurable conclusions can be drawn from it. An example could be a survey of structured questionnaires sent out to a sample of a population.

**Qualitative data** is not measurable, but it is useful to get people to say what they feel and think, as opposed to giving relatively simple answers to unstructured questions.

## 6.1.2 Primary vs secondary data

In marketing research, primary data is collected specifically for the purpose of the research in question. Secondary data has not been specifically collected for the research.

| Secondary data | |
|---|---|
| **Source** | **Uses** |
| **Internal** <br><br> • From existing information systems <br> • Accounting data <br> • Customer databases <br> • Data produced by other departments (eg complaints) <br><br> **External** <br><br> • Published statistics from government, professional/ trade bodies <br> • Review of journals <br> • Research already collected by market research agencies can be purchased, eg Nielsen Index on grocery chains and random surveys | • Before primary research to give guidance <br> • Instead of expensive primary research; some questions may already be answered <br> • Some information can only be acquired via secondary data <br> • Where primary research is not possible |

Secondary data is normally insufficient for a complete marketing research exercise.

| Primary data | |
|---|---|
| **Source** | **Uses** |
| From inside or outside the organisation | Can be qualitative or quantitative; described in detail below. |

## 6.1.3 Collecting information

Once the sample has been established, data has to be collected. Possible methods include the following.

| Data collection method | Comment |
|---|---|
| **Questionnaires**, such as the following. <br><br> • Post surveys <br> • Telephone <br> • In street, via market researchers <br> • Over the Internet to people who log in to a site <br> • At home <br> • In hotels <br> • In shops | A number of precise questions requiring precise responses. Ensuring questions are free of ambiguity is absolutely vital. <br><br> Survey must be relevant to statistical analysis. <br><br> Questionnaires often move from the general to the specific. <br><br> The interviewer always has to locate suitable respondents. <br><br> A danger with postal questionnaires is that response is self-selected. |
| **Experiment** | The researcher may set up artificial surroundings or may test a product in real surroundings (eg asking software purchasers to try out Beta versions of certain packages). |
| **Observation** | People can be observed using product. |
| **Unstructured interviews** | There is no structure to what is effectively a conversation but the interviewer may have a checklist of topics to be covered. |

| Data collection method | Comment |
| --- | --- |
| Depth interviews | The aim is to explore attitudes and motives for behaviour that may not be conscious. If conducted properly, respondents can be encouraged to say what they feel. |
| Projective techniques | People often say that they will act in a different way than they do, in fact, behave. Researchers have borrowed methods from psychologists, and seek to uncover unconscious motives.<br><br>Examples include:<br><br>• Inkblot tests ('What images do you see in this inkblot?')<br>• Word association<br>• Thematic apperception tests ('What is going on in this picture?') |
| Focus groups | Focus groups usually consist of 8 to 10 respondents and an interviewer taking the role of group moderator. The group moderator introduces topics for discussion and intervenes as necessary to encourage respondents or to direct discussions if they threaten to wander too far off the point. The moderator will also need to control any powerful personalities and prevent them from dominating the group. |

## 6.2 Sales potential

The amount of sales that a product can achieve is known as **sales potential**. Not all competing products in a market will have the same potential as it will vary for each individual product due to **selling price** and the amount it is **promoted**.

Other factors influencing sales potential include:

• How '**essential**' the product is to consumers
• The **overall size** of the **market**
• The **level of competition** in the market
• Whether consumers may **delay purchasing** the product (non-essential luxury items)

## Question

Market research

Which of the following options show five steps that could be used in a typical market research programme?

A    Define problem, develop hypothesis, collect data, analyse data, report findings
B    Develop hypothesis, collect data, define problem, analyse data, report findings
C    Analyse data, define problem, develop hypothesis, collect data, report findings
D    Define problem, collect data, develop hypothesis, analyse data, report findings

## Answer

A    Refer to Section 6.1 of this chapter.

**Exam focus point**

The November 2007 exam offered twenty marks (in two ten-mark questions) for an explanation of how an organisation should segment its market and how income potential can be estimated.

# Chapter Roundup

- 'The customer' in a transaction can involve a number of different roles

- **Buyer behaviour** describes the activities and decision processes relating to buying. **The process** describes a sequence of steps, from need recognition, through information search, evaluation of alternatives, purchase decision and post-purchase evaluation.

- Overall, factors affecting customer behaviour are **social** (such as reference groups, roles and status), **cultural**, **personal** (eg age, economic status, lifestyle) and **psychological** (eg attitudes).

- Organisations are viewed as more rational than individuals. The buying **decision process** is likely to be **formal**.

- A **segment** is a group of customers with similar characteristics who can be **targeted** with the same marketing mix. Segmentation bases can include objective classifications (eg age) as well as more subjective approaches such as lifestyle or attitudes.

- **Segmentation** enables firms to **differentiate** their product to meet customer needs. It enables alternatives to mass marketing, by targeting particular groups of buyers.

- **Sales forecasting** can involve complex relationships. It's debatable whether demand forecasting is a science or an art – as it involves methods that derive from **judgmental sources** and from **statistical sources** it is probably a bit of both.

- **Market research** is needed to obtain the type of data about customers and their needs that is necessary for marketing plans. Both **quantitative** and **qualitative** data have an important role.

# Quick Quiz

1   Distinguish between 'buyer', 'payer' and 'user'.

2   List four types of factors that influence consumer buying.

    1      .................................................................

    2      .................................................................

    3      .................................................................

    4      .................................................................

3   A transaction between an electronic component supplier and a factory that makes electronic devices is a business-to-consumer transaction.

    True   ☐

    False   ☐

4   List five possible bases for market segmentation.

    1      .................................................................

    2      .................................................................

    3      .................................................................

    4      .................................................................

    5      .................................................................

5    Which of the following are factors of 'current demand'?

   A    Area Market Potential
   B    Total Industry Sales
   C    Relative Market Share
   D    All of the above

6    Market research only relates to new products or services.

   True    ☐

   False   ☐

# Answers to Quick Quiz

1    The buyer is the person who selects the product/service.
     The payer finances the purchase.
     The user receives the benefit.

2    Social factors, cultural factors, personal factors and psychological factors.

3    False. It is a business-to-business transaction.

4    Geographical area, age, gender, income level, occupation, lifestyle etc. Refer to Section 4.5 for other examples.

5    D    They are all factors.

6    False. Market research also relates to existing products and services.

Now try the question below from the Exam Question Bank

| Number | Level | Marks | Time |
|--------|-------|-------|------|
| 11 | Examination | 30 | 54 mins |

# The use of technology in a marketing context

## Introduction

In this chapter we look at the role of **information technology in marketing** – with particular emphasis on the **Internet**.

The Internet has had a significant effect on marketing activities. It enables goods (and some services) to be sourced worldwide, easily and cheaply; it also enables them to be promoted globally at relatively low cost. The Internet therefore drives prices downwards, with implications for marketing, margins, infrastructure costs, and customer dynamics.

Towards the end of the chapter we look at how the effectiveness of online marketing may be measured. Finally, we outline the role technology may play in managing customer relationships.

| Topic list | Learning outcomes | Syllabus references | Ability required |
|---|---|---|---|
| 1 The marketing information system | D(iv) | D(4), D(5) | Evaluation |
| 2 The Internet | D(v) | D(11), D(13) | Evaluation |
| 3 Electronic commerce (e-commerce) | D(v) | D(11), D(13) | Evaluation |
| 4 Mobile phones ('M-marketing') | D(v) | D(11), D(13) | Evaluation |

# 1 The marketing information system

Organisations are using ever more sophisticated **marketing information systems** to gather information and **manage customer relationships**.

## 1.1 Marketing and competitor research: the traditional view

A traditional source of information about environmental conditions has been the **marketing information system** (MkIS) (*Kotler*, 1994). This consists of people, equipment and procedures to gather, sort, analyse, evaluate, and distribute needed, timely and accurate information to **marketing** decision makers.

| Elements of the marketing information system | |
|---|---|
| **Internal records system** | This includes reports of orders, sales, dispatches, accounts payable and receivable etc which provide a store of historical customer data. |
| **Marketing intelligence system** | This is the term used for information gathered on the market place by managers on a day-to-day basis. It is derived from **continual monitoring** of the environment to alert managers to new trends. |
| **Marketing decision support system (MDSS)** | Covered in the next section. |
| **Marketing research system** | Marketing research aids management decision making by providing specified information in time for it to be of value. Marketing research covers **general research** into trends as well as specific surveys, both quantitative and qualitative. It **normally** relates to **current** customers and **current** policies. |

## 1.2 Marketing Decision Support Systems (MDSS)

*Kotler* (1991) defines a **Marketing Decision Support System (MDSS)** as a set of decision models with supporting hardware and software available to marketing managers to assist them in analysing relevant business data and making better marketing decisions.

This is a very wide ranging definition which could encompass a wide range of separate systems (eg spreadsheet models, expert systems, database systems, analytical packages etc).

Managers today are often faced with an ever increasing amount of information on which to base decisions upon. Models are often used to provide a structure that enables this information to be organised and analysed in a way that aids decision-making. Models may also allow the creation and testing of various scenarios.

### 1.2.1 Marketing databases

A **marketing database** is a central hub of information concerning an organisation's markets and customers.

**Sources of data**

- **Published** market research data
- **Marketing research** carried out by the organisation
- Data acquired about **customers** (through previous dealings or the Internet)
- **Internally generated data** on competitors, trends and products

The **benefits** of a marketing database include:

- **Centralises data** for whole organisation
- **Maximises** the use of IT
- **Integrates knowledge** from various sources
- **Structures** and **aids** decision making and problem solving

Some of the most advanced MDSS are based upon Expert Systems.

### 1.2.2 Using expert systems in marketing

An **Expert System** (ES) is defined by the British Computer Society as: 'the modelling, within a computer, of expert knowledge in a given domain, such that the resulting system can offer intelligent advice or take intelligent decisions'.

The most important modules that constitute a rule-based expert system are the knowledge base, the inference engine and the explanation subsystem. We covered the different elements of an expert system in Chapter 1.

In the field of marketing management, expert systems that contain the appropriate data and rules may be useful in a number of areas, for example:

- To facilitate the exploration of options and changing assumptions for a given problem
- To enable the combination of expertise from different experts and sources
- The transfer of knowledge and expertise
- Building a knowledge base helps to establish generalisations and identify gaps and inconsistencies in current knowledge
- Improved problem-solving by means of extensive analysis and explanatory functions

Many marketing decisions are based by necessity on uncertain or 'fuzzy' information. Fuzziness occurs when a fact or rule cannot be defined precisely. More advanced expert systems are able to make educated assumptions based upon the data held in the system. Recent models also allow the formulation of hypothesis in natural language, removing the need for complicated mathematical and statistical assumptions – this simplifies the model building and specification process.

As with any information system, manual or computerised, a MDSS should be used as an aid to decision making rather than being seen as providing a definitive 'must be right' answer.

# 2 The Internet

FAST FORWARD

The **Internet** is a worldwide computer network. **Websites** are points which it uses for dissemination of information, product/service development, transaction processing and so on. **The Internet** challenges business as it **avoids intermediaries** – small companies can also benefit through 'affiliated programmes'. The Internet is widely used by children, tomorrow's consumers. The Internet reduces transactions costs and switches **power to sellers**.

## 2.1 What is different about the Internet?

There are several features of the Internet which make it radically different from what has gone before.

(a) It **challenges traditional business models** – because, for example, it enables product/service suppliers to interact directly with their customers, instead of using intermediaries (like retail shops, travel agents, insurance brokers, and conventional banks).

(b) Although the Internet is global in its operation, its benefits are not confined to large (or global) organisations. **Small companies** can move instantly into a global marketplace.

(c) It offers a **new economics of information** – because, with the Internet, information is much more widely available.

(d) It supplies virtually instant access to organisations, plus the capacity to complete purchasing transactions. This is only truly impressive if it is accompanied by equal speed so far as the delivery of tangible goods is concerned.

(e) It has created **new networks of communication** – between organisations and their customers (either individually or collectively), between customers themselves (through mutual support groups), and between organisations and their suppliers.

(f) It has led to **affiliate programmes** – through which small enterprises can gain access to customers on a scale which would have been viewed as impossible a few years ago.

(g) It **promotes transparent pricing** – because potential customers can readily compare prices not only from suppliers within any given country, but also from suppliers across the world.

(h)    It makes possible **sophisticated market segmentation opportunities**. Visualising and approaching such segments may be one of the few ways in which e-commerce entrepreneurs can truly create competitive advantage.

(i)    The web can either be a **separate** or a **complementary** channel.

## Case Study

Amazon.com, one of the most celebrated website enterprises, aims to become the Internet's first one-step store, and has already diversified from its original bookshop business into such fields as electronic consumer products, mobile telephones, cars, leisure, gardening equipment, holidays, travel and toys. Its diversification programme has undoubtedly given it substantial breadth, helping to reduce the likelihood that its customers will feel the necessity to go elsewhere for some of their needs.

On the other hand, there are considerable cost burdens involved, not least in delivery. If customers order a variety of product items, it is likely that they will be delivered separately, from separate locations, with shipping expenses that vastly exceed the cost when goods are sent all at once.

Note, too, that Amazon, unlike many other 'dot.com' enterprises, does not subcontract its delivery activities, but undertakes them all through its own employees. This is cited as one of the explanations for its exceptional performance record.

Among Amazon's major assets is a massive customer database (29 million people) and an almost unparalleled level of information and insight into customer preferences and behaviour patterns. Cross-selling opportunities are accordingly impressive, and the company has embarked upon a number of co-branding arrangements with complementary retailers.

# 3 Electronic commerce (e-commerce)

**FAST FORWARD**

> **Electronic commerce** (or e-commerce) means conducting business electronically via a communications link.

**Key term**

**E-commerce** involves conducting transactions using electronic means (eg the Internet).

An older technology that is covered under the electronic commerce umbrella is Electronic Data Interchange (EDI).

## 3.1 Electronic Data Interchange (EDI)

EDI is a form of computer-to-computer data transfer. For instance instead of sending a customer a paper invoice through the post the data is sent over telecommunications links. This offers savings and **benefits** to organisations that use it.

(a)    It reduces the **delays** caused by postal paper chains.

(b)    It avoids the need to **re-key** data and therefore saves time and reduces errors.

(c)    It provides the opportunity to reduce administrative **costs** eg the costs associated with the creation, recording and storage of paper documents.

(d)    It facilitates shorter **lead times** and reduced inventory holdings which allow reductions in working capital requirements (eg just-in-time policies).

(e)    It provides the opportunity to improve **customer service**.

## 3.2 E-commerce and the web

Over the last few years, electronic commerce or **e-commerce** has increasingly been used to describe the use of the Internet and websites in the sale of products or services. A simple definition for this context is that 'e-commerce is the process of trading on the Internet'.

### 3.2.1 Distribution

The Internet can be used to get certain products **directly into people's homes**. Anything that can be converted into **digital form** can simply be uploaded onto the seller's site and then **downloaded** onto the customer's PC at home. The Internet thus offers huge opportunities to producers of text, graphics/video, and sound-based products.

## 3.3 Electronic marketing

For **customers** the Internet offers a **speedy and impersonal** way of getting to know about the services that a company provides. For **businesses** the advantage is that it is much cheaper to provide the information in electronic form than it would be to staff phones, and more effective than sending out mailshots.

Websites can provide **sound and movement** and allow **interactivity**, so that the user can, say, drill down to obtain further information or watch a video of the product in use, or get a virtual reality experience of the product or service.

Case Study

Peapod.com is an online supermarket and one of the more sophisticated recorders and users of customers' personal data and shopping behaviour. With over 200,000 customers in various US cities, Peapod's website sells groceries that are then delivered to customer's homes. A list of previous purchases (including brand, pack size and quantity purchased) is kept on the site, so the customer can make minor changes from week to week, saving time and effort.

Peapod creates a database on each shopper that includes their purchase history (what they bought), their online shopping patterns (how they bought it), questionnaires about their attitudes and opinions, and demographic data (which Peapod buys from third parties). A shopper's profile is used by the company to determine which advertisement to show and which promotions/electronic coupons to offer. Demographically identical neighbours are thus treated differently based on what Peapod has learned about their preferences and behaviours over time.

Shoppers seem to like this high-tech relationship marketing, with 94% of all sales coming from repeat customers. Manufacturers like it too. The more detailed customer information enables them to target promotions at customers who have repeatedly bought another brand, thereby not giving away promotion dollars to already loyal customers.

### 3.3.1 Collecting information about customers

People who visit a site for the first time may be asked to **register**, which typically involves giving a name, physical address and post code, e-mail address and possibly other demographic data such as age, job title and income bracket.

When customers come to the site on subsequent occasions they either type their (self-chosen) username and password or more usually now, if they are using the same computer, the website recognises them using a **cookie,** which is a small and **harmless** file containing data that uniquely identify the computer.

From the initial registration details the user record may show, say, that the user is male, aged 20 to 30 and British. The **website can respond** to this by displaying products or services likely to appeal to this segment of the market.

### 3.3.2 Clickstreams

As users visit the site more often, more is learned about them by **recording what they click on**, since this shows what they are really interested in. On a news site for instance, one user may always go to the sports pages first, while another looks at the TV listings. In a retail sense this is akin to physically following somebody about the store recording everything they do (including products they pick up and put back) and everything they look at, whether or not they buy it.

 Case Studies

(1) **Airlines**

The impact of the web is seen clearly in the transportation industry. Airlines now have a more effective way of bypassing intermediaries (ie travel agents) because they can give their customers immediate access to flight reservation systems. In the UK, EasyJet, became the first airline to have over half of its bookings made online.

(2) **Travel agents**

The web has also produced a new set of on-line travel agents who have lower costs because of their ability to operate without a High Street branch network. Their low-cost structure makes them a particularly good choice for selling low margin, cheap tickets for flights, package holidays, cruises and so forth.

These low-cost travel agents have been joined, furthermore, by non-travel-agents who simply specialise in opportunistic purchasing (eg lastminute.com).

(3) **Tesco**

In another arena, Tesco is already the UK's largest Internet grocery business, but other companies are rapidly developing new initiatives. Waitrose@work allows people to order their groceries in the morning (typically through their employer's intranet communication system) and then have them delivered to the workplace in the afternoon: this approach achieves significant distribution economies of scale so far as Waitrose is concerned.

(4) **Financial services**

The impact of the Internet is especially profound in the field of financial services. New intermediaries enable prospective customers to compare the interest rates and prices charged by different organisations for pensions, mortgages and other financial services. This means that the delivering companies are losing control of the marketing of their services, and there is a downward pressure on prices, especially for services which can legitimately be seen as mere commodities (eg house and contents insurance).

## 3.4 Challenges of e-commerce

E-commerce involves an unusual mix of people – security people, web technology people, designers, marketing people – and this can be very difficult to manage. The e-business needs supervision by expensive specialists.

In spite of phenomenal growth the market is still fuzzy and undefined. Many e-businesses have only recently reported making any **profit**.

Unless the e-business is one started completely from scratch, any new technology installed will **need to link up with existing business systems**.

The international availability of a website means that the laws of all countries that transactions may be conducted from have to be considered. The legal issues surrounding e-commerce are complex and still developing.

Above all, e-commerce faces a lack of **trust**. In most cultures, consumers grant their trust to business parties that have a close **physical presence**: buildings, facilities and people to talk to. On the Internet these familiar elements are simply not there. The seller's reputation, the size of his business, and the level of customisation in product and service also engender trust.

Internet merchants need to address issues such as fear of **invasion of privacy** and abuse of customer information (about their **credit cards**, for example) because they stop people even considering the Internet as a shopping medium.

 Case Study

### E-commerce

'For some the Internet is a necessary evil – others browse and surf the net with that obsessive drive that is peculiar to any new technology. But the Internet is not just any new technology. It is the most important communications development since the advent of the telephone, and like the telephone it has created its own culture and given birth to new businesses and new possibilities.

'Early confusion about the Internet meant that many companies built their own websites after learning the rudiments of HTML. They had registered their company name and done everything by the book. The website went on-line and they all waited with baited breath. Nothing happened. No new business arrived and nothing changed, and they couldn't understand why.

'E-commerce is a tidal wave; if you choose to participate you either 'sink or swim'. You must be daring enough in design to achieve something quite different from the ways things have been done in the past.

'A website is a shopfront that must be located in the centre of town in the full gaze of everyone. A good one can make a small business as powerful and competitive as some of the largest players. It just needs flair and commitment to succeed. But to do so there are some measures that must be used.

'Marketing outside the web, in the press or even on the radio can alert the market to the website. The site itself should be properly identified by name, registered competently with the appropriate search engines and it must look good.

| Website essentials |
| --- |
| • Integration with all company systems (ie back office) |
| • Speedy implementation |
| • Quick and easy updating by own staff to retain topicality |
| • Self producing audit records |
| • Promotion via the Internet |
| • Press and PR for website |
| • Attractive design but appropriate for the web |
| • Scope to interact with visitors |
| • Planned structure to include profitable business concept |
| • Control and maintenance by owner, without developer involvement |

'The appearance of a website is extremely important. Attractive and easy to fill interactive forms can lure a sales prospect into being a buyer. One has seconds in which to achieve this end. Too many graphics slow down the procedure. The experience of visiting and browsing through the shop and responding to the goods on offer must be clever, intriguing, quick and efficient. Millions of pounds worth of business is lost on the Internet every day as a result of so-called interactive websites that are difficult to operate and dull.

'The **key to success**, and the true working system is to be found in the **back office**. This invisible component is frequently overlooked. You can have the most seductive website in the world, but without a robust, secure, integrated back office system it's worth nothing. The website designer makes the shop window look good but cannot be expected to address the back office system.

'Installing e-commerce can bring about overall improvements in accounting and management systems across the board. One bookseller never realised that he had fundamental problems in terms of dispatching stock and warehouse management. This is now being solved by the introduction of an integrated website that will interact with his financial and accounting system.

'There are so many new possibilities and ventures created by this new technology, and the most inspired e-commerce enterprises will empower small and medium sized concerns to compete as never before.

*Adapted from Management Accounting, February 2000*

**Exam focus point**

Exam questions may focus on practical considerations of website design including compatibility with browsers, telling customers that the site is secure, staying in contact with them without being intrusive and data protection/consumer protection issues.

### 3.4.1 Security risks

**FAST FORWARD**

Establishing links to the Internet brings **security risks**. Suitable systems, policies and procedures should be implemented to minimise these risks.

Computer systems with links to other systems such as the Internet are exposed to security risks. Some of the main risks are explained below.

| Security risks associated with the Internet and e-commerce | |
|---|---|
| **Risk** | **Explanation** |
| **Hackers and eavesdroppers** | Hackers attempt to gain unauthorised access to computer systems. They may attempt to damage a system or steal information. Hackers use tools like electronic number generators and software which enables rapid password attempts. |
| | Data that is transmitted across telecommunications links is exposed to the risk of being intercepted or examined during transmission (eavesdropping). |
| **Viruses** | A virus is a small piece of software which performs unauthorised actions and which replicates itself. Viruses may cause damage to files or attempt to destroy files and damage hard disks. When transmitted over a network, such as the Internet, into a 'clean' system, the virus reproduces, thus infecting that system. |
| | Types of virus include: |
| | E-mail viruses spread using e-mail messages and replicate by mailing itself to addresses held in the user's contacts book. |
| | Worms copy themselves from machine to machine on a network |
| | Trojans or Trojan horses are hidden inside a 'valid' program but perform an unexpected act. Trojans therefore act like a virus, but they aren't classified as a virus as they don't replicate themselves. |
| | Trap doors are undocumented access points to a system allowing controls to be bypassed. |
| | Logic bombs are triggered by the occurrence of a certain event. |
| | Time bombs are triggered by a certain date. |

| Security risks associated with the Internet and e-commerce | |
|---|---|
| **Risk** | **Explanation** |
| Hoaxes | An associated problem is that of hoax virus warnings. There are a vast number of common hoaxes, most of which circulate via e-mail. Many are a variation of one of the most 'popular' early hoaxes – the Good Times hoax. This hoax takes the form of a warning about viruses contained in e-mail. People pass along the warning because they are trying to be helpful, but they are in fact wasting the time of all concerned.<br><br>A number of websites provide information on hoaxes and 'real' viruses – for example www.sophos.com. If you receive a warning of a virus or the promise of rewards for forwarding an e-mail to a number of others, this is a good place to look to establish if the warning is a hoax or not. |
| Denial of service attack | A fairly new threat, relating to Internet websites is the 'denial of service attack'. This involves an organised campaign to bombard an Internet site with excessive volumes of traffic at a given time, with the aim of overloading the site. |

## 3.5 Controls

The risks identified above can be minimised through a variety of controls that provide network and communications security.

### 3.5.1 Anti-virus software

The main protection against viruses is anti-virus software. Anti-virus software, such as McAfee or Norton searches systems for viruses and removes them. Anti-virus programs include an auto-update feature that downloads profiles of new viruses, enabling the software to check for all known or existing viruses. Very new viruses may go undetected by anti-virus software (until the anti-virus software vendor updates their package – and the organisation installs the update).

Additional precautions include disabling floppy disk drives to prevent viruses entering an organisation via floppy disk. However, this can disrupt work processes. At the very least, organisations should ensure all files received via floppy disk and e-mail are virus checked.

### 3.5.2 A firewall

External e-mail links can be protected by way of a firewall that may be configured to virus check all messages, and may also prevent files of a certain type being sent via e-mail (eg .exe files, as these are the most common means of transporting a virus). Firewalls can be implemented in both hardware and software, or a combination of both. A firewall disables part of the telecoms technology to prevent unauthorised intrusions. However, a determined hacker may well be able to bypass this.

### 3.5.3 Encryption

Data that is transmitted across telecommunications links is exposed to the risk of being intercepted or read during transmission (known as 'eavesdropping'). Encryption is used to reduce this risk. Encryption involves scrambling the data at one end of the line, transmitting the scrambled data, and unscrambling it at the receiver's end of the line. A person intercepting the scrambled data is unable to make sense of it.

### 3.5.4 Electronic signatures

One way of providing electronic signatures is to make use of what is known as public key (or asymmetric) cryptography signatures. Public key cryptography uses two keys – public and private. The private key is only known to its owner, and is used to scramble the data contained in a file. The 'scrambled' data is the electronic signature, and can be checked against the original file using the public key of the person who signed it. This confirms that it could only have been signed by someone with access to the private key. If a third party altered the message, the fact that they had done so would be easily detectable.

An alternative is the use of encryption products which support key recovery, also known as key encapsulation. Such commercial encryption products can incorporate the public key of an agent known as a Key Recovery Agent (KRA). This allows the user to recover their (stored or communicated) data by approaching the KRA with an encrypted portion of the message. In both cases the KRA neither holds the user's private keys, nor has access to the plain text of their data.

### 3.5.5 Authentication

Authentication is a technique of making sure that a message has come from an authorised sender. Authentication involves adding extra data in a form previously agreed between sender and recipient.

### 3.5.6 Dial-back security

Dial-back security operates by requiring the person wanting access to dial into the network and identify themselves first. The system then dials the person back on their authorised number before allowing access.

## 3.6 B2B e-commerce

The major growth so far in the field of e-commerce has concentrated on the business-to-business (B2B) sector. Here are some examples to show the growing significance of the Internet in many business-to-business sectors.

(a)   **Major companies** are setting themselves up as e-businesses.

(b)   IBM now requires all its suppliers to **quote and invoice electronically** – no paper documentation is permitted.

(c)   Many firms are using the Internet to **exploit the transparency of supplier prices**, and to maximise their purchasing benefits from the availability of world-wide sourcing. Robert Bosch, the German kitchen appliance manufacturer, requires all its suppliers to have web-based catalogues and prices.

(d)   Companies are also **increasing their customer service** through the web. Dell, the computer company, has created extranets for its major business customers, enabling them to receive personalised customer support, their own price lists, and some free value-added services.

Question                                                                                    Website

Learning outcome: D(v)

Advise a company providing holidays how value could be added to its product by provision of information or other features on a website.                                                               10 marks

Answer

A company selling holidays via a website could add value to the service it provides by providing information and other features on the site:

**Information provided on the site**

•   Details of the holiday including information relating to the hotel facilities, meals included etc

•   Comments from satisfied customers explaining what they enjoyed about the holiday

•   General information regarding usual weather patterns, currency, customs such as tipping etc. (or links to sites that provide this information)

•   Possibly price comparisons showing more expensive competitor prices

•   Details of related services such as holiday insurance and currency exchange facilities

•   General travel tips – such as take an electric plug converter, beware of unauthorised taxis, get to the airport in good time etc

**Other features provided on the site**

- Clear, logical efficient layout including ensuring pages are not too complicated as this slows down loading and may result in frustrated customers leaving the site
- A secure facility to enable the purchase of the holiday online
- Contact details including both e-mail and telephone for queries. Some customers may prefer to speak to a staff member or book over the telephone
- Links to other travel related sites
- The site name should be easy to remember to encourage repeat visits from users who fail to 'bookmark' the site

# 4 Mobile phones ('M-marketing')

 Marketing techniques that utilise mobile phone technology are sometimes referred to as '**M-marketing**'.

**M-marketing techniques** include:

- Calling customers and/or potential customers on their mobile phones
- Texting customers and/or potential customers on their mobile phones using Short Message Service (SMS) technology
- Marketing using websites specially designed for users accessing the site using a mobile phone handset or similar hand-held device

One risk for the marketer is that, even more so than 'landline' phones, mobile phones are seen as a personal item. Therefore, marketing material sent to mobile phones may cause resentment.

# Chapter roundup

- Organisations are using ever more sophisticated **marketing information systems** to gather information and **manage customer relationships**.

- The **Internet** is a worldwide computer network. **Websites** are points which it uses for dissemination of information, product/service development, transaction processing and so on. **The Internet** challenges business as it **avoids intermediaries** – small companies can also benefit through 'affiliated programmes'. The Internet is widely used by children, tomorrow's consumers. The Internet reduces transactions costs and switches **power to sellers**.

- **Electronic commerce** (or e-commerce) means conducting business electronically via a communications link.

- Establishing links to the Internet brings **security risks**. Suitable systems, policies and procedures should be implemented to minimise these risks.

- Marketing techniques that utilise mobile phone technology are sometimes referred to as '**M-marketing**'.

# Quick Quiz

1   What does MDSS stand for?

    A       Marketing data software system

    B       Marketing decision support system

    C       Marketing data support system

    D       Marketing decision service system

2   Which type of programme introduced as a result of the Internet is often beneficial to small companies as it allows them access to customers on a large scale?

    A       Agent programme

    B       Affiliate programme

    C       Access programme

    D       Global programme

3   Distinguish between encryption and authentication.

4   What is a virus?

5   Texting customers' mobile phones is a form of 'M-marketing'.

    True   ☐

    False  ☐

# Answers to Quick Quiz

1   B    MDSS stands for marketing decision support system

2   B    Affiliate programmes allow small enterprises access to customers on a scale that would have been virtually impossible before the Internet

3   Encryption involves scrambling and unscrambling data to prevent unauthorised 'eavesdroppers' obtaining useful information. Authentication ensures a message gave come from an authorised sender.

4   A small program that infects systems and possibly damages them.

5   True. M-marketing relates to mobile phones.

Now try the question below from the Exam Question Bank

| Number | Level | Marks | Time |
|--------|-------|-------|------|
| 12 | Examination | 30 | 54 mins |

# Managing change

# Organisational development

## Introduction

Over time an organisation will **change** and **develop**.

Change occurs in the organisation's environment and in turn this requires the organisation to change. This chapter explores issues relating to how organisations may change over time.

We start by describing how organisations typically have to introduce, develop and change as a result of environmental turbulence.

Then we explore issues relating to the organisational life cycle, before covering Greiner's model which suggests that the size and range of a business's activities pose particular problems.

Later, we explain how growth and decline can require structural change, and look at how organisational development may be sustained in the long term.

| Topic list | Learning outcomes | Syllabus references | Ability required |
|---|---|---|---|
| 1 Organisational development | B(i) | B(1) | Comprehension |
| 2 Models of growth and development | B(i) | B(1) | Comprehension |
| 3 Contraction and decline | B(i) | B(4) | Comprehension |
| 4 Structural reorganisation and divestment | B(i) | B(4) | Comprehension |
| 5 Change triggers | B(i), B(iii), B(iv) | B(1), B(3), B(4) | Evaluation / Comprehension |

# 1 Organisational development

FAST FORWARD

> **Organisational development** is a term used to group together a wide range of elements that attempt to improve the performance and effectiveness of an organisation and often intervene into the social processes of an organisation.

**Key term**

> **Organisational development (OD)** is an integrated process that attempts to improve the overall performance and effectiveness of an organisation by developing the individuals and groups it is composed of. It has a number of elements, each of which will have different relevance to any given organisational situation.

As the definition above states, organisational development encompasses a wide range of activities aimed at improving organisational performance.

Because it is so wide-ranging, it is not possible to define specific stages and activities for an OD programme. However, the following general **framework** may be useful.

- Management awareness of need
- Disclosure of objectives
- Data gathering and diagnosis
- Consensus on strategy
- Implementation and monitoring

## 1.1 Processes relevant to organisational development

A number of processes may be regarded as central to OD.

(a) **Change management** is dealt with in the next chapter.

(b) **Management development** is a holistic process, both responding to the organisation's needs and promoting individual personal development. The aim is to develop management skills *throughout* the organisation, not just among those labelled 'manager' so that everything encompassed in the management of the organisation is improved.

(c) Development of **organisational culture** where required, so that it supports aims and processes involved in developing the organisation.

(d) Improvement of the **motivational element**, which includes employee attitudes, commitment and morale.

(e) Resolution of **conflict** within the organisation.

OD makes use of a range of **intervention strategies**, including those listed below.

(a) Management **training** based on maximum concern for both people and production.

(b) **Sensitivity training**. Small, unstructured group meetings (sometimes called **therapy groups** or T-groups) may be used to increase sensitivity to emotional reactions in others and in oneself.

(c) **Team building** attempts to improve work group performance by attention to task procedures, interpersonal relationships and patterns of interaction within the group.

(d) **Attitudes** are investigated by the use of **survey questionnaires**. Work groups are involved in the interpretation of the data and the development of action plans.

(e) In some circumstances, **managed confrontation** may be encouraged to resolve differences.

Some of these factors may involve the use of **third party consultants**.

*Mullins* sums up OD like this.

> 'OD is action-oriented and tailored to suit specific needs. It takes a number of forms with varying levels of intervention. OD concerns itself with the examination of organisational health and the implementation of planned change. This may include training in interpersonal skills, sensitivity training, and methods and techniques relating to motivational processes, patterns of communication, styles of leadership and managerial behaviour.'

## 1.2 Levels at which OD efforts may focus

Some writers classify the levels at which **OD initiatives** may be directed. The emphasis given to each level depends upon the situation facing the organisation.

There are three main levels.

(a) **Individual level**: If managers believe that the behaviour of individuals requires development or improvement OD efforts will focus on improving individual skill levels, attitudes and motivation. Techniques employed could include education and training, management development, coaching and counselling, team building activities, inter-group activities, role analysis, job re-design, planning and objective setting activities and process consultation.

(b) **Organisation structure and systems level**: If investigations indicate that organisational behaviour is being adversely affected by the characteristics of the organisational situation in which people work, then OD initiatives will focus upon organisation structure and processes. The aim is to make structural and procedural modifications (eg job redesign, reward systems, setting clear objectives) that help achieve organisational goals.

(c) **Organisational climate and interpersonal style levels**: Some managers believe that the social and other informal processes among organisation members are important determinants of organisational behaviour. An OD initiative in this area would aim to create a system with a wide climate of high interpersonal trust and openness and a reduction in the negative consequences of excessive social conflict and competitiveness.

# 2 Models of growth and development

## 2.1 Growth

**FAST FORWARD**

Many organisations pursue **growth**, which can be defined in many ways such as increases in profits, market share etc.

**Organisations may grow in a number of ways**, for example:

- Sales revenue (a growth in the number of markets served)
- Profitability (in absolute terms, and as a return on capital)
- Number of goods/services sold
- Number of outlets/sites
- Number of employees
- Number of countries

**Reasons for growth** could include:

(a) **A genuine increasing demand for the products/services**. For example, there is likely to be a growth in the number of UK hospitals specialising in geriatric illnesses, simply because the number of elderly people in the population is expected to rise.

(b) **Growth can be necessary for an organisation to compete effectively. Economies of scale** can arise from producing in bulk, as high fixed costs can be spread over more units of output.

(c) **The managers of the organisation like growth**, as it increases their power and rewards.

(d) **Shareholders can see growth as a means of increasing their wealth**, in many cases.

(e) Companies take over in order to gain **control over resources**, or the value added at different stages of the supply chain.

Organisational growth in size can occur by **acquisition** or **organically** (ie generated by an expansion of the organisation's activities). It is to **organic growth** that we shall now turn.

## 2.2 The organisational life cycle

The 'S-curve hypothesis' is a theory devised by economists to explain organisational growth.

It suggests that organisations have a relatively short period of establishment, followed by rapid growth before tailing off into stability and eventual decline.

The curve is shown below.

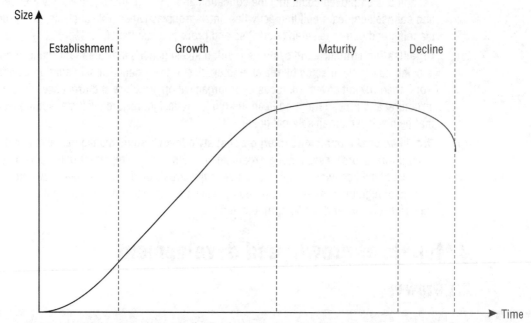

The organisational life cycle ('S curve')

## 2.3 Greiner's stage model of growth

FAST FORWARD

> *Greiner* suggests that organisations grow in phases, in which evolutionary growth is punctuated by revolutionary crises. Growth is driven by creativity, direction, delegation, co-ordination and collaboration. Growth is punctuated by crises of leadership, autonomy, control and red tape respectively.

A **stage model of growth** was suggested by *Greiner*. It assumes that, as an organisation **ages**, it grows in **size**, measured, perhaps by the **number of employees** and **diversity** of activities. This growth takes place in discrete phases. Each phase is characterised by two things.

(a) **Evolution**. This is a distinctive factor that **directs** the organisation's growth.

(b) **Revolution**. There may be a **crisis**, through which the organisation must pass before starting the next phase.

*Greiner* identified five phases.

**Phase 1**

(a) **Growth through creativity**. The organisation is small, and is managed in a personal and informal way. The founders of the business are actively involved in operations, personnel issues and innovation. Apple Computers, for example, started up in a garage. The product range is probably limited. A key goal is survival.

(b) **Crisis of leadership**. Sooner or later there comes a need for distinct **management skills**, relating less to products and marketing issues and more to the co-ordination of the organisation's activities.

## Greiner's growth model

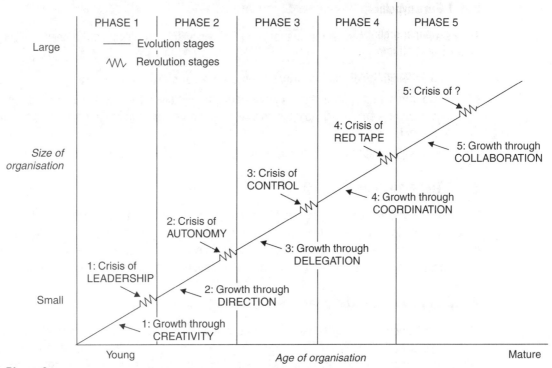

### Phase 2

(a) **Growth through direction**. Clear direction is provided in response to the crisis of leadership by **professionalising** the management. At the same time, there are more employees. Their initial enthusiasm might be tempered by loss of autonomy and the growth of hierarchy.

(b) **Crisis of autonomy**. Delegation becomes a problem. The top finds it harder and harder to keep in detailed control as there are too many activities, and it is easy to lose a sense of the wider picture. **Employees resent the lack of initiative and their performance falters**.

### Phase 3

(a) **Growth through delegation**. The response to the crisis of autonomy in Phase 2 is delegation. This has the advantage of decentralising decision-making and giving confidence to junior managers.

(b) **Crisis of control**. Delegation leads to additional problems of co-ordination and control. **Over-delegation can result in different departments acting sub-optimally**, in other words pursuing their own departmental goals to the detriment of the organisation as a whole.

### Phase 4

(a) **Growth through co-ordination**. The addition of internal systems, procedures and so forth aims to ensure co-ordination of activities and optimal use of resources, without reverting to the detailed hands-on methods in Phase 1. You might expect to see more complex management accounting systems, transfer pricing procedures, and some central management functions.

(b) **Crisis of red tape**. The new procedures **inhibit useful action**.

### Phase 5

(a) **Growth through collaboration**. The crisis of red tape is resolved by **increased informal collaboration**. **Control is cultural rather than formal**. People participate in teams.

(b) This growth stage may lead to a '**crisis of psychological saturation**', in which all become exhausted by teamwork. (Greiner did not name this crisis, hence the question mark in the diagram.) *Greiner* postulates a sixth growth phase involving a dual organisation: a 'habit' structure for daily work routines and a 'reflective structure' for stimulating new perspectives and personal enrichment.

*Greiner's* model refers to evolutionary organisational **growth** punctuated by revolutionary **crisis**.

## 2.4 Criticisms of organisation life cycle models

### 2.4.1 Formation

**Early stages**. Not all organisations are founded by a visionary controlling entrepreneur, selling a product or service.

(a)     A new organisation can be formed from the **merger of two existing ones**.

(b)     Two or more companies might **collaborate on a joint venture**. The Airbus project, for example, did not start as a small business, but as a result of co-operation between governments and existing companies.

(c)     New organisations are created by existing ones and have a substantial complement of staff.

### 2.4.2 Too many issues

**The models combine too many issues**: organisation structure, organisation culture, product/market scope, leadership, management style and reward systems. A business can grow quickly in some aspects but not in others. The UK **niche retailers** of the 1980s expanded in terms of the number of sites, locations, employees, and profits growth, but the **product/market scope was very restricted**.

### 2.4.3 Growth is not the same as effectiveness

Many organisations can be **effective without growth**. In fact, growth is **not** the normal state of affairs for many organisations. For example, a doctors' practice can be effective without treating ever-increasing numbers of patients, and an orchestra reaches a maximum size when it needs no more players.

It is possible to combine a bureaucratic obsession with procedures and efficiency with a strong sense of purpose. Hospitals depend on the devotion and professionalism of staff – but clinical procedures have to be adhered to.

### 2.4.4 No timescale

**It gives no idea of the timescale involved**.

(a)     For example, the early stages may be very rapid, or may take several years. The longer it takes, the easier, it might be for the organisation to adjust, and no crises may punctuate the process.

(b)     Growth models imply a **linear development** over time, whereas the organisation might enjoy different rates of growth at different times of the life cycle, or even decline.

(c)     It is not always easy to assess the phase of the life cycle any organisation is actually going through.

### 2.4.5 Ignores environment and competition

**The models do not clearly indicate the relationship with the environment**. Organisational growth partly depends on environmental factors.

The growth of the business can be curtailed by the **growth of competition**. In other words, a business can be hemmed in, but still survive and even prosper.

 Case Study

Some years ago, an American firm saw a sudden surge in demand for Cabbage Patch dolls, which were relatively unsophisticated toys. The manufacturer expanded operations rapidly, but by the next year, demand had faded significantly.

# 3 Contraction and decline

Corporate **decline** is caused by poor management, poor financial controls, high cost, poor marketing, a variety of competitive weaknesses, a failure of big projects, and financial policy. **Turning the situation** or acquisition **round** can mean addressing these issues independently of preconceptions.

## 3.1 Causes of decline

Three important causes of organisational decline are:

(a) **Environmental entropy**. The organisation's environment may change to such an extent that it may no longer provide conditions in which the organisation can flourish. For example, a decline in the housing market could put many estate agents out of business. The decline may be temporary or in some situations permanent.

(b) **Vulnerability**. The organisation may for some reason fail to prosper in its environment. It may not pursue the right strategy or choose the right business. It may not be large or strong enough to cope with sudden shifts in demand or strong competition.

(c) **Organisational atrophy**. The organisation may lose its ability to cope. Its managers may be complacent and unable to adapt.

## Question

September 11

The airline industry and the travel industry in general suffered following the terrorist attacks in the United States on September 11 2001.

Which of the following terms best describes the events of September 11 from the point of view of an airline?

A    Organisational atrophy
B    Environmental atrophy
C    Requisite variety
D    Vulnerability

## Answer

B    The best description in these circumstances is environmental atrophy. The resulting downturn in demand was eventually reversed.

### 3.1.1 Specific causes of decline

**Causes of decline** and the **strategies** to deal with them are outlined below.

(a) **Poor management**. This should be dealt with by the introduction of new management and perhaps organisation restructuring (this should only be embarked upon once the new executive knows how the firm *really* works, including its informal organisation).

(b) **Poor financial controls**. This can be dealt with by new management, financial control systems which are tighter and more relevant, and, perhaps, decentralisation and delegation of responsibility to first line management of all aspects except finance.

(c) **High cost structure**. Cost reduction is important in improving margins in the long term. New product-market strategies are adopted for the short term (to boost profitability and cash flow). Growth-orientated strategies are only suitable once survival is assured. A focus strategy (whether cost-focus or differentiation-focus) is perhaps the most appropriate.

(d)   **Poor marketing**. The marketing mix can be redeployed. *Slatter* believes that the sales force of a crisis-ridden firm is likely to be particularly demotivated.

(e)   **Competitive weakness**. This is countered by cost reduction, improved marketing, asset reduction (eg disposing of subsidiaries, selling redundant assets), even acquisition, and of course, a suitable product-market strategy.

(f)   **Big projects/acquisitions**. Acquisitions can go bad, or there can be a failure of a major project (eg Rolls Royce aerospace once went into receivership because of the cost of developing the RB211 engine).

(g)   **Financial policy**. Firms might suffer because of high gearing. Arguably, organisations subject to management buyouts financed by interest-bearing loans are vulnerable. Converting debt to equity and selling assets are possible options to deal with this.

## 3.2 Managing decline

Companies who realise they are in decline must stop and reverse the trend if they are to survive in the long term. Whether a company does recover depends on the actions they choose and how they implement their recovery strategy. Four possible approaches are:

- Retrenchment
- Turnaround

- Divestment
- Liquidation

### 3.2.1 Retrenchment

Retrenchment involves performing the same activities as before but cutting costs drastically.

### 3.2.2 Turnaround

**Turning a company round requires an able top management, with the right mix of skills and experience**. Substantial changes at the top may be needed. The development of an effective top management team requires attention to the points below.

(a)   What resources does the team have to work with within the company and what could it obtain from the industry?

(b)   What is the *ideal* management team given the nature of the crises facing the organisation. For example a firm with poor financial controls may require a team with a financial or systems bias, whereas a firm whose problem was lacklustre products may need a team with a marketing bias.

(c)   Against this ideal team, how does the current team shape up? New expertise may need to be imported, or a plan may be needed to enhance the capability of the existing team.

The top management team need to:

- Create a new vision for the organisation
- Gain acceptance of the new vision
- Force through and 'refreeze' the change

Successful leadership is more likely to occur when the person in charge of an organisation possesses some generic leadership characteristics (ie suitable 'traits') and is then able to customise them (ie operate on a 'contingency' basis) to that particular context.

### 3.2.3 Divestment

Divestment involves the external sale of part of the organisation, or the closure of a unit or operation (a rationalisation). See later in this chapter.

### 3.2.4 Liquidation

Liquidation involves selling the business to one or more buyers. This is the 'last resort' – in effect it represents an admission that the business (or the managers) have failed.

Learning outcome: B(i)

The XZY Company is well-established and has many long-standing customers. Although the market the XYZ Company operates in has been expanding, the company's sales levels have remained stable.

XYZ Company has approached a firm of management consultants to establish why their sales have not increased in proportion to the market. The consultants have informed XYZ that their specialist in organisational development (OD) will be leading their investigation.

The Managing Director of XYZ has never heard of OD and has asked for your advice.

*Required*

Explain the nature of OD and describe how it might be used to assist the XYZ Company.          20 marks

## Answer

Organisational development (OD) involves an organisation-wide drive to increase organisation effectiveness through improving the organisation's processes. OD attempts to change beliefs, attitudes, values and the structure of an organisation so that the organisation is then more able to adapt to and prosper in their environment. OD is necessary whenever an organisation is not progressing in a sustainable manner.

OD is concerned with all levels of a company's operations. There are many versions of OD approaches; the common ground is that an initial diagnosis stage determines where the organisation currently stands when measured against its target for that aspect.

The consultant would gather information – probably from outside as well as inside the organisation as the processes XYZ needs to develop must meet external (customer) needs. Attitudes and opinions may be investigated by observation and interviews. Questionnaires may be used to achieve wide coverage.

An OD programme for XYZ would involve a planned approach to introduce improvement through change. XYZ is failing to attract new customers, which would imply that it has 'lost touch' with the market. This would be the starting point for the consultant's work.

Once the key problems have been identified, managers can focus their change efforts at a specific level within the organisation. There are three main levels:

- **Individual level**: this is appropriate when managers believe that organisational behaviour is determined by the characteristics of its members. The aim is to improve individual skill levels, attitudes and motivation. OD specialists employ a range of techniques for this purpose. These include education and training, management development, coaching and counselling, team building activities, inter-group activities, role analysis, job re-design, planning and objective setting activities and process consultation.
- **Organisation structure and systems level**: this is appropriate when it is felt that organisational behaviour is determined by the characteristics of the organisational situation in which people work. The aim is to direct employee behaviour to organisational goals and techniques involving structural and procedural modifications such as divisionalisation, job redesign, reward systems and the setting of clear objectives.
- **Organisational climate and interpersonal style levels**: some managers believe that organisational behaviour is determined by emotional and social processes, which characterise the relations among members. They aim to create a system with a climate of high interpersonal trust and openness and reduced dysfunctional consequences of excessive social conflict and competitiveness.

No one level should be focused on exclusively and it would seem that a balance of approaches would be necessary at the XYZ Company.

# 4 Structural reorganisation and divestment

**Acquisitions** and **divestments** are examples of growth and decline. Acquisitions can be problematic if there are cultural differences. Divestments enable a firm to concentrate on its core businesses, or to realise a profit on the original investment in the acquisition.

## 4.1 Factors creating pressure for change in organisations structure

Pressure for change to the structure of an organisation could come from a variety of areas.

(a) **Changes in the environment of the organisation**. For example, greater competition might create pressures for cost-cutting, and so staff cuts.

(b) **Diversification into new product-market areas**. There is a need for better lateral and vertical integration as an organisation becomes more complex and differentiated. A possible role for special co-ordinators can be found. Another issue which might be addressed is when to switch from a functional to a divisional organisation structure.

(c) **Growth**. Employing more people creates problems of extended management hierarchies and poor communication.

(d) **New technology**.

(e) **Changes in the capabilities of personnel employed.** These can include changes in education levels, the distribution of occupational skills, employee attitudes to work etc.

(f) **Crisis and turnaround** might require changes in the organisation structure.

(g) The existing organisation might be showing signs of **weakness and strain,** such as management overload, poor integration, co-ordination and decision-making, insufficient innovation and weakening control. These are common management problems, but made worse by deficiencies in the organisation structure.

Restructuring is not always necessary every time that changes take place in an organisation's circumstances. When a problem arises with an organisational deficiency, management has to analyse and diagnose the fault.

(a) What is the **scope** of the problem?

(b) What is the **source** of the problem? (It is relatively easy to spot personal problems, when a manager is not doing his job properly, or there are personal rivalries and conflicts, but it is not so easy to diagnose faults in organisational structure.)

(c) Is the problem **temporary** or **permanent**, **unique** or **recurrent**?

(d) At what **level** in the management hierarchy and organisation structure is the problem located? This is the point where restructuring will be needed.

## 4.2 Acquisitions and mergers

A company which is planning to grow must decide on whether to pursue a policy of organic growth (ie growing its own operations) or a policy of taking over other established businesses, or a mix of the two.

(a) Acquisitions can be made to enter new product areas, or to expand in existing markets, much more quickly. Organic growth takes time. With acquisitions, entire existing operations are assimilated into the company at one fell swoop.

(b) Acquisitions can be made without cash, if share exchange transactions are acceptable to both the buyers and sellers of any company which is to be taken over.

(c) When an acquisition is made to diversify into new product areas, the company will be buying technical expertise, goodwill and customer contracts and so on which it might take years to develop if it tried to enter the market by growing organically.

However, **acquisitions do have their problems**.

(a) They might be too expensive: some might be resisted by the directors of the target company. Others might be referred to the government under the terms of anti-monopoly legislation.

(b) Customers of the target company might resent a sudden takeover and consider going to other suppliers for their goods.

(c) In general, the problems of assimilating new products, customers, suppliers, markets, employees and different systems of operating might create 'indigestion' and management overload in the acquiring company.

### 4.2.1 Guidelines for acquisitions

The management writer *Drucker* (1982) identified five guidelines when one company acquires another.

| Guideline | Comment |
|---|---|
| **Contribution** | The company acquiring the other company must know exactly how it will enhance the acquired company. |
| **Common core** | The companies should have some common core in markets, operations or technology. |
| **Value** | The acquiring company should value the products, services and customers of the company being acquired. |
| **Management cover** | The acquiring company should have some top management capable of managing the acquired company (as senior managers may choose to or be required to leave). |
| **Linkage** | Within a year some managers should have 'crossed' over between the previously separate companies. |

### 4.2.2 Mergers

A **merger** involves the coming together of two or more organisations to become one. The organisations involved are usually of similar size.

Mergers have similar advantages and disadvantages to other types of acquisitions. A possible complicating factor with mergers is that as there is no dominant original organisation there may be problems establishing a new identity and culture. There may also be 'power-struggles' between staff from the different organisations.

 Case Study

An example of growth which had to be pursued through diversification and acquisition is Fujitsu. By acquiring the UK firm ICL, not only did Fujitsu find an entry to the European market, but also acquired ICL's experience in *open systems technologies*.

## 4.3 Non-growth strategies and de-growth strategies

Most strategies are designed to promote growth, but management should consider what rate of growth they want, whether they want to see any growth at all, or whether there should be a contraction of the business. It might be difficult to envisage a company that is hostile to growth, but think of family companies where members of the family wish to retain personal control and so do not want to see any expansion which calls for substantial new funding.

### 4.3.1 Divestment

Divestment means getting rid of something. In strategic planning terms, it means selling off a part of a firm's operations, or pulling out of certain product-market areas (ie closing down a product line).

(a) A company might decide to concentrate on its core businesses and sell off fringe activities, or to sell off subsidiaries where performance is poor, or where growth prospects are not good.

(b) Selling off subsidiaries at a profit can be a means of raising finance.

(c) Selling attractive subsidiaries can thwart a takeover bid.

One term that describes divestment is 'demerger'. This is sometimes referred to as 'unbundling'. Demergers are the opposite of mergers. The main feature of a demerger is that one corporate entity becomes two or more separate entities. The newly-separated businesses might have the same shareholders, but they will usually have different people on their boards of directors.

A demerger might take one of two forms.

(a) A **management buyout** (see below).

(b) A **major demerger of a group**: a well known and successful example is the break up of ICI into its pharmaceuticals and chemicals components (Zeneca and ICI) in order to release more value for shareholders. This in part resulted from a takeover bid.

### 4.3.2 Rationalisation

Rationalisation involves reviewing a (usually failing) area of the business and making changes. Typically rationalisation involves streamlining processes and reorganising the way things are done – often including a reduction in staffing levels. If the process is carried out effectively, rationalisation can result in a turnaround in the area of business concerned. In many cases however the term rationalisation is used as a 'catch-all' phrase to justify cutbacks.

## 4.4 Management buyouts

When a firm decides to divest itself of a part of its operations, it will try to get what it can by selling off the business as a unit, or by selling individual assets. Typically, a better price can be obtained by selling the business as a unit, and there might well be many other firms interested in buying it.

In recent years, however, there have been a large number of management buyouts, whereby the subsidiary is sold off to its managers. The managers put in some of their own capital, but obtain the rest from venture capital organisations (eg banks), and hope to make a bigger success of the business than the company who is selling it off.

Management buyouts are often associated with ailing subsidiary companies, where the group's management agree to sell off the subsidiary as an alternative to closing it down.

### 4.4.1 Strategic factors in a buyout decision

A management buyout team must answer three important questions.

(a) Can the buyout team raise the finance to pay for the buyout. Buyouts are well-favoured by venture capital organisations, which regard them as less risky than new start-up businesses, and so access to funds is often not a serious problem.

(b) Can the bought-out operation generate enough profits to pay for the costs of the acquisition – ie interest payments on the borrowed finance? If the buyout price is too high, the answer would be no.

(c) Can the buyout team convince its co-investors that it has the management skills, as well as the enthusiasm, to succeed?

## 4.5 Terminology

Structural reorganisation seems to attract jargon! A few common terms are explained in the table below.

| Term | Explanation |
|---|---|
| **Spinning off** or **unbundling** | Selling off parts of an organisation that don't fit strategically, even though they may have potential. |
| **Downsizing** | Reducing the size of existing operations – usually through redundancies. |
| **Rightsizing** | Term used to describe a rationalisation that occurs following an acquisition. |

# 5 Change triggers

Change can be triggered by **internal** and **external** factors (strategic).

## 5.1 Internal change

The need for an organisation to change or develop could be caused (or 'triggered') by a number of factors.

(a)   **Changes in the products the organisation makes, or the services it provides**. These are made in response to changes in customer demands, competitors' actions, new technology, and so on.

(b)   **Changes in technology and changes in working methods**. These changes are also in response to environmental change such as the advent of new technology and new laws on safety at work.

(c)   **Changes in management and working relationships**. For example, changes in leadership style, and in the way that employees are encouraged to work together. Also changes in training and development.

(d)   **Changes in organisation structure or size**. These might involve creating new departments and divisions, greater delegation of authority or more centralisation, changes in the way that plans are made, management information is provided and control is exercised, and so on. Organisation re-structuring will be made in response to changes of the types discussed above.

### 5.1.1 The nature of internal change

Some common reasons for, or examples of, significant change include the following:

(a)   **New technology** could impact in a number of areas.
- Computerisation of operations
- New products
- New working methods
- Better management information systems

We look at issues related to information technology and change management in the following chapter.

(b)   **Reorganisation**, such as the following.

(i)   A company is **taken over**, and so has to adopt the organisational policies of the new parent company.

(ii)   A **merger** (full joining together or two previously separate organisations). The two cultures and operations need to combine to become one.

(iii)   Growth causes reorganisation into **divisions**, or more specialist **functional departments**.

(iv)   Divestment or **rationalisation** of businesses.

(v)   A drive to **keep costs down** leads to cost cutting measures such as job losses.

(c)    Changes to **working conditions**, such as:
   (i)    New offices
   (ii)   Shorter working week
   (iii)  More varied work times (flexible working)
   (iv)   More outsourcing, ie giving work to outsiders
   (v)    Greater emphasis on occupational health
(d)    **Personnel policies**, such as:
   (i)    Changes in rules and procedures – for instance, about use of the internet.
   (ii)   Promotions, transfers, separation of employees, training and development, problems perhaps growing in complexity.
(e)    **Philosophy of management** (relations between management and employees), for example:
   (i)    A new senior manager may introduce new style of leadership.
   (ii)   The attitudes of managers and employees may change over time, perhaps leading to greater participation of subordinates in decision-making.
   (iii)  Communications with employees may become more open.
   (iv)   There may be greater collaboration between management and trade unions in labour relations.

### 5.1.2 Change through organisational learning

**Key term**

A **learning organisation** is one that constantly increases its ability to control and shape its future.

To achieve this *Senge* (1992) explained that continual learning must become a 'way of organisational life'. He believed this required the breaking down of traditional hierarchies to allow all to work towards a shared vision with a common sense of purpose. The learning organisation constantly adapts to changes in the external environment. Change therefore becomes natural, expected and accepted. *Senge* identified five core competences of learning organisations.

| Competence | Explanation |
|---|---|
| **Build a shared vision** | Provides a common sense of purpose that brings everyone together. |
| **Mastery of learning** | Individuals continually develop in areas important to them. |
| **Challenge assumptions of learned behaviours** | Individuals should recognise how alternative actions of taken could create a new reality. |
| **Team learning** | Individuals should form and act in teams. |
| **System thinking** | Problems should be viewed as complex interrelationships rather than discrete parts. |

## 5.2 External (strategic) change

**FAST FORWARD**

**Organisational changes need careful planning**. This is true of all but the smallest changes, and it is especially true of major changes.

Strategy can be seen as a process of adapting the organisation to its environment. By devising and following a prescribed strategy an organisation is in effect agreeing to the likelihood of frequent change – as an organisation's environment is subject to constant change and the organisation must then react appropriately if strategic goals are to be achieved.

Major organisational changes should be planned for during the corporate planning process.

## 5.2.1 The nature of strategic change

**FAST FORWARD**

Change itself may be divided into two types, **incremental** and **transformational** and so may the management approach to change be divided into **reactive** and **proactive**.

**Key terms**

> **Incremental change** is characterised by a series of small steps. It is a gradual process.
>
> **Transformational change** is characterised by major, significant change being introduced relatively quickly.
>
> **Step change** describes an unexpected jump (upwards) or drop (downwards) in the pace of change. The step is caused by an unexpected event (eg environmental disaster, unexpected change in government etc).
>
> **Planned change** involves following a series of pre-planned steps.
>
> **Emergent change** views change as a series of continuous open-ended adjustments to the environment.

*Johnson and Scholes* suggest the model of change shown below.

Nature of change

|  | Incremental | Transformational |
|---|---|---|
| **Pro-active** | Tuning | Planned |
| **Reactive** | Adaptation | Forced |

*Management role* (vertical axis label)

The importance of **proactive management** is that it implies that organisational change may be undertaken *before* it is imposed by events. It may, in fact, result from the process of forecasting and be a response to expected developments. **Forced change** is likely to be both painful and risky.

The need for change can affect any aspect of the organisation. The creation of **new products and services** is an obvious area for change, as is the development of the processes by which they are created and delivered. However, change can also become necessary in **support activities**.

**Cultural change** has been a preoccupation of senior managers for some time, reflecting the need to deliver significant improvements in quality, efficiency and service. We consider this further later in this chapter.

## 5.2.2 Drivers of strategic change

**External developments**, whether or not forecasted, are the most usual drivers of change. These can be analysed using the PESTEL approach.

(a)   **Political changes** may be brought in by a new government.

(b)   Routine economic developments are unlikely to lead to transformational change, but the possibility of sudden **economic shock**, such as occurred in SE Asia in 1998, may do so.

(c)   **Social developments** include improvements in education and the increasing number of women who wish to combine work with child-rearing. This has led to major changes in the labour market, including the expansion of job-sharing and part-time work.

(d)   **Technological developments** can lead to new products and processes, possibly making existing ones obsolete.

(e)   **Environmental** agreements and legislation may require the organisation to change its activities.

(f)   **Legal changes** must be complied with, but a proactive approach, including lobbying, may steer the change in a business friendly direction.

Change may also be driven by factors internal to the organisation including internal technical, administrative, financial and social developments.

### 5.2.3 A systematic approach to implementing change

For an organisation to be innovative, and continually responsive to the need for change, a systematic approach should be established, for planning and implementing changes.

### 5.2.4 A step-by-step model for change

Although each situation should be considered individually, the following general steps can be identified in a major change initiative.

**Step 1**     Determine need or desire for change in a particular area.

**Step 2**     Prepare a tentative plan. Brainstorming sessions are a good idea, since alternatives for change should be considered.

**Step 3**     Analyse probable reactions to the change.

**Step 4**     Make a final decision from the choice of alternative options. The decision may be taken either by group problem-solving (participative) or by a manager on his own (coercive).

**Step 5**     Establish a timetable for change.

    (a)    'Coerced' changes can probably be implemented faster, without time for discussions.

    (b)    Speed of implementation that is achievable will depend on the likely reactions of the people affected.

    (c)    Identify those in favour of the change, and perhaps set up a pilot programme involving them. Talk with any others likely to resist the change.

**Step 6**     Communicate the plan for change. This is really a continuous process, beginning at Step 1 and going through to Step 7.

**Step 7**     Implement the change.

**Step 8**     Review the change. This requires continuous evaluation.

 Case Study

In the UK public sector over the past 20 years, turbulence has been the norm. The transfer of public corporations to the private sector required new organisation structures and management styles.

## 5.3 Other approaches

### 5.3.1 Use a change agent

*Buchanan* and others have emphasised the role of change agents.

**Key term**

> A **change agent** is an individual (or sometimes a group) with the responsibility for driving and 'selling' the change – they are often used in programmes of organisational development.

The role of the change agent varies depending on the brief they are given. It may include:

- Defining the problem
- Suggesting possible solutions
- Selecting and implementing a solution
- Gaining support from all involved

To be effective a change agent should have the following skills and attributes.

- Communication skills
- Negotiation and 'selling' skills
- An awareness of organisational 'politics'
- An understanding of the relevant processes

## 5.3.2 Integrative v segmentalist

In *The Change Masters*, *Kanter* distinguished between firms with an **integrative** approach and those with a **segmentalist** approach. The integrative approach is taken by innovative firms that see problems as wholes and produce visionary solutions, developing their abilities in the process. Segmentalist firms stifle entrepreneurial innovation by taking narrow, functionally based views of any problem. The integrative, innovative approach is monitored in a variety of ways.

(a) Encouragement of a culture of pride in the organisation's achievements.

(b) De-layering the hierarchy.

(c) Improvement of lateral communication and working across functional boundaries.

(d) Wide distribution of information about company plans.

(e) Decentralisation and the empowerment of entrepreneurially inclined people at junior levels in the organisation.

## 5.3.3 Beer and Nohria: Theory E and Theory O

Beer and Nohria identified two theories of change – **Theory E** (based on economic value) and **Theory O** (based on organisational capability).

**Theory E** change strategies believe in a '**hard**' approach to change. They see shareholder value as the only legitimate measure of business success. Theory E change often involves heavy use of economic incentives, layoffs, downsizing, and restructuring.

Managers who subscribe to **Theory O** believe that if they were to focus exclusively on economic value (ie return to shareholders) they might in fact harm their organisation in the long term. Therefore, they favour a '**soft**' approach to change.

Because theories E and O are so different it's hard to manage them simultaneously – employees tend to distrust leaders who alternate between nurturing and ruthless behaviour.

One possible solution *Beer* and *Nohria* explored was using the two approaches sequentially – change managers could start with one approach then move to another. However, they found that in most situations this would take too long (sometimes decades) to be practical – and would often require two different leaders to implement.

*Beer* and *Nohria* concluded that it **is** possible to apply theories E and O together – however it requires great skill. They also found that because it is more difficult than mere sequencing, the **simultaneous use of O and E strategies** is more likely to be a source of sustainable **competitive advantage**.

An explanation of this integrated approach is shown in the following table.

| Dimension of change | Theory E | Theory O | Integrated approach (Theories E and O combined) |
|---|---|---|---|
| Goals | Maximise shareholder value. | Develop organisational capabilities. | Explicitly embrace the paradox between economic value and organisational capability. |
| Leadership | Manage change from the top down. | Encourage participation from the bottom up. | Set direction from the top and engage the people below. |
| Focus | Emphasise structure and systems. | Build up corporate culture: employees' behaviour and attitudes. | Focus simultaneously on the hard (structures and systems) and the soft (corporate culture). |
| Process | Plan and establish program. | Experiment and evolve. | Experiment and evolve; plan for spontaneity. |
| Reward system | Motivate through financial incentives. | Motivate through commitment – use pay as fair exchange. | Use incentives to reinforce change but not to drive it. |
| Use of consultants | Consultants analyse problems and shape solutions. | Consultants support management in shaping their own solutions. | Consultants are expert resources who empower employees. |

 Case Study

One company that exemplifies the reconciliation of the hard and soft approaches is ASDA, the UK grocery chain. Archie Norman took over as CEO of ASDA in the early 1990s, when the retailer was nearly bankrupt.

Norman laid off employees, flattened the organisation, and sold off loss making businesses. These acts usually result in distrust among employees. Yet during Norman's eight-year tenure as CEO, ASDA also became famous for its atmosphere of trust and openness.

With his opening speech to ASDA's executive team Norman indicated clearly that he intended to apply both E and O strategies in his change effort. He said: 'Our number one objective is to secure value for our shareholders and secure the trading future of the business. I intend to spend the next few weeks listening and forming ideas for our precise direction. We need a culture built around common ideas and goals that include listening, learning, and speed of response, from the stores upwards. [But] there will be management reorganisation. My objective is to establish a clear focus on the stores, shorten lines of communication, and build one team.'

If there is a contradiction between building a high-involvement organisation and restructuring to enhance shareholder value, Norman embraced it.

# Chapter Roundup

- **Organisational development** is a term used to group together a wide range of elements that attempt to improve the performance and effectiveness of an organisation and often intervene into the social processes of an organisation.

- Many organisations pursue **growth**, which can be defined in many ways such as increases in profits, market share etc.

- **Greiner** suggests that organisations grow in phases, in which evolutionary growth is punctuated by revolutionary crises. Growth is driven by creativity, direction, delegation, co-ordination and collaboration. Growth is punctuated by crises of leadership, autonomy, control and red tape respectively.

- Corporate **decline** is caused by poor management, poor financial controls, high cost, poor marketing, a variety of competitive weaknesses, a failure of big projects, and financial policy. **Turning the situation** or acquisition **round** can mean addressing these issues independently of preconceptions.

- **Acquisitions** and **divestments** are examples of growth and decline. Acquisitions can be problematic if there are cultural differences. Divestments enable a firm to concentrate on its core businesses, or to realise a profit on the original investment in the acquisition.

- Change can be triggered by **internal** and **external factors** (strategic).

- **Organisational changes need careful planning**. This is true of all but the smallest changes, and it is especially true of major changes.

- Change itself may be divided into two types, **incremental** and **transformational** and so may the management approach to change be divided into **reactive** and **proactive**.

- *Beer and Nohria* identified two theories of change – **Theory E** (based on economic value) and **Theory O** (based on organisational capability).

# Quick Quiz

1   List the three levels at which OD efforts may focus.

    1   .......................................................

    2   .......................................................

    3   .......................................................

2   List four examples of types of growth (eg sales revenue).

    1   .......................................................

    2   .......................................................

    3   .......................................................

    4   .......................................................

3   Which of the following is not a cause of decline?

    A   Requisite variety
    B   Vulnerability
    C   Environmental entropy
    D   Organisational atrophy

4   Briefly explain the difference between divestment and rationalisation.

5   Which type of change is described below?

    'Change is a series of continuous open-ended adjustments to the environment'

    A   Incremental
    B   Transformational
    C   Emergent
    D   Step

# Answers to Quick Quiz

1   Individual; Organisation structure and systems; Organisation climate and interpersonal style.

2   Growth may occur in sales revenue, profitability, volume of goods or services sold, number of outlets, number of employees and other matters.

3   A   Requisite variety is an element of systems theory not a cause of corporate decline.

4   Divestment means to get rid of an area of a business – Rationalisation involves reviewing it and making changes often resulting in 'turning it around'.

5   C   The statement describes emergent change.

| Now try the question below from the Exam Question Bank | | | |
|---|---|---|---|
| **Number** | **Level** | **Marks** | **Time** |
| 13 | Examination | 30 | 54 mins |

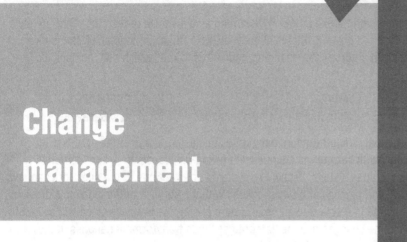

# Change
# management

## Introduction

Change is a feature of the organisation's environment and requires the organisation to change as well in many different ways.

In this chapter we take a closer look at the **nature of change** and various aspects of **change management**.

We explain why people resist change and how such resistance is articulated (through words and actions).

Later, we explore the possibilities of culture change across organisations. You should be able to assess the ingredients for an effective culture transformation programme in an organisation.

The final section looks at information technology (IT) and change – in the context of IT being a trigger or cause of change and also how IT may assist in change management.

| Topic list | Learning outcomes | Syllabus references | Ability required |
|---|---|---|---|
| 1 The process of changing human behaviour | B(iii) | B(2), B(3) | Evaluation |
| 2 Resistance to change | B(ii) | B(3) | Evaluation |
| 3 Commitment, co-ordination and communication | B(iii), B(iv) | B(3), B(4) | Evaluation |
| 4 Successful change | B(iii) | B(3) | Evaluation |
| 5 Information technology and change management | A(v), A(vi) | A(7) | Evaluation |

# 1 The process of changing human behaviour

## 1.1 The three stage approach

**FAST FORWARD** ⟩⟩

The Lewin/Schein three stage **model of change** identifies key steps as Unfreeze, Move and Refreeze.

In the words of *John Hunt* (*Managing People at Work*): 'Learning also involves re-learning – not merely learning something new but trying to unlearn what is already known.' This is, in a nutshell, the thinking behind *Lewin/Schein's* **three stage approach** to changing human behaviour, which may be depicted as follows.

| **UNFREEZE** | | **MOVE** | | **REFREEZE** |
|---|---|---|---|---|
| existing behaviour | → | attitudinal/behavioural change | → | new behaviour |

**Step 1**   **Unfreeze** is the most difficult (and in many cases neglected) stage of the process, concerned mainly with **selling** the change, with giving individuals or groups a **motive** for changing their attitudes, values, behaviour, systems or structures. If the need for change is immediate, clear and perceived to be associated with the survival of the individual or group (for example change in reaction to an organisation crisis), the unfreeze stage will be greatly accelerated. Routine changes may be harder to sell than transformational ones, if they are perceived to be unimportant and not survival-based.

Changing organisational **culture** is perhaps hardest of all, especially if it involves changes to long-held cultural values. Unfreezing processes require four things.

- A trigger
- Someone to challenge and expose the existing behaviour pattern
- The involvement of outsiders
- Alterations to power structure

**Step 2**   **Move** is the second stage, mainly concerned with identifying what the new, desirable behaviour or norm should be, communicating it and encouraging individuals and groups to 'own' the new attitude or behaviour. This might involve the adoption of a new culture. To be successful, the new ideas must be shown to work.

**Step 3**   **Refreeze** is the final stage, implying consolidation or reinforcement of the new behaviour. Positive reinforcement (praise and reward) or negative reinforcement (sanctions applied to those who deviate from the new behaviour) may be used.

This model is based on the view that change is capable of being planned. You should note that this is not always possible in real life.

# 2 Resistance to change

**FAST FORWARD** ⟩⟩

Change involves **structural** and **behavioural** factors. **Resistance** to change results from individual uncertainties and distrust of management. Some resistance may result from **uncertainty** about the nature of the change itself, or from poor information.

## 2.1 How change affects individuals

Change may affect individuals in several areas.

(a)   There may be **physiological** changes in a person's life, both as the natural product of development, maturation and ageing, and **as the result of external factors**: (a change in the pattern of shift-working, for example, may temporarily throw the individual's eating, waking and sleeping routine out of synchronisation with the body's sense of time).

(b) **Circumstantial** changes – living in a new house, establishing new relationships, working to new routines – will involve letting go of things, perhaps 'unlearning' old knowledge, and learning new ways of doing things.

Above all, change affects individuals **psychologically**.

(a) It may create **feelings of disorientation** before new circumstances have been assimilated.

(b) Uncertainty may lead to insecurity. This is especially acute in changes involving work, where there can be very great pressures for continuity and fast acclimatisation.

(c) The secure basis of warm, accepting relationships may be up-rooted; the business of forging new relationships can be fraught with personal insecurity.

### 2.1.1 Types of change experience

Four types of change experience have been identified (*Torrington and Weightman* (1994)).

| Type | Comment | Reaction |
|------|---------|----------|
| **Imposition** | Initiated and driven by someone else | Resistance |
| **Adaptation** | A change in attitude or behaviour as a result of changes by others | Uncertainty |
| **Growth** | A response to opportunities | Delight |
| **Creativity** | The individual instigates and controls the change process | Excitement |

## 2.2 Resistance to change at work

Resisting change means attempting to preserve the existing state of affairs against pressure to alter it.

Sources of resistance to change itself may include age and inflexibility, strong needs for security and emotional instability. Sources of resistance to particular proposed changes, (eg in location, methods of working, pay structure), may include the following:

(a) **Attitudes or beliefs**, perhaps arising from cultural, religious or class influences (for example, resistance to changes in the law on Sunday trading).

(b) **Loyalty to a group and its norms**, perhaps with an accompanying rejection of other groups, or outsiders (for example, in the case of a relocation so that two departments share office space). Groups tend to close ranks if their independent identity is threatened.

(c) **Habit, or past norms**. This can be a strong source of clinging to old ways, whether out of security needs, respect for tradition, or the belief that 'you can't teach an old dog new tricks' (for example, resistance to the introduction of new technology).

(d) **Politics** – in the sense of resisting changes that might weaken the power base of the individual or group or strengthen a rival's position.

(e) The **way** in which any change is put forward and implemented.

## 2.3 Reactions to proposed change

There are a range of possible reactions to a proposed change.

(a) **Acceptance** (whether enthusiastic espousal, co-operation, grudging co-operation or resignation)

(b) **Indifference** (usually where the change does not directly affect the individual: apathy, lack of interest, inaction)

(c) **Passive resistance** (refusal to learn, working to rule)

(d) **Active resistance** (deliberate 'spoiling', go-slows, deliberate errors, sabotage, absenteeism or strikes)

*John Hunt* highlights a number of responses that may not **look** like resistance on the face of things, but are **behaviours aimed at reinforcing the** *status quo*. There are a number of responses that the manager should learn to recognise.

(a)     Pleas of ignorance: ('I need more information').

(b)     Delayed judgement: ('let's wait and see ...'), perhaps stalling for time with comparisons ('there are other ways ...').

(c)     Defensive stances: ('This isn't going to work', 'It'd be too expensive', 'It's the wrong time to ...').

(d)     The display of various personal insecurities: ('I won't be able to cope', 'I won't see my team anymore', 'We won't have control over our planning any more', 'Why can't we just go on as we are?'); fear, anxiety, resentment at the manner of change, frustration at perceived losses.

(e)     Withdrawal, or disowning of the change: ('Oh well. On their heads be it', 'I'm not interested in flexitime anyway').

 Case Study

It is interesting to set side by side the comments of Sainsbury's director of personnel and a senior official of the shop worker's union . It isn't difficult to tell which is which!

(a)     'I have taken a close personal interest to ensure that in every branch the people who are working are those who volunteered. Not working on Sunday is not going to affect promotion prospects, it is not going to affect people's pay, and it is not going to affect our attitude to them.'

(b)     'Retailers have ways of making Sunday working become the norm. Employers work through the ranks. First they approach the weakest, the people who have less than two years' experience and who have no rights for unfair dismissal, then they pick the starry-eyed people who think they are going to be managing director, then they pick the people who work low hours and need a few bob. Then they come to the resolute minority and say: "You are out of step".'

## 2.4 Overcoming resistance to change

### 2.4.1 Force field analysis

It is also necessary to assess the impact of change on the political system of the organisation.

*Kurt Lewin* developed a simple technique of visualising the change process called **force field analysis**. This can be used to identify ways of dealing with an unsatisfactory situation. It is based on the idea that in any group or organisational situation there is an **interplay of restraining and driving forces that keeps things in equilibrium**.

**FAST FORWARD**

Lewin's **force field analysis** maps the forces that are pushing **toward the preferred state** and the restraining forces, which are **pushing back to the current state**. They can then be presented in a chart.

The example below describes a public sector organisation whose management are introducing a performance review system.

Let us imagine a group of workers who are producing at 70% of the efficiency that might be expected on purely technical grounds. This being so, their output can be visualised as a **balance** between two opposing sets of forces, ie **driving forces** which are propelling their output upwards and **restraining forces** which are preventing it from going beyond the 70% level.

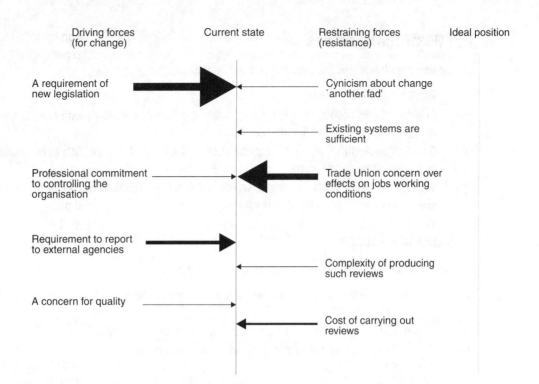

Note that these driving forces and restraining forces represent **perceptions** entertained by the workers themselves. They are not merely a list of impersonal advantages and disadvantages because, as is often the case with complex scenarios, an advantage for one person turns out to be a disadvantage from someone else's point of view.

If the workers in question were to increase their output, that may prove beneficial for the organisation's management team, but the workers themselves would feel their job security to be threatened.

## 2.4.2 Dealing with resistance

*Kotter and Schlesinger* (1979) identified six methods of dealing with **resistance to change**. They are:

(a)   **Education** and **communication**

This method is effective where the cause of the resistance is lack of information about the change.

(b)   **Participation** and **involvement**

Where those affected by the change have the power to resist it, this method reduces the resistance by taking their views into account.

(c)   **Facilitation** and **support**

Where the cause of the resistance is anxiety and insecurity, support such as training is effective.

(d)   **Negotiation** and **agreement**

Compensating those who lose out (for example redundancy packages) may be appropriate in some instances.

(e)   **Manipulation** and **co-optation**

This method involves the presentation of partial or misleading information to those resisting change or 'buying-off' the main individuals who are at the heart of the resistance.

(f)   **Explicit** and **implicit coercion**

Ultimately the use or threat of force to push through the change and the crush resistance may be the only option.

The six approaches are not intended to be used separately in isolation – a combination of them is likely to be required.

## 2.5 Restraining forces

Forces that may hinder the introduction and acceptance of change include:

(a)     Dislike of the work itself.

(b)     Fear that if they produce more, the organisation will then be unable to sustain sales at the higher level of output, so redundancies will ensue.

(c)     Fear that once higher output norms have been established, the organisation will expect such norms to be sustained permanently.

(d)     Dislike of the supervisor, the management and even the organisation as a whole, thereby making the workers unco-operative and resentful.

## 2.6 Driving forces

Forces that may be used to drive change through include:

(a)     Fear of dismissal if output falls below a reasonably well-defined rate acceptable to or tolerated by the management.

(b)     Financial incentives, without which output would be significantly lower than 70%.

(c)     Fear of losing special privileges, such as concessionary prices for the organisation's products or services.

(d)     Response to pressure from the management – and thus a desire to reduce that pressure to acceptable proportions.

Once the equilibrium has been established, the organisation may be content. Alternatively, management may believe that the disruption 'costs' arising from any disturbance to the *status quo* may outweigh the potential 'benefits' involved.

On the other hand, if management wants to increase output levels to, say, 80%, then logically this can only be done in **either** of the following ways.

(a)     **Overcoming resistance** through strengthening the driving forces, ie increasing management pressure, enhancing fears of dismissal and so forth

(b)     **Reducing resistance** by weakening the forces that currently hold down output, for example through job redesign, adoption of a more people-centred management style

**Exam focus point**

> In May 2005, candidates were required to discuss potential strategies for overcoming resistance to change and identify which would be most suitable for the organisation in the scenario.
>
> The November 2007 exam gave ten-marks for an evaluation of how an organisation has managed resistance to a change.

## 2.7 Introducing the change

There are three important factors for managers to consider when dealing with resistance to change.

*   The **pace** of change
*   The **manner** of change
*   The **scope** of change

Changes ought generally to be introduced slowly. Apart from 'people problems', there may be a long planning and administrative process and/or financial risks to be considered. For example, in a re-location of a factory a range of alternatives will have to be considered.

### 2.7.1 Pace

The more gradual the change, the more time is available for questions to be asked, reassurances to be given and retraining (where necessary) embarked upon. People can get used to the idea of new methods and become acclimatised at each stage.

(a)　Presenting the individuals concerned with change as a *fait accompli* may avoid resistance at the planning stage, but may result in resistance surfacing later – probably strengthened by resentment.

(b)　**Timing** will also be crucial: those responsible for change should be sensitive to incidents and attitudes that might indicate that 'now is not the time'.

## 2.7.2 Manner

The manner in which a change is put across (communicated) is very important. The need for change must made clear, fears soothed, and if possible the individuals concerned positively motivated to embrace the changes as their own.

(a)　**Resistance should be welcomed and confronted**, not swept under the carpet. Talking thorough areas of conflict may lead to useful insights and the adapting of the programme of change to advantage. Repressing resistance will only send it underground.

(b)　**There should be free circulation of information** about the reasons for the change, its expected results and likely consequences. That information should appear sensible, clear, consistent and realistic. There is no point issuing information which will be seen as a blatant misrepresentation of the situation.

(c)　**The change must be sold to the people concerned**. Objections must be overcome, but it is also possible to get people behind the change in a positive way. If those involved understand that there is a real problem, which poses a threat to the organisation and themselves, and that the solution is a sensible one and will solve that problem, there will be a firm rational basis, for implementing change. It may even be possible to get staff excited by the change, by emphasising the challenge and opportunity and perhaps by offering rewards and incentives.

(d)　**Individuals must be helped to learn**, that is, to change their attitudes and behaviours. Few individuals will really be able to see the big picture in a proposed programmed of change. In order to put across the overall objective, the organisation should use **visual aids** to help conceptualise. Learning programmes for any new skills or systems necessary will have to be designed according to the abilities of the individuals concerned.

(e)　The effects of **insecurity** and **resentment** may be lessened if people are **involved** in the planning and implementation of the change, so that it is not perceived to have been imposed from above.

## 2.7.3 Scope

The scope or extent of the change is important and should be reviewed. Total transformation will create greater insecurity – but also provides the opportunity for greater excitement – than moderate innovation.

There may be hidden changes to take into account: a change in technology may necessitate changes in work methods, which may in turn result in the breaking up of work groups. Management should be aware of how many various aspects of their employees' lives they are proposing to alter – and therefore on how many fronts they are likely to encounter resistance.

 Case Study

Watch out for examples of organisations undergoing change in the press and see how it is being handled. Technological change, takeovers, new conditions of work and relocations are amongst the many examples you may see reported.

**Exam focus point**

Change management is something of a 'hot topic' in today's business environment. It is therefore highly likely to be examined regularly. The syllabus specifically mentions theorists such as *Senge*, *Lewin*, *Peters*, and *Beer and Nohria*, so make sure you learn this material.

# 3 Commitment, co-ordination and communication

Commitment, co-ordination and communication play an important role in the context of introducing any form of change.

(a) **Commitment.** Commitment to the change must be universal including all involved. Senior management must demonstrate commitment in the allocation of resources required (people, money, time etc) to achieve change.

(b) **Co-ordination.** To implement change successfully requires co-ordination. This involves ensuring those involved in the process work in an efficient and effective way towards an agreed common goal. This requires planning and control.

(c) **Communication.** Successful change is extremely unlikely to be achieved without good communication. The right people must communicate the right things at the right time and in the right way. Good communication early in the process should ensure all are aware of what the process hopes to achieve. Communication during the process should aid co-ordination and to maintain momentum. Upon completion, communication is likely to focus on ensuring there is no revision to the previous behaviour – and a review of the process itself to see if any lessons may be learnt.

## Case Study

**Change Management, a pragmatic approach in Abbey National plc**

There have been many internal changes in Abbey National since becoming plc.

- Change from 49 to 5 mortgage administration centres.
- Set up of 3 Teleservice Centres.
- Introduction of postal accounts.
- Reduction in the number of branches.
- Combine administrations of Scottish Mutual and Abbey National Life under same customer service structure and systems.

People resist what they perceive that they will lose. Perception = reality. **Communication is critical. The effects of good communication**:

- Reduces uncertainty
- Builds commitment
- Shapes assumptions
- Involve the people in the process

**COMMUNICATE TO GAIN COMMITMENT**

**The communication process**

Step 1     Project team 'sell' concept to managers and supervisors

Step 2     Supervisors present to their team with support from project team

Step 3     Two day briefing/training for supervisors

Step 4     On-ground support for supervisors throughout implementation

Step 5     Remove support gradually

Step 6     Continuous improvement course

Step 7     Formal handover to managers

## Change issues encountered at Abbey National plc

- Supervisor's confidence destroyed (security blanket removed)
- No PC experience to operate spreadsheets
- Task of planning day takes too long, no time to do other work
- This would not work in our area because we are different
- Frightened of raising issues
- Focus on backlogs – no time to do process management

## Summary

- Involve the people who are impacted at all stages
- Caveat on initial stages or market sensitive projects
- Communicate, communicate, communicate – tailored, early, often – if you have nothing to say people may believe you have a hidden agenda
- Consider the cultural differences
- Do not forget managers

## What if you do not have the time to go through all the stages and give the level of support people require?

- Anticipate as many issues as possible
- Mobilise maximum power
- Expect/prepare for resistance

*Source: CIMA articles database*

## Question

*Change management*

Learning outcome: B(iii)

The recently-appointed Chief Executive Officer (CEO) of the F Steel Company is intent on making the organisation more competitive. He has made it clear that he considers current operational performance to be below acceptable levels. He recently stated, 'Costs are too high and productivity is too low'.

Demand for steel is growing, particularly in export markets such as countries in the Pacific rim, and the CEO believes F Steel should capitalise on this. To do this he believes some change to working conditions at F Steel will be required. A reduction of import duty in some proposed export markets would also be required for profitable trading.

The trade union that represents the steel workers in F Steel Company is well-organised and has promised the workers that it will defend their wage levels and working conditions.

*Required*

(a) List the forces for change and causes of resistance in the F Steel Company. Classify these according to whether they can be considered as deriving from internal or external sources.

10 marks

(b) Recommend how the newly-appointed Chief Executive Officer in the F Steel Company might go about managing the process of change.

10 marks

**(Total = 20 marks)**

## Answer

(a) **Forces for change – internal**

- Forceful new CEO
- Poor operational performance
- High costs
- Low productivity

**Forces for change – external**

- High export demand
- Only steady domestic demand for steel
- Customer complaints

**Forces resisting change – internal**

- Long-serving managers' complacency
- The trade union's attitude

**Force resisting change – external**

- High import duties in some export markets

(b)  Lewin suggests that after the forces for and against change have been established, effort should be put not only into breaking down those opposing it (which is a natural management response), but also into building up the influence of those supporting it.

This process is the first or 'unfreeze' phase of the Lewin/Schein change model. The CEO will have to set up both a programme of education and support for the complacent managers and enter into forceful negotiations with the trade union. The basic aim is to frighten both parties with evidence of looming disaster. This is clear enough from the company's competitive situation. Ansoff points out that an early crisis can be triggered in order to improve willingness to change.

The second phase of the Lewin/Schein change model requires action to change behaviour, laying down new patterns and reinforcing them. Residual resistance should be confronted with free circulation of information about plans for the future and why they are required. Individuals must be helped to change their attitudes and behaviours. An extensive programme of organisational development is probably required for the F Steel Company. There should be proper application of positive and negative reinforcement in the shape of rewards and sanctions.

The final phase of the model is 'refreeze'. This prevents the staff from slipping back into their old ways and attitudes by a combination of exhortation, reward for good performance and sanctions against the backsliders.

External forces are less susceptible to this treatment than internal ones. In the case of the F Steel Company, representations could be made to government about both the exchange rate and the unfair competition, perhaps through a trade association or other umbrella body. However, it is necessary to recognise that even if action is forthcoming, it is unlikely to be prompt.

# 4 Successful change

FAST FORWARD
*Daft* (1998) identified **four parameters** that are needed for change to be successful.

| Parameter | Explanation |
|---|---|
| The need for change is identified | A perceived need for change is required if proposals are to be taken seriously. |
| Adoption of the proposed change | Key decision-makers, managers and employees must agree to adopt the change. |
| Resources are available | Resources such as finance, time and management support must be made available. |
| Implementation | Materials and equipment must be purchased; employees must be trained. |

*Daft* also described managerial barriers to successful change.

| Barrier | Explanation |
|---|---|
| Excessive focus on cost | Managers may focus on cost at the expense of employee motivation or customer satisfaction. |
| Failure to highlight benefits | The positive benefits must be communicated so it is perceived that they outweigh any negatives. |
| Lack of co-ordination and co-operation | Incompatible systems and internal conflicts between departments may slow down or prevent a successful implementation. |
| Uncertainty avoidance | Managers naturally fear uncertainty that change brings. They should seek to prevent a 'blame culture' developing by constantly communicating with their team, helping to reduce uncertainty. |
| Fear of loss | Uncertainty causes fear in managers that their power, status or even job is at risk. The organisation should focus attention on management to reduce this fear. |

# 5 Information technology and change management

## 5.1 Introducing a new information system

FAST FORWARD

Research seems to indicate that the major cause of information systems failure is **inadequate user involvement**. Users need to be involved in the development process at all stages – including system design.

One example of change is the implementation of an information system using information technology. Unfortunately, new information systems often fail to bring the benefits expected.

One common cause of dissatisfaction with new information systems is **insufficient user involvement** when establishing requirements for the new system. This is particularly true if the traditional systems development life cycle is followed.

Other **common causes of dissatisfaction** with information systems include:

(a)   IS project managers are often **technicians**, not managers. Technical ability for IS staff is no guarantee of management skill – an individual might be a highly proficient analyst or programmer, but **not a good manager**.

(b)   The project manager may accept **an unrealistic deadline** – the timescale is fixed early in the planning process. User demands may be accepted as deadlines before sufficient consideration is given to the realism of this.

(c)   **Poor or non-existent planning** is a recipe for disaster. Unrealistic deadlines would be identified much earlier if a proper planning process was undertaken.

(d)   A lack of **monitoring** and **control**.

(e)   Users **change their requirements**, resulting in changes to the system as it is being developed.

(f)   **Poor timetabling and resourcing**. It is no use being presented on Day 1 with a team of programmers, when there is still systems analysis and design work to do. The development and implementation of a computer project may take a considerable length of time (perhaps two years for a relatively large installation). Major projects require formal planning and scheduling.

The project manager has a number of **conflicting requirements**.

(a)   The **systems manager**, usually the project manager's boss, wants the project **delivered on time**, to specification and within budget.

(b)   **User** expectations may be misunderstood, ignored or unrealistic.

(c)   The project manager has to plan and supervise the work of **analysts** and **programmers** and these are rather different roles.

A project is affected by a number of factors, often in **conflict** with each other.

(a) **Quality** of the system required, in terms of basic system requirements.

(b) **Time**, both to complete the project, and in terms of the opportunity cost of time spent on this project which could be spent on others.

(c) **Costs** and resources allocated to the project.

The balance between the constraints of time, cost and quality will be different for each project. If a system aims to provide competitive advantage then time will tend to be the dominant factor. If safety is paramount (eg an auto-pilot system) then quality will be most important. If the sole aim of a project is to meet administrative needs that are not time dependent, then cost may be the dominant factor.

The relationship can be shown as a triangle.

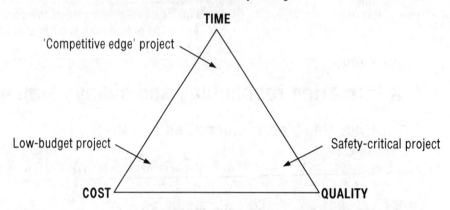

**The Time/Cost/Quality Triangle**

The balance of time, cost and quality will influence decision making throughout the project – for example whether to spend an extra £5,000 to fix a problem completely or only spend £1,000 on a quick fix and implement a user work-around.

## 5.2 Problems in the development process

Problems that occur when implementing a new information system can usually be traced to **deficiencies in the development process**. The table that follows outlines some common mistakes that adversely affect the implementation process – and the systems development stage or activity they relate to.

| Stage/activity | Problems |
|---|---|
| **Analysis** | The problem the system is intended to solve is not fully understood. |
| | Investigation of the situation is hindered by insufficient resources. |
| | User input is inadequate through either lack of consultation or lack of user interest. |
| | The project team is unable to dedicate the time required or insufficient time spent planning the project. |
| **Design** | Insufficient user input. |
| | Lack of flexibility. The organisation's future needs are neglected. |
| | The system requires unforeseen changes in working patterns. |
| | Failure to perform organisation impact analysis. An organisational impact analysis studies the way a proposed system will affect organisation structure, attitudes, decision making and operations. The analysis aims to ensure the system is designed to best ensure integration with the organisation. |
| | Organisational factors sometimes overlooked include: |
| | • Ergonomics (including equipment, work environment and user interfaces) |
| | • Health and safety |
| | • Compliance with legislation |
| | • Job design |
| | • Employee involvement |

| Stage/activity | Problems |
|---|---|
| **Programming** | Insufficient time and money allocated to programming. |
| | Programmers supplied with incomplete or inaccurate specifications. |
| | The logic of the program is misunderstood. |
| | Poor programming technique results in programs that are hard to modify. |
| | Programs are not adequately documented. |
| **Testing** | Insufficient time and money allocated to testing. |
| | Failure to develop an organised testing plan. |
| | Insufficient user involvement. |
| | User management do not review and sign-off the results of testing. |
| **Conversion** | Insufficient time and money allocated to data conversion. |
| | Insufficient checking between old and new files. |
| | The process is rushed to compensate for time overruns elsewhere. |
| **Implementation** | Insufficient time, money and/or appropriate staff mean the process has to be rushed. |
| | Lack of user training increases the risk of system under-utilisation and rejection. |
| | Poor system and user documentation. |
| | Lack of performance standards to assess system performance against. |
| | System maintenance provisions are inadequate. |

## 5.3 Overcoming user resistance

A recurring theme when examining the reasons for information system failure is user resistance. We will now examine the findings of research into causes of user resistance. Three types of theory that explain user resistance are explained in the following table.

| Theory | Description | Overcoming the resistance |
|---|---|---|
| **People-oriented** | User-resistance is caused by factors internal to users as individuals or as a group. <br><br> For example, users may not wish to disrupt their current work practices and social groupings. | User training. <br> Organisation policies. <br> Persuasion. <br> User involvement in system development. |
| **System-oriented** | User-resistance is caused by factors inherent in the new system design relating to ease of use and functionality. <br><br> For example, a poorly designed user-interface will generate user-resistance. | User training and education. <br> Improve user-interface. <br> Ensure users contribute to the system design process. <br> Ensure the system 'fits' with the organisation. |
| **Interaction** | User-resistance is caused by the interaction of people and the system. <br><br> For example, the system may be well-designed but its implementation will cause organisational changes that users resist eg reduced chance of bonuses, redundancies, monotonous work. | Re-organise the organisation before implementing the system. <br> Redesign any affected incentive schemes to incorporate the new system. <br> Promote user participation and encourage organisation-wide teamwork. <br> Emphasise the benefits the system brings. |

## 5.4 IT and change: other issues

### 5.4.1 Constant change

A reliance on IS/IT commits an organisation to continual change. The pace of technological change is rapid. Computer systems – both hardware and software – are likely to be superseded after a few years.

### 5.4.2 Information technology (IT) as an enabler of change

FAST FORWARD IT can play a significant role as an **enabler** in the change management process.

In some circumstances information technology may be the driving force or trigger of organisational change. Even when IT is not a significant factor in the actual change, it can play an important part in the change management process.

| IT's possible role in organisational change | Comment |
|---|---|
| The type of products or services that are made and sold | For example, companies like Sony manufacture home computers, Virgin have an Internet Service Provider business. Technological changes affect many products, for example the introduction of tennis and squash rackets with graphite frames. |
| The way in which products are made | There is a continuing trend towards the use of automation and computer aided design and manufacture. The manufacturing environment is undergoing rapid changes with the growth of advanced manufacturing technology. For example, Computer Integrated Manufacturing (CIM) changed the methods and cost profiles of many manufacturing processes. The techniques used to **measure and record costs** have also adapted to the use of IT. |
| The way in which employees are mobilised | Computerisation encourages de-layering of organisational hierarchies and greater workforce empowerment and skills. Using technology frequently requires changes in working methods. |
| The way in which services are provided | High-street banks encourage customers to use 'hole-in-the-wall' cash dispensers, or telephone or Internet banking. Most larger shops now use computerised **Point of Sale terminals** at cash desks. Many organisations use **e-commerce**: selling products and services over the Internet. |
| IT acts as an enabling technology | IT can produce dramatic changes in individual businesses and whole industries. For example, competition in the airline industry has intensified due to information systems that allow easy fare comparison and booking. IT can be both a **cause** of major changes in doing business and a **response** to them. |
| Communication and co-ordination | As explained earlier in this chapter, co-ordination is essential when introducing change. IT can facilitate this through the use of e-mail, project management software, an intranet, groupware etc. |
| Source of unity and structure | In times of restructuring, information systems can be a visible sign of the new situation. For example, an organisation-wide network perhaps with an intranet provides evidence of and encourages acceptance of the new situation. |

## 5.5 Change and real-life

It is worth remembering that change theory is just that – theory. In the real world nothing is ever straightforward and you should bear in mind that not all theories are workable in a given situation and that parts of theories may be used together to manage change.

*Michael Jarrett* (2005) touched on this when he identified 7 'myths of change'. These myths are: change creates value; resistance can be overcome; change is constant and can be managed; the change agent knows best; change requires following prescribed steps and that big change requires big changes. You should bear these in mind when tackling exam questions.

## Question

Which of the following types of system could be used to help with co-ordination and communication in change management?

A     Intranet
B     Project management software
C     E-mail
D     All of the above

## Answer

D     All of these systems could be used to aid co-ordination and communication in the change process.

**Exam focus point**

In May 2006, a 20-mark Section C question required candidates to analyse a scenario facing some organisations and:

(a)     Discuss the dangers of it not responding to change.
(b)     Discuss the types of change they could make in order to survive and prosper.

# Chapter Roundup

- The Lewin/Schein three stage **model of change** identifies key steps as Unfreeze, Move and Refreeze.

- Change involves **structural** and **behavioural** factors. **Resistance** to change results from individual uncertainties and distrust of management. Some resistance may result from **uncertainty** about the nature of the change itself, or from poor information.

- Lewin's **force field analysis** maps the forces that are **pushing toward the preferred state** and the restraining forces, which are **pushing back to the current state**. They can then be presented in a chart.

- **Commitment**, **co-ordination** and **communication** play an important role in the context of introducing any form of change.

- *Daft* (1998) identified **four parameters** that are needed for change to be successful.

- Research seems to indicate that the major cause of information systems failure is **inadequate user involvement**. Users need to be involved in the development process at all stages – including system design.

- **IT** can play a significant role as an **enabler** in the change management process.

# Quick Quiz

1   State the three stages of Lewin's model for changing the behaviour of individuals.

2   What causes resistance to change?

3   What is force field analysis?

4   *Fill in the gaps.*

    C..................., c.................. and c.................. play important roles when introducing change to an organisation.

5   Most research indicates that the major cause of information systems failure is inadequate user involvement.

    True    ☐

    False   ☐

# Answers to Quick Quiz

1   Unfreeze, change (or move) and refreeze.

2   Attitudes, beliefs, loyalties, habits and norms, politics.

3   Lewin's analysis of the driving and restraining forces which underlie any group or organisational equilibrium.

4   Commitment, co-ordination and communication.

5   True. Inadequate user information is a common cause of information system failure.

Now try the question below from the Exam Question Bank

| Number | Level | Marks | Time |
|--------|-------|-------|------|
| 14 | Examination | 30 | 54 mins |

# Objective test
# question and answer bank

Each of the questions numbered **1** to **10** has only ONE correct answer. Each of these questions is worth **2 marks**.

1  Which one of the following statements explaining examples of the advantages that a computer-based accounting system has over a manual system is false?

   A    A computer-based accounting system is easier to update as new information becomes available

   B    A computer-based accounting system will always reject inaccurate financial information

   C    Financial calculations can be performed more quickly and accurately

   D    The management accountant can more readily present financial information to other business departments in a variety of forms

2  The systems development life cycle model, as developed by the National Computing Centre in the 1960s, has six stages. Four of these are: Feasibility study; Systems analysis and design; Systems implementation; Review and maintenance. What are the other two stages in the systems development life cycle model?

   A    Budgeting and systems management

   B    Systems control and systems acceptance

   C    Problem identification and systems investigation

   D    Systems investigation and systems management

3  Duplication of data within a database is referred to as which one of the following?

   A    Data independence

   B    Data redundancy

   C    Data sufficiency

   D    Data warehousing

4  Which one of the following statements relating to systems investigation is correct?

   A    Interviews with user staff are not an effective method of fact finding in a system investigation

   B    A cost-benefit analysis is performed at the system investigation stage

   C    During the system investigation phase of a project development, an assessment is made of the strengths and weaknesses of the proposed system

   D    Some aspects of systems investigation may be carried out during the feasibility study for an information systems development project

5  An employee who exposes the ethical misconduct of others in an organisation is known as a(n):

   A    Ombudsman

   B    Whistleblower

   C    Mentor

   D    Monitor

6  Group selection methods are most often used when selecting for management positions. Why is this?

   A    Applicants for other positions may not understand the process

   B    They are proven to always result in the correct applicant being selected

   C    These methods tend to be expensive

   D    To flush out those unwilling to participate

7   To be of use for marketing research purposes a segmentation variable must define a market segment that has three characteristics. What are they?

   A   Measurability, stability, accessibility
   B   Stability, substantiality, measurability
   C   Substantiality measurability, accessibility
   D   Stability, accessibility, substantiality

8   Environmental entropy can lead to an organisation's demise. Which of the following is an example of environmental entropy?

   A   Environmental legislation imposing a 'carbon tax' on power generation
   B   A falling birth rate
   C   The imposition of a luxury tax on certain goods
   D   All of the above

9   Which of the following is not part of the 'unfreeze' stage of the Lewin/Schein change model?

   A   Provision of motivation for change
   B   Alterations to the power structure
   C   Adoption of a new culture
   D   A trigger for the change process

10  Which of the following are attributes of an effective change agent?

   (i)     Communication skills
   (ii)    Political awareness
   (iii)   Understanding of relevant processes
   (iv)    Negotiation skills

   A   (i), (iii) and (iv) only
   B   (ii), (iii) and (iv) only
   C   (iii) and (iv) only
   D   All of the above

---

Each of the questions numbered **11** to **15** require a brief written response. The response should be in note form and should not exceed 50 words. Each of these questions is worth **4 marks**.

---

11  Explain what is meant by the term business-process re-engineering.

12  Describe the philosophy of lean production.

13  Distinguish quality assurance from quality control.

14  Explain why three additional Ps are sometimes added to the original four Ps of the marketing mix.

15  Explain the meaning and the thinking behind employee empowerment.

1  B  Statement B is false as, even with built in safeguards, some incorrect information may be input into a computer system.

2  C  The systems development life cycle begins with the identification of a problem or opportunity. The next stages, in sequence, are carrying put a feasibility study, systems investigation (fact finding), systems analysis and design, systems implementation and review and maintenance.

3  B  Duplication of data within a database is known as redundancy. Data independence refers to the independence of the logical data in a database from its physical storage location, and the independence of the data from the programs that access it.

4  D  Some aspects of systems investigation may be carried out largely during the feasibility study of an information systems project.

5  B  A whistleblower reveals devious, unethical or illegal practices.

6  C  Group selection methods are time consuming and require the presence of skilled observers/interviewers. They are particularly useful for assessing interpersonal skills and personality traits. They are usually considered too expensive to be justified for many positions. (Note - option B is incorrect as no recruitment technique is guaranteed to result in the best candidate being chosen in all cases.)

7  C  Stability might seem like a desirable feature in its own right, but it is covered by substantiality.

8  D  All are examples of change in the environment - which in systems terminology may be referred to as environmental entropy.

9  C  This would form part of the 'move' or 'change' phase.

10  D  They are all attributes of an effective change agent.

11  **Business Process Re-engineering** (BPR) involves the radical redesign of business processes to achieve improvements in areas such as cost, quality, service and speed. BPR is more than the automation or computerisation of existing ways of doing things – it involves significant redesign of working methods.

12  **Lean production** aims to minimise the amount of resources (including time) used in all activities of an enterprise. It involves identifying and eliminating all non-value-adding activities. Lean production involves the systematic elimination of all forms of waste.

13  **Quality assurance** focuses on the way a product or service is produced. Production procedures and standards are introduced that aim to prevent defects before the good/service is produced. Quality control focuses on the checking of work that has been done – finding mistakes after the event rather than eliminating them.

14  The **traditional 'four Ps'** (product, price, place, promotion) were related to consumer goods. The three extra Ps (People, Processes, Physical evidence) were added to more accurately reflect the issues relating to services (eg for insurance: representative, the policy setting and selling process, insurance certificate).

15  **Employee empowerment** means giving staff at all levels the authority and freedom to make decisions that affect how they do their job. The thinking behind the theory is that those who actually do the work are best positioned to make decisions relating to how their work is done.

# Exam question and answer bank

# What the examiner means

The table below has been prepared by CIMA to help you interpret exam questions.

| Learning objective | Verbs used | Definition |
|---|---|---|
| **1 Knowledge**<br>What you are expected to know | • List<br>• State<br>• Define | • Make a list of<br>• Express, fully or clearly, the details of/facts of<br>• Give the exact meaning of |
| **2 Comprehension**<br>What you are expected to understand | • Describe<br>• Distinguish<br>• Explain<br>• Identify<br>• Illustrate | • Communicate the key features of<br>• Highlight the differences between<br>• Make clear or intelligible/state the meaning of<br>• Recognise, establish or select after consideration<br>• Use an example to describe or explain something |
| **3 Application**<br>How you are expected to apply your knowledge | • Apply<br>• Calculate/ compute<br>• Demonstrate<br>• Prepare<br>• Reconcile<br>• Solve<br>• Tabulate | • Put to practical use<br>• Ascertain or reckon mathematically<br>• Prove with certainty or to exhibit by practical means<br>• Make or get ready for use<br>• Make or prove consistent/compatible<br>• Find an answer to<br>• Arrange in a table |
| **4 Analysis**<br>How you are expected to analyse the detail of what you have learned | • Analyse<br>• Categorise<br>• Compare and contrast<br>• Construct<br>• Discuss<br>• Interpret<br>• Produce | • Examine in detail the structure of<br>• Place into a defined class or division<br>• Show the similarities and/or differences between<br>• Build up or compile<br>• Examine in detail by argument<br>• Translate into intelligible or familiar terms<br>• Create or bring into existence |
| **5 Evaluation**<br>How you are expected to use your learning to evaluate, make decisions or recommendations | • Advise<br>• Evaluate<br>• Recommend | • Counsel, inform or notify<br>• Appraise or assess the value of<br>• Advise on a course of action |

# 1 External information

**Learning outcomes: A (iv), A (vii)**

JM Ltd is a private company which manufactures a range of packaging materials for customers in the fresh and frozen food industries. Before his recent retirement, the company's chairman and founder was the main source of external information – he kept his 'finger on the pulse' of the industry utilising his network of personal contacts built up over a period of some twenty years. Since his retirement, the board has felt that external information has been lacking. They wish to implement a formal system to capture relevant external information.

*Required*

(a)   Describe the aspects of its environment that JM Ltd should gather information on and the sources that may provide it. (22 marks)

(b)   Explain four ways the board could use the captured information. (8 marks)

(Total = 30 marks)

# 2 ERM, stages of development MIS

54 mins

**Learning outcomes: A (iii), A (v)**

ABC Ltd supplies small tools, fixings such as nails and screws, paint and similar DIY materials to individual customers and small home improvement and decorating businesses. Sales are made from a central warehouse in a large city. Sales to private customers are usually on a cash basis, most sales to small companies are on credit, with up to 30 days' payment terms being offered. Most invoices are for a relatively low value, with £42 being the average invoice amount.

The company has been relatively successful, and has made a small profit in each of the last five years of trading. However, there has been a lack of investment in IT systems.

Many of the employees at ABC (there are 24 full-time staff) have a long service history, and the directors tend to run the company on the basis of trust, rather than 'waste time', as they put it, introducing complicated systems.

**Current systems and problems with them**

ABC operates various computer systems; they are old, but generally reliable. The directors had no specific plans for upgrading the systems until a series of incidents which took place in the last few weeks:

1   Significant delays were noted and errors found in the credit sales system.

2   A review of the stock system found that cost price of stock purchased for resale was based on the historical prices of five years ago, rather than the current price. This was in effect under-pricing goods.

3   There are no up-to-date management accounts and very limited management information. A Management Information System proposed two years ago was not implemented due to lack of time on the part of the Chairman (who was also the nominal IT Director because no other director wanted the job).

The directors are now considering introducing an integrated accounts package. An initial review of current systems included a detailed review of the existing credit sales system. Notes from this review are shown below:

**Existing Sales System – Credit sales**

The system is partly manual and partly computerised, having been written in-house about 15 years ago by the chairman's son as a software project at university. It is basically a recording system only, it lacks the controls found as standard in most modern computerised accounting system packages.

The main steps in the system are:

**Step 1**    Goods are despatched to customers using one despatch note per delivery. Despatches are made either by the customer collecting the goods from the company directly, or via a courier service.

**Step 2**    Despatch note information is transferred daily onto a sales invoice proforma produced using a PC and word processing software. More than one despatch note can appear on one sales invoice where a customer places more than one order during a day. For example, Despatch Note numbers 10109 and 11092 for customer Jones both appear on invoice 66203. Transposition errors occur frequently when the despatch note numbers are entered onto the sales invoice.

**Step 3**    Despatch notes are filed in date order with no check to ensure the numeric sequence is complete.

**Step 4**    After printing out, sales invoices are re-input individually into the sales day book and sales ledger. These computer systems are maintained in another department.

**Step 5**    Copy sales invoices are sent to each customer at the end of each week. More than one sales invoice may be sent to one customer if the customer has made purchases on more than one day during that week. For example, Sales Invoice 66203 for sales made on Tuesday will be sent to the customer with invoice 67321 for sales made on Friday.

**Step 6**    Customers pay invoices by cheque. Payments normally relate to more than one sales invoice. For example, cheque number 100976 from customer Jones may pay Sales Invoices 66203, 67321 and 68903.

**Step 7**    Cheque are recorded individually in the cash book.

**Step 8**    Cheques are also recorded in the sales ledger from CB information. However, some invoices are only partly paid where queries about individual despatches have not been cleared. For example, Cheque 100976 paid invoices 66203 and 67321 in full, but only partly paid sales invoice 68903. The remaining amount on Invoice 68903 will be paid on cheque 101076 in the following week.

**Step 9**    All cheques are grouped together and banked on a daily basis.

**Step 10**    A report of all overdue debts is produced on a weekly basis from the sales ledger. The part payment of invoices causes difficulties for debt collection, because the computer system flags a part payment as fully paying the invoice and moves the remaining balance into a global 'part-paid invoices' section of the ledger. This account was used because it was thought that part-payments would be relatively rare; however, about one in a hundred payments fall into this category making the system very difficult to maintain.

**Lack of management information**

The lack of management information has concerned the board, although to date, provision of this information has not been a major objective. A consultant has been appointed to review the existing systems and implement a high-level Management Information System for use by the directors and other strategic managers.

*Required*

(a)    Prepare an Entity Relationship Model for the sales and cheque receipts system.    (10 marks)

(b)    Explain the main stages involved in the SDLC and describe the main issues/activities required at each stage of the SDLC for the proposed MIS at ABC.    (20 marks)

**(Total = 30 marks)**

# 3 Service level agreement; obtaining IT services    54 mins

**Learning outcome: A (vii)**

The directors of DS are not satisfied with the GDC Ltd facilities management company. The appointment of GDC Ltd was relatively rushed and although an outline contract was agreed, no detailed Service Level Agreement was produced. Details of the contract follow.

---

The contract can be terminated by either party with three months' notice.

GDC Ltd will provide IT services for DS, the services to include:

- Purchase of all hardware and software
- Repair and maintenance of all IT equipment
- Help desk and other support services for users
- Writing and maintenance of in-house software
- Provision of management information

Price charged to be renegotiated each year but any increase must not exceed inflation, plus 10%.

---

*Required*

(a)  Explain, from the point of view of DS, why it might have received poor service from GDC Ltd, even though GDC Ltd has met the requirements of the contract.    (12 marks)

(b)  Explain the courses of action now available to DS relating to the provision of IT services. Comment on the problems involved in each course of action.    (8 marks)

(c)  Explain the benefits of outsourcing that DS would have enjoyed if the contract and SLA had been drafted properly.    (10 marks)

**(Total = 30 marks)**

# 4 Operations strategy    27 mins

**Learning outcome: C (i)**

Six factors that should be taken into account when devising an operations strategy are:

- Capability
- Range and location of operations
- Investment in technology
- Strategic buyer-supplier relationships
- New products/services
- Structure of operations

*Required*

Briefly describe what each of the six factors identified above mean in the context of operations strategy.

Illustrate your answer with examples related to a retail supermarket chain.    **(15 marks)**

# 5 Inventories and JIT    54 mins

**Learning outcomes: C (i), C (iii)**

(a)  In relation to inventory control levels, briefly explain the following.

|  |  |  |
|---|---|---|
| (i) | Reorder level | (2 marks) |
| (ii) | Minimum level | (2 marks) |
| (iii) | Maximum level | (2 marks) |
| (iv) | Reorder quantity | (2 marks) |
| (v) | Average inventory | (2 marks) |

(b)  Identify and explain five features of a just-in-time (JIT) production system.    (15 marks)

(c)  Identify the financial benefits of JIT.    (5 marks)

**(Total = 30 marks)**

# 6 Business process re-engineering (BPR)                54 mins

**Learning outcome: C (ix)**

AB Ltd was established over a century ago and manufactures water pumps of various kinds. Until recently it has been successful, but imports of higher quality pumps at lower prices are now rapidly eroding its market share. The managing director feels helpless in the face of this onslaught from international competitors and is frantically searching for a solution to the problem. In his desperation, he consults a range of management journals and comes across what seems to be a wonder cure by the name of Business Process Re-engineering (BPR). According to the article, the use of BPR has already transformed the performance of a significant number of companies in the USA which were mentioned in the article, and is now being widely adopted by European companies. Unfortunately, the remainder of the article which purports to explain BPR is full of management jargon and he is left with only a vague idea of how it works.

*Required*

(a)     Explain the nature of BPR and describe how it might be applied to a manufacturing company like AB Ltd.                                                                                  (10 marks)

(b)     Describe a five-step process that AB Ltd can use to develop and implement BPR.     (10 marks)

(c)     Describe the major pitfalls for managers attempting to re-engineer their organisations.   (10 marks)

**(Total = 30 marks)**

# 7 Job descriptions                                        54 mins

**Learning outcome: E (iii)**

(a)     Discuss the following issues related to job descriptions.

    (i)      Their purpose                                                                  (5 marks)

    (ii)     Their benefits                                                                 (6 marks)

    (iii)    Their possible disadvantages                                                  (6 marks)

(b)     Identify (very briefly) six characteristics or features of an effective job description.     (3 marks)

(c)     Describe five attributes that a person specification may include.                          (10 marks)

**(Total = 30 marks)**

# 8 Carrot and stick                                        36 mins

**Learning outcome: E (iv)**

In *Turning People On: The Motivation Challenge*, Andrew Sargent states that: 'Gone the days when managers could resort to the 'carrot and stick' approach to motivate the workforce.'

Explain what you believe Sargent means by this remark, and comment on the extent to which you agree with his sentiments.                                                                       **(20 marks)**

**Note**: You don't need to be familiar with Sargent's writing to answer this question – it is sufficient to know that carrot means 'reward' and stick means 'punishment'.

# 9 Appraisal                                               54 mins

**Learning outcomes: E (ii), E (iii)**

(a)     Explain the reasons why appraisals are needed to effectively review performance and improve it in the future.                                                                           (10 marks)

(b)     Identify and explain the features of an effective performance appraisal system.          (10 marks)

(c)     Discuss the advantages and disadvantages of performance appraisal systems.             (10 marks)

**(Total = 30 marks)**

# 10 The marketing concept                                    36 mins

**Learning outcome: D (i)**

Explain what is meant by 'the marketing concept'. Compare this with a product orientation and a sales orientation.                                        **(20 marks)**

# 11 Marketing research                                       54 mins

**Learning outcomes: D (ii), D (iv)**

An organisation wishes to improve customer service through better distribution of its product lines to retail stores. Currently, the computerised ordering system is linked directly to major retail customers (who represent more than 70% of total business) through Electronic Data Interchange (EDI). Using this technology the firm is able to supply 90% of its product lines in less than three working days and 50% within 24 hours.

The organisation is planning to carry out specific marketing research with the aim of identifying areas of possible improvement in the distribution and logistics function.

*Required*

Produce a report for the marketing manager that identifies and explains:

(a)    The key stages necessary in conducting such research.                    (15 marks)

(b)    Specific objectives for the marketing research and how the research should be conducted.
                                                                               (15 marks)

                                                                    **(Total = 30 marks)**

# 12 Internet-based marketing communications          54 mins

**Learning outcome: D (v)**

For many organisations, business-to-business marketing communications have been transformed by the development of the Internet and related digital technologies. Prepare notes for a meeting at which you are expected to argue the case **for** the development of Internet-based marketing communications (you may base your answer on a business or company of your choice).                    **(30 marks)**

# 13 Organisation life cycle and corporate decline    54 mins

**Learning outcome: B (i)**

(a)    Describe the stages of an organisation's life cycle, according to Greiner's model. Comment on how useful you think models of an organisation life cycle are.                (14 marks)

(b)    Briefly explain how the management information required would change as an organisation moves through the phases of the life cycle.                                (6 marks)

(c)    (i)     List four causes of corporate decline.                          (2 marks)
       (ii)    Briefly describe four strategies companies can use to manage corporate decline.
                                                                               (8 marks)

                                                                    **(Total = 30 marks)**

# 14 Change

**54 mins**

Learning outcomes: B (i), B (ii), B(iii), B (iv)

(a)     Explain five drivers of change that organisations may face.                                    (10 marks)

(b)     Identify and explain the main reasons why it is often difficult to introduce change in organisations.
                                                                                                        (10 marks)

(c)     Identify and explain the key processes that help to bring about the successful implementation of
        change in organisations.                                                                         (10 marks)

**(Total = 30 marks)**

# 1 External information

(a)     Some aspects of JM Ltd's **external environment** will be more important for the company than others. Just what the most important aspects are vary from organisation to organisation. The first step that should therefore be taken is for an individual or a committee to be appointed to establish (and subsequently review) what aspects of the external environment should be monitored by formal methods and procedures.

The aspects of the environment that might be monitored include the following.

(i)     **Competitors**. Information should be gathered about what competitors are doing, how successful they are and how much of a threat they are. New contracts awarded by food companies will be of interest to JM Ltd.

(ii)    **Suppliers**. Information should be gathered about suppliers and potential suppliers, their prices, product or service quality and delivery dates etc.

(iii)   **Customers**. An organisation should always try to be aware of the needs of its customers, to identify changes in these needs, to recognise potential market segments, and to assess the size of a potential market. Customer awareness is vital for new product development and successful selling.

(iv)    **Legal changes**. Changes in the law might affect how an organisation operates, and any such changes should be monitored. For example, changes in data protection legislation.

(v)     **Political changes**. Some organisations are affected by national or local politics. If politics can be important, the organisation should try to monitor political decisions at both national and local level.

(vi)    **Financial and economic conditions**. Most organisations have to monitor developments in financial and economic conditions. As just one example, a company's treasury department must be aware of current money market interest rates and foreign exchange rates. As another example, the general rate of inflation is significant for decisions about wage increases for employees.

(vii)   **Environmental pressures**. The use of CFCs in packaging has been identified as contributing to the hole in the ozone layer. Companies such as JM Ltd therefore need to find alternative materials to use in their products.

Once the main types of environmental information have been identified, JM Ltd should then establish the following.

(i)     The most **appropriate sources** for obtaining this information. This will vary according to the nature of the information.

(ii)    The individuals or departments **whose task** it should be to gather the information, and where appropriate, disseminate it through the organisation to other people who might need it.

(iii)   The **form** in which the information should be disseminated through the organisation.

**Sources of information**

(i)    **Suppliers'** price lists and brochures.

(ii)    **Published reports and accounts** (of competitors, suppliers and business customers).

(iii)    **Government** reports (often, reports on specific topics. Economic and trade reports, for example, are frequently produced by central government).

(iv)    Government statistics.

(v)    External databases, provided by specialist organisations and often available over the **Internet**. Treasury departments, for example, use external databases to obtain information about current interest rates and foreign exchange rates.

(vi)    Newspaper and other **media** reports.

(b)    The board will take a **strategic approach** when using the captured information. It is likely to use the information for:

    (i)    **Planning**. The information will help JM Ltd to formulate a plan to react to the external environment and therefore assist with, among other things, **resource** planning, assessing possible **time-scales** for implementation and the likely impact of **alternative scenarios** on the company.

    (ii)    **Controlling**. Once the plan is implemented, its actual performance must be controlled. Information is required to assess **whether it is proceeding as planned** or whether there is some unexpected deviation from plan. It may consequently be necessary to take some form of corrective action.

    (iii)    **Performance measurement**. Overall performance of the plan must be measured in order to enable its success or failure to be determined. Constant monitoring of the external factors will help the board keep the plan on course.

    (iv)    **Decision making**. The board requires information to make informed decisions. Without it they cannot react logically to the situation that faces JM Ltd.

# 2 ERM, stages of development MIS

**Top tips**. Although it is unlikely you will be asked to draw a diagram such as an ERM, DFD or ELH in the exam, your understanding of these models may be tested. By drawing a model you should gain the knowledge and understanding required – but don't panic if your model is not 'perfect'.

(a)    See the ERM on the following page.

(a)

Entity Relationship Model - ABC Ltd Sales and cheque receipts

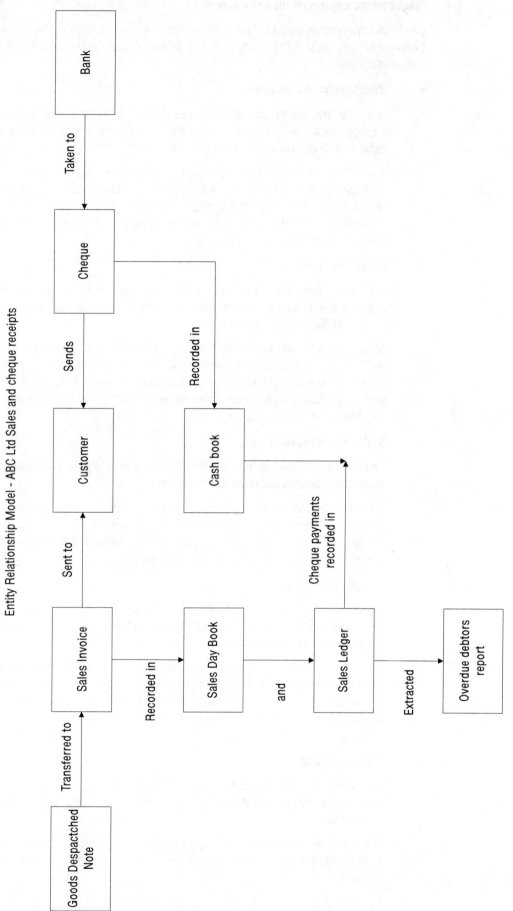

(b)    **Stages for the implementation of a new MIS**

One model that may be used as a guide when implementing a new MIS is the Systems Development Life Cycle (SDLC), although other techniques are just as valid. The SDLC has the following stages.

- **Identification of a problem**

    This stage involves an analysis of an organisation's information requirements. The analysis is carried out in conjunction with the users of the system so that the actual requirements, rather than likely requirements, can be determined.

    Within ABC Ltd there is already a recognised need for a new MIS. Recent errors within the stock system also highlight the need for additional management control. Discussions should be held with the various managers /board members to identify exactly what information they require, and this should be compared to a review of the existing manual system and the information this provides.

- **Feasibility study**

    This stage normally involves a review of the existing system and the generation of a range of possible solutions for the new MIS. One system will be selected based on the costs and benefits of the available systems.

    At ABC this will involve using the requirements identified in the problem identification stage and a review of what MIS's are available. A summary of the costs and benefits of the most suitable systems should be produced, and a decision made at the end of this stage on which system to implement. An Important consideration will be compatibility with the proposed new integrated accounts package.

- **Systems investigation**

    This is a detailed investigation into the existing system to obtain information on response times, data volumes and other key indicators.

    Given that there is no existing computerised MIS, this stage will focus on checking what information is already produced by the current systems in ABC, and then determining how this can be incorporated into the new MIS. It is now that standards should be set as to how information will be held and produced by the MIS.

- **Systems analysis**

    Systems analysis involves a detailed analysis of existing systems to determine why methods are being used, what the alternative methods are and what the performance criteria for the systems should be.

    Due to the lack of up-to-date systems within ABC, this stage will involve checking documentation like the Entity Relationship Model (from part (a)) to ensure an understanding of how systems in ABC actually work. A review of the specification of the integrated accounts package that will be purchased to ensure it fits the expected working methods and will be able to 'talk' to the MIS.

- **Systems design**

    Having obtained all the information about the existing systems, the proposed accounts package and the possible MIS's, this stage involves producing a detailed systems design for the new MIS.

    This would involve showing the outputs to be produced, how those outputs will be produced by the MIS, and what inputs and processes will be required to provide the outputs.

- **Systems implementation**

    As the name suggests, in this stage the MIS will be implemented into ABC Ltd.

    The main issues with implementation are likely to be the linking to other accounts packages, and ensuring that staff are aware of new working methods. The MIS should be thoroughly tested before implementation, particularly checking of the accuracy and suitability of management information produced.

- **Review and maintenance**

    This is an ongoing process which checks that the objectives set at the beginning of the feasibility study have been met, and that the performance of the system is satisfactory.

    At ABC this stage will involve checking again that the system is meeting user requirements on an on-going basis.

# 3 Service level agreement; obtaining IT services

**Top tips.** In part (a), think about what is in the SLA, and also what isn't. For example, there isn't a clause detailing any financial penalty for providing poor service. Part (b) requires you to think more widely about IT/IS service provision. Consider the general benefits of outsourcing in part (c) and apply to DS.

As a guide, marks could be awarded as follows:

| | | |
|---|---|---:|
| (a) | Award up to 3 marks for each valid point and explanation | 12 |
| (b) | Award up to 3 marks for each valid course and associated problems - to a maximum of 8 marks | 8 |
| (c) | Award up to 2 marks for each valid benefit and explanation | 12 |
| | | 30 |

(a)    GDC Ltd appears to have met its legal obligations even though the level of service it has provided to DS has been poor. There are a number of reasons for this.

DS rushed the appointment of GDC and did not insist on a **detailed Service Level Agreement (SLA)**. The contract does not specify the level of service that GDC will provide.

For example, GDC is obligated to provide 'management information', but there is no detailed definition of what this information will entail, and no deadline for the provision of the information. (eg '...within 5 working days of month-end').

DS handed **complete control** of its IT systems to GDC Ltd. The absence of IT expertise within DS puts it at a **disadvantage** when arguing its case with GDC Ltd.

For example, GDC could spend significant amounts of DS money on sub-standard hardware and software. DC Ltd would **not have the expertise to question** or challenge this purchase, resulting in poor use of DS funds and a poor level of service. However, even when purchasing sub-standard hardware GDC would not have breached the requirement of the contract to 'purchase all hardware and software'.

GDC Ltd is also responsible for the writing and maintenance of in-house software. **Unless GDC has a detailed understanding of DS the software written may not be suitable**. As GDC receives a set annual fee, it may be tempted to produce software as quickly and cheaply as possible. As the contract has no mention of software standards, GDC would be meeting its legal obligations.

Another reason that could be contributing DS receiving poor service is that **the agreement is now two years old**. Changes could have taken place inside DS within the past two years that an outside organisation such as GDC does not understand. The nature of management information required now may be different to that required two years ago.

Service levels could also be suffering because **GDC has no financial incentive to provide a good standard of service.** GDC Ltd has the right under the contract to increase the annual fee, above the rate of inflation, without any consultation and with no reference to the satisfaction of DS.

(b) The courses of action now available to DS relating to the provision of IT services, and the problems involved in each, are outlined below.

(i) **DS could carry on under the existing agreement**, protecting the knowledge that GDC has built up on the provision of IT services to DS, **but applying 'moral' pressure** (in the form of complaints and meetings with GDC management) to obtain a better level of service. The main problem with this course of action is that the level of service may not improve at all.

(ii) DS could terminate the existing contract by giving three months' notice, and **negotiate a new contract with GDC with a well-defined SLA**. Possible problems include the fact that GDC may not wish to negotiate a new SLA leaving DS with no IT services, or GDC may agree a new SLA but still provide the old shoddy service.

(iii) DS could terminate the existing contract by giving three months' notice and **look for a new supplier** of all its IT services. However, this would mean 'starting from scratch'. Even an efficient provider would take time to develop a feel for the requirements at DS, and build up their expertise. There is no guarantee the new service provider would be better than GDC, although a more detailed SLA would help.

(iv) **DS could establish its own in-house IT team**, probably using a combination of contractors and 'permanent' employees. The main problems with this option are the time and cost of finding setting up the team and that the team would be 'starting from scratch' and may only receive limited help from GDC during the hand-over.

(c) The **advantages** to DS of outsourcing are as follows.

(Any five from the following.)

- Outsourcing would remove uncertainty about **cost**, as the annual contract price is **fixed** in advance. If computing services are inefficient, the costs will be borne by GDC Ltd.

- Successful contracts build a stable relationship over the long-term. This would encourage DS to **plan** for the future.

- Outsourcing would bring the benefits of **economies of scale** to DS. GDC Ltd may conduct research into new technologies or agree deals with equipment suppliers that that benefit a number of their clients including DS.

- Specialist organisations, such as GDC Ltd, are able to retain **skills and knowledge**. DS may not have a sufficiently well-developed IT department to offer IT staff opportunities for career development. Talented staff would leave to pursue their careers elsewhere.

- New skills and knowledge become available. A specialist company such as GDC Ltd can **share** staff with **specific expertise** (for example, with experience of writing in-house software) between several clients who would not otherwise benefit from them.

- **Flexibility**. GDC Ltd can scale resources up or down depending upon demand. For instance, during a major changeover from one system to another the number of IT staff needed may be twice as large as it will be once the new system is working satisfactorily.

# 4 Operations strategy

Brown identified six factors important to operations strategy. Each of these is described below, with examples relating to a retail supermarket chain.

- **Capability required**. Any operations strategy will be influenced by what it is that the organisation 'does'.

  For example, a supermarket chain sells food and other items to consumers.

- **Range and location of operations**. The operations strategy will be affected by the scale and geographical spread of the organisation's operations.

  For example, a supermarket chain with say 10 outlets in one region of a country will face different operation strategy issues than a nationwide chain.

- **Investment in technology**. Technology will impact upon operations and therefore operations strategy as it has the potential to change the processes associated with operations.

  For example, a supermarket chain operating using an EFTPOS system linked to their stock (logistics/warehousing systems will operate differently to a chain relying on less-automated systems).

- **Strategic buyer-seller relationships**. Who key strategic partners are will affect operations strategy.

  For example, a supermarket may have a preferred supplier for canned food items. Operations may then be designed to help facilitate this relationship. Relationships with 'buyers' (consumers) may be developed using loyalty card schemes – and operations changed based on what the scheme reveals.

- **New products/services**. This relates to how long the business will be able to do what it is currently doing (in the same way).

  A supermarket may find it also needs to offer on-line shopping and home delivery. It could also decide to move into non-traditional areas such as consumer electronics – or even consumer insurance or finance. These types of changes require changes to operations strategy.

- **Structure of operations**. Operations strategy will also be influenced by how staff are organised and managed.

  For example, will 'regional managers' have responsibility and complete control over all stores in one region – or will one national strategy apply?

  Issues such as staff levels, shift patterns and human resources policies will also affect operations strategy. For example, will stores be open 24 hours – and if so how will this be staffed?

# 5 Inventories and JIT

(a)  (i)   **Reorder level**. When inventories reach this level, an order should be placed to replenish stocks. The reorder level is determined by considering the rate of consumption and the lead time (lead time is the time between placing an order with a supplier and the stock becoming available for use).

   (ii)  **Minimum level**. This is a warning level to draw management attention to the fact that inventories are approaching a dangerously low level and that outages are possible.

   (iii) **Maximum level**. This also acts as a warning level to signal to management that stocks are reaching a potentially wasteful level.

   (iv)  **Reorder quantity**. This is the quantity of inventory which is to be ordered when stock reaches the reorder level. If it is set so as to minimise the total costs associated with holding and ordering inventory, then it is known as the **economic order quantity**.

   (v)   **Average inventory**. This is a calculation of the average inventory level that assumes actual levels fluctuate evenly between the minimum (or safety) inventory level and the highest possible inventory level (the amount of inventory immediately after an order is received, ie safety inventory + reorder quantity).

(b)  JIT production systems will include the following features.

### Multi-skilled workers

In a JIT production environment, production processes must be shortened and simplified. Each product family is made in a workcell based on flowline principles. The variety and complexity of work carried out in these work cells is increased (compared with more traditional processes), necessitating a group of dissimilar machines working within each work cell. Workers must therefore be more flexible and adaptable, the cellular approach enabling each operative to operate several machines. Operatives are trained to operate all machines on the line and undertake routine preventative maintenance.

### Close relationships with suppliers

JIT production systems often go hand-in-hand with JIT purchasing systems. JIT purchasing seeks to match the usage of materials with the delivery of materials from external suppliers. This means that material stocks can be kept at near-zero levels. For JIT purchasing to be successful this requires the organisation to have confidence that the supplier will deliver on time and that the supplier will deliver materials of 100% quality, that there will be no rejects, returns and hence no consequent production delays. The reliability of suppliers is of utmost importance and hence the company must build up close relationships with their suppliers. This can be achieved by doing more business with fewer suppliers and placing long-term orders so that the supplier is assured of sales and can produce to meet the required demand.

### Machine cells

With JIT production, factory layouts must change to reduce movement of workers and products. Traditionally machines were grouped by function (drilling, grinding and so on). A part therefore had to travel long distances, moving from one part of the factory to the other, often stopping along the way in a storage area. All these are non-value-added activities that have to be reduced or eliminated. Material movements between operations are therefore minimised by eliminating space between work stations and grouping machines or workers by product or component instead of by type of work performed. Products can flow from machine to machine without having to wait for the next stage of processing or returning to stores. Lead times and work in progress are thus reduced.

### An emphasis on quality

Production management within a JIT environment seeks to both eliminate scrap and defective units during production and avoid the need for reworking of units. Defects stop the production line, thus creating rework and possibly resulting in a failure to meet delivery dates. Quality, on the other hand, reduces costs. Quality is assured by designing products and processes with quality in mind, introducing quality awareness programmes and statistical checks on output quality, providing continual worker training and implementing vendor quality assurance programmes to ensure that the correct product is made to the appropriate quality level on the first pass through production.

### Set-up time reduction

If an organisation is able to reduce manufacturing lead time it is in a better position to respond quickly to changes in customer demand. Reducing set-up time is one way in which this can be done. Machinery set-ups are non-value-added activities which should be reduced or even eliminated. Reducing set-up time (and hence set-up costs) also makes the manufacture of smaller batches more economical and worthwhile; managers do not feel the need to spread the set-up costs over as many units as possible (which then leads to high levels of stock). Set-up time can be reduced by the use of one product or one product family machine cells, by training workers or by the use of computer integrated manufacturing (CIM).

(c) JIT systems have a number of **financial benefits**.

- Increase in labour productivity due to labour being multiskilled and carrying out preventative maintenance
- Reduction of investment in plant space
- Reduction in costs of storing stock
- Reduction in risk of stock obsolescence
- Lower investment in stock
- Reduction in costs of handling stock
- Reduction in costs associated with scrap, defective units and reworking
- Higher revenue as a result of reduction in lost sales following failure to meet delivery dates (because of improved quality)
- Reduction in the costs of setting up production runs
- Higher revenues as a result of faster response to customer demands

# 6 Business process re-engineering (BPR)

**Top tips.** The key to providing a good answer to this question is ensuring that you **refer** wherever possible to the **scenario** provided in the question. Here are the **key phrases** in the scenario that you should have highlighted for part (b) and associated comment.

- **Rapidly eroding its market share/onslaught from international competitors** – but is another reaction more appropriate than the implementation of BPR?
- **Helpless/frantically searching/desperation** – but BPR should not be implemented unless there is good reason.
- **Management journals/wonder cure** – but the company needs to consider the value of using a consultant.

(a) **The nature of BPR and its application to AB Ltd**

A **process** is 'a collection of activities that takes one or more types of input and creates output that is of value to the customer'.

Part of this process is manufacture of goods, and so is relevant to AB Ltd. However, a process is more than just manufacturing, it involves the ordering and delivery of goods to the customer. Arguably, AB Ltd does not need to manufacture. All aspects of the process, from ordering to delivery, must be considered.

**Key features of BPR**

(i) Focus on the **outcome**, not the task.

(ii) **Ignore the current way** of doing business. For example, AB Ltd may be divided into departments. The current organisation structure is not relevant to the process. Indeed having a large number of departments may make the process harder to manage, as it is split between several different responsibilities. The same customer's order may be passed from department to department.

(iii) Carefully determine how to use **technology**. IT has often been used to automate existing processes rather than redesign new ones. This means that **AB Ltd must have an information strategy** for the company as a whole.

(iv) **Review job design**. Scientific management split jobs into their smallest components. BPR suggests that, in some cases, **enlarged jobs** are more efficient if they lead to fewer people being involved in the process.

(v) **Do the work where it makes most sense**. This might affect where sales order processing and credit controls are carried out.

(vi) Work must be done in **logical sequence**. This can affect factory layout but also the sequence of clerical activities.

(vii) **Those who perform the process should manage it**. The distinction between managers and workers should be eroded; decision aids such as expert systems should be provided.

(viii) **Information provision should be included in the work** that produces it.

(ix) The customer should have **a single point of contact** in the organisation.

In effect, BPR requires the asking of the fundamental question: 'If we were starting from scratch, what would we do?'

(b) *Davenport* and *Short* prescribe a **five-step approach** to BPR that AB Ltd can adopt.

(i) Develop a **business vision and process objectives**.

BPR is driven by a business vision which implies specific business objectives such as cost reduction, time reduction, output quality improvement, Total Quality Management and empowerment. The vision and objectives must be developed before AB Ltd can continue onto the other stages.

(ii) **Identify the processes** to be redesigned.

AB Ltd can either take a 'high impact' approach whereby the most important processes, or those which conflict with it are redesigned; or it can take an 'exhaustive' approach where all processes are identified and prioritised for re-engineering.

(iii) Understand and **measure the existing processes**.

AB Ltd should ensure previous mistakes are not repeated by understanding how they are caused. This will also provide it with a baseline to help the business make future improvements.

(iv) **Identify IT levers**.

AB should be aware of potential IT capabilities that could prove useful when designing processes.

(v) Design and **build a prototype** of the new process.

AB Ltd should not view the actual design as the end of the BPR process but as a prototype, with successive alterations. The use of a prototype enables the involvement of customers.

(c) **Pitfalls**

    (i)    BPR is an **all or nothing proposition**. It is thus expensive and risky, requiring major expenditure on consultancy, investment in IT systems and disruption. It is not worth doing unless there is a good reason.

    (ii)    AB Ltd is concerned about overseas competition. There may be other **competitive responses more appropriate than BPR**, such as improving quality, outsourcing, a focus strategy or a differentiation strategy.

    (iii)    **Implementation is difficult**, as organisations fail to think through what they are trying to achieve, and the process becomes captured by departmental interest groups. In AB Ltd, the production director, sales director and finance director may well conflict. The customer may deal with all three of them.

    (iv)    Managers take a **departmental view**, rather than the view of the business as a whole.

    (v)    BPR becomes **associated only with across the board cost cutting** rather than a fundamental re-evaluation of the business. Managers will fight very hard to avoid any threats to their position.

    (vi)    Management consultants responsible for the ideas often fail to come up with realistic strategies for implementation. Managers are thus left with a BPR formula that they may not fully understand and have to implement it in a hostile work environment.

# 7 Job descriptions

> **Top tips.** Good answers to part (a) would provide a rounded argument - showing the possible disadvantages of job descriptions as well as potential benefits. Your answer should have focused on job description policy rather than about the detailed contents.
>
> You may have generated other attributes to include in a person specification in part (c). For example, the *Alec Rodgers* framework, such answers are equally valid.

(a)    (i)    **Purpose of job descriptions**

        A job description is a written statement of the main responsibilities of a job, and the role's organisational and operational interrelationships. Although they vary from firm to firm, a typical job description might contain the job title, a list of duties, reporting relationships, and hours of work.

        In recruitment, a job description can the used to determine identify the skills needed from the new recruit. (A person specification can be developed from a job description.)

        A job description makes clear what a person is expected to do, and thus makes it easier for the organisation to function.

        Job descriptions can be used for job evaluation purposes, as they focus the attention on the job, in comparison with other jobs.

    (ii)    **Benefits of job descriptions**

        Job descriptions are an essential way in which the organisation allocates labour and carries out its activities. If work processes are standardised, as in a bureaucracy, then the job description will function as a part of the socio-technical system of the organisation. A job description, by defining the relationships of the position to other positions, is a part of organisation structure.

        One of the economic benefits of organisations is that they permit division of labour and specialisation. Job descriptions can enforce these features by writing them into the work that people do.

        Some people value certainty and security, and a job description, by precisely delineating what a person must do, can provide such psychological assurance.

They can be used in the appraisal, discipline or grievance process, so that the employee is appraised as to what he or she is expected to do. They can be appealed to in case of dispute.

They can pinpoint weaknesses in the organisation structure, if there are disputes as to authority.

### (iii) Possible disadvantages of job descriptions

The modern organisation should be flexible. Flexibility may require employees to perform functions in addition to those in their job description. If job descriptions attempt to include flexibility by including phrases such as 'any other duties as required', there may be no point in having the description at all.

Job descriptions can discourage teamworking and encourage commitment to the job as such, rather than to the firm or its wider mission.

However, many organisations require a continual redefinition of roles in the light of the organisation's wider mission. Job descriptions that focus on the detail of the job not on the wider mission of the firm may be counterproductive.

Job descriptions assume that the job designer knows best in advance how a job should be done. This could inhibit individual and organisational learning by inhibiting creative team work. Moreover, many job descriptions do not employ the wider systems thinking perspective which might be considered necessary for organisational learning.

Formal descriptions may be inappropriate for some jobs, especially those which cannot be broken down into a sequence of repetitive routine tasks. For certain jobs, such as customer care, the job description may not outline those items which make a particular difference.

## (b) Job description characteristics/features

> **Top tips.** Here is one set of suggestions, but you could quite easily have come up with something different that would also have scored well.

(i) Job descriptions should be as brief as possible while still capturing the essence of the role.

(ii) They should focus on what the employee is expected to achieve, as opposed to how this is done, except where there are vital reasons to specify procedures.

(iii) Job descriptions should contain information explaining the context of the job.

(iv) They should encourage teamwork rather than allowing employees to evade tasks not specified in the description.

(v) Job descriptions should facilitate the staff appraisal process.

(vi) Job descriptions should reflect the reality of operations – not some ideal of how things should be.

## (c) A **person specification** may cover attributes such as:

### (i) Personal skills

These are skills that the person may have acquired or developed over time, for example, communication or negotiation skills.

### (ii) Qualifications

These include academic or vocational attainments such as a university degree or the CIMA qualification.

### (iii) Innate ability

This is a person's natural ability to do something. It usually cannot be taught or acquired, although training may develop it further. Examples include manual dexterity or mental sharpness.

(iv) **Motivation**

This specifies what motivates the person. It may be financial reward, promotion or overcoming challenges. The person filling the position must be motivated by the rewards on offer.

(v) **Personality**

A person's personality describes their inner disposition, for example, whether or not they can stay calm under pressure or whether they 'get on with the job' rather than thinking about it before they start. Certain roles require certain personalities to be successful or to fit in with staff already employed.

# 8 Carrot and stick

**Top tips.** This is a simple example of the relatively common type of question in which a character makes a short remark that has major theoretical and practical implications. It is an important part of examination technique to be able to assess such remarks and decide whether you recognise the theory that is being referred to. You then have to decide whether or not you know enough about it to be able to produce an answer!

The 'carrot and stick' approach to motivation uses both **rewards** and **punishments** to motivate behaviour in employees.

**Rewards**, or **positive motivators** could include extrinsic rewards (eg more pay) and intrinsic rewards (eg a sense of recognition). Punishments include dismissal, demotion and reprimand.

An implication of the carrot and stick approach could be that it assumes that all human beings have the same attitude to work and motivation. This suggests that good behaviour can be encouraged by rewards and punishments of a fairly simple kind.

Sargent's statement implies that this model of motivation, where manipulative managers can dangle rewards and threaten punishments as a means to generate higher levels of performance, is out of date and **no longer appropriate**.

In its place, some argue that management now have a more sophisticated repertoire of motivational techniques. There is now a recognition that, as human beings are complex, so too are their expectations of, and behaviour in, the workplace.

The argument that the carrot and stick approach is a thing of the past is developed from a number of trends in management that have been apparent over the past few years.

More complex theories of motivation, such as Maslow's hierarchy of needs and Herzberg's two factor theory have been around for some time. HR departments or interviewers generally attempt to take into account factors of individual personality (eg is the interviewee by nature industrious?) when interviewing. In practice, therefore, the carrot and stick approach, which suggests that all people can be motivated in the same way, is now seen as too simplistic.

Organisations now look at **management techniques** that have been successful in other areas of the world or in other industries and attempt to apply them in their workplaces. For example, it has been common to attribute part of the success of Japanese companies to employee motivation and participation (empowerment).

Another factor in the decline of the simple 'carrot and stick' approach has been the growth in the service sector, where 'people' issues are often more important than technical ones in **providing services** and generating repeat business. The increasing use of technology and flexible working patterns further changes the old traditional employer/employee relationship.

Broadly speaking then, Sargent is proposing that management is (or if not, should be) much more sophisticated in its approach to motivation. Ways should be found to **involve employees** more in decision making. This should reduce the potential for conflict between managers and staff – and hopefully also lead to better quality decisions as those involved in 'doing the work' are often best qualified to understand the implications of a decision.

However, Sargent's statement is contradicted by some evidence.

(a) 'Carrots' certainly have are a **motivating factor** in some cases - many employees depart to different employers offering more money.

(b) The **stick** is still used in **disciplinary matters** (eg adherence to rules).

(c) The **biggest stick** of all is, arguably, **redundancy**, although management can shift the blame for wielding it on to general economic conditions.

(d) In industries with **skills shortages** management tries to keep those workers whose skills it most values, and to **employ** their **services productively**. This may mean satisfying an employee's higher needs (on Maslow's hierarchy), but this is more out of necessity (offering a carrot to keep the person on-board) than because of any change in management philosophy.

(e) The increase in **part-time employment** has also increased manager's power to use the stick to enforce discipline, as some would argue part-time workers are more easily replaced.

So, the carrot and stick approach is definitely less prevalent today, but occasionally it may still be a valid approach to certain work situations.

# 9 Appraisal

> **Top tips**. Appraisal is a quite a popular examination topic. This question covers a great deal of important basic material related to appraisal. In part (c) you need to apply your knowledge to come up with advantages and disadvantages.

(a) Face-to-face appraisals are needed for a number of reasons.

    (i) Managers and supervisors may obtain **random impressions** of employees' performance (perhaps from their more noticeable successes and failures), but **rarely form a coherent, complete and objective picture** as they may not work closely with them on a day-to-day basis.

    (ii) They may have a fair idea of their employees' **shortcomings** – but may not have devoted time and attention to the matter of **improvement and development**. Appraisals focus their attention on these matters.

    (iii) **Judgements are easy to make, but less easy to justify** in detail, in writing, or to the subject's face. Therefore, appraisals force managers to think carefully before judging their staff.

    (iv) **Different assessors may be applying a different set of criteria, and varying standards of objectivity and judgement**. This undermines the value of appraisal for comparison, as well as its credibility in the eyes of the appraisees.

    (v) Unless stimulated to do so, **managers rarely give their staff adequate feedback on their performance.** Appraisals require feedback to be accurate and effective, therefore improving future performance.

(b) Most large firms have a regular system of appraising staff. The objectives of staff appraisal systems are to help in developing staff members to their full potential and to enable the organisation to allocate their human resources in the most efficient way possible. To achieve these objectives an effective appraisal system is likely to incorporate certain key characteristics.

    (i) Appraisal reports should be made out in **writing** and at **fixed intervals**. Staff appraisal is a sensitive operation and a written record of the assessment may remove any doubts or uncertainties which arise at a later date. The report is part of a record, the personnel file, which charts an employee's progress within the organisation. The intervals at which the appraisal should be carried out depend on the nature of the employee's work. For specialist staff who move from one long-term assignment to another, appraisal may be appropriate after each assignment is completed. For staff engaged in more routine work, an interval of six months or a year may be suitable.

(ii)     Written reports should be **objective**. An employee's superior may be inclined to assess harshly to excuse his own poor performance; alternatively, an easy-going relationship during day-to-day work may make a superior feel reluctant to be critical, especially if his subordinate's promotion prospects may be harmed. One way of improving objectivity is to make the assessment form very detailed: the more specific the assessor is required to be, the less margin there is for subjective responses.

(iii)    Appraisal should be **consistent** throughout the organisation. This can cause problems in organisations which, like banks, have many semi-autonomous branches. Again, the use of detailed assessment forms (standard throughout the organisation) will help, but the assessment form is only the beginning of the appraisal process and care must be taken to ensure consistency in the later stages too.

(iv)    Assessments should be **discussed** with the person assessed. If employees do not know what is being written about them they will not be able to improve in areas where shortcomings have been noted. This could cause particular frustration if the assessment system is used as part of a process of selecting staff for promotion.

(v)     Persons conducting the appraisal interviews should be **trained** and ideally experienced in the necessary techniques.

(vi)    The employee should be encouraged to **contribute** to the appraisal process. Ideally, the employee should have sight of the written assessment in time to consider a response before being called to interview. During the interview the emphasis ought not to be on problems and obstacles, but on opportunities. The interviewee should be encouraged to talk about their career plans, their knowledge and skills and how they could be put to better use, and to make suggestions for improving the way their work is carried out.

(vii)   There should be adequate follow-up after the interview has taken place. If the system is to be effective, staff must have confidence in it. This will only happen if results are seen to follow from the assessments.

(c)   **Advantages of appraisal systems**

(i)     They enable the organisation to gather information about the skills and potential of employees and to identify training needs.

(ii)     They provide a system on which salary reviews and promotions can be based.

(iii)    They help to develop the employee's potential by directing his attention to particular strengths and weaknesses.

(iv)    They allow the employee and his assessor to discuss and agree on personal objectives.

(v)     They may contribute to staff motivation.

**Disadvantages of appraisal systems**

(i)     The **subjective** element in such systems cannot be entirely eliminated.

(ii)     They depend for their success on a mutual confidence between the assessor and the employee assessed. In practice, it is **difficult to achieve that confidence**.

(iii)    It is difficult to go beyond appraisal of **past performance**, which may be an inadequate guide to future performance in a different job. If an appraisal scheme is used as a guide to promotion potential this is a serious disadvantage.

(iv)    They **often do not lead to improvements** in performance. Criticism of areas where performance has been weak can lead to a defensive response and future performance may actually deteriorate.

(v)     There are many posts, particularly in technical roles, where **further promotion is impossible**, performance is standardised at a high level and experience is infinitely valuable. To the incumbents of such posts a formal appraisal system may seem like a waste of time.

# 10 The marketing concept

> **Top tips**. The standard of discussion in this suggested solution is similar to that expected in the exam – preparing your own solution will provide you with good reinforcement of the Study Text material.

One definition of the marketing concept is 'a management orientation or outlook, that accepts that the key task of the organisation is to determine the needs, wants and values of a target market and to adapt the organisation to delivering the desired satisfaction more effectively and efficiently than its competitors'.

In other words, customer needs and the market environment are considered of paramount importance. Since technology, markets, the economy, social attitudes, fashions, the law and so on are all constantly changing, customer needs are likely to change too. The marketing concept is that changing needs and attitudes must be identified, and products or services adapted and developed to satisfy them. Only in this way can a supplier hope to operate successfully and profitably (if the supplier of the goods or service is a profit-making organisation).

Some firms may be **product oriented** and others **sales oriented**, although it is generally accepted that most firms should be **marketing oriented** to be successful in the longer term.

(a)    A **product-oriented** firm is one which believes that if it can make a good quality product at a reasonable price, then customers will inevitably buy it with a minimum of marketing effort by the firm. The firm will probably concentrate on product developments and improvements, and production efficiencies to cut costs. If there is a lack of competition in the market, or a shortage of goods to meet a basic demand, then product orientation should be successful. However, if there is competition and over-supply of a product, demand must be stimulated, and a product-oriented firm will resort to the 'hard-sell' or 'product push' to 'convince' the customer of what he wants.

(b)    A **sales-oriented** firm is one which believes that in order to achieve cost efficiencies through large volumes of output, it must invest heavily in sales promotion. This attitude implies a belief that potential customers are by nature sales-resistant and have to be persuaded to buy (or buy more), so that the task of the firm is to develop a strong sales department, with well-trained sales people. The popular image of a used car salesman or a door-to-door sales representative would suggest that sales orientation is unlikely to achieve any long-term satisfaction of customer needs.

The **marketing concept** should be applied by management because it is the most practical philosophy for achieving any organisation's objective. A profit-making company's objective might be to achieve a growth in profits, earnings per share or return on shareholder funds. By applying the marketing concept to product design the company might hope to make more attractive products, hence to achieve sustained sales growth and so make higher profits.

Another implication of the marketing concept is that an organisation's management should continually be asking 'what business are we in?' This is a question which is fundamental to strategic planning too, and the importance of developing a market orientation to strategic planning is implicit in the marketing concept.

(a)    With the **product concept** and **selling concept**, an organisation produces a good or service, and then expects to sell it. The nature of the organisation's business is determined by what it has chosen to produce, and there will be a reluctance to change over to producing something different.

(b)    With the **marketing concept**, an organisation commits itself to supplying what customers need. As those needs change, so too must the goods or services which are produced.

If the marketing concept is to be applied successfully, it **must be shared** by all managers and supervisors in an organisation. 'Marketing' in its broader sense covers not just selling, advertising, sales promotion and pricing, but also product design and quality, after sales service, distribution, reliability of delivery dates and in many cases (such as the retailing industry) purchasing supplies. This is because the customers' needs relate to these items as well as more obvious 'marketing' factors such as sales price and how products are promoted.

Another way of expressing the important point made above is: 'most firms have a marketing or sales department, but the marketing concept should be shared by managers in every department'.

It could also be suggested that marketing should aim to **maximise customer satisfaction**, but within the constraints that all firms have a responsibility to society as a whole and to the environment. Not only is there the idea that 'high gross national product also means high gross national pollution' but also there is a need to make efficient use of the world's scarce and dwindling natural resources.

(a)     Some products which consume energy (motor cars, houses) should perhaps make more efficient use of the energy they consume.

(b)     It may be possible to extend the useful life of certain products.

(c)     Other products might be built smaller, so that they make use of fewer materials.

# 11 Marketing research

**Top tips.** The question asks how the research should be conducted – this requires you to make some assumptions. Our answer assumes that the organisation has a field sales force, but does not employ a specialist market research analyst. If you struggled with this question, use this answer to help your understanding of this area.

REPORT

To:          Marketing Manager
From:       A Candidate
Date:        21 January 20X5
Subject:    Identifying areas of improvement in the distribution and logistics function

This report outlines the marketing research process, giving the key stages in undertaking research and the specific research objectives and methodology to be followed.

(a)     **Marketing research process – key stages**

(1)     Set the objectives of the research
(2)     Define the research problem
(3)     Assess the value of the research
(4)     Construct the research proposal
(5)     Specify data collection method(s)
(6)     Specify technique(s) of measurement
(7)     Select the sample
(8)     Collect the data
(9)     Analyse the result
(10)    Present the final report

The following points relating to each key stage should be considered.

(i)      **Research objectives** need to be **SMART** – Specific, Measurable, Actionable, Reasonable and Timescaled.

(ii)     Some **exploratory research** may be necessary to clarify problem areas and further understand customer requirements.

(iii)    A **cost benefit exercise** will need to be carried out to ensure that undertaking the research is cost-effective.

(iv)    **Proposals need to be submitted** for the category of research to be undertaken and must be agreed by all parties.

(v)     **Data** can be **primary** (field research) or **secondary** (desk research). Collection methods will vary according to the type of research.

(vi)    At the **measurement stage**, all the factors under investigation will need to be converted into quantitative data to allow for analysis.

(vii)   **Sample size** will be dependent on time and resources but must be sufficient to be statistically significant.

(viii)  **Decisions** as to who will undertake the research and how will it be carried out must be made.

(ix) **Statistical analysis** may involve using manual techniques, computer techniques or a combination of both.

(x) Findings will need to be **presented** and a **formal report** submitted.

(b) **Specific research objectives and method of conducting research**

    (i) **Research objectives**

        Separate objectives are needed for the two groups of customers, those using Electronic Data Interchange (EDI) and those not using it.

        (1) **Customers using EDI**

- To establish how they rate current distributive and logistics processes
- To identify areas where improvements can be made
- To establish to what extent perceived customer service levels can be improved by better distributive and logistics processes

        (2) **Customers not using EDI**

- To establish reasons for non-use of EDI
- To identify incentives to encourage non-users to invest in EDI technology
- To quantify the likely benefit in improved customer service

    (ii) **Conducting the research**

        The most cost-effective way to undertake the research is likely to be a combination of in-house and external agency resource. My proposal is as follows.

        (1) Draw up a research brief internally.

        (2) Short list and then commission a specialist marketing research agency.

        (3) Ask the agency to compile questionnaires (one for EDI customers, one for non-EDI users).

        (4) Use the company's sales representatives to collect questionnaire data.

        (5) Await questionnaire analysis and presentation of findings by the agency.

The **questionnaire format** should be such that the sales team can conduct semi-structured interviews. This would facilitate the collection of quantitative data (tick box, pre-coded choices) and qualitative data (views and opinions recorded from open-ended questions).

Probing questions, such as 'What other factors are there?' can also be used to clarify responses or gather additional information. They are also useful for triggering further responses. More skill is required in conducting semi-structured interviews, but these should be within the capabilities of the sales team, provided that they are given an adequate brief.

# 12 Internet-based marketing communications

**Top tips.** This is a straightforward question with an easy format. Facts about the Internet need to be related to the context of the question. Better answers will recognise the development of relationships as an important factor, and address the strategic aspects. Don't worry if your answer differs from ours, you will gain credit for relevant points made.

In business-to-business (B2B) markets, organisational **buying behaviour** is more complex than in consumer markets. This is because of the increased number of people involved in the **decision making process**.

Marketing communications in the **B2B** market is traditionally characterised by the predominance of **personal selling**. This contrasts with business-to-consumer based promotional activity **(B2C)** where **mass media communications** have tended to be the most important route to the target audience.

The development of the **Internet and related digital technologies** has introduced new ways in which audiences in both sectors can be reached. These notes will concentrate on communications in the B2B sector.

Very briefly, the Internet and digital technologies can lead to

- Faster communication
- More information being available at a lower cost
- Cheaper transactions
- Improved relationships with intermediaries
- Potential for improved levels of customer satisfaction
- Speedier problem resolution
- Improved communication

In the B2B sector, the development and maintenance of **profitable relationships** is important. Part of marketing communications' role is to develop these relationships by **reducing perceived risk and uncertainty**. It also needs to provide **clarity** and provide fast, pertinent and timely **information** in order that decisions can be made.

### Loyalty

Loyalty between organisations can be improved by **targeting information and customised messages** at the right people within the partner organisation. **Speed of response** to customer questions, and the **clarity of the information** provided, is important for the development of trust and loyalty.

### Productivity

Productivity should be increased as electronic communication not only saves time, but also **shortens the time between order and delivery**.

### Costs

The costs of our communications can also be considerably reduced. Paper and printing costs associated with sales literature and demonstration packs can be reduced.

Further website development will enable us to collect names and addresses, respond to **e-mail** questions and provide **data** for our sales force. If we develop the website still further, then **e-commerce transactions** will enable routine orders to be completed quickly and at a lower cost.

This frees up the sales force to visit and manage the accounts of established customers more often, referred to as **key account management**.

### Marketing communications mix

Digital technologies enable the **collection of data** for use through online and offline sources. So our **direct marketing** activities can be improved, and our **sales promotions** targeted to provide real and valued incentives. Even our **public relations** activities can benefit by placing suitable material on our web pages.

### Effectiveness

Finally, digitally-based communications can improve the **timeliness** of the information we provide and help us to measure the **effectiveness** of our marketing communication activities.

### End notes

To conclude and summarise, our marketing communications with business partners will improve through improved efficiency and effectiveness, which in turn will be reflected in the nature and **quality of the relationships** we hold. This will ultimately be reflected in our overall performance in meeting our corporate goals.

**Improved trust, commitment and a higher propensity to share information must lead to increased business performance**. The development of Internet based communications is a strategic decision that needs to be thought through in terms of the impact it will have on the way we and our partners do business.

# 13 Organisation life cycle and corporate decline

(a)     **Greiner's model**

The **organisation life cycle model** was suggested by Greiner. It assumes that, as an organisation ages, it grows in *size*, measured perhaps by the number of employees and diversity of activities. This growth is characterised by a number of discrete phases. Each phase is characterised by:

(i)     A distinctive factor that directs the organisation's growth.

(ii)    A crisis, through which the organisation must pass before achieving the next phase.

       (1)     **Phase 1**. The organisation is small, and is managed in personal and informal ways. The founders of the business are actively involved in operations. Apple Computers, for example, started up in a garage. However, sooner or later there comes a need for distinct management skills, relating less to products and marketing issues and more to co-ordination of the organisation's activities. This is a **crisis of leadership**.

       (2)     **Phase 2**. Clear direction is provided by professionalising the management. At the same time, there are more employees. This initial enthusiasm might be tempered by loss of autonomy and the growth of hierarchy. The problem arises in that of delegation. The top finds it harder and harder to keep in detailed control as there are too many activities and it is easy lose a sense of the wider picture. Employees resent the lack of initiative and their performance falters. There is a **crisis of autonomy**.

       (3)     **Phase 3**. The response to the problems of Phase 2 is delegation. This has the advantage of decentralising decision-making and giving confidence to junior managers. However, this in itself leads to additional problems of co-ordination and control. Over-delegation can result in different departments acting sub-optimally. There is a **crisis of control**.

       (4)     **Phase 4**. The addition of internal systems, procedures and so forth to ensure co-ordination of activities, optimal use of resources etc. This increased complexity results in a **crisis of red tape**.

       (5)     **Phase 5**. The crisis of red tape is resolved by increased informal collaboration. Control is cultural rather than formal. People participate in teams. Greiner thinks that this growth stage may lead to a crisis of psychological saturation, in which all become exhausted by teamwork. He postulates a sixth growth phase involving a dual organisation: a 'habit' structure for daily work routines and a 'reflective structure' for stimulating new perspectives and personal enrichment.

Greiner's model describes organisational growth as inevitably punctuated by crisis. A different approach is the **'S' curve hypothesis** devised by economists to explain organisational growth. This suggests organisations have a short period of establishment, followed by rapid growth before trailing off into stability and eventual decline.

**Criticisms** of these models include the fact that they often assume organisations are founded by a visionary controlling entrepreneur, selling a product or service. This excludes many organisations.

(i)     A new organisation can be formed from the merger of two existing ones.

(ii)    Two or more companies might collaborate on a joint venture. The Airbus project, for example, did not start as a small business, but as a result of co-operation between governments and existing companies.

(iii)   New organisations are created by existing ones and have a substantial complement of staff.

Greiner's model perhaps combines too many issues: organisation structure, organisation culture, product/market scope, leadership and management style.

It is possible to combine an obsession with procedures and efficiency (bureaucracy) with a strong sense of mission. Hospitals depend on the devotion and professionalism of staff - but clinical procedures *have* to be adhered to.

By their very nature, models have to generalise. These models therefore provide a framework for thought, rather than a prescription for growth.

(b)   **The management information required in each phase**

The management information should enable informed decision making and facilitate control over operations.

In **Phase 1**, it is unlikely that there would be formal management information produced at all. This is because the organisation is small, and those involved are likely to feel they know all they need to know without formal mechanisms.

In **Phase 2**, the management as a whole becomes professionalised, and you would expect to see the finance function growing in importance. This would include the production of some management information (probably with an internal focus) for senior management.

In **Phase 3**, extensive delegation would suggest a need for systems of performance evaluation, profit centre analysis etc. A specific management accounting department or team may be established in this stage.

**Phase 4** is characterised by extensive controls and procedures. Managers are likely to request much more information relating to budgets and expenditure levels.

**Phase 5** should engender a more rounded examination of the information that should be provided to allow improved decision-making. Information should have both an internal and external focus. Informal collaboration should be encouraged and be supported by information systems which contain modelling facilities. Executive information systems should allow high level analysis with the ability to drill down into basic data.

(c)   (i)   Causes of **corporate decline** include [only four required]:

- Poor management
- Poor financial controls
- High cost structure
- Poor marketing
- Competitive weakness
- Big projects/acquisitions
- Financial policy

(ii)   **Companies who realise they are in decline must stop** and **reverse the trend** if they are to survive in the long term. Four possible approaches are:

- Retrenchment
- Divestment
- Turnaround
- Liquidation

**Retrenchment**

Retrenchment involves performing the same activities as before but cutting costs drastically. Decline is reversed as the operations become more profitable.

**Turnaround**

Turnaround involves **senior management** making **substantial changes** to the company in all aspects of its operation. The change reverses the company's fortunes.

To achieve a successful turnaround, the senior management team need to:

- Create a new vision for the organisation
- Gain acceptance of the new vision
- Force through and 'refreeze' the change

**Divestment**

Divestment involves the **external sale** of part of the organisation, or the closure of a unit or operation (a rationalisation). By removing parts that are 'dragging down' the rest of the business, the fortunes of the remaining parts should improve.

**Liquidation**

Liquidation involves **selling the business** to one or more buyers. This is the 'last resort' – in effect it represents an admission that the business (or the managers) have failed.

# 14 Change

> **Top tips**. Part (a) uses knowledge from Chapter 13. There are many drivers of change, think about all the PESTEL factors. The answer in part (b) provided represents one possible approach – other points could have scored equally as well. The same could be said for part (c) – don't panic if the processes you included are slightly different.

(a)   **Drivers of change**

(i)   **Regulatory changes**

Legal or other regulatory changes to how the company must operate, or to the goods and services it produces will affect the company as it must adapt to meet them.

(ii)   **Economic developments**

Changes to the economy of where it operates or where it trades will drive change within the company as it must alter its operations to meet these challenges. For example, high inflation will force a company to reduce its costs to remain competitive.

(iii)   **Social developments**

Developments within a culture or society may require a company to adapt to meet them. For example, it may be required to improve childcare facilities or introduce flexible working to enable employees to balance their work/home life.

(iv)   **Technological developments**

Technology creates opportunities and threats to an organisation. It must keep up-to-date on developments to ensure its technology does not become obsolete, but it also offers more efficient ways of operating. Companies must continually adapt to this change to be successful.

(v)   **Internal company factors**

Internal factors such as finance, administration and its culture may drive change. For example, the company's ethics may develop and it may wish to operate in an environmentally friendly way, thus requiring changes in its processes.

(b)   **Reasons for difficulties in bringing about change**

(i)   Change may be **expensive**, particularly if major innovations in working procedures are planned. There may be a tendency to assume that the present methods are working satisfactorily and that any marginal improvement will not be worth the cost.

(ii)  Change involves **planning** in advance, consultation and negotiation. Managers who are thinking of introducing change may be daunted by the administrative hurdles to be overcome.

(iii) Policies and procedures become **fixed and inflexible**. It can be difficult for people who have become accustomed to them to understand that alternative methods are possible to achieve the same aims.

(iv)  Employees often **resist change** which:

- Alters the pay or status of an individual relative to that of other individuals
- Lessens the value of their experience
- Causes disruption to their social life (eg shift-working or relocation)
- Is associated with job insecurity (eg technological innovation)

(c)   **Key processes in successful implementation of change**

(i)   **Planning**. This should begin with a definition of the objectives to be achieved by the proposed change. In environments where change takes place at a rapid pace this may be more of an ideal than a target achievable in practice, but in principle all change should be planned. Where major changes are proposed, this is obviously all the more important and a significant amount of time may need to be devoted to planning.

(ii)  **Consultation**. Interested parties should be invited to express their views on the need for the proposed change and on the methods for implementing it. It is possible that quite different means may be proposed at this stage for achieving the defined objectives. At the least, the process of consultation should help to minimise opposition to change: people will be unable to complain that the change has been forced on them if they have been given the opportunity to suggest alternative approaches.

(iii) **Communication**. This is important before, during and after the change. Before the change takes place, all employees affected by it should be notified of its aims and its intended effects. Efforts should be made to **minimise resistance**; this may involve explaining that the change will not lead to redundancies, that adequate training will be given to all staff in any new procedures and that benefits for employees are expected to arise from the change. As the change is introduced steps should be taken to **communicate progress** so that employees are not left in the dark. Any transitional procedures should be clearly explained; for example, if a computerised system is being introduced a form of parallel running may be needed. In that case staff would need to know that for a time they are expected to process data through two systems in parallel.

(iv)  **Monitoring and review**. At all stages the progress of the change should be monitored and employee reactions recorded. Comparison with the original plan will show where implementation of the plan is being carried out successfully and where improvements are needed. Finally, review of the whole process after it is complete will indicate where follow-up action is required to tidy up loose ends. It will also provide benefits when future changes are planned because lessons will have been learnt.

# Index

**Review Form & Free Prize Draw – Paper P4 Organisational Management and Information Systems (5/08)**

All original review forms from the entire BPP range, completed with genuine comments, will be entered into one of two draws on 31 January 2009 and 31 July 2009. The names on the first four forms picked out on each occasion will be sent a cheque for £50.

Name: _____    Address: _____

_____

_____

**How have you used this Study Text?**
*(Tick one box only)*

☐ Home study (book only)

☐ On a course: college _____

☐ With 'correspondence' package

☐ Other _____

**Why did you decide to purchase this Study Text?** *(Tick one box only)*

☐ Have used BPP Texts in the past

☐ Recommendation by friend/colleague

☐ Recommendation by a lecturer at college

☐ Saw information on BPP website

☐ Saw advertising

☐ Other _____

**During the past six months do you recall seeing/receiving any of the following?**
*(Tick as many boxes as are relevant)*

☐ Our advertisement in *Financial Management*

☐ Our advertisement in *Pass*

☐ Our advertisement in *PQ*

☐ Our brochure with a letter through the post

☐ Our website www.bpp.com

**Which (if any) aspects of our advertising do you find useful?**
*(Tick as many boxes as are relevant)*

☐ Prices and publication dates of new editions

☐ Information on Text content

☐ Facility to order books off-the-page

☐ None of the above

*Which BPP products have you used?*

| | | | | | |
|---|---|---|---|---|---|
| Text | ☑ | Success CD | ☐ | Learn Online | ☐ |
| Kit | ☐ | i-Learn | ☐ | Home Study Package | ☐ |
| Passcard | ☐ | i-Pass | ☐ | Home Study PLUS | ☐ |

*Your ratings, comments and suggestions would be appreciated on the following areas.*

| | Very useful | Useful | Not useful |
|---|---|---|---|
| Introductory section | ☐ | ☐ | ☐ |
| Chapter introductions | ☐ | ☐ | ☐ |
| Key terms | ☐ | ☐ | ☐ |
| Quality of explanations | ☐ | ☐ | ☐ |
| Case studies and other examples | ☐ | ☐ | ☐ |
| Exam focus points | ☐ | ☐ | ☐ |
| Questions and answers in each chapter | ☐ | ☐ | ☐ |
| Fast forwards and chapter roundups | ☐ | ☐ | ☐ |
| Quick quizzes | ☐ | ☐ | ☐ |
| Question Bank | ☐ | ☐ | ☐ |
| Answer Bank | ☐ | ☐ | ☐ |
| OT Bank | ☐ | ☐ | ☐ |
| Index | ☐ | ☐ | ☐ |

| | Excellent | Good | Adeqate | Poor |
|---|---|---|---|---|
| Overall opinion of this Study Text | ☐ | ☐ | ☐ | ☐ |

**Do you intend to continue using BPP products?**    Yes ☐    No ☐

**On the reverse of this page are noted particular areas of the text about which we would welcome your feedback. The BPP Learning Media author of this edition can be e-mailed at: stephenosborne@bpp.com**

**Please return this form to: Nick Weller, CIMA Publishing Manager, BPP Learning Media Ltd, FREEPOST, London, W12 8BR**

## Review Form & Free Prize Draw (continued)

**TELL US WHAT YOU THINK**

Please note any further comments and suggestions/errors below.

## Free Prize Draw Rules

1   Closing date for 31 January 2009 draw is 31 December 2008. Closing date for 31 July 2009 draw is 30 June 2009.

2   Restricted to entries with UK and Eire addresses only. BPP Learning Media Ltd employees, their families and business associates are excluded.

3   No purchase necessary. Entry forms are available upon request from BPP Learning Media Ltd. No more than one entry per title, per person. Draw restricted to persons aged 16 and over.

4   Winners will be notified by post and receive their cheques not later than 6 weeks after the relevant draw date.

5   The decision of the promoter in all matters is final and binding. No correspondence will be entered into.